Corinna Assmann
Doing Family in Second-Generation British Migration Literature

Media and Cultural Memory/ Medien und kulturelle Erinnerung

Edited by
Astrid Erll · Ansgar Nünning

Editorial Board
Aleida Assmann · Mieke Bal · Vita Fortunati · Richard Grusin · Udo Hebel
Andrew Hoskins · Wulf Kansteiner · Alison Landsberg · Claus Leggewie
Jeffrey Olick · Susannah Radstone · Ann Rigney · Michael Rothberg
Werner Sollors · Frederik Tygstrup · Harald Welzer

Volume 25

Corinna Assmann

Doing Family in Second-Generation British Migration Literature

—

DE GRUYTER

Dissertation, Ruprecht-Karls-Universität Heidelberg, 2017

ISBN 978-3-11-076377-5
e-ISBN (PDF) 978-3-11-060508-2
e-ISBN (EPUB) 978-3-11-060387-3
ISSN 1613-8961

Library of Congress Control Number: 2018950638

Bibliographic information published by the Deutsche Nationalbibliothek
The Deutsche Nationalbibliothek lists this publication in the Deutsche Nationalbibliografie;
detailed bibliographic data are available on the Internet at http://dnb.dnb.de.

© 2021 Walter de Gruyter GmbH, Berlin/Boston
This volume is text- and page-identical with the hardback published in 2018.
Printing and binding: CPI books GmbH, Leck

www.degruyter.com

Acknowledgements

This book is the slightly revised version of my PhD thesis submitted under the title "Family Matters in Second-Generation British Migration Literature" at the University of Heidelberg in the summer of 2017. For the last decade during my studies and the time of my PhD, I was most fortunate to have received the unwavering support of my supervisor Vera Nünning, whose on-going encouragement and constructive advice was always extremely reassuring. I would also like to express my deep gratitude to my second supervisor Astrid Erll, whose profound knowledge of the field, informed criticism, and invaluable feedback helped me to reshape the manuscript for this book. I am most thankful to her and Ansgar Nünning for giving me the opportunity to publish my book in their series. Great thanks also go to Stella Diedrich and Nancy Christ at de Gruyter for their untiring help and assistance during the last stages of making this book.

Over the years of writing, I have been very lucky to be surrounded by a wonderful group of colleagues and friends at the English Department in Heidelberg, who have shaped the process of my thesis in various ways. I want to thank Caroline Lusin for her guidance during my studies and in the early stages of this project, and Jan Rupp for his useful advice in many delightful and informed conversations. Incalculable is the gratitude I feel for the generations of colleagues with whom I not only shared countless technical discussions but also many emotional ups and downs that come with the writing process: first of all, my office mate of many years, Stephanie Frink, followed by Bernard Woodley, Gesine Heil, Claudia Falk, and Christine Schwanecke. I am particularly indebted to Claire Earnshaw and Jennifer Smith for their feedback, last-minute corrections, and support in the final stages of my project. Claire has been the most untiring reader of this work and an incredibly resourceful help with stylistic and other detail.

Apart from this professional framework, I benefited immensely from being a part of two groups that were a constant source of intellectual debate, inspiration, and emotional motivation. My warmest thanks go to all the members of *Discover Football* in Berlin, and to the global network of wonderful women football players, as well as to the group *schwarzweiss* in Heidelberg, in particular to Caroline Authaler, Jan Becht, Christiane Bürger, Danijel Cubelic, Philmon Ghirmai, Diana Griesinger, and Carolin Liebisch for their friendship and long hours of discussion on issues of post-colonialism, global history, intersectionality, and what not.

What most kept me going over the last years were the wonderful times I spent with friends with whom I grouped up for various 'writing retreats' in

Malmö, Ratingen, the Spessart, or on Lake Traunsee. At these, the combination of exercise, food, discussion, and feedback created a space and time that helped me to bring the material into shape. For this and more I am tremendously thankful to Sarah Ablett and Friederike Faust. I also want to thank Anna Hartmann, Antony Pattathu, Jan Rupp, and my sister Valerie for their contributions to these retreats.

Last but not least, I want to thank my family for their overwhelming support. I feel grateful beyond words for the many ways and forms of doing family that we share. Aleida, Jan, Vincent, David, Marlene, and Valerie, to you and the extended family beyond our circle of seven this book is dedicated. Since I started working on this project, I have learnt as much about family relationships from my sisters, brothers, and parents as I have from my reading, and I was fascinated by the way these two spheres of learning entered a mutually stimulating dialogue. Special thanks are due to my brother David and my sister Marlene for proof-reading parts of my thesis and for sacrificing precious hours of sleep in order to help me bring my bibliography into shape before submission. Finally, for her great support – technical and otherwise – in applying the final touches to this book, very special thanks go to my partner Kristin.

The photographs arranged for the cover image of this book stem from a batch of family photos I bought at a small antique shop in Istanbul. Only through my travel back to Germany (and through their framing in the context of this book), did these pictures enter a context of migration (that I know of). The pictures' temporal setting, however, as well as the combination of family practices depicted in the images with the act of doing family that has to do with collecting such pictures, justify their use for this book.

Corinna Assmann
Heidelberg
1 July 2018

Contents

1		Introduction: Family Matters in Contemporary British Migration Literature —— 1
1.1		Family and Migration —— 2
1.2		The Family as a (New?) Field for Literary Studies: Aims and Methodology —— 7
1.3		Family and Migration in Literature: State of Research —— 12
2		Family Practices and Cultures of Relatedness —— 20
2.1		Family and Identity: Related and Relational Selves —— 22
2.1.1		Doing Family: The Social Construction of Relatedness —— 23
2.1.2		Family and the Social Development of the Self —— 37
2.2		Family (Hi)Stories and the Genealogical Imagination —— 48
2.2.1		Family Memory and Narrative —— 50
2.2.2		Genes and Genealogies —— 70
2.3		Doing Family as a New Field for Literary Analysis —— 77
3		Uncovering Family History: The Intergenerational Construction of Identity through Family Memory —— 81
3.1		"Divided loyalties": In-Betweenness and British-Asian Identity in Meera Syal's *Anita and Me* (1996) —— 82
3.1.1		Family Cultures and Differences —— 83
3.1.2		The Past Is a Foreign Country: Memory and Longing in the Diasporic Family —— 85
3.1.3		Anita Rutter: Meena's "passport to acceptance" —— 90
3.1.4		"Help from overseas": Meena's Initiation into Family History —— 95
3.2		"Everyone should know where they come from": Genealogical Identity in Andrea Levy's *Fruit of the Lemon* (1999) —— 102
3.2.1		The Family Tree Stub: Migration as a Narrative of Arrival and Beginning —— 103
3.2.2		Models of 'Rooted' Englishness: Genealogies, Family Traditions and Cultural Identity —— 110
3.2.3		The Fruit of the Family Tree: Appropriating Family History and Re-claiming Englishness —— 117
3.3		"Past tense, future imperfect": Breaking Free from Tangled Family Roots in Zadie Smith's *White Teeth* (2000) —— 121

3.3.1	Root Canals: The Inescapability of (Family) History —— 123	
3.3.2	Families of Choice: Irie's Search for 'Pure' Englishness —— 126	
3.3.3	"The perfect blankness of the past": Claiming Family History as a Chance for New Beginnings —— 131	
3.4	Concluding Thoughts: Family History and Genealogy as a Framework for Narratives of the Self —— 138	
4	**Family Secrets and Religious Conflict in the Muslim Diaspora —— 141**	
4.1	Migration and Loss: Family Relationships under the Burden of Cultural Trauma in Nadeem Aslam's *Maps for Lost Lovers* (2004) —— 143	
4.1.1	Mapping Loss: Inside and Outside of the 'Desert of Loneliness' —— 147	
4.1.2	A House "full of disappearances": Memories and Silences —— 154	
4.1.3	Body and Self: The Disintegration of Family —— 159	
4.2	Discovering Secrets, Unsettling Scripts: (Family) Identity and Islam in Robin Yassin-Kassab's *The Road from Damascus* (2008) —— 166	
4.2.1	Self-Fashioning and Postmodern Identities in the Multicultural Sphere —— 168	
4.2.2	Family Legacy as Life Script: Setting a 'Straight Path' —— 173	
4.2.3	Memory, Narrative, and Family Secrets —— 177	
4.3	Concluding Thoughts: Trauma and Silence —— 185	
5	**Family Memoirs: Relational Life Writing —— 188**	
5.1	"An ongoing story": Hanif Kureishi's Collective Family Memoir *My Ear at His Heart: Reading My Father* (2004) —— 191	
5.1.1	Affiliation and Disaffiliation: Becoming a Writer in Fulfilment of and through Rebellion against the Family Ideal —— 193	
5.1.2	"Dad is speaking to me again": The Memoir as a Multi-voiced (and Multi-modal) Transgenerational Family Dialogue —— 200	
5.1.3	"Trying to bring everything together": The Multifarious Voices of the Relational Self —— 205	
5.2	"Made up from a mixture of myth and gene": Family and Relatedness in Jackie Kay's Adoption Memoir *Red Dust Road* (2010) —— 210	
5.2.1	Family Storytelling as a Way of Doing Family —— 212	
5.2.2	"What makes us who we are": Stories as Inheritance —— 218	
5.2.3	Searching for "the place I come from": Locating the Diasporic Self —— 223	

5.3   Concluding Thoughts: Narratives of Filiation —— 232

6 Four Topoi of 'Doing Family': Food, Home, Photography, and the Body —— 235
6.1   Food —— 236
6.2   Home —— 242
6.3   Photography —— 248
6.4   The Body —— 253

Works Cited —— 263

Index —— 285

1 Introduction: Family Matters in Contemporary British Migration Literature

Stuart Hall was 18 years old when he immigrated to the UK, an age that symbolically marks the entry into adulthood and the corresponding dissociation from the family of origin. As he points out in his 1986 essay "Minimal Selves", family, however, remains a crucial framework for the constitution of the self – even if spatially removed:

> It wasn't a joke when I said that I migrated in order to get away from my family. I did. The problem, one discovers, is that since one's family is always already 'in here,' there is no way in which you can actually leave them. [...] I wish they were still around, so that I didn't have to carry them around, locked up somewhere in my head, from which there is no migration. So from the first, in relation to them, and then to all the other symbolic 'others,' I certainly was always aware of the self as only constituted in that kind of absent-present contestation with something else, with some other 'real me,' which is and isn't there. (Hall 1996, 116)

In this impressive self-portrait Hall expounds self-formation as a process that is never performed independently of others but is intrinsically intersubjective and always relational, and as such, continuously changing and unstable. The migration experience described by Hall shows how persistently the family continues to shape identity-building processes; even when it is no longer part of his immediate environment, it haunts his existence as 'symbolic other'. The context of migration creates a specific frame for the "absent-present contestation" that Hall ascribes to the family and which is closely linked to questions of cultural identity, home and belonging. The continuing presence of the absent family establishes a link between past and present, the old and the new. This connection connotes constancy and coherence in the face of the rupture of migration, which is often accompanied by a strong sense of change and loss. At the same time, there is a 'haunting' quality to this idea of family: it cannot be evaded or escaped but demands to be dealt with in some way. In this light, family may be experienced as at odds with a person's self-image, or as a constrictive determinant regarding adaptation processes in the new surrounding.

Hall's observation of the internalisation of the family as a 'symbolic other' is striking in its compact precision regarding the complex nature of identity, family, and migration. He develops this even further through his metaphoric description, where he touches on the intertwinement of the cognitive 'symbolic other' "in [his] head" and the corporeal dimension of self and other in the family context. The family is "carr[ied] around", one cannot "leave it", it is "in here" – incorporated. This description testifies to the strong affective bonds within the family. Taken literally, however, it can also be read to refer to the bodily connection one bears to one's family through genetic descent. Family is thus not only a primary point of reference and framework for the social construction of identity, it is also the basis for the genetic code. What makes family such an interesting analytical framework for the construction of identity is the interplay and tension between social and biological factors of identity, between heredity on the one hand – the genetic transmission of physical or mental traits – and (cultural) heritage – traditions, values, and norms that are passed on from generation to generation – on the other. Any engagement with family-related negotiations of the self will consequently also deal with the intersections of constructionist and essentialist concepts of identity.

Considering the fact that the family plays such a major role in identity construction, it is surprising that this specific interrelation has not gained more attention in literary studies. The process of identity formation begins and evolves in the family as an 'interactively lived community' (cf. Brinker-von der Heyde 2004, 8). Roles, relationships, behavioural patterns, and social structures as they are practised within the family permeate all other social interactions and areas of life. This study brings together the two topics of family and migration, with the aim of providing a systematic exploration of the role of the family under the pressure of migration as reflected in migration literature.[1]

1.1 Family and Migration

Migration has a strong impact on family relations and identity construction. What had been experienced as self-evident and taken for granted in the home country is now rendered strange, complex, and fraught with contradictions. The

---

[1] The intention behind this choice of term is to evade, on the one hand, politicised debates of representation, and, on the other hand, to be as all-encompassing as possible. The term emphasises the experience of migration (also as part of the authors' biographical background) instead of a specific ethnicity, which makes it as potentially open for white authors as for writers of colour. Nevertheless, 'Black British' is still the most widely used term, although with the introduction of more differentiated labels like British Asian or British Muslim it progressively loses its inclusive meaning as a "political signifier" (McLeod 2010, 46) derived from late twentieth century identity politics and activism. For a discussion of these terms see Baker et al. (1996, 5), McLeod (2010, 46), Stein (2004, 8–18), or Weedon (2016).

disintegration of established alliances and networks necessitates a search for new points of reference. The intercultural experience produces a radical proliferation of social and cultural frameworks of identity that transforms and overturns accepted family relations and roles. This often posits a challenge to families, which have to come to terms with the re-evaluation of family values, roles, and traditions from the first generation to the next. This 'disruptive' experience turns the world of the family upside down, and is the reason for migration theory to start counting generations from this new 'point of origin'. The distinction between first, second, or third generation is used broadly to characterise different points of view and experiences in the shared history of migration that change with the socio-historical context, resulting in different national affiliations, modes of belonging, and cultural identities from one generation to the next.[2] For members of the second generation, those born in Britain or immigrated at a childhood age, the process of identity construction in multicultural societies is often particularly intricate and tension-laden. Not surprisingly, many texts of migration literature deal with questions of transcultural identities and belonging precisely from this second-generation perspective (cf. Korte 1999).

The different 'generations' of migration literature written in the twentieth century can also be read in light of the political debate and the discourse on multiculturalism in Britain, as many outlines of British Black and Asian writing demonstrate.[3] While British Black and Asian authors from the first generation largely dealt with problems of social belonging and racism in the difficult context of arrival and accommodation in new and often hostile surroundings,[4] writers of the second generation have programmatically called for and induced a re-

---

[2] Cf., e.g., King et al. (2014); Sürig and Wilmes (2015); Wessendorf (2013); Esser (1990).
[3] Cf. Sommer (2001), Procter (2006, with regard to the politics of representation), Weedon (2016), or Sesay (2004). Although Sommer does not exclusively focus on post-colonial diasporic fiction with his term 'fictions of migration', there is a clear emphasis on what could otherwise be termed 'ethnic minority literature' or 'Black British literature' (see Sommer 2001, 6 and 3 respectively). Sommer puts his concept of 'fictions of migration' in the context of more general attempts to introduce new approaches to postcolonial literary studies that move away from binary oppositions central to postcolonial discourse such as that of periphery and centre, or self and other (cf. Sommer 2001, 2). For a similar discussion see also Nadia Butt (2015, 6–7), who delineates the advantages of the concept of transcultural memory over using postcolonial theory for the study of the contemporary Indo-English novel.
[4] Cf., e.g., Sam Selvon, *The Lonely Londoners* (1965), and Joan Riley, *The Unbelonging* (1985). See Sommer (2001, 75, 105–106), who classifies these novels as *Migrationsromane* as they deal primarily with the experience of immigration. Weedon (2016, 46) stresses the distinction of second-generation writers from authors such as Rushdie and Naipaul, "whose work is framed by the experience of empire, anti-colonial struggles and post-colonial legacies".

definition of "Englishness" as an open concept of national and cultural identity that is more true to the changed situation in the UK.[5] The 1980s and 90s are generally seen as a watershed period in Black British cultural politics and aesthetics that is decidedly influenced and advanced by a "new generation", or a "new breed" of writers (Sesay 2004, 107, 100). Chris Weedon (2016, 40) defines the period between 1980–2010 as one of "an increase and diversification in writing by black and Asian writers in the UK, augmented thematically and aesthetically by work from generations born and/or educated in Britain and their new configurations of questions of difference and identity". According to John McLeod's (2010, 46) cogent outline of a genealogy of black writing in Britain,[6] the second generation is characterised by its particularly rich creative output and its key role in the evolvement of Black British politics and aesthetics in the 1980s and the following final decades of the twentieth century. This view is supported by Daniela Berghahn (2013, 7) with regard to cinema when she describes the second generation of European filmmakers with migrant backgrounds as being responsible for "the development of a vibrant diasporic film culture". In his widely influential study on the Black British *bildungsroman*, Mark Stein (2004, 171) also emphasises this "transformative potential" in much second-generation writing that aims at "describing and inciting cultural changes", or, in other words, at "'re-writing' Britain" (Stein 2002, 34–35). Such a transformation, however, is no simple and easy process, as Hanif Kureishi's much-quoted beginning to his debut novel *The Buddha of Suburbia* (1999 [1990], 3) demonstrates: "I am an Englishman born and bred, almost." This instance of conditional 'self-ascription' hints at the problematic negotiation of a second-generation migrant identity through conflicting social demands, expectations, self-images, and the perception that others have of them. It is in the nature of things – of being born and bred, so to speak – that the family becomes a prominent and pressing issue in second-generation writing. As the selection of books to be examined in this book will show, second-generation writers increasingly bring into focus family constellations and connections, and thus – via the diachronic (and diasporic) perspective of family history – extend the temporal and

---

[5] Cf., e.g., Andrea Levy, *Fruit of the Lemon* (1998), and Zadie Smith, *White Teeth* (2000). See also Stein (2004, 4–7) for an overview of post-WW II migrant authors as well as a more general critical discussion of the definition of generations of (Black British) writers.

[6] Although McLeod (2010, 46) differentiates different generations of Black British writing here, he is wary of the connotations of the concept of genealogy and rejects the idea of an evolutionary model in the sense of presenting mere continuity and a neat progression of concerns and themes. Instead, he argues that the different generations need to be considered in light of their distinct and separate concerns and perspectives.

spatial framework in which questions of memory, identity, and belonging are explored to include long-term historical entanglements and (post-)colonial involvements.[7] In following this shift in focus to family-related issues, and therefore to more 'local affairs', I take my cue from McLeod's (2010, 46–47) important observation that contemporary British Black writing is not always and not solely concerned with "the refashioning of 'British identities'" at a personal psychological as well as national level.

From here, I will proceed to analyse migration literature at the turn of the twentieth century in light of the ways in which family informs identity construction.[8] Focusing on second-generation writers, I want to look into the changing roles and meanings of the family as well as intergenerational family relations in a migration setting. I will aim to highlight the specific challenges, problems, and possibilities that arise in the process of identity construction as they are conveyed through the prism of the family – a dimension of experience that has, as yet, been largely neglected in the study of migration literature. The family is not only "the crucible of society" (Vangelisti 2003, ix), it is also, generally speaking, the context in which the groundwork for a person's identity is laid. The family as reference point for the formation of the self sheds light on key aspects of identity construction, bringing together and creating a fruitful tension between social constructionist and biological determinist concepts of identity.[9] Zadie Smith's seminal debut novel *White Teeth*, for example, plays with the contradictions and friction resulting from these two models of heteronomous determination vs. autonomous self-definition. This not only involves the issue of genetic inheritance, when the body takes on significance as a carrier of family history, and family memory emerges as inscribed into the genetic code as

---

[7] Although there is an emphasis on the entangled histories of Britain and its former colonies in this study, the term 'migration literature' (rather than, e.g., diasporic or Black British literature) indicates that the conceptual and theoretical base established here can also be applied to literature in other migration contexts such as in the case of more recent A8 migrants.

[8] The text corpus mainly features novels, i.e. works of fiction. The inclusion of two memoirs, however, prompts me to use the more general term 'literature', although only prose writing is considered in this thesis. The framework of analysis could nevertheless easily and very fruitfully be extended to other literary genres such as drama and poetry (including spoken word and performance poetry). Jackie Kay, whose memoir is analysed here, is a case in point, as much of her poetry, in particular *The Adoption Papers* (1991), could be read from a similar perspective. This example moreover hints at the applicability of the approach elaborated here to writing beyond the field of 'migration literature'.

[9] The family as a framework of identity encourages us to recognise the importance of the body for subjectivity and selfhood and the fact that "psychology and physiology are intimately linked" (Eakin 1999, 20), thus expunging the "venerable mind/body split" (Eakin 1999, 25).

an inalienable part of the self.¹⁰ The aspect of the body also opens up important concerns particularly with regard to Black and Asian British literature, in which racism, discrimination, and the attempt to cast off imposed stereotypes are common motifs. Against the background of this dimension of 'family resemblances', the body cannot be exclusively considered as a medium of performative constructions of identity, it now also becomes a site of racialisation, an important carrier of identity that involves a great potential for conflict in negotiating identity and ethnic and cultural belonging. As the locus of genetic transmission, the family plays a pivotal role in this negotiation and is intractably linked to the conflict.

A frequently used and popular plotline in migration fiction is based on the intergenerational conflict in the family that arises from issues of cultural belonging and affiliation, in which characters of the second generation are presented as having to position themselves between the values and views of their parents on the one hand, and those of the host society and their social generation on the other.¹¹ Mark Stein (2004, 29) emphasises the importance and frequency of this trope in second-generation migration literature, where it is usually cast as a "blending of what could vaguely be referred to as generational and cultural conflicts" (see also Stein 2002, 34). While such social dynamics set in motion by the family members' dissimilar processes of acculturation take place on the synchronic axis of the family, the diachronic axis introduces the perspective of family history – a perspective that has not received due attention in literary studies thus far.¹² If we take serious Chris Weedon's (2016, 46; emphasis in the original) assertion that a primary aspect of second generation writing is that it "draws on family and community *memories of migration*", then a closer focus on the familial context and framework of memory and the processes of trans-

---

10 Cf. the character of Millat in *White Teeth* (525–526): "His is an imperative secreted in the genes and the cold steel in his inside pocket is the answer to a claim made on him long ago. He's a Pandy deep down. And there's mutiny in his blood."
11 The most famous examples of this plotline can probably be found in film, as for example in the two box office hits *East Is East* (1999) and *Bend It like Beckham* (2002). Ken Loach's *Ae Fond Kiss* (2004) about an interracial love relationship could also be named here. See Weedon (2016, 47) for an overview of these thematics in literature.
12 Stein's monograph on the *bildungsroman* (2004) is indicative of this prioritisation: Although he deals in depth with constructions of genealogical identity (with reference to Abdulrazak Gurnah's *Dottie*, 1990, 41–42, Levy's *Fruit of the Lemon*, 1999, 67–73, and Bernardine Evaristo's *Lara*, in the 1997 version, 80–96), he continuously stresses the importance of intergenerational conflict as the main topic through which family is thematised in the novel of transformation (cf. e.g. 25, 29, 58, 66). Exceptions to this focus are referenced in the state of research section of this introduction.

mission it involves seems warranted. In many novels, the characters are not just members of a modern 'nuclear' family; they also evolve as part of a transgenerational network of relations. The aim of this study is to explore such historical extensions of the individual self-narrative in interconnection with the other factors mentioned above, namely the body and social interaction. It will, moreover, be interesting to see how "[w]e can gauge this shift in concerns by attending to changes in literary form" (McLeod 2010, 47), namely, how the interplay between the synchronic and diachronic dimension of the family also influences the formal level of the written text. We can assume that the role of the family at the story level has implications at the discourse level and affects the modes of representation. This may concern genre-related features of the novels, with regard to genres such as the *bildungsroman* or family novel, narrative mode, or other narratological aspects such as the semanticisation of time and space.

1.2 The Family as a (New?) Field for Literary Studies: Aims and Methodology

Although the family is one of the biggest and most common topics in literature, it is still largely under-theorised in literary studies.[13] The topic does, however, neatly dovetail with a number of research areas that have recently gained ground in literary studies, and which serve as a fruitful starting point for a more detailed investigation into (migrant) families in literature. Three concepts will be of particular importance for this thesis in order to create a theoretical frame of reference: the relational self, generations and genealogies, and the nexus of

---

[13] This is true not only with regard to Black and Asian British literary studies but applies to the study of contemporary English literature in general. This is different for other literary periods, as, for example, James Kilroy's (2007) insightful study of representations of domesticity and the ideological discourse of the family in the nineteenth-century novel. His literary analysis is embedded in historical, anthropological, as well as sociological research of the development of family life, from extended family structures to the nuclear family of the industrial age, and gives an interesting overview of the family in nineteenth-century society and culture in England. A different example of this approach is offered by Golightly (2012). In their edited volume, O'Reilly Herrera et al. (1997) deal with selected aspects or dimensions of the family, including motherhood, the patriarchal family, and children. Prillinger's (2000) analysis of the family in the late twentieth-century Scottish Working-Class Novel follows the sociological model of the family life cycle, which is, as a concept of family, more restricted than envisaged in this study. Here, the primary focus on the nexus of family and identity in a migrant context calls for an understanding of family that is connectible with prevalent concepts in the field of diasporic literature and postcolonial studies.

memory and narrative. Each of these research areas have drawn a great deal of attention from the field of narratology recently, and consequently offer a broad basis of theoretical conceptualisation around questions of identity construction and, as will be shown, family matters.

As this study aims to put the individual into the context of the family, it seems natural to turn to the concept of the *relational self* as developed by John Paul Eakin, which emphasises the importance of personal relationships and the positioning of the individual within a larger network of relations for the construction of identity (cf. Eakin 1999, 43ff.). The family as "primary social unit" (Visser 2005, 5) naturally plays a crucial role in this context. Consciousness of the self does not develop in isolation, independent of others, because self-formation has at its very core an intersubjective dimension in that we depend on others to recognise and affirm how we see ourselves (cf. Eakin 1999, 52). Beyond this very basic aspect of intersubjectivity, identity is always constructed in relation to others, whether through aspects of sameness, affiliation, imitation, or through differentiation and distinction. The self cannot be conceptualised without the other as a foil against which it takes on its shape. Identities, therefore, are essentially relational, as well as dynamic and always in development. Eakin highlights the role of the family in this process of creating a collaborative and collectively built identity. The family constitutes a social unit that we usually share an intimate space with over a long period of time,[14] and therefore takes a special place in the dynamics of identification and differentiation. Although the concept of the relational self has recently gained prominence in literary studies, the specific role of the family has received comparatively little attention in this field of research, especially if understood as a configuration that goes beyond individual family relationships such as father-son, for example. Here, I employ the concept of the relational self not only to investigate identity construction in relation to individual significant others, but also to look deeper into the interrelations and tensions of individual and collective identities in the family.

The intersection of individual and collective identities is also a central concern in the research on *generations and genealogies*. The field of generation studies has evolved quickly since the 2000s, establishing 'generation' as a noteworthy cross-disciplinary concept in history, the social sciences, cultural

---

[14] Definitions of family usually emphasise the aspect of shared residence alongside that of kinship/blood relation (cf. Berghahn 2013, 18). However, when the interest in family relations broadens to account for transgenerational constellations, it quickly becomes evident that the idea of a shared household is not necessarily central to understandings of family, especially in a diasporic context.

theory, and in literature.¹⁵ This line of research, rather than treating generations as naturally 'given', is interested in generations as 'imagined communities' that are constituted or strengthened through narrative (cf. Roseman 2005), and highlights the fact that 'generation' is first and foremost a concept of identity (Jureit and Wildt 2005, 9). The concept of generation involves two dimensions, a synchronic dimension of social or historical generations based on "collectively held ideas and shared formative experiences" (Rupp 2017, 105),¹⁶ and a diachronic dimension as represented by family generations. The diachronic perspective highlights intergenerationality and the temporal succession of generations, that is, how they form a genealogy on the basis of patterns of descent and lineage. Here, identification takes place not on the horizontal axis of synchronicity, but on a vertical axis of sequence and diachronic interrelations. In contrast with social generations, generational positioning within the family supports an individualised concept of identity rather than the process of collective identity formation. Yet, the concept of generation continues to link the family to larger social or historical contexts and developments, and stresses the intersection of family and society, the personal and the collective, the private and the public. The two temporal dimensions are thus closely connected, not least because the discourse of generations in different contexts is always to a certain degree informed by the model of generational succession in the family.

The third conceptual field I turn to here, the nexus of narrative and memory, is located on a superordinate level since the other two areas of research build on ideas and assumptions that stem from memory studies and the theory of narrative identity. Indeed, the two concepts of the relational self and generations/genealogy are firmly embedded in the findings and conceptualisations that have proceeded from the continuously expanding field of memory

---

15 These studies are concerned with the discourse of generations, the contexts and ways in which the concept is employed and how it relates to specific historical constellations. For the social sciences see Mannheim 2009 [1928; 1952], Eyerman and B. Turner (1998), Edmunds and B. Turner (2002); in memory studies see A. Assmann (2007), Kansteiner (2012); in history see Fietze (2009); as a subject for interdisciplinary cultural theory see, first of all, the work produced by Sigrid Weigel and her research group: Weigel (2002), Weigel (2006), Weigel et al. (2005), Parnes et al. (2008), but also Jureit and Wildt (2005), Künemund and Szydlik (2009), Bohnenkamp et al. (2009); in literary studies see Sollors (1988), Kraft and Weißhaupt (2009), Lauer (2010), Sobral (2012).
16 Karl Mannheim (the founding father of sociological research on generations) speaks of the "stratification of experience" (*Erlebnisschichtung*), where "[a]ll later experiences [...] tend to receive their meaning" from an "original set" of first impressions and decisive childhood experiences (Mannheim 2009 [1952], 177).

studies. The 'lens of memory studies' (Erll 2017, 111) brings to the fore both these concepts' concerns with the interconnections of individual/autobiographical memory with different frameworks of collective memory, as well as with the way these memory frameworks are intertwined and permeate each other. The idea of the relational self, having originated in literary research on autobiography, quite naturally connects with theories of *narrative identity* and *memory*. Dan P. McAdams defines identity as the integration of "disparate roles, talents, proclivities, and social involvements into a patterned *configuration* of thought and activity that provides life with some semblance of psychosocial *unity and purpose*" (2003, 188; emphasis in the original). It is through narrative that such a sense of coherence and continuity is achieved as the synchronic and diachronic dimensions of identity are "brought meaningfully together in a temporally organized whole" in the form of the life story (ibid, 189). The life-story theory of identity revolves around the nexus of memory and narrative.[17] The emergence of autobiographical memory in early childhood is also closely connected to the development of narrative ability (cf. Nelson 2003). This process of social learning in interaction with significant others usually takes place to a large extent in the realm of the family, which constitutes the framework of the transmission of cultural and social narrative forms for structuring past experiences and projecting the life narrative into the future. The embeddedness of autobiographical memory in family memory is an important source of meaning and coherence for the life story and the identity construction of the individual. The interrelations between family memory and narrative with individual levels of identity construction and the life story on the one hand, and with collective structures of meaning production and identity on the other, are manifold and highly complex (cf. Erll 2011a). The focus on family, central to the human experience, offers an excellent vantage point for examining the interconnections and tensions of individual and collective identity.

With the support of these concepts, which are well-established in interdisciplinary literary studies, my aim is to bring the family into the centre of literary analysis. Family seems to be a simple enough matter at first. Due to its ubiquity in everyday personal life, its pervasiveness in public discourse, and its wide

---

[17] Given the close connection of memory and narrative, this has, not surprisingly, become a vast field of research in literary studies. Research here concentrates mostly either on autobiographical memory (cf. Birke 2008; Bruner and Weisser 1991; Eakin 2001; Neumann 2005), cultural memory (cf. the section on "Literature and Cultural Memory" in Erll and A. Nünning 2008; Erll 2014; Erll and Rigney 2009), or the intersection of both (cf. Gymnich and A. Nünning 2006).

dispersal over numerous and diverse academic fields of research, family appears natural, unquestioned and unquestionable. Digging deeper into sociological, anthropological, and psychological theories of family in chapter 2.1, I want to show that this assumed naturalness is exactly why it is worthwhile to establish a concept of family that determines the object of analysis more clearly and outlines possible approaches for the study of family matters in literature. The notion of 'family' is to a great degree ideologically saturated and much contested (cf. Smart 2007, 27; Morgan 2011, 50; Edwards et al. 2012, 732).[18] It also tends to be over-charged with meaning: "Family is an idea constituted in and through the images produced by family researchers, by families themselves, and by canonical narratives of family circulating through culture." (Jorgenson and Bochner 2003, 513)

The associations and meanings surrounding the term 'family' are neither stable nor clearly definable. In order to arrive at a more complex and precise conceptualisation, it is important to break up the monolithic notion of family and to make room for divergent concepts and transformations of family life and family values under the condition of social change and cultural diversity. In order to be able to recognise different forms and interpretations of family life, it is useful to take into consideration recent re-theorisations of the concept from the fields of sociology and anthropology that propose a more open definition. Here, the breadth of the meaning of 'family' has been highlighted by the introduction of a variety of alternative terms, such as 'personal life', 'cultures of relatedness', or 'family configurations'. These hint at the different approaches that are present in the field, which has recently diversified to include a greater variety of facets, such as 'intimacy', 'family lives', 'family practices', 'displaying family', 'doing family', etc. (cf. Edwards et al. 2012, 733).[19] Furthermore, moving away from family as something that is predetermined increases awareness for the way ideas of family and of family life are informed by a variety of factors such as class, ethnicity, culture, or time and place in history (cf. Brinker-von der Heyde 2004, 7–8). A more open conceptualisation also recognises the family as an intersectional field in which other identity categories such as ethnicity, gen-

---

18 This ideologically charged assumption of family refers mostly to the prototypical notion of the heterosexual, white, middle-class nuclear family. See also Brinker-von der Heyde (2004, 7).
19 For an overview and critical discussion of these new approaches to family see Morgan (2011a, 33–53). For a summary of "the sociological battle over the family", its "great debates" and new directions see Smart (2007, 7–31). For an historical introduction of family theories see Crosbie-Burnett and Klein (2009). See also Carsten (2000, 2–4); D. Chambers (2012, 1, 34); Cheal (2002, 12); Finch (2007, 66); Galvin (2006, 15); Jallinoja and Widmer (2011, 5); Jamieson (2011, 1.2).

der, class, age, or generation overlap (cf. J. Scott et al. 2003, xvi). The theme of family as a lens for reading migration literature thus corresponds with the concerns of transcultural studies, in particular the transcultural perspective in memory studies that aims to question and steer clear of the "grids (territorial, social, temporal, which we tend to superimpose upon the complex realities of remembering in culture" (Erll 2011b, 8).

1.3 Family and Migration in Literature: State of Research

The family is the primary site of transmission of cultural values, norms, and traditions, albeit in close interaction with other social networks and institutions that are part of the greater societal and cultural context. It constitutes the framework and informs the ways in which personal identities emerge and narratives of the self are constructed. This function of the family as 'cradle of culture' gains even higher significance and becomes more complex when regarded in light of the migration experience. Migration dramatically impacts on all aspects that constitute family life, as it entails an often drastic change in the living situation and the social and cultural context.[20] The post-migration condition in multicultural societies is highly sensitive to potential conflict between family, the community, other cultural/ethnic groups and/or the majority society. Conflict, however, not only arises at the borders of the family in contact with the outside world, frictions also erupt within the family group, and typically affect generational and gender relationships. The intricacies of the nexus of family and migration thus involve a "varied spectrum of aspects of interculturality that trigger conflict and/or initiate re-negotiations" (Holdenried 2012, 13; my translation). As Cornelia Helfferich (2012) elaborates, the impact of migration on families moves between the poles of being a 'crucial test' to family identity and of 'reinforcing family togetherness'.[21] Family memory and identity gain a heightened significance against the background of migration, change, and separation, but also become more fragile, as the tensions between old and new, and be-

---

[20] Migration is to be understood not as a uniform process but as highly differentiated with regard to divergence in historical, social, regional contexts, reasons of migration, etc., and thus needs to be considered in its heterogeneity (cf. Helfferich 2012). The focus of this study on specific novels and the experiences depicted therein will hopefully help to keep the problem of generalisation at bay.

[21] Cf. the title of Helfferich's (2012) article: "Migration – Zerreißprobe oder Stärkung des Familienzusammenhalts?".

tween different cultural influences and values, often give rise to conflict and threaten family ties.²²

Black and Asian British writing has, since the 1980s, established itself as a prolific and progressively important branch of contemporary literature. Its relevance emerges in literary productivity, heightened media coverage, and growing numbers of new releases, which all attest to what Graham Huggan (2001, vii) compellingly calls "the booming 'alterity industry'", yet is not confined to these fields. Migration literature also meets with increasing critical recognition, to which literary awards and rising attention in academia can testify.²³ The abundance of research published in this area since the beginning of the twenty-first century documents the fact that Black (and Asian) British culture has become firmly established as a field of study in its own right within literary and/or cultural studies.²⁴ While questions of identity construction and belonging are top-ranking research topics in this field,²⁵ the role of the family in relation to these concerns needs yet to be explored in detail. If, as Michaela Holdenried (2012, 13) claims, the impact of migration on the family is as yet a largely overlooked topic in sociological research, this is definitely the case in literary studies. Therefore, this study on the one hand advances considerations around the family, both synchronic and diachronic, to enhance the rapidly growing field of research on contemporary migration literature in Britain. On the other hand, however, the books analysed here can be seen to provide a fruitful commentary and addition to research on migration and the family beyond the field of literary studies, as the "proto-empirical dimension" (Holdenried 2012, 13; my translation) of literary writing offers us a privileged window unto the experiences and challenges that migrant families face.

A few studies, however, have put a spotlight on family matters in migration literature, setting the agenda for further research. In her essay on "Accultura-

---

22 Hence the perhaps overstated trope of the intergenerational/cultural conflict in representations of migrant families. Cf. Berghahn (2013, 2): "The family, as the smallest unit of society and as the prime site of socialisation and identity formation, plays a pivotal role in the provocative evocation of such culture clash scenarios, given that, in public discourse and political rhetoric, society's ills are regularly attributed to the decline or failure of the family."
23 Huggan makes a point to not exclude academia (and thus also himself) from the processes surrounding the "material conditions of production and consumption of postcolonial writings" (2001, vii) and the commodification of postcolonial studies and aesthetics.
24 Some examples are Reichl (2002); Procter (2003); Arana and Ramey (2004); Stein (2004); Kadija (2005); Low (2006); Eckstein et al. (2008); Rupp (2010); Upstone (2010); Gunning (2010); Osborne (2016).
25 See, e.g., Bromley (2000); Stein (2002, 34); Weedon (2004a); Weedon (2004b); Frank (2010).

tion and Family Structure", Silvia Mergenthal (1996) provides an interesting perspective by describing the impact of the post-migration condition on family configurations and relationships in an analysis of three novels.[26] In a similar vein, Janet Wilson's (2005) insightful article on "The Family and Change: Contemporary Second-Generation British-Asian Fiction"[27] compares two novels, analysing the changes in attitude in the respective protagonists towards their families. Her readings are guided by the question of whether these characters confirm traditional ideas of family unity by identifying with their existing family network, or whether they drift apart from their family in search of alternative models of family.[28]

While these two examples deal mainly with the synchronic family, the present study aims to broaden this scope by placing the synchronic family in a diachronic perspective. The complex interplay of, on the one hand, "continuity and growth", the family as the "locus of tradition, [...] as the place where core values of the preceding generations and the ancestors are transmitted and lived" (Visser 2005, 5), and the family as a place of disruption and social and cultural change on the other hand, necessitates an approach that involves both perspectives. Irene Visser (2005, 5) emphasises that "[i]n contemporary postcolonial literatures in English the theme of the family is particularly rich and diversified", as it draws together many of the issues central to understanding multicultural societies and the concerns of marginalised groups within them:

> As the custodian of tradition and memory, the family fulfils an important function, transmitting and mediating the memories, mores, and myths of the preceding generations and the community. Rituals, customs, spirituality, morality and religion all have their place within the family structure, themselves forming family fictions of a unique and, most often, communal nature. (Visser 2005, 5)

---

26 Timothy Mo's *Sour Sweet* (1982), Hanif Kureishi's *The Buddha of Suburbia* (1990), and Kazuo Ishiguro's *A Pale View of Hills* (1982).
27 Wilson's (2005) article is part of the proceedings of a conference on *Family Fictions: The Family in Contemporary Postcolonial Literatures in English*, edited by Irene Visser and Heidi van den Heuvel-Disler. This online publication presents the only volume that is focussed exclusively on family in contemporary postcolonial literature.
28 Wilson's analysis comprises Syal's *Anita and Me* (1996), Ali's *Brick Lane* (2003), and Kureishi's *The Buddha of Suburbia*. Both Mergenthal's (1996) and Wilson's (2005) study focus on the interconnection between family roles and identity on the one hand and cultural belonging on the other, albeit without a clearly stated theoretical or conceptual basis for their analysis. In sum, Wilson's conclusion that the family provides a "crucial origin and point of departure for [the novels'] protagonists" (Wilson 2005, 118) is a promising presupposition for further explorations of the field.

What Visser's important enumeration of the forms of family communication does not take into account is another dimension that is crucial with regard to 'postcolonial families', namely family as a medium of historical experience and its transmission. The prism of family therefore also invites us to follow up on questions raised by Barbara Korte and Ulrike Pirker (2011, 12) regarding a "history boom" in the late twentieth century in the United Kingdom, which has induced "a new historical culture for a 'multiethnic Britain'" (Korte and Pirker 2011, 13). Issues concerning historical entanglements and the interconnections between power and constructions of the historical narrative lie at the centre of postcolonial theory; such issues also constitute a crucial part of the more hidden and suppressed forms of family interaction. A closer look at the way history is transmitted within families thus duly recognises and gives prominence to the "essential plurality of memory" (Rupp 2010, 1), an insight that is fundamental to the discussion around discourses of national, transnational, or postcolonial memory and history from the stance of transcultural memory studies.[29] Diasporic and transnational family narratives per se open up perspectives on the construction of collective memory that reach beyond the national framework and emphasise the dynamics of memory and the importance of performativity in remembering, aspects that are central also to transcultural memory studies (see Brunow 2015, 3).

With her contribution on the genre of 'family and generational novels' in contemporary British literature, Astrid Erll (2007) has made an important advance in the field of migration literature. Her 'exemplary reading' of Zadie Smith's *White Teeth* reveals how, in the genre of the family novel, the dimension of colonial history and its ramifications come to the fore in the frameworks of family memory and genealogical (dis)continuities.[30] As her essay shows, a look into the role of family memory and history in novels like *White Teeth* might provide routes that connect the study of British migration literature with other fields such as transcultural memory studies. The insights into family memory that these novels offer attest not only to "the great internal heterogeneity of cultural remembering within the nation-state" (Erll 2011b, 8), but the represented families, being diasporic families, are themselves deeply affected by transcultural movements, migration, and travel (reaching back to colonial times). As Nadia Butt (2015, 19) contends, "[t]here is no doubt that memories of migrants are a site of transcultural memory, but it is to be noticed that cultural interac-

---

29 See Rothberg (2013) for a discussion of the relations and overlaps between (trans)cultural memory studies and postcolonial studies.
30 Cf. also Weingarten's (2012) reading of *Brick Lane* as "interkultureller Familienroman".

tions are no longer merely a sphere of migrants".[31] Second- or third-generation writing in particular meets this concern, as the issues of identity and belonging raised in these novels are closely connected to the larger-scale "process of redefining Britishness" and the social sphere in Britain (cf. Stein 2004, 30).

Novels and other forms of writing such as the non-fictional memoirs included in this study thus attest to the role of literature as an important medium for the production of cultural memory that "give[s] insight into what is a highly diverse and contested historical culture" (Korte and Pirker 2011, 14). The dual national and transnational orientation of migration literature (cf. Brunow 2015, 53) serves to challenge monolithic notions of memory and national frameworks for the construction of the past and the historical narrative. This can similarly be said of the perspective of family memory as an approach to tackle contemporary issues of identity and belonging in the selected novels. It should not surprise us that "the heightened presence of memory issues in public discourses on immigration in the past two decades" (Erll 2017, 110; cf. Korte and Pinker 2011; cf. Holdenried 2012, 14–17) finds expression in a growing literary interest in themes of family remembering and genealogical identity. Indeed, Erll (2017) assesses the expanding field of "Fictions of Generational Memory", thus highlighting "the significant role that memory, generationality, and genealogy play in structuring contemporary literature". Examining the family as a site of memory not only compellingly conjoins chief concerns of both memory and generational studies, it also incorporates many of the aspects of 'memory in culture'[32] that Erll (2011b, 14) highlights: "It involves knowledge, repertoires of stories and scripts, implicit memory, bodily aspects such as habitus, and – next to remembering – also that other basic operation of memory: forgetting."

Propelled by a boom in the genre of the 'multigenerational' or 'family novel' by writers of the second and third post-World War II generation, the intersections of generation, genealogy, family memory, and (trans)national history have been the object of extensive research and discussion in German literary and cultural studies since the 1980s. Although the family constellation and the historical context is considerably different in the German case, some concepts developed with respect to German family novels can also be applied to contem-

---

31 In a similar vein, Brunow (2015, 18) emphasises that "[t]he case of migrant memories shows the need for memory scholars not to 'other' migrant or diasporic persons in the research process by situating them outside a national framework".

32 Erll introduces the phrase "memory in culture" in contradistinction to 'the memories of cultures' in order to emphasise the meaning of culture in this context as relating to the sociocultural contexts of memory production and to avoid "tying culture – and by extension cultural memory – to clear-cut territories and social formations" (2011b, 6).

porary British literature.[33] In the following, I will distinguish between the family novel in the more narrow sense of the genre, for which I will use the term 'multigenerational novel', and 'family writing' as a broader and more general indication of content. In family writing, the family is not only the context of an individual development (as, for example, in the *bildungsroman*) but is at the heart of the novel.[34] The multigenerational or family novel, as a genre, involves two main aspects:[35] Firstly, a plot-line that follows the chronology of two or more family generations, focusing on family relationships and intergenerational conflict. This entails an extended time frame of 80 to 100 years (corresponding to the time span of the communicative memory in the family), and includes an extended cast of characters and perspectives. Secondly, the story of the family is interwoven with socio-historical events and developments, which is often done through the characters' generationality.[36] In addition, Erll (2007, 118; my translation) emphasises the "critical discussion of the topics 'generationality' and/or 'genealogy'".[37]

With the exception of *White Teeth*, the texts selected for this study do not closely (nor sometimes even broadly) fall into the genre category of the multigenerational novel, but they nevertheless show considerable overlap with the features listed above, which prompts us to group them as family writing. The books, published between the years 1996 and 2010, were written by writers from the second immigrant generation and, with one exception, put this specific experience at their centre. The selection of texts attempts to map a broad spec-

---

[33] There is considerable confusion and lack of clarity in the usage of genre denominations concerning those novels that are, in German, referred to as 'family' or 'generational novels'. In the scope of this thesis, however, it is impossible to go into this discussion in detail. Even in the German context, which has seen numerous publications on the genre in the last years, the terminology is complex, and the two terms are often used interchangeably, but also with variations in meaning (see Galli and Costagli 2010, 8ff.). In English, there seems to be even more confusion as regards genre denominations, and the multigenerational novel, the family saga or family chronicle, and the family novel exist side by side. The most widely cited monograph on the genre in the realm of Anglophone literature is Yi-ling Ru's *The Family Novel* (1992). See also Boyers's essay on "The Family Novel" (1974) and Erll (2007, 117).
[34] Cf. Galli and Costagli (2010, 8) for this usage of the term 'family novel'.
[35] Cf. Erll (2007, 117) and Galli and Costagli (2010, 8ff.).
[36] Lutosch (2007, 9–10) criticises that this is often understood to imply that the family serves as a 'mirror' for society, or a microcosm that resembles the macrocosm of society, both of which are widely inaccurate assumptions.
[37] Ru's list of features of the 'family novel' is geared towards the big modernist family chronicles like *Buddenbrooks* and therefore features, in addition to the characteristics above, "the decline of the family" (1992, 2).

trum of Black and Asian British writing that has a common epicentre in the theme of the family. To begin, Chapter 3 looks at three works that have long reached canonical status in contemporary British literature and are frequently cited as prime examples of what I here call 'migration novels'. It is due to their elevated status that these novels are particularly well suited to demonstrate that the tendencies that are described in this study have relevance for the overall field of Black and Asian British writing. Meera Syal's *Anita and Me* (1996) and Andrea Levy's *Fruit of the Lemon* (1998) are generally read as paradigmatic of the Black British *bildungsroman*, an interpretation that I want to supplement by drawing attention to the dimension of family history opened up in these novels. From this perspective, the two novels suddenly show astonishing similarities with Zadie Smith's millennial bestseller *White Teeth* (2000), which carves out the full potential of these themes for the genre of the multigenerational novel – a genre that at first glance seems to differ widely from the themes, structure, and narrative form of the *bildungsroman*. Chapters 4 and 5 proceed from here to deal with lesser-known texts that each add new aspects to the complex topic of family and migration. With Nadeem Aslam's *Maps for Lost Lovers* (2004) and Robin Yassin-Kassab's *The Road from Damascus* (2008) a still somewhat marginal, albeit steadily growing field of Black and Asian British literature is taken into consideration, namely Muslim writing. The focus here is on the interwovenness of 'family culture' and religion, which borders on the idea of 'family as religion'. The last chapter looks at two 'family memoirs', Hanif Kureishi's *My Ear at His Heart: Reading My Father* (2004) and Jackie Kay's *Red Dust Road* (2010), and thus acknowledges the cultural significance of the recent wave of relational autobiographies, a trend that is currently remoulding the genre(s) of life writing. What these texts of family writing share is their centre of gravity in London or other British cities, while the migration stories follow the routes of the former British Empire to the West (the Caribbean) and to the East (South Asia).

The selection could well be extended to include other texts that invite readings along similar lines and that give an impression of the diversity, scope, and extent of the field of family writing. Bernardine Evaristo's family verse chronicle *Lara* (2009), in particular, shares many themes with the novels discussed in Chapter 3, while exploring the protagonist's biracial family history as 'doubly postcolonial', rooted in Catholic Ireland on her mother's side and in Nigeria and Brazil on her father's. *Travelling with Djinns* (2003) by Jamal Mahjoub adds yet another dimension to the quest of self-discovery through an investigation of family history and relationships by involving the third generation in form of the protagonist's seven-year-old son. Irenosen Okojie's multigenerational novel

Butterfly Fish (2015) provides an original take on the topic by interweaving different time layers from nineteenth-century Nigeria to present-day London. The field of relational life writing, of course, offers a great variety of further examples that deal with the nexus of personal identity, family, entangled histories, and transcultural memory, such as Vikram Seth's *Two Lives* (2005) and Michael Ondaatje's *Running in the Family* (1982), a family memoir that precedes the bulk of this study's corpus by roughly twenty years. Linda Grant's *The Clothes on Their Backs* (2007) is yet another example of the complexity of the topic of migration and family identity, which, in this case, is dealt with in the context of an Eastern-European Jewish family in Britain. The novel thus demonstrates that the relevance of the questions that fuel this study exceed the realm of Black and Asian British writing – and may serve as an invitation to further research in other areas of migration literature. Moreover, a comparison of family writing in the migration context, as it is discussed here, with literature from the broader field of postcolonial New Anglophone Literatures would be likely to present interesting new perspectives; Kamila Shamsie's *Kartography* (2002), for example, offers a fascinating take on the complex interlacing of family, history, and memory that corresponds closely with the analyses offered here. John McLeod's (2010) analysis of Caryl Phillips's novel *In the Falling Snow* (2009) demonstrates the potential of extending the approach to include the distinct perspective of the third generation, and to see how that changes family constellations and generational identities (see also Erll 2017).

Given the huge productivity and amazing variety of Black and Asian British literature, this study can by no means provide a representative overview of its genres, narrative forms, and literary motifs. What this book offers, however, is a new approach to, and a deeper understanding of, the long-term continuities and aftereffects of colonial history and the way the ramifications of postcoloniality and globalisation find expression in the lives, practices, and structures of diasporic families. With its focus on the second generation, this approach not only allows us to explore the tensions that arise from this history and put pressure on the fragile system of the migrant family, but it also points to the potential for enabling change and offering new ways of belonging that lie in a 'usable' past.

2 Family Practices and Cultures of Relatedness

In contrast to predictions during the 1960s and '70s that announced the 'decline' and even the 'death of the family' (cf. Cooper 1976 [1971]), the institution of the family seems to have survived deep cultural and social transformations. At the beginning of the twenty-first century, it is still very much alive and – judging by the number of recent publications in sociology and anthropology – continues to provide fertile soil for scholarly discussion.[1] It is obvious that the family has not lost its social and cultural relevance, indeed contrary to previous fears, it has become a central area of research as well as an animated focus of public debate. This is confirmed by Jacqueline Scott and her colleagues (2003, xvi), who write in their preface to *The Blackwell Companion to the Sociology of Families* that the field of family studies

> has moved from being at the fringes of the discipline [of sociology] to being one of the key areas for understanding the structural and life-course transformations that are taking place across the globe. The upheavals of the late twentieth century have left social researchers keen to understand how individuals are responding to and shaping the rapid changes that are occurring in economic, political, and cultural spheres. For examining the impact of globalization and the ramifications of individualization, there is no better test-bed than the family setting.

In short, the family not only provides a significant milieu for the individual's social formation of self, but is also seen as an ideal microcosm for the study of much larger economic, social, and cultural developments. As the quote shows, the family is no longer solely perceived as a self-sufficient nucleus of society but is recognised more and more for its interrelatedness with continuous transformations and exchanges on a global level. Writers and novelists, I would like to add, who have explored the social net and living conditions of the family under the stress of political and economic changes, have contributed important insights to this new concept of the family in a global context. Before turning to

---

[1] See, for example, Smart 2007, Edwards et al. 2012 for sociology and Carsten 2004 for the field of cultural anthropology. The EU-financed research project FAMILYPLATFORM (2009–2011; 1.400.000 €) that spans 12 organisations from nine different European countries testifies to the topicality and political significance of the issue. The huge success of the US TV-series such as *Modern Family* (premiered in 2009), *Transparent* (2014 onwards), and other family-focused formats like *Black-ish* (2014ff.), points to a greater interest in the family and its changing forms.

these works and analysing their aesthetic input, we have to examine some of the theories that provide us with a better working knowledge of the interconnections between individual and collective identity construction within the family.

Family is a topic that can be accessed from a variety of angles relating to different areas of study such as sociology, psychology, communication, anthropology, and history – to name only the most prominent fields engaged in this "inherently interdisciplinary" (J. Scott et al. 2003, xvii) research area. The aim of this chapter is to present some of the concepts, theories and concerns developed in these fields in order to identify important issues of the discourse on the family in the late twentieth and early twenty-first century. In this context, a special emphasis will be placed on the role of the family in identity building processes at the level of the individual, as well as on its role with regard to the family's embeddedness in larger-scale social processes relating to migration and transculturality.

Family relations can be described as being organised along two axes: the horizontal and the vertical. The horizontal axis is the location for the 'synchronic family', which stands for the configuration of mutual relationships between family members co-existing in time. The members of a household prototypically comprise of parent(s) and child(ren), but can also include (great)grandparents and members of extended family, including friends and pets. The emphasis in this case is on the family as a system interacting in a shared space and time continuum. The second axis runs vertically in time and produces the 'diachronic family' that is shaped by genealogy, family history, and memory.[2] Families exist always in and through time and are subject to change. From an external perspective, it is therefore common to refer to the family life cycle, stages in family life, or family development in this context.[3] Yet, it can also be said that if considered from within, the family exists in a diachronic dimension. Our idea of

---

[2] Sara Maza (1997, 208) uses the same terminology in distinguishing the "synchronic family of love" from "the diachronic family of bloodlines".

[3] Moreover, this distinction along two temporal axes is not to be confused with that between the 'family of origin' (or 'family of orientation') one is born or adopted into and the 'family of choice' (or 'family of (pro-)creation') one establishes in adult life, for example by marriage. With regard to the temporal axes introduced here, family of origin and family of choice are both 'synchronic families'. These two forms of family are relevant from a biographical perspective, or in terms of generational succession and the time frames of individual families. In the two-generation model of the family prevalent in sociological studies of the family today, these two forms of family are mostly regarded in isolation, unconnected. The idea of the horizontal and the vertical axis assists in making us aware of the temporal connection of smaller family units.

family encompasses more than an interactive relationship of its members in a shared present; it can be extended to the ancestors of the past and makes room for future generations. Both axes are, of course, closely intertwined, but the heuristic distinction is important for analytical purposes to highlight different perspectives and functions that are important for the development of the self, the relationship between self and family, forms of connectedness and the production of family identity.

This chapter roughly follows these two axes, horizontal and vertical, in its analysis of family practices and notions of relatedness. The first part will look at the synchronic family according to current concepts and theories, focusing on the interrelations between the self and the family in society and culture. While it is important to point out the culture-specificity of family relations and structures, the focus of this chapter will not be to identify specific cultural forms of family but rather to find concepts and approaches that can be applied to different social, cultural, or historical settings and situations. The second part deals with the formation of family identity over time, focusing on the intergenerational construction of family memory. It asks how the diachronic family of history and memory plays back into the synchronic family, shaping its members and impacting on their relationships.

2.1 Family and Identity: Related and Relational Selves

Since the 1990s, the discourse on the family has been fundamentally shaped by the theory of individualisation and detraditionalisation, which attracted great public attention and expressed widespread "moral panics" about the 'decline of the family' (D. Chambers 2012, 2; cf. Fink 2002). Although the theory has increasingly been met with scepticism, it has nevertheless initiated a reworking of the field of family sociology, based on a reconceptualisation of the notion of family that shifts the focus from structure to meaning. This approach involves a rethinking of embeddedness and connectedness as conceived within families and thus also emphases the way identity is negotiated in the relational context of the family. The perspective on relationality runs counter to the priority given to individual identity construction by late modernist thinking in that it concentrates on the way "the self is defined by – and lives in terms of – its relations with others" (Eakin 1999, 43).

This subchapter approaches the issue of family and relational identity from two distinct angles, firstly, by focusing on the family and its specific practices of identity construction and meaning-making, and secondly, by looking at the embedded individual and analysing the role of the family and its interconnections with society and culture in the production of the self. By thus combining the findings of current research on the family, relatedness and intimacy in sociology and anthropology with the concept of 'relational selves' (or 'relational identity') as discussed mainly in (developmental) psychology, this chapter aims to shed light on how family life and practices are closely intertwined with processes of the formation of the self.

The emphasis on meaning-making processes in the family provides an ideal platform for the analysis of literary narratives because it allows room for more openness and greater complexity instead of setting a fixed framework of preconceived definitions and notions – which had long been the main preoccupation of family sociology. Moreover, the family is not only an "inherently interdisciplinary" (J. Scott et al. 2003, xvi) subject matter, but can also be seen as an essentially intersectional field, where "gender, age and generation and other social divisions" (Morgan 1996, 33) constitute significant conditions that shape family life and perspectives on the family. It therefore touches on a great variety of aspects of identity that are in turn connected to social and cultural systems of meaning. As a key site of socialisation, the family brings to the fore these "crucial intersections, with individuals interlinked with other family members, and families interlinked with other institutions" (J. Scott et al. 2003, xvii).

2.1.1 Doing Family: The Social Construction of Relatedness

Individualisation and Detraditionalisation: The Decline of the Family in Modernity

Public discourse on the family is often marked by angst and neurosis (cf. Minkmar 2014, 37): new living arrangements or forms of reproduction and child rearing are commonly seen as a threat to family values. In France, for instance, the widespread and vehement protest against same-sex marriage in 2013 was fuelled less by homophobia than by the fact that French marriage law now included the right of adoption and assisted reproduction. The predominantly middle-class demonstrators, although not generally opposed to equal rights for same-sex couples, nevertheless felt the need to stand up in "defense of children and the family", as one protester stated (qtd. in Heneghan 2014). Heated debates like the one in France signify the persisting strong influence of the construct of 'the family' and its power as a cultural symbol. This may strike as remarkable considering the prevalence of the individualisation thesis and its central assertion of the loss of meaning of the family. Has the family atrophied to become a mere "zombie category", as Ulrich Beck has labelled it, dead but still alive (cf. Rutherford 2013, 204)?

The individualisation thesis[4] characterises modernity as an age focused on individual self-fulfilment in the light of growing freedom and new possibilities. Accordingly, value is ascribed to 'personal identity' and individuality rather than 'social identity' (cf. Gross 2005, 290). These changes, of course, have their effect on personal relationships. In his key work, *The Transformation of Intimacy* (1992), Anthony Giddens describes how institutionalised 'expert systems', such as the medical system or the financial system, gained power in late modernity and superseded more traditional institutions, whose former social functions consequently became less significant. As concerns intimate relationships, this means a move away from "older, more traditional narratives of romantic love, which stressed the obligations of lifetime commitment" (Gross 2005, 289–290), towards the ideal of the "pure relationship". As opposed to the "ethos of romantic love" that "helped to put women 'in their place' – the home" (Giddens 1992, 2) in a male-dominated modern society, the 'pure relationship', egalitarian and democratic in nature, is centred on individual growth and emotional fulfilment.[5] Sexuality, rather than simply fulfilling the role of reproduction, became an important aspect of the self, and a site of emancipation.[6]

The concept of 'individualisation' was introduced by Ulrich Beck and Elizabeth Beck-Gernsheim in their highly influential book *The Normal Chaos of Love* (2004 [1995], 1–10). Like Giddens, they traced the origins of social transformations to changes in the "ways of living and loving" (Beck and Beck-Gernsheim 2004 [1995], 2) through establishing intimate relationships and living arrangements as their focus of discussion. They state that the present age is characterised by "a collision of interests between [...] family demands and personal freedom, or between family demands and love" (Beck and Beck-Gernsheim 2004 [1995], 1–2). As a result, "[t]he nuclear family, built around gender status, is falling apart on the issues of emancipation and equal rights" (Beck and Beck-Gernsheim 2004 [1995], 2). In Beck and Beck-Gernsheim's view, 'labour market individualism' promotes personal development over "traditional social identities" and gender roles, which, in turn, heavily affects domestic

---

4 For a critical overview of this thesis see also Gross (2005), D. Chambers (2012, 3ff.), or Smart (2007, 17ff.).

5 For a more detailed definition of the 'pure relationship' see Giddens (1992, 58).

6 Giddens (1992, 27) calls this "plastic sexuality", which, "severed from its age-old integration with reproduction, kinship and the generations, was the precondition of the sexual revolution", and runs parallel to the development of the pure relationship (cf. Giddens 1992, 58).

relationships. Individualisation signifies the trend of "mass exodus from the family circle" because people "prefer to live on their own, pursuing ideas like independence, diversity, variety, continually leafing over new pages of their egos" (Beck and Beck-Gernsheim 2004 [1995], 4). Traditional institutions and normative narratives that guide the development of the self give way to open "decision-making and individual initiative [...]. Standard biography is transformed into 'choice biography'" (Beck and Beck-Gernsheim 2004 [1995], 5). In his seminal book on *Liquid Modernity* (2000), Zygmunt Bauman, another important proponent of the thesis, similarly describes the "increasingly short supply" of "such patterns, codes and rules to which one could conform, which one could select as stable orientation points and by which one could subsequently let oneself be guided". These are "no longer 'given', [...] with the burden of pattern-weaving and the responsibility for failure falling primarily on the individual's shoulders" (Bauman 2000, 7–8).[7] In a similar way, the family's previous position as a fixed social category is transformed and culturally dissolved so that it is no longer a fixed condition of life, but a matter of individual choice (cf. Beck and Beck-Gernsheim 2002, 28). The concept of 'individualisation' goes hand in hand with the term 'detraditionalisation', because "the rise of individual agency" comes at the cost of "the erosion of traditional values" (D. Chambers 2012, 35).

It is interesting to look at how migrant families are positioned within this discourse through the ambivalent ascriptions attached to them in media representations. On the one hand, the "social and cultural values by which diasporic families [...] abide are stigmatised as archaic" (Berghahn 2013, 2), on the other hand, "idealised depictions of diasporic families [are deployed as] an appealing counterfoil to the selfish pursuit of individual desire, which is often blamed for the alleged decline of the family in the West" (Berghahn 2013, 3). In this context, the role of the second generation may not simply consist of being caught 'in-between' autonomy, individualism, and self-fulfilment as opposed to heteronomy, tradition, and family loyalty. Indeed, identification with and valorisation of the family may also be presented as a positive act of choice and connected with the realisation and constitution of the self.

---

7 In *Liquid Love* (2003), Bauman explores the consequences of "the liquid modern setting of life" (viii) on human relationships and interpersonal bonds *in extenso*. Since the perspective of these studies tends to focus on inter-couple relationships and the conditions of starting a family more than on the relationships within a family and between different family generations, this short overview suffices in the context of this study.

Although extremely influential, the individualisation theory has recently been criticised by family sociologists. A major point of criticism is that the thesis fails to convince on an empirical level (cf. D. Chambers 2012, 39–40; Gross 2005, 288; Smart 2007, 20; Holdenried 2012, 12). In what she calls "the sociological battle over the family", Carol Smart (2007, 8) makes a distinction between two major strands in family-centred sociological studies since the 1950s; on the one hand, there are the 'grand theories', whose abstract "approaches have developed as explanations of social change and social relationships rather than specifically in relation to family life". Here, the idea of the family as the 'nucleus of society' serves to exemplify social transformations and processes on a large scale. Empirical analyses of families, on the other hand, are focused more on social realities and are thus also more comprehensive in covering a greater variety of living arrangements and forms of family life. Such empirical studies unveil persisting inequalities in gender relationships and constraints of social class that qualify the freedom of individual choice (cf. D. Chambers 2012, 5, 40). In this discussion, literature may offer an interesting alternative to the opposition of empirical studies and grand theorising as methods of knowledge production. Literature offers a rich field of exploration for approaches that investigate small-scale changes, details of everyday life, emotions and personal attitudes, along with the concept of meaning-making. Literary representations of the family leave room for ambiguities, contradictions, and different perspectives. At the same time, literature is an integral part of social and cultural discourses and often provides important commentary on and insights into more general issues of society.[8]

As Beck and Beck-Gernsheim (1995, 2) note, the void left by the family will be filled by the family, "[o]nly different, more, better" – the singular family will be taken over by a plurality of families: "the negotiated family, the alternating family, the multiple family, new arrangements after divorce, remarriage, divorce again, new assortments from your, my, our children, our past and present families". Quality makes way for quantity with tight bonds being replaced by looser ties, and so this list traces shifting family alliances over the course of a lifetime and ultimately the loss of meaning of each and every one. Critics of the individualisation thesis, however, suggest that pluralisation of families does not necessarily entail a decline in the cultural and personal significance of the fami-

---

8 Interestingly, both Giddens and Beck and Beck-Gernsheim begin their argument with examples taken from contemporary literature, Julian Barnes's *Before She Met Me* (1982) and Michael Cunningham's *A Home at the End of the World* (1990) as well as Scott Turow's *The Burden of Proof* (1990) respectively.

ly. In his essay, "The Detraditionalization of Intimacy Reconsidered" (2005, 288), Neil Gross makes the useful distinction between 'regulative traditions', which are central to a community's identity and determine membership of that community, and 'meaning-constitutive traditions', intergenerationally transmitted patterns of sense-making. This distinction also helps us to address family-related values in connection with the wider cultural and group-related context in a more differentiated and complex way. In Western society, for example, while the coercion of traditional – i.e. "lifelong, internally stratified" – marriage and sanctions against deviations from associated regulations and practices have faded, traditional marriage and the family still function as the "hegemonic ideal" (Gross 2005, 288). Thus, although the traditional structure of the 'nuclear family' is changing and makes room for new and diverse forms of family life, it "remains a powerful icon of tradition and stability, often still perceived as an antidote to today's social problems" (D. Chambers 2012, 2).[9]

The family can consequently only be declared dead if one continues to apply fixed definitions and specific institutional criteria. Instead, the focus in contemporary (qualitative) sociological research has shifted to "how people understand their close relationships and emotional connections, behavior and activities together, obligations and responsibilities, everyday lives and interactions, within and across households" (Edwards et al. 2012, 730). The singular term of 'the Family' has come under question as a conceptual misnomer in the face of the growing diversity and fluidity of family structures and experiences (Widmer 2010, 2). Although the term 'family' still carries associations of gendered and generational hierarchies and traditional obligations that are implicit in the idea of the 'nuclear family',[10] it nevertheless remains important as "a vital cultural and personal signifier of deep and ambivalent desires for and fear about togetherness, belonging and connectedness" (Edwards et al. 2012, 735).

The wide array of (emotional and cultural) connotations that come with the term 'family' also provides the basis for it being the explicit focus of this study – as opposed to related concepts that have enjoyed greater academic attention in

---

9 This very iconicity of the family is the basis of "idealised depictions of diasporic families [in fiction that function as] an appealing counterfoil to the selfish pursuit of individual desire, which is often blamed for the alleged decline of the family in the West" (Berghahn 2013, 3).
10 The concept of the 'nuclear family' was initially introduced by anthropologist Peter Murdock (1949) as a "residence unit" of husband and wife and their child/ren (biological or legal). In the context of the mid-twentieth-century structural-functionalist definition of the family, gendered role allocations of male breadwinner and female homemaker were added (cf. Widmer 2010, 2; see Parsons 1955).

recent years, such as generations or genealogies.[11] This study's particular interest in the ways that ideas and meanings of the family play a constitutive part in self-formation processes also makes it necessary to adhere to the term 'family'. I will nevertheless concentrate on approaches in contemporary family sociology that aim to reconceptualise the field of family relationships.[12] Besides the use of the plural in order to acknowledge a variety of family forms and relationships,[13] new concepts, such as configurations, intimacy, and personal life, and different perspectives on diverse aspects of the 'family', as, most prominently, 'family practices' and 'displaying family', have been introduced (cf. Edwards et al. 2012, 733). These recent approaches share a critical perspective on past sociological research and its ethnocentric bias, which has, by privileging white, heterosexual, middle-class family norms and values, reified and naturalised the 'nuclear family' (cf. D. Chambers 2012, 6).[14] In contrast, these new approaches are all designed to "go beyond" traditional models of the family and extend the scope of relationships and activities that are subsumed into the field in one way or another (cf. Morgan 2011b).

New Approaches in Family Studies: Relatedness, Practices, Rituals and Routines, Myths, and Stories

The most influential new approach in family sociology in the past two decades – and also a key example of new ways of thinking beyond or in response to the

---

11 Cf. for example Weingarten 2014; Erll 2017. See also Erll's chapter on "Familien- und 'Generationenromane': Zadie Smith", which, in line with the genre that the chapter introduces, focuses mainly on the diachronic family and consequently on the topics of generations and genealogies.

12 In this, I focus primarily on trends in British sociology, which have proven to be the most fruitful and creative in this field, and, I would say, hold the greatest potential for application to literary studies. In German sociology, by contrast, it seems still acceptable for a newly revised text book on the foundations and theoretical perspectives of family sociology (Hill and Kopp 2013 [1996]) to begin with an extremely narrow definition of the family based on 1) a long-term relationship between a man and a woman, who 2) cohabit, and 3) have at least one biological or adopted child (Hill and Kopp 2013 [1996], 10). Other approaches, although open to change and new forms of family, focus primarily on structure (such as Nave-Herz 2007, 2014) and are therefore less relevant for this study.

13 These are, for example, cohabitation, 'living apart together' couples (LATs), single-parent families, same-sex partnerships and families, 'fictive kin', post-divorce families, etc.

14 For a concise historical overview of traditional approaches in family sociology and the socio-historical and economic background of the cultural ideal of the 'nuclear family' see, e.g. D. Chambers (2012, 14ff.).

individualisation thesis (D. Chambers 2012, 41)[15] – is David Morgan's 'family practices' approach.[16] Introduced in his book *Family Connections* (1996), the approach has a dual focus, the first of which is based on the connections among family members, while the second targets the connections between families and other areas of social enquiry. The basic premise of the approach is that "'family' [...] is not a thing, but a way of looking at, and describing, practices" (Morgan 1996, 199). In other words, 'family' is not simply there, but has to be produced and maintained in active everyday interaction. The idea of 'doing family' "radically shifts sociological analysis away from 'family' as a structure to which individuals in some sense belong, towards understanding families as sets of activities which take on a particular meaning, associated with family, at a given point in time" (Finch 2007, 66). Importantly, these practices constitute family membership and define familial relationships: Family practices are relational in that they are generally oriented towards others, and "in enacting these practices, the other is defined as a family member" (Morgan 2011b, 3.3). Furthermore, the approach concerns itself with the connections of family practices and relationships with other interrelated practices that have to do with, for example, gender, class, care or work (cf. Morgan 2011b, par. 3.17, 4.5). It therefore reveals the "particularly strong links between self and society" (Morgan 1996, 193) as provided by family practices in their interconnections with other social sites.

In his "Conclusion", Morgan (Morgan 2011b, 188ff.) defines the concept of practices in more detail and names six key features: The term 'practices' (1) allows for a certain discrepancy between the perspectives of the observer and the actor. As an example, he suggests the activities of 'mowing the lawn' and 'feeding the children', which might be interpreted as 'gendered social practices' without being understood as such by the actors themselves; (2) it conveys a sense of the active (in comparison to 'family structures'); (3) it carries a sense of the everyday and (4) of regularity; (5) it denotes fluidity, as any set of practices can be described in different ways depending on the specific focus (family practices vs. gendered practices, consumption practices, etc.), and is therefore open to interpretation, depending on the perspective chosen; and finally, (6) the term establishes a link between history and biography in that practices are historical-

---

15 See Morgan (1996, 197ff.) for his explicit engagement with theories about the decline of the family in 'high modernity'. He identifies the debates about the centrality or decline of the family as "themselves family practices" (198), they are socially constructed and have specific histories and social meanings (cf. also 194–195).
16 Although, from the British point of view, "[o]ne of the first conceptual foundations of the new approach to a sociology of family life" (Smart 2011b, 13), Morgan's concept of family practices goes largely unmentioned in German textbooks on family sociology.

ly constituted and embedded in a host of factors regarding expectations, rules, norms, values, etc. The most prominent family practices usually revolve around shared activities such as meals, conversations, or holidays.

The concept of family practices works similarly to the way that the family is understood in communication studies, which deal with "how families are created, shaped, and sustained through social interaction" (L. H. Turner and West 2006, x).[17] Here, storytelling figures as a key communication practice that "forms families" (Langellier and Peterson 2006, 109) in a threefold way: firstly, by putting experience into a certain form and creating coherence; secondly, by producing patterns of family interaction (with regard to the story content as well as in the situation of telling and listening); and finally, thirdly, as a key site for identity construction for the family as a whole and its members individually (see Langellier and Peterson 2006, 111ff.).[18] This pattern alone highlights the complexity and multi-dimensionality of family practices. Stories are "at the center of daily, communicated family life" (Koenig Kellas and Trees 2013, 391) and are thus a crucial element of routine family interaction; as such, they have a prominent function in family life, which Jane Jorgenson and Arthur Bochner (2003, 515) describe as "a continuous struggle to create, maintain, and/or restore narrative coherence in the face of unexpected contingencies of lived experiences". Storytelling not only creates connectedness through bringing people together at the moment of narration, but also "produces sociability and socialness through connecting people at the level of shared (or comparable) imaginings and experiences" (Smart 2007, 82).[19]

---

[17] The "communication view of the family as a dynamic, socially constructed system of relationships" (Rogers 2006, xv) was developed in communication studies since the 1970s with recourse to the concepts of family introduced much earlier, during the 1920s, by theorists of symbolic interactionism and the Chicago school, but widely neglected until the second half of the twentieth century (see Rogers 2006, xvi). Another important strand of influence is system theory and its concern with interaction processes and interconnected relationships (see also Vangelisti 2003, ix).

[18] All of these functions are very closely related and play into the processes of identity construction in different ways, the last of which being the only one that is most obviously and explicitly concerned with identity. Koenig Kellas and Trees (2013) suggest three different functions of family stories: creating (identity construction), socialising (teaching lessons), and coping (as used in family narrative therapy, e.g.). I find Langellier and Peterson's distinction useful because it applies to a more basic level of family interaction, whereas the categorisation by Koenig Kellas and Trees denotes functions that build on the identity-creating function of family stories (such as socialising and coping).

[19] The subject of family stories and narrative will be dealt with in more detail in chapter 2.2.1.

Family practices, in general, are practices that involve "those relationships and activities that are constructed as being to do with family matters" (Morgan 1996, 192). This construction of the meaning of 'family' engaged with here contains two levels: Firstly, that of individual perception and interpretation of the actors involved, and secondly, that of a cultural understanding of 'family' and its historical evolution. The family-practices approach thus combines two aspects of 'family culture': the everyday regularity of family life, and the dimension of the family imaginary. The family is not only a unit of biological reproduction, it is also an 'imagined community' (Anderson 1991). In the terminology of historian John Gillis (1996), there are the families we live *with* and the families we live *by*, the latter being constituted through myth, ritual and image.[20] Gillis (2002, 2) claims that "a substantial dimension of family life today is experienced as dream", located in the imaginary, in the past or in the future, and is typically aligned with the culturally dominant ideal of family. However, the family imaginary is not confined to the realm of dreaming or imagination, but "constantly impinge[s] on our actual routine practices" (Smart 2007, 51); it is realised and actualised through key family practices centred around planning, collective remembering, storytelling, and family photographs,[21] among others. In this way there is a constant interplay between praxis and imagination, between the family we live with and the family we live by (cf. Jorgenson and Bochner 2003, 518). In fact, "rituals of remembering or of narrating stories about family are constitutive of a cultural level of meaning about families and relationships" (Smart 2007, 51) and are therefore central to the linking of history and biography that Morgan claims is a key feature of the practices approach (Morgan 2011b, 1.4).

The family imaginary holds great significance for migrant families as it not only strengthens relationships amongst present members of the family, but

---

[20] Even before Gillis, the psychiatrist Ronald D. Laing noted the difference between the observable family and the internalised 'family' as "a fantasy structure" (Laing 1971, 5) that exists in the modality not of perception but of "imagination, memory, dreams" (Laing 1971, 7). See also Jorgenson and Bochner (2003, 514ff.), who distinguish between "the observable, 'practicing family'" and "the subjectified family".

[21] Gillis (2002, 6) quotes Susan Sontag (1977, 8) with this interesting observation on the link between a rise in practices of the family imaginary (particularly photography) and the 'decline of the family': "Photography becomes a rite of family life just when, in the industrializing countries of Europe and America, the very institution of the family starts undergoing radical surgery".

expands family life in space and time.²² Past- or future-oriented practices are able – as Susan Sontag (1977, 8–9, cf. Gillis 1996, 78) notes with regard to photography – "to memorialise, to restate symbolically, the imperilled continuity and vanishing extendedness of family life. Those ghostly traces, photographs, supply the token presence of the dispersed relatives." Two decades later, Marianne Hirsch (2012a [1997]) drew attention to these symbolic practices with her investigation into the connection between family photos, postmemory and historical trauma. As the example of family photography shows, the constituents of the family imaginary – myth, ritual, image as "forms of symbolic production" (Jorgenson and Bochner 2003, 517) – are closely interrelated and work together to "serve the practical function of organizing and structuring the indefinite flow of family experiences into meaningful coherence" (Jorgenson and Bochner 2003, 518). While image refers back to the idea of the family symbolically visualised in the family photograph, myth and ritual emphasise the key roles of narrative and memory-practice respectively in the construction of family identity.²³

In the constructivist perspective of 'doing family', stories hold a central place as a "scaffold for a family's identity" (Galvin 2006, 14). Family myth, specifically, refers to those narratives that have a symbolic function for the family: they reflect important truths, define family relationships and roles, and convey values and goals across generations.²⁴ Family myths are similar to what Jody Koenig Kellas and April Trees (2013, 392) refer to as "family legacies": "stories that last across generations and teach simple, straightforward themes about family identity [...] – stories used to evaluate the overall sense of who a family is and how an individual can evaluate him or herself in relation to the family". Family myth can be understood as providing an overarching theme that comprises of and interconnects decisive and constitutive family stories such as, for

---

22 The family imaginary involves both the synchronic and the diachronic axis of the family. Family practices, therefore, are important means of linking the two dimensions of family life by creating a meaningful connection across generations and at specific moments in time. This holds similarly for the transnational connection between family members on the synchronic axis.

23 In this study, I will use the concepts of 'myth' and 'ritual' in the way they have been made fruitful in the context of family studies (as, for example, by The Emory Center for Myth and Ritual in American Life, cf. Shore 2003). However, even in this context the meanings may slightly vary due to the interdisciplinarity of the field, and the concepts are not always clearly defined in each case. I will therefore use this definitional freedom to push both terms in the direction that best suits the purpose of this work.

24 For a more detailed discussion of the definition of family myth, see Box (1979, 79), who tentatively defines family myth as "a manifest enacted picture or story presented by the family and consisting of a mutually accepted set of images and roles".

instance, 'entrance stories' or 'narratives of origin' (cf. Koenig Kellas and Trees 2013, 392).[25] Myths are closely related to rituals in that "[t]hey frequently have a foundational quality similar to rituals and the telling of myths often follows a ritual or ritualized pattern" (V. Nünning and Rupp 2013, 16). Thus, it may be said that the stories told to perpetuate the family myth are intimately connected to the practices of storytelling that are based on these stories and which serve to significantly contribute to their meaning as well as to the sense of belonging and shared identity that they provide. Family myths are dependent, like all narratives, on the perspective and context of narration, and may thus be subject to change, adjustments or adaptations as the family changes and develops over time. It is therefore important to consider "the reciprocal relation between the family's explanatory story and the actual behaviour of the family members" (Box 1979, 79), as well as the specific contexts of such stories and their "narrative performance[s]" (Jorgenson and Bochner 2003, 525), along with whether and how they stand out from patterned family interaction. Furthermore, the idea of myth carries with it the notion of something "both true and not true", a "duet of fact and fiction" (Shore 2003, 2) that might "emerge from a selective, intentional distortion in the representation of family experiences [...] designed to reflect the family's values" (Sabourin 2006, 47). The production of family myths is intricately linked to more general practices of family storytelling and remembering, which play an essential role in creating and maintaining family and individual identity.[26]

Family ritual as the third constituent of the family imaginary ties in with Morgan's concept of practices, at least with regard to their performative quality. However, the more routine, instrumental family practices are regular everyday activities, whereas rituals are – by definition – "marked off from the routine of everyday life" (Snoek 2006, 11).[27] Most importantly, though, family rituals carry "a symbolic component that fosters group identity and meaning-making in group situations" (Fiese and Parke 2002, 382). Family rituals are at the heart of

---

[25] Galvin here cites such examples as stories about how parents met, or birth and adoption narratives.
[26] The key fields of family memory and narrative will be dealt with in more detail in chapter 2.2.1.
[27] Snoek (2006) offers a whole list of characteristics of rituals found in common definitions; this, however, is one of only four 'monothetic' features (that are found in any definition), and can therefore be regarded as a central factor. For a more elaborate distinction between family rituals and family routines see Spagnola and Fiese (2007, 285), who contrast the concepts "along the dimensions of communication, commitment, and continuity" (cf. also Fiese et al. 2002, 382–383).

family culture and play a key role in "transmitting the family's enduring values, attitudes, and goals" across generations (Wolin and Bennett 1984, n.p.). Steven Wolin and Linda Bennett (1984) distinguish three kinds of rituals in the family ranging from "the most extreme to the least formal of family behaviors": family celebrations (holidays and festivities deeply embedded in the cultural context such as, for example, Christmas, weddings, Bar/Bat Mitzwah, etc.), family traditions (including more family-specific activities like summer vacations, birthday customs, etc.), and patterned family interactions (less standardised, more variable, routine-like practices such as family meals, leisure activities, and other techniques of organising daily life).[28] These activities share the properties of transformation, communication and stabilisation, which mark them out as rituals.[29] As such, they serve to build family identity, define and strengthen family roles and relationships, facilitate emotional exchange, and help to manage continuity and change throughout the developmental cycle of the family and in times of transition (cf. Fiese and Parke 2002, 383–384).

In summary, one can say that family myths and rituals play an important role both at the level of synchronic as well as diachronic family construction and shed light on the way in which the two axes interconnect. Firstly, these "symbolic productions operate reflexively to shape family experience" (Jorgenson and Bochner 2003, 519). Through practices of conversational remembering and storytelling, for instance, families build a corpus of self-defining stories that carry information about their specific family identity, its values and principles, and the identities and roles of each family member (cf. Jorgenson and Bochner 2003, 524). As such, these practices can be crucial community-building activities that strengthen family ties and affirm solidarity. Secondly, narratives and rituals build a link to previous generations of a family and are an important means of transmitting family traditions, values, and knowledge across genera-

---

[28] Shore (2003, 3) refers to "canonical rituals" and "interaction rituals" in order to point to the fact that family life involves *"formalized patterns* of behavior" (Shore 2003, 4; emphasis in the original) that are more or less elaborate, or vary in scale of their ritualisation.

[29] These properties also appear in Snoek's (2006) list of characteristics of rituals in one way or another. However, here and in the following I will adhere to the concept of ritual used in family studies (mostly from the perspectives of communication studies and psychology). Given the elusiveness of ritual as a concept, it is helpful to regard single rituals in their specific context and to adapt the term to its use for a given purpose, in this instance, it is the construction of family identity (cf. Snoek 2006, 12). As Fiese et al. (2002, 383) point out, family studies dealing with rituals are generally concerned with three main topics: "(a) routines and rituals as patterned interactions, (b) the developmental course of routine and rituals, and (c) psychological health and well-being in relation to routines and rituals".

tions. They play a central role in ensuring continuity and continuance of the family over time. Besides these positive functions of strengthening cohesion, stories and rituals may also carry a symbolic meaning in order to express tensions within the family, as well as disaffection and ambivalence (cf. Jorgenson and Bochner 2003, 519).

While the elements of family culture listed above serve to construct and strengthen a sense of identity within the family, the notion of 'displaying families' deals with the way family identity is communicated to the outside world. Extending Morgan's concept of 'doing', Janet Finch (2007) highlights the performative[30] quality of family practices. Family display constitutes an important supplement to the concept of 'doing family' because it emphasises how the family imaginary and everyday practices converge. Family display is as much about the families we live by as the families we live with, if not more so. In addition to having the effect of constituting family membership for those involved, practices that 'display' family need to be "both conveyed to and understood by relevant others [...] as carrying meaning associated with 'family'" (Finch 2007, 66). Family practices, therefore, are embedded into the wider systems of meaning based around what constitutes a ('working') family in a given cultural setting (cf. Morgan 1996, 190). According to Finch, all family relationships must be displayed in order to gain social reality; however, the degree of intensity of the need for display varies and is likely to be more intense in circumstances of change or renegotiation of relationships (e.g. in post-divorce families) as well as for non-conventional family relationships (e.g. same-sex partners; cf. Finch 2007, 71–72).[31] Conversely, an apparent need for display – and affirmative feedback on the quality of a relationship – may be indicative of a level of insecurity, the precarious nature of a relationship, or a person's familial role. Moreover, 'display', with its corresponding notion of social recognition, also highlights the way in which larger social networks and communities with specific values and norm systems shape family practices. Given the symbolic power of the idea of

---

30 For an elaboration on how the concept of 'display' differs from that of performance and performativity, see Finch (2007, 76).
31 Family display thus also touches on the question of what is considered as (ideal) family and what it represents: "definitional concerns surface as members face outsiders' challenges regarding the veracity of their claims of relatedness" (Galvin 2006, 4). Under these circumstances, families rely on "external and internal boundary management practices" to build, delineate and maintain identity. On the inside, the "internal sense of family-ness" is established via such family practices as outlined above, e.g. narrative, ritual, or also naming. To the outside, boundary management practices include labelling, legitimising, defending (Galvin 2006, 9ff.).

family, the importance ascribed to the display of family practices may also provide us with an insight into the role of the family as a carrier of cultural identity in a specific (migrant) community. Particularly in a post-migrant setting, the way in which family roles and relationships are negotiated within the family, where different cultural influences often have an impact, may differ with the way a family presents itself to the rest of the community.

To sum up, the focus of scholarly analysis has shifted away from the family as an institution, to the realm of practices, intimate relationships, and one's personal life – in other words, to significant aspects of social life that need not be exclusively defined through 'the family'. The research questions connected to this shift move the debate away from the question of the decline of the family to the ways family life is constituted and the meanings that individual people draw from their family (cf. D. Chambers 2012, 41). The question is not whether families still exist or whether they are still important – obviously they do and they are. The question is how family life is lived in certain cases and what specific family practices tell us about the significance of family relationships for the individuals within it. Family practices, rituals, stories, and myths are not only significant in that they provide a sense of group belonging, they also "tap the intersection between the individual and the whole family" (Fiese and Parke 2002, 386) and serve to highlight the interconnection between personal identity construction and family processes.[32] Although the concept of 'family' is becoming more fluid and shifting, the persistent "popularity of the term 'family', which is even being extended to describe close friendships and alternative kinds of intimacies, suggests a strong social desire to preserve principles of commitment and reciprocity that bind members of society together" (D. Chambers 2012., 1).[33] Modernity's plurality of possibilities for individual identity construction and life choices are thus not necessarily a threat to the family but can, conversely, be seen as increasing the relevance of the family and family practices, which, in this context, are less regulated or normativised, and are more open to individual processes of meaning-making – and thus more dependent on individual choice.

---

[32] This aspect is foregrounded in psychological studies that analyse the role of family rituals with regard to coping strategies in families, high-risk conditions or mental and physical health (cf. Fiese et al. 2003, n.p.).
[33] See also Gross (2005) for the continuance of patterns of meaning-making that concern the family.

2.1.2 Family and the Social Development of the Self

While the approaches presented in the last chapter deal with the way "the family, as a group, is organized and finds meaning as a collective unit" (Fiese and Parke 2002, 381), the next subchapter examines how these family practices influence self-development and individual identity building processes. The new preoccupation of family studies with how people live their relationships and invest them with meaning has resulted in a stronger emphasis on, firstly, relationality and, secondly, family embeddedness. While the former is concerned with (inter)active forms of establishing and maintaining relationships, the latter describes the state of being related, of being connected to others in a network of relationships that are not chosen but that people are (in most cases) born into.

The current response to the individualisation thesis also involves a new perspective on identity construction that moves away from the idea of the isolated, autonomous individual towards the conception of 'social selves': "When challenging individualism as an omnipotent sociological tool kit, family sociologists found, or more correctly, rediscovered relationality, or the embeddedness of the individual in family and kin relationships." (Jallinoja and Widmer 2011, 5; see also Smart 2007, 28) Overall, the crucial role of 'the family' in the (cognitive and psychological) development and socialisation of a person is undisputed. Nevertheless, the shift in "focus away from individuals to relationships and to socially significant ensembles that are constituted by these relationships" (Jallinoja and Widmer 2011, 5) is relatively recent, yet it builds on a long line of theory on social identities in psychology and sociology that stretches back to William James and, most importantly, the tradition of symbolic interactionist theory based on George Herbert Mead's work (cf. Lawler 2014, 6). The "growing sense of discontent with psychological approaches to identity that are seen as excessively individualistic and atomistic" (Schachter 2005, 376) raises new questions concerning the process of identity construction that point towards the connection of individuality and a sense of belonging. This dynamic of individuation and relatedness is an important driving force in family relationships, where "[f]amilies and individuals continually negotiate the twin demands of autonomy and connectedness across the stages of individual and family development" (Benson and Deal 1995, 563). These mechanisms within families are indicative of the more general process of socialisation and human development, which is "based on the paradoxical association between two seemingly opposing factors; that is, the duality between agency and communion, individuality vs. collectivity, self vs. other" (Adams and Marshall 1996, 430). This dialectic lies at the heart of socialisation and a relational concept of identity.

Relational Selves, the Self in Context

This discussion acquires a further dimension through Paul Eakin's (1999) concept of 'relational selves' and the aspect of narrative identity.[34] Eakin's concept proceeds from the theory of a gendered model of identity construction in autobiographical writing. In this model, which ties in with prevalent assumptions about dichotomous gender identities in modern Western culture, masculine identity construction is attributed with a drive towards individualism while feminine identity is seen as being formed "through relation to the chosen other" (M. Mason 1980, qtd. in Eakin 1999, 47). Following on from Jessica Benjamin (*The Bonds of Love*, 1988), Eakin deconstructs the gender binaries of 'individual vs. collective' and 'autonomous vs. relational' as merely "developmental tendencies that are inextricably intertwined in a complex process of individuation" (Eakin 1999, 52) and which pivot on the paradox that "at the very moment of realizing our own independence, we are dependent upon another to recognize it" (Benjamin 1988, 33, qtd. in Eakin 1999, 52). It is this important "dynamic of recognition" that for Eakin (1999, 52; emphasis in the original) makes all identity "*necessarily* relational". Identity is thus discursively transacted: the 'I' is interpellated by the 'you' (Eakin 1999, 63).[35] In this idea of inter-subjectively constructed identity, social interaction is essential for psychological and cognitive development. Ian Burkitt (2008) makes a similar point with his concept of 'social individuality', which emphasises that individuality and relationality are not oppositional or mutually exclusive positions, but, on the contrary, closely intertwined; the term expresses the conundrum "that to become an individual self with its own unique identity, we must first participate in a world of others that is formed by history and culture" (Burkitt 2008, 1).

---

[34] This study focuses on Eakin's understanding of relationality as derived from literary study; the concept itself originated in psychology, where it is most widely used and theorised on (see Gergen's 'relational being', 2009). However, a due consideration of psychological research on the relational self or relationality would lie beyond the scope of this thesis. The psychological concept of "a 'self-within-relationships'" (Chen et al. 2011, 150) also prioritises synchronic over diachronic relationships, a weighting I aim to re-balance here by emphasising the genealogical depth of the relational (and related) self.

[35] Eakin here refers to psychologist John Shotter's theory of social accountability and selfhood. This idea of self-awareness as dependent on recognition through others is similar to G.H. Mead's understanding of an experience of the self being possible not directly or immediately as a subject (as 'I'), but as an object experienced by others (as 'me') in a shared social environment or context (cf. Burkitt 2008, 38; Winkle-Wagner 2010, 28; see also Smart 2007, 28, who also links her concept of 'personal life' to Mead's distinction between 'I' and 'me').

This is, in a nutshell, also what is referred to by Gerard Adams and Sheila Marshall (1996) in their definition of 'socialisation', which they understand as a process that, firstly, governs the dynamics of relations between individuals, and, secondly, ensures "the integration and respect of individuals as participants within a society that regulates behaviours according to societal codes" (Adams and Marshall 1996, 430). This definition points to the interconnectedness of interpersonal relationships and interaction (e.g. in the family) on the one hand and the individual's relationship with wider social networks and larger contexts that are outside the family on the other. Socialisation, at its core, deals with the interface between the subject and his or her surrounding social structure (Geulen 2004, 6). More generally, the concept of socialisation is based on the assumption that a person's material, social, and cultural environment works as a constitutive (not merely accidental) condition of individual personality development, which is thereafter conceived as an interactive (not unidirectional) and lifelong process (Geulen 2004, 4). Talcott Parsons (1955), a leading scholar in the field of socialisation, has already emphasised the family's paramount role in this process in modern society. In his so-called structural-functionalist approach, he conceives of the family as having two key functions: The first function is to provide primary socialisation by transmitting cultural values, norms and codes of conduct; in this way the family serves as a safeguard for social and cultural continuity. The second function is to offer emotional and economic stabilisation for its members (cf. D. Chambers 2012, 21; Hill and Kopp 2012, 61).

We may sum up this discourse by saying that socialisation in general, and the development of the individual in the family in particular, are marked by the inherent tension between heteronomy and autonomy.[36] The dialectical interplay between individual development and group processes needs to be considered as part and parcel of a person's social identity formation. As Adams and Marshall (1996, 431) suggest, social and psychological well-being depends on a balance between the dynamics of differentiation and integration, or, in other words between the individual and the social dynamic of the socialisation process. In this view, an over-emphasis on either connections or on differentiation may impede individual autonomy or compromise continuity and cohesion of a given

---

[36] Dieter Geulen (2004, 8) sees an inherent contradiction in the concept of socialisation between the idea of the individual as governed by internalised norms on the one hand, and his or her claim to be an autonomously acting subject on the other hand. This contradiction between autonomy and connectedness is one of the key causes of tension in the family (cf. Benson and Deal 1995, 563).

'life system' – such as, for instance, the family (cf. Adams and Marshall 1996, 431–433). This balance is crucial because, "as humans, we are relationally embedded. Context is an essential feature of the self." (Adams and Marshall 1996, 437)

Identity formation of the 'person-in-context' is influenced on both the macro- and micro-level, i.e. by larger social, political, cultural, economic features as well as through interpersonal communication and interactions (cf. Adams and Marshall 1996, 438). Eakin (1999, 85) constructs the cultural and societal framework of the relational self as having a layered structure, with the "identity-shaping environments […] nested one within the other – self, family, community set in a physical and cultural geography, in an unfolding history". In this model, the family not only takes a decisive role as "the key environment in the individual's formation" but also acts as a link between self and society, due to the fact that it "serves as the community's primary conduit for the transmission of its cultural values" (Eakin 1999, 85). This notion coincides with Urie Bronfenbrenner's ecological model, which was first introduced in the 1970s and is similarly concerned with the way human development takes place in its interaction with its immediate environment. In his model, "the ecological environment is conceived as a set of nested structures, each inside the other like a set of Russian dolls" (Bronfenbrenner 1993, 38). The model demonstrates how different systems from the micro- to the macro-level interconnect and interact, and thus directly, as well as indirectly, influence the development of the individual through proximal processes.[37] The family, due to the regularity of the (face-to-face) interaction that it provides over an extended period of time, must be seen as a particularly influential microsystem.[38]

The influence of the family on identity formation processes, besides being dependent on individual factors, is also culture-specific and determined by its socio-historical context, since the value and functions ascribed to family in a society or community may differ. Furthermore, the role of the family as a source

---

[37] Bronfenbrenner (1993, 39–40) understands the environment as structured on five levels: microsystems (face-to-face interactions and relations, e.g. the family), mesosystems (interconnections between two or more settings, a system of microsystems, e.g. family and school), exosystems (linkages between microsystems and environments of indirect influence, such as a parent's workplace), macrosystems (the overarching pattern of the lower systems), and chronosystems (time as property of the environment, this includes both historical time and the individual life course).

[38] Microsystems are defined as "a pattern of activities, social roles, and interpersonal relations experienced by the developing person in a given face-to-face setting with particular physical, social, and symbolic features" (Bronfenbrenner 1993, 39).

of socialisation is contingent on the socialisation practices dominant in a community or society. Jeffrey Arnett (1995), for instance, distinguishes two general types of cultures that differ with regard to the range of individual differences that are encouraged or allowed in identity formation and that can be classified as either broad or narrow socialisation. While the first promotes individualism, independence, and self-expression, the second values obedience and conformity. In a similar vein, James Côté (1996) examines forms of identity formation practices and types of identity based on Margaret Mead's (1970) model of cultural patterns that determine the socialiser-socialisee relationship. Likewise, these differ with regard to choice and commitment and the relationship between individual and community. Although Côté uses a chronological classification of three types of societies (pre-modern, early-modern, and late-modern),[39] for the purpose of this study it is more useful to understand their respective characteristics as often contradictory and conflicting tendencies and values within a society that encompasses quite different cultural or ethnic groups and communities. The disparity between a family's or its local community's values regarding individual choice vs. collective commitment and the values propagated by the majority society may put pressure on a family and its individual members, often resulting in family discord. In diasporic or migration literature (and film), this is often a primary source of intergenerational conflict in families.[40]

For a closer look at the process of relational identity construction within the framework of the family, Carol Smart's (2007) notion of 'personal life' proves useful.[41] Introduced as an alternative concept to 'the family', it directs attention to the individual person within the family rather than focus on the family as collective unit. Intended to broaden the scope of analysis in family studies, the concept is not only open to diverse forms of family and relationships, it also involves reconfigured kinship networks and friendships, and therefore does not a priori prioritise family relationships over other close relationships. In this

---

[39] Mead's model is interested in social change, and therefore follows a diachronic perspective. Roughly summarised, the three cultures are "*postfigurative*, in which children learn primarily from their forebears, *configurative*, in which both children and adults learn from their peers, and the *prefigurative*, in which adults learn also from their children" (Mead 1970, 1; qtd. in Côté 1996, 418). Côté further develops this model by introducing distinct levels of analysis for different aspects of identity (social, personal, and ego identity), as well as the level of social interaction.
[40] The widely popular film productions of *East Is East* (1999) and *Bend It like Beckham* (2002) are vivid examples of this generic narrative of intergenerational division in migrant families.
[41] See Morgan (2011a, 37ff.) for a detailed differentiation of Smart's concept and his concept of 'family practices'.

respect, the concept also considers the specific role and significance of the family in relation to a larger network of different social relationships. The term of the 'personal' is used here as a counter-term to the 'isolated individual' (of the individualisation thesis) and stresses the social, interconnected aspect of personhood, which "requires the presence of others to respond to and to contextualize [... the individual's] actions and choices" (Smart 2007, 28; cf. Smart 2011b, 13). The concept of personal life thus posits at its core the idea of a "reflexive (social) self" (Smart 2011b, 13), which dovetails closely with Eakin's theory of relational selves.[42]

Personal life as a concept is geared towards understanding and representing family life in "a more textured way" that captures "the multi-dimensionality of relationships" and relational selves (Smart 2011b, 14). To this end, Smart discerns five overlapping core concepts that expand the notion of family practices by putting emphasis on the realm of "thinking and imagining family relationships" (Smart 2011b, 38) in order to better work out the interconnections between the mental and the physical aspect of 'doing family': Biography, Memory, Imaginary, Relationality, and Embeddedness.[43] 'Biography' refers to the fact that the approach is concerned primarily with the individual, and, consequently, with identity, which is seen as processual, as a life story based on personal experience and the narrative processes of meaning-making (cf. Smart 2011b, 42).[44] It therefore relies on 'Memory', which, as an essentially social phe-

---

[42] Despite the proximity of her theory to Eakin's concept of 'relational selves', Smart does not reference him in in her book; she does, however, highlight the gap between the two domains of psychology and her own field of research, sociology (Smart 2007, 35). In contrast, the sociologist Burkitt, who is also referred to extensively by Eakin, plays a more prominent role in her development of the concept of relationality. Moreover, the field of kinship anthropology has a dominant impact in this area of research and provides the basic impetus in what Smart (2007, 33) refers to as "the cultural turn in the sociology of family life".

[43] The original order in which Smart presents these concepts is: Memory, Biography, Embeddedness, Relationality, and Imaginary. I have chosen to rearrange them for the sake of argument.

[44] While this focus on the individual agent may seem natural to literary scholars, it is more exceptional in the field of sociology, where the individual needed to be discovered as an object of study in the first place. Smart (2007, 42) here cites the 'biographical turn' in sociology, which refers to the development and growing recognition of biographical methods and case-study approaches ('thick descriptions') in the discipline in the wake of an "increased interest in literature, art, and narrative as well as the more obvious areas of the media and film" (see also Michael Rustin's "Reflections on the Biographical Turn in Social Science", 2000). The term of 'biography' here refers to a concern with individual identity that takes the "movement through the life course" (Smart 2007, 42) into account. I use this notion in order to align it with theories regarding the narrative construction of identity and Dan McAdams's concept of 'identity as life

nomenon, links the individual to its social context (cf. Misztal 2003, 4–5).[45] The family plays a central role in such an "intersubjectivist approach" (Misztal 2003, 6) to memory:[46] Not only is individual memory crucially shaped by the family, acts of remembrance also shift the family of origin "into a special place in our internal calibrations of personal significance" (Smart 2007, 39). The 'Imaginary', as expounded above, brings in the social, cultural and historical contexts within which relationships are formed, life stories constructed and memories shaped. With 'Relationality' and 'Embeddedness' Smart distinguishes two qualities of relational selves: First, relationality is based on the assumption that the self is inherently relational and intersubjectively constituted in social interaction as well as in webs of relationships. This understanding of relationality derives from the way kinship studies have converged in anthropology and sociology to devise the concept of relatedness, which recasts kinship as "*negotiated relationships* [...] constituted in *relational practices*" (Finch and Mason 2000, 164, qtd. in Smart 2007, 48; emphasis in the original). Relationality, then, "emphasizes the active nature of relating and reduces the idea that relationships are simply given (and hence unchanging) through one's position in a family genealogy" (Smart 2007, 49). The second quality, embeddedness, is concerned with 'linked lives' and chains of relationships across generations that one does not actively choose nor maintain, but find themselves in due to various given circumstances. Moreover, embeddedness is not in itself necessarily positive: while it can offer security, it may also be experienced as suffocating, since kin or family constitute "sticky relationships" and tenacious bonds that are seen to have "haunting powers" (Smart 2007, 45) and are not easily dissolved. Both aspects, relationality and embeddedness, are tightly intertwined, and together constitute the specific nature of family relationships between belonging and independence.

---

story' (2003), consequently putting more emphasis on the aspect of narrativity than Smart herself does.

45 Smart here draws on Barbara Misztal (2003, 5), who approaches the interdisciplinary field of memory studies from a sociological perspective, and recognises an "individualistic bias" in cognitive psychology, a field that has, in her words, come "under attack for ignoring the social context of remembering, and for overlooking social rules of remembrance".

46 According to Misztal (2003, 6), in this approach it is assumed that while the remembering subject is an individual, their memory only exists in relation to others, and, moreover, refers to an intersubjective past.

The Body and Identity: Bridging the Nature/Culture Divide

The concept of the relational self is based on a constructionist concept of identity as formed through interaction and communication, which runs counter to an understanding of identity as a person's "true, 'inner core' [...], unknown and unknowable" (Lawler 2014, 16). Such an essentialist notion of identity is grounded in "the philosophical image of the self-contained individual" (Burkitt 1994, 7; cf. Keupp 2008, 101)[47] and consequently sees the process of identity formation as existing within rather than between individuals (cf. Lawler 2014, 17).[48] Ian Burkitt (1994, 8) discerns a similar bias against the interactive dimension of the self in constructionist theories, for which he attests a tendency of "over-concentrat[ing] on discourse at the expense of understanding humans as embodied social beings". In his essay on "The Shifting Concept of the Self" (1994), he tracks the influence of Michel Foucault and Jacques Derrida on structuralist and postmodern notions of a contingent, fluid self as text produced by discourse. According to Burkitt, such a notion of the discursive construction of self leaves room for criticism because it does not pay enough attention to *practice* ("in respect of the formation of discourses and texts", 1994, 13), *communication* (with regard to language as a practical instrument rather than simply a system of signs), and, thus, ultimately the *context* of social relations and interactions:

> People are located not just in texts but also in social relations and practices: the elemental forms of 'context'. Self is not, then, purely a creation of discourse but a product of social relations and embodied actions within those relations. (Burkitt 1994, 15)

In his effort to give more prominence to the body in concepts of the self, Burkitt (1994, 16) draws on the work of sociologists Norbert Elias and Pierre Bourdieu to show how the discourses on identity are "actually linked to the changing *experience* of individuals" in a network of social relations, and shape bodily dispositions through social practices.

Burkitt's emphasis on relations, communication, and bodily practices ties in with the idea of 'doing family' presented above, and hints at the way that acts

---

[47] Steph Lawler here refers to Norbert Elias, who identifies "this notion of an 'inner' 'hidden' core to the self" as a product of the civilising process, and, consequently, as particular to Western culture and intellectual history.
[48] Essentialist concepts of identity often focus on body features as determinants of identity. Prominent examples are the construction of 'race' or 'sex' not as social categories, whose meaning is historically, culturally, and/or socially contingent, but as physical determinants that produce absolute 'natural' qualities.

of meaning-making and identity construction in the family are interlinked with the formation of relational selves. Burkitt (cf. 1994, 24–25) connects this idea of an embodied self to Ulric Neisser's concept of the 'ecological self', the first stage of his "Five Kinds of Self-Knowledge" (1988), which includes one's sensory perception and activity as part of the physical environment. The body forms the basis of the self in that it figures not only as the "corporeal substratum of identity" (Eakin 1999, 67) but also as interface to the outside world.[49] However, the focus on family highlights yet another dimension of the embodied self: the way in which we are linked to our family via genetic inheritance. Genes act not only as the basic material of our physical makeup, which in turn informs our self-perception and body image as well as other people's image of ourselves. Biological factors play an important role in shaping who we are, but are generally disregarded in social or constructionist theories of the self.

In questions of identity and human development, the nature versus nurture debate has long given way to a view that sees both aspects – personal experiences and the environment on the one hand, and genetic inheritance on the other – as being interlinked as opposed to mutually exclusive. The fields of epigenetics and behavioural genetics conceive the influence of genetics as effecting individual development in dynamic and interactive interplay with social and environmental factors. In this view, the genome can be compared to a text, of which only parts will be read over the course of a lifetime (Asendorpf 2004, 37); and, one should add, which can also be rewritten, since a person's genetic layout is not immutable but reacts to outside influences.[50] The role of the family in the construction of identity brings together both factors, as the connection one builds to one's blood relations is not only grounded in social interaction but also draws on physical resemblance and genetic inheritance:

> A blood relationship is a relationship of identity. People who are blood relatives share a common identity, they believe. [...] It is a belief in common biological constitution, and aspects like temperament, build, physiognomy and habits are noted as signs of this shared biological makeup, this special identity of relatives with each other. (D. Schneider 1968, 25, qtd. In Lawler 2014, 51)

---

[49] This understanding is based on a "composite definition of the self [... as] based on having a physical body, experiencing reflexive consciousness, having interpersonal connections and belonging to small groups, and exercising the executive functions of decision-making and self-regulation" (Baumeister and Muraven 1996, 406). These different aspects correspond with Neisser's concept of different levels of self-understanding.
[50] See, for instance, Bronfenbrenner (1993, 41), who states that heritability is "in fact highly influenced by events and conditions in the environment".

Bodily characteristics and mental features or personality traits are often referred back to parents or grandparents and establish a feeling of similarity and belonging based on the 'idiom of nature' (Carsten 2000, 7). However, such a link is not necessarily and exclusively 'natural', as 'blood relationships' have a symbolic quality and the meanings assigned to them are cultural: "ties considered to be 'given in nature' are intrinsically bound up with what people *make* of those ties" (Lawler 2014, 48; cf. Carsten 2000, 7). Incorporating the aspect of biological givens does not necessarily produce essentialist identities; the question is, rather, how and to what end different variables of the self are employed in the process of "active identity work" (Lawler 2014, 52). As Steph Lawler (2014, 52) states, the salient point here is recognition, which works as "a nodal point" between choice and determinism: "Some traits [can] be disowned and others embraced." (Lawler 2014, 52)

Such an approach to kin-based identification is compelling because

> [t]his form of identity constitution raises important questions about individualism and collectivism, about the place of various forms of inheritance, and about the shifting relations between 'nature' and 'culture'. Ultimately, it exposes some of the contradictory ways in which identity is understood and 'done' […]. (Lawler 2014, 46)

It is, therefore, important to acknowledge that there are different ways of doing identity in the context of family and kinship, even with regard to such seemingly fixed factors as genetic inheritance. In Western discourse, blood and DNA are extremely powerful metaphors for creating ties and establishing relationships that are significant for a person's identity. New kinship studies over the course of the last decades have reconfigured the understanding of kinship in an analogous way so as to bypass the nature/culture divide. In a movement similar to the rebranding of the field of family studies in sociology, the term 'relatedness' has been introduced in anthropology as an alternative to the concept of kinship, which has come under increased criticism since the 1970s for its Western-biased perspective and definitions.[51] With the concept of 'relatedness', anthropologists such as Janet Carsten (2000, 4) wish to convey "a move away from a pre-given analytic opposition between the biological and the social on which much anthropological study of kinship has rested". Initially criticised by David Schnei-

---

[51] In the introduction to her central work, *After Kinship*, Janet Carsten (2004, 10) shows how the concept of kinship has, from the start, been at the very heart of anthropological studies, being understood as "constituting the political structure and providing the basis for social continuity in stateless societies", and was therefore seen as the key to and 'natural' foundation of social organisation in different cultures.

der (1968; 1984), this binary was effectually dismantled by Marilyn Strathern (1992), who, with reference to the consequences of new reproductive technologies, began to question "the opposition between a fixed or given nature and a changeable or contingent culture" (Carsten 2004, 21). The destabilisation of nature "as the grounding for culture, or as simply there to be revealed or discovered" (Carsten 2004, 21) challenges the Western notion of knowledge as derived from the facts of nature (cf. Carsten 2000, 9).[52] Kinship, being "simultaneously part of nature and part of culture" (Carsten 2000, 10), has been recast in the concept of 'relatedness' as a realm where the two interconnect in different ways. In this vein, the contrast between the biological and the social, then, can be re-conceptualised as a key feature of a specific cultural (e.g. northern European) discourse of kinship (Carsten 2000, 26–29).[53] As such, "biological relatedness continues to have a powerful impact on ideas about the structuring of kin [... just as] genetic connection remains a paramount element of identity" (D. Chambers 2012, 16).[54] Overall, the concept of relatedness provides a more fluid and malleable notion of kinship that recognises different elements of negotiated relationships such as substance, feeding, cohabitation, procreation, emotion, etc., and thus incorporates both of the processes of meaning-making through practices and biological/genetic bonds (cf. Carsten 2000, 17–18, 34).

This mapping of personal life does justice to the multidimensionality of family relationships as it allows for different approaches and recognises the correlations between diachronic and synchronic perspectives. As Smart shows in her study (2007), it provides a theoretical framework for the exploration of meaning-oriented questions that deal with such different aspects of family life as emotions, connections, secrets, home, and objects.[55]

---

[52] Carsten (cf. 2004, 21) links this criticism of the nature/culture dualism to a similar development in gender and queer studies that moved away from the sex/gender-divide to a social constructionist (and performative) view of gendered bodies (cf. Butler 1990).
[53] Carsten (2000, 21) draws from examples of different ethnic groups (Rajasthani and Nuer people) in order to show how the relation of biological and social aspects of relatedness is not universal but always part of specific discourses that may involve either place ('village kinship') or shared (bodily) substance (blood ties, nurturance; see also the concept of 'milk kinship' prevalent in many Muslim communities, cf. Eviatar 2012, 60; Carsten 2013, S7).
[54] Deborah Chambers (2012, 16) cites as an example the common practice whereby adopted people will search for their birth parents at some point in their lives, which "indicates the fascination in western societies for discovering the 'self' through biological heritage".
[55] These are the concerns raised in different chapters of Smart's book on *Personal Life*. The focus on narrative augurs particularly well for an investigation of the overlapping domains of personal life in order to see how individual identity construction relies on the family as a framework of meaning. See chapter 2.3.

2.2 Family (Hi)Stories and the Genealogical Imagination

We do not choose our parents or our relatives. There is an inescapability to family relations and family identity that is most strongly expressed in the idea of DNA, genetic inheritance, and bloodlines, which means that we carry elements of our forebears within us, in one way or another. But this is not the whole story: "As surely as we are born into genes, genealogy, and a body of relatives of blood, marriage, and bonds, we are 'born into' family stories and histories, family myths and metaphors, family rituals and routines, family language and secrets." (Langellier and Peterson 2006, 109) We are not only part of our biological gene pool but also a part of our family tradition. After a long history of emphasising the exceptional individual in Western culture, there is a growing awareness that our families and family histories shape our understanding of who we are and what we might become. In the last decade, there has been a notable boom in genealogy and the 'family heritage industry' (cf. Kramer 2011, 380; Lawler 2014, 45), promoted by a growing number of online resources, websites, and handbooks such as ancestry.co.uk or familysearch.org that encourage the reader and user to "discover your ancestors". Knowing your ancestry and toolboxes for genealogical research have become key elements in the exploration, understanding, and construction of the self (cf. Kramer 2011, 380).[56] The popular BBC series, *Who Do You Think You Are?* (running weekly since 2004), which presents celebrities in the process of researching their family history, attests to this boom. The programme is designed to answer the title's question with reference to the past as a hitherto largely unacknowledged resource of identity construction, and emphasises the connection between identity and inheritance (cf. Lawler 2014, 45–46). The new importance attached to notions such as 'origin', 'genealogy', 'heritage', and 'rootedness' for processes of identity construction not only complicates modern notions of individualism but also challenges the dichotomy between 'post-modern' concepts of constructivism and 'pre-modern' ideas of essentialist identity.

This preoccupation with family history and genealogy has prompted a new sense of the self that extends into the past beyond a person's life span, thus adding a further important dimension to Eakin's concept of relational selves.

---

[56] Kramer (2011, 380) summarises some of the explanations that are given for the boom, which is alternatively described as a "reaction to depersonalized modernity and mobile lifestyles [...], social dislocation and/or migration [...], a crisis in belonging in postcolonial societies [...], a weakening of family bonds [...] or, at the very least, evidence of public concern over the durability of the family". What all these explanations share is a concern with anxieties of belonging with regard to place, history, and relationships.

Narratives of relational lives, according to Eakin (1999, 69), are "developed collaboratively with others, often family members" (Eakin 1999, 57, 88). Eakin's referencing of the family focuses exclusively on social interaction in the synchronic family context. There is no regard for the larger diachronic processes of family history and references to older generations. While many sociological and psychological studies that examine constructions of self are limited to the synchronic context, this study aims to expand the scope beyond this temporal horizon and take into account the relations between generations in a diachronic perspective.[57] From a psychological point of view, Robyn Fivush emphasised the importance of this diachronic intergenerational frame and of the larger temporal dimension for a person's psychological well-being.[58] New

> findings point to the critical importance of placing one's own life in the context of familial history that provides a framework for understanding one's self as a member of a family that extends before one's birth and provides a stage on which one's individual life will be played out. One's own story is embedded in the story of others in the past and in the present. (Fivush 2008, 55)

The first part of the following chapter looks at the nexus of memory and narrative within families. It will focus in detail on this new insight about the long-term embeddedness of the individual in collective stories, and the ways in which the construction of the personal life story is bound up with family memory and family practices of storytelling. It will also raise the question of how the experience of migration affects family memory and forms of transmission in families. Family memory often comes under pressure as immigrants are expected to adapt and "forget, or at least relegate, the past so that the memory of what is here and now [...] becomes dominant" (Chamberlain and Leydesdorff 2004, 229). The second part of the chapter deals with the role of the "genealogical imagination" (Zerubavel 2012, 3) in linking past and present generations in families. 'Genealogy' implies an understanding of family that moves beyond the nuclear family to a more extended family network within which the link between grandparents and -children is of particular importance in forging a historical image of the family. The chapter will investigate how the concept of family

---

57 This same focus on the synchronic family can be observed in research on family memory and practices of storytelling in communication studies. See Bohanek et al. 2009, Bietti 2010, Langellier and Peterson 2006, Koenig Kellas and Trees 2013. A more intergenerational approach can be seen in the study of so-called ‚family legacies' (see B. Thompson et al. 2009).
58 Robyn Fivush's diachronic approach is a notable exception in the field. See also Fivush et al. 2008.

changes as the temporal perspective expands from a two-generation to a three-generation model, and will look at the "mental threads we envision as linking past and present members of families" (Zerubavel 2003, 8).

2.2.1 Family Memory and Narrative

This chapter concentrates on the two aspects of narrative and memory as a basis for investigating how family identity is shaped and interrelates with forms of individual identity construction. Following the premise of narrative psychology, narrative is understood here to be not only a feature of storytelling, "but a fundamental way of organising human experience and knowledge" (Neumann and A. Nünning 2008, 8; cf. Bruner 1991a). This view of narrative as an omnipresent aspect of the human experience, as a 'tool for thinking' and as a 'means of worldmaking' has entered into a wide range of different fields of study as part of the 'narrative turn' in human sciences (V. Nünning 2013, 1; cf. Rimmon-Kenan 2006, Herman 2007).[59] When this is extrapolated to the realm of family matters, we see that different aspects of narrative begin to come into play. The role of narrative in identity construction, on both the individual and the collective level, is particularly important in this context. Dan P. McAdams (2003, 187; emphasis in the original) encapsulates the concept of 'narrative identity': "The *self* is many things, but *identity* is a life story." Identity, understood in its most basic sense as "what people *make* of themselves" (Lawler 2014, 8), relies on narrative in order to take shape and to be communicated. Since identity has to be thought of as plural and shifting, narrative in all its adaptability is important in order to bridge incoherencies and create unified meaning.[60] In families, the processes of individual and collective identity construction through narrative are interconnected on many levels, and the degree to which family narrative

---

[59] Bruner (1991a) discerns a 'paradigm shift' in psychology concerning narrative's role in constituting reality, which he dates to the appearance of the collection of essays *On Narrative*, published in 1981, in which Hayden White and Paul Ricoeur are represented among others (see Mitchell 1981).

[60] This roughly follows a sociological definition offered by Jonathan Turner (2013, 333) with reference to Sheldon Stryker (as part of an introduction to "Symbolic Interactionist Theories of Identity"): "[I]dentities are parts of larger sense of self [sic], and as such, they are internalized self-designations associated with positions that individuals occupy within various social contexts." In this view, the self encompasses "a set or series of identities that can be invoked individually or simultaneously in situations" (J. Turner 2013, 331–332).

and individual life stories are compatible or correspond with one another yields deep insights into family dynamics.

Self-narratives, apart from transforming the self into an identity, work to connect the past and the future: "[P]eople make sense of their own lives in terms of self-defining stories – integrative narratives of self that reconstruct the past and anticipate the future in such a way as to provide life with identity, meaning, and coherence." (McAdams 2006, 110) The same can be said of family stories and the construction of an overarching family narrative. By creating coherence, causality, and intentionality, narratives are the "most important resource for the forging of a successful identity" (Birke 2008, 23; see also Fivush and Haden 2003, viii). The life story, projecting into the past as well as into the future, has a prospective and a retrospective aspect to it, in which both equally adhere to socially sanctioned forms of narrative (cf. Eakin 1999, 110). Available life scripts are limited and strongly subject to cultural and societal norms as transmitted through the family: Consciously or unconsciously, the patterns of our life stories echo the norms of class, gender, and race or ethnicity (McAdams 2003, 201). Rule-governed and bound to convention, "narrative is necessarily normative" (Bruner 1991, 15). The French sociologist Maurice Halbwachs introduced the concept of 'social frameworks' in order to describe this mechanism of adaptation in conjunction with constraint in his seminal work on collective memory (Halbwachs 1992 [1925]; see also Eakin 2008, 30). Such frameworks denote the social context of remembering, as memories are always constructed, developed, and maintained in interaction and in social exchange with significant others (cf. A. Assmann 2006, 213; see also Misztal 2003, 1). It is in these social contexts that we see that the narrative patterns for identity are quickly established and internalised. From this follows that it is crucial to focus more on the family as a primary site and medium for the construction and transmission of cultural and social norms to create a life story is crucial, while it is also essential to study the transmission of family-specific values, goals and legacies, which play a vital role in shaping life scripts. Self-narratives are thus intricately bound up with narratives of the family and with family memory in general.

Three Aspects of Family Memory
Family memory is something that is difficult to escape from because "[n]o matter how we enter a family – by birth, marriage or some other way – we find ourselves to be part of a group, where our position is determined [...] by rules and customs independent of us that existed before us" (Halbwachs 1992, 55; qtd. in Erll 2011a, 306). Carol Smart's (2007, 48–49) helpful differentiation between

'relationality' and 'embeddedness' points to the difference between a biographical disposition and a potential for agency. Embeddedness defines constraints and possibilities, whereas relationality describes the scope within which individuals create their own worlds.[61] In this sense, the growing popular interest in family history and genealogy has to be conceived not in terms of a fixed imprinting but as a new premise for formations of the self. The analysed novels demonstrate this interplay between taking over established patterns and the process of tapping into the possibilities of transcending them.

The interrelation between the individual and the collective that can be observed in identity formation processes in the family also informs the different ways that memory plays a role with regard to family. In her essay on "Locating Family in Cultural Memory Studies", Astrid Erll (2011a, 308) lays the foundations for a family-focused perspective in memory studies. In examining the role of the family in Halbwachs' theory of collective memory, she identifies three aspects:[62]

1) Family as a social framework of memory (*cadre social*)
2) Family memory as collective memory
3) Family as a link between individual memory and larger formations of collective memory

These three aspects are closely interconnected and overlap in many ways, which presents difficulties in treating them as separate entities. Any instance of family reminiscing may very well show features relating to all three of these aspects of family memory. Nevertheless, the following is an attempt to understand in more detail what is meant by each of these points, and how they are distinct from one another.

1) Family as a social framework of memory
First of all, the family is a basic component of an individual's social framework of memory because it forms the main setting for cognitive development in early childhood. It is primarily within the family and in interaction with her parents (or other significant others in a family-like setting) that a child learns to remem-

---

61 See also chapter 2.1.2.
62 In his work *The Social Frameworks of Memory* (originally published 1925, transl. in *On Collective Memory*, 1992), Halbwachs dedicates a whole chapter to "The Collective Memory of the Family".

ber.⁶³ This collaborative construction of storied memories, most often in the family, i.e. between parent(s) and child(ren), is referred to as 'memory talk' in developmental psychology. In Eakin's theory of the relational self, the practice of memory talk serves as a prime example of a child's "intersubjective instruction in personhood" (Eakin 1999, 63). Katherine Nelson and Robyn Fivush (2004) among others have shown parent-child talk about the past to be a key factor in forming a concept of self through the attainment of autobiographical memory in social interaction.⁶⁴ Providing a setting for cognitive development in early childhood, family relationships play a key role in fostering memory and narrative ability – two prerequisites for the construction of a "narrative self understanding" (Nelson 2003, 7).

With his concept of social framworks, Halbwachs has taught us to focus more closely on the immediate social environment of remembering as an interpersonal and interactive practice. This seminal interactive nucleus, however, is much more than just the context and site for the production and re-production of family memories. Memory frameworks, such as the family, "that permit and fashion recollection are not merely social but also socially and culturally specific" (Chamberlain and Leydesdorff 2004, 229). The family is thus, in a much broader sense, the medium and site of introduction and learning of basic cultural values, narratives, and schemata. It is in the family that the transmission of the "collective symbolic order" is performed (Erll 2011a, 305). In this sense, the family as a social framework of memory plays a crucial part in providing "the culturally available narrative forms" (Fivush and Reese 1992, 115; qtd. in Eakin 2001, 295) for structuring past experiences and shaping the future. Each life narrative is "embedded in sociocultural frameworks that define what is appropriate to remember, how to remember it, and what it means to be a self with an autobiographical past" (Fivush and Haden 2003, vii; cf. also Misztal 2003, 5).⁶⁵ Social frameworks provide the coordinates for remembering by transmitting social and cultural knowledge of collective concepts of time and space and ways of thinking and experiencing, "cognitive schemata that steer our perception and memory in particular directions" (Erll 2011a, 305; 313). Forms and functions of life stories are "socially and culturally constructed"

---

63 Cf. Erll (2011a, 305): "Family members are the people who usually constitute the first, and often most important, social frameworks for a child."
64 See also Fivush and Haden (2003) and Eakin (1999, 110ff.).
65 Eviatar Zerubavel (2003, 4) similarly refers to "filters" that govern what and how we remember, and that are "highly impersonal, as they are rarely ever grounded in individuals' own experience". These filters, which "fit certain (unmistakably cultural) mental schemata [... are] evident in the highly formulaic plot structures we often use for narrating the past."

(Fivush 2008, 51), and individual narratives may more or less conform to, or deviate from, the script. This also indicates that there are concepts of self and identity that find shape in life scripts and are culturally contingent. Examples of this include the individual's relationship with family and the wider community and whether the self is defined as more independent and autonomous or more other-directed and interpersonal (Fivush 2008, 51–52). Parent-child memory talk is "enveloped in a society's metaphors and narratives", and "the fact that the culture is instantiated in the parental mind and is made visible through and in the language used to communicate [...] gives these exchanges their cultural power" (Nelson 2003, 23). In this way, family narratives and stories of the self are always constructed with reference to the available "sociocultural schemata" (Erll 2011a, 305).

The family as a social framework of memory thus also plays an important function in socialising "children into cultural and familial expectations for what to value and how to behave" (Koenig Kellas and Trees 2013, 397). Parents' stories of their childhood experiences may serve as guidelines for children to evaluate their own actions and experiences (cf. Koenig Kellas and Trees 2013, 397; see also Segrin and Flora 2011, 59). Narrative socialisation not only transmits themes such as achievement and personal success, but also allows for transgressions, and thus sets out future roles to be enacted by children (cf. Segrin and Flora 2011, 60). The process of narrative socialisation is closely embedded in cultural and social norms and values, and is accordingly gendered – so that there may be a variation between a mother's and a father's stories, while they may also change depending on the gender of the addressee and/or their corresponding role expectations with regard to themes such as achievement, independence, and autonomy (cf. Koenig Kellas and Trees 2013, 397).[66] On a more

---

[66] It is not solely in the area of parental storytelling that we see gender differences emerge, they often occur in the general narrative interactions within the family, with "parents with daughters engag[ing] in more detailed and more relationship-oriented reminiscing than do parents with sons". This, in turn, tends to "allow for the direct socialization of gendered modes of self" that correspond with cultural expectations of relational (female) and individuated (male) selves (Bohanek et al. 2006, 41). See also Buckner and Fivush (2000) for an extensive study on "Gendered Themes in Family Reminiscing". In this study, as elsewhere (cf. Koenig Kellas and Trees 2013), narratives about shared parent-child activities are examined in addition to narratives that parents recount of their own childhood. The socialisation process thus involves building a bridge across generations by emphasising experiential sameness, and accordingly continuity – children are made to understand that their parents were also children once, and that values and rules carry validity across time. See Fivush et al. (2009) for the gender differences that exist between the family reminiscing styles of the father and the mother respectively.

general level, the memories and stories shared in a family produce narrative patterns and plot structures that not only express a certain sense of family identity but also shape the available life scripts of the individuals in that family. In this way, family 'myths' or legacies, which may evolve over several generations, transport themes, values, and goals that offer orientation (or delineate limits or boundaries) for the prospective self-narrative. This leads seamlessly to the second aspect, family memory as collective memory.

2) Family memory as collective memory
As the concept of social frameworks indicates, individual memories are unthinkable in the absence of the larger webs of memory that they are set in relation to. The construction of personal memories is always tied to other memories and memories of others; these interrelations not only help the individual to "acquire coherence and consistency, but also create social bonds" (A. Assmann 2006, 213). The family, accordingly, not only provides a vital social framework of memory, but also a stock of memories and an archive of stories that build up the context for the individual's memories and which adapt to become part of their own life story: "Our personal memories include much more than what we, as individuals, have ourselves experienced. [...] Individuals' personal and collective memories interact." (A. Assmann 2006, 211; cf. also Misztal 2003, 76) Memory is not a given 'thing', it relies on a dialogic context to be activated and constructed; it is therefore essentially social and interactive in nature. While other forms of collective memory may play a crucial part in providing a frame for an individual's self narrative, as in, for example, generational memory,[67] family memory is characterised by a high degree of social interaction and exchange. Consequently, the line between "appropriated memories and personally acquired memories" (Misztal 2003, 76) becomes blurred in families.[68] There is

---

[67] Cf. A. Assmann (2006, 214). See also Erll (2014, 388ff.) for an elaboration on generations as mnemonic communities, and "the permeability between our own and other people's memories" (Erll 2014, 389) in this context. Erll, moreover, details the way memories are 'mediated' through "all kinds of representations [that] preform as well as retrospectively shape our autobiographical memories" (Erll 2014, 389).

[68] With regard to the 'appropriation' of memories that are not 'personally acquired', Barbara Misztal (2003, 76–77) points to how "memory is produced by an individual but is always produced in relation to the larger interpersonal and cultural world in which that individual lives – for example, one remembers one's childhood as part of a family". With reference to Jeffrey Prager's theory of 'false memory', she draws a line between "memory's *embeddedness*" (the role of the present in remembering) and "its *embodiedness*" (how past feelings and sensations

a pool of common and shared experiences, although, of course, individual perspectives clash within family memory and may give rise to considerable conflict. Anecdotal repetition and shared commemorative practices therefore enhance the effect of shared and appropriated memories. It has been established as an important psychological fact that the telling of family stories creates shared knowledge among family members even where there is no shared experience of the narrated events. Recurring stories are often told collaboratively and in a ritualised way, with parents actively engaging children in the conversation so that the stories become the very medium for building connections between the generations and their respective experiences (cf. Fivush et al. 2008, 139). From the point of view of the younger generation, this means that through their involvement in the shared activity of family reminiscing, they are able to incorporate events that lie outside their realm of direct experience into their own history and identify with them. On a thematic level, these stories work horizontally as well as vertically, building connections between the members of both the synchronic as well as the diachronic family. This is done by emphasising similarities among family members and laying down larger patterns for recurrent themes of family memory. In this way, certain stories may develop into long-term traditions and become part of the family legacy – stories that "are passed down from generation to generation, creating multigenerational threads of meaning in both family and individual identity" (Koenig Kellas and Trees 2013, 392). Family memories thus form a type of collective memory that

---

help a person to interpret the past; Misztal 2003, 77; emphasis in the original). This ties in with Alison Landsberg's concept of 'prosthetic memory', which – despite the fact that this concept denotes a very specific case of memory construction – shows parallels to processes of memory formation in the family. Landsberg (2004, 19) shows how "memories originate outside a person's lived experience and yet are taken on and worn by that person". The significant difference in Landsberg's concept is, however, that she considers memories that are not "necessarily and substantively shaped by lived social content" (Landsberg 2004, 19) and are therefore "transportable" and consequently potentially connecting across class, ethnicity, gender, nationality, and other differences. With the concept of prosthetic memory, Landsberg (2004, 19) hopes to "move beyond the familiar opposition between social construction and essentialism". I would argue, however, that in the family, processes of memory transmission also cannot be conceived of as happening "in a straightforward, hereditary fashion" (Landsberg 2004, 10) but also challenge a distinction between 'organic' and constructed memories. See Landsberg (2004, 7) for a critique of 'organic memory' as a theory of inherited memory.

provides a particularly important frame of reference for individual memory (cf. Erll 2011a, 306–307).[69]

The collective and shared aspect of family memory is also stressed in the theory of 'communicative memory', which is based on the family framework of three interacting generations with a time span of 80 to 100 years (J. Assmann 1995, 126–127).[70] The concept of communicative memory passes over the life span of the individual to focus on the inter- and transgenerational production of family stories. Importantly, communicative memory, in contrast to 'cultural memory' is "non-institutional" and "not [or only to a small degree] formalized and stabilized by any forms of material symbolization" (J. Assmann 2008, 111).[71] It relies on personal transmission and on those who 'own and inhabit' (A. Assmann 2006, 213) these memories, and therefore seems to periodically vanish.[72]

The idea of communicative memory highlightes the way in which family memory is constituted of a host of embodied memories, and is realised in social interaction and interpersonal acts of transmission (cf. A. Assmann 2006, 213). It is therefore important to not only consider the content of family memory, but to also look at its actualisation in "specific mnemonic practices" (Erll 2011a, 308) and the acts of family reminiscing. Fivush and colleagues (2008) distinguish between two important psychological functions of family reminiscing: The first concerns parent-child memory talk (family as social framework of memory), which forms a substantial part of a child's formation of a 'subjective self' with a unique perspective on past experiences; the second regards stories told in the family concerning others (family as collective memory), through which children

---

[69] As Astrid Erll (2008, 4) points out, the notion of 'collective memory' has to be understood as an "operative metaphor" that transfers the concept of remembering as individual cognitive process to the collective level of culture (or the family).
[70] See also J. Assmann (2008, 111) and A. Assmann (2006, 213).
[71] There are, of course, a variety of material carriers of family memory, of which family photographs stand out as being the most pertinent example. Nevertheless, these photographs also rely on their connection to embodied memories of individuals as a frame of reference. Family memory is thus still largely limited to the "cycle of oral interaction" of three generations. "Even if these memories are anecdotalized and regularly rehearsed or stabilized by letters or photographs, they remain volatile and subject to change and fading away." (A. Assmann 2006, 214)
[72] With this I do not mean to suggest that 'cultural memory' (as counter-concept to 'communicative memory') exists only in materialised and institutionalised forms; as the metaphor of 'memory' suggests, it depends on individual acts of remembering. Cf. Erll (2008, 5): "a 'memory' which is represented by media and institutions must be actualzed by individuals, by members of a community of remembrance".

(and adolescents)[73] learn to develop an 'intergenerational self' that helps them to understand their own life stories in the context of other people's lives and within an on-going narrative. The reservoir of shared family stories acts in extending the experiences and life spans of the individual family members involved. Family stories thus constitute an important frame of reference for the construction of autobiographical memory that embeds the individual self within a social framework of other people's lives and also within larger structures of meaning. Empirical psychological research confirms that this intergenerational perspective can be an important resource in the processes of identity formation:

> [F]amily stories create meaning beyond the individual, to include a sense of self through historical time and in relation to family members [...]. Part of who a person is is defined by the experiences of his or her parents and their parents before them. (Fivush et al. 2008, 134)

Family stories not only receive their unique mark and signature from the 'what' of the narrative but also from the 'how' of the narration; often the tone in which a story is told, as well as the specific rituals or routines that have been established around the practice of telling, can be more important for the emotional quality of a memory than the event itself. Barbara Fiese and Marcia Winter (2009) have examined the diverse ways that families engage in storytelling and reminiscing from the perspective of communication studies and came up with a classification of 'couple narrative styles', which makes a connection between narrative interaction and the well-being of families. The spectrum of their categorisation ranges from 'disengaged', 'conflictual/disruptive', and 'conflictual/contained' couple narrative style on the lower end to 'cooperative' and, finally, 'collaborative'. For each of these styles, they analyse the 'process' of narration and the way that the narrative style affects the story 'content'. So, for example, both the disengaged and conflictual/disruptive narrative style are characterised by such a major amount of disagreement expressed during its narration that the family's story itself becomes indiscernible. While the first, however, is marked by "decidedly cool and distant" interaction between the narrators, the latter will reveal "several episodes of moderate-to-high-intensity anger/rejection/conflict that linger in the interaction" (Fiese and M. Winter 2009, n.p.). In the conflictual/contained narrative style, the conflict largely remains concealed and contained in such a way that a "conjoint story" can be

---

[73] It is not before adolescence that the life narrative takes on a more complex form "that links events across time and places the self in relation to others, embedded in an unfolding human drama of interconnected stories" (Fivush 2008, 54).

told. On the highest end of the spectrum, 'collaborative storytelling' is described as the most satisfactory and integrated form of storytelling in families, both with regard to content (as concerns richness, coherence, and continuity of the story) and to the process of narration (involving "synthetic, synergistic exchanges", Fiese and M. Winter 2009, n.p.). As studies of communication among family members and couples in general show, story content and narrative interaction directly relate to "how satisfied couples were with their relationships", a "focus[...] on the 'we-ness' of their early dating relationships" (Fiese and M. Winter 2009, n.p.) indicating a high degree of 'marital functioning' that translates into a collaborative style of family storytelling (cf. Koenig Kellas and Trees 2013, 395).[74]

Jennifer Bohanek and her colleagues (2006) have conducted a similar study with a focus on the way families manage to acknowledge and integrate different perspectives in the narrative interaction between parents and children. They discern three styles: coordinated, individual, and imposed perspective. Families creating a coordinated perspective in intergenerational storytelling will gain "a more complex understanding of one's own perspective, the perspective of others, and the integration of the self with others" (Bohanek et al. 2006, 48).[75] It is not surprising that a coordinated perspective style, which results in "a cohesive, unitary collaborative narrative", contributes to "creating interconnectedness as a whole family" (Bohanek et al. 2006, 48). Indeed, Bohanek et al. make a valuable point in drawing attention to the aspect of perspective in family narrative, its correlation with "broader overall family communication patterns" (Bohanek et al. 2006, 49), and the interrelation of such features of communication with family cohesiveness. Perspective, in this context, can well be understood in the sense that Vera and Ansgar Nünning (2000, 10; cf. also Surkamp 2003, 37) employ in their theory on the perspective structure of narrative texts. This philosophical concept of perspective encompasses all aspects involved in shaping a person's subjective model of reality, which also includes their understanding of family.[76] The ways in which meaning is created both within and through the

---

[74] See chapter 5.2 on Jackie Kay's *Red Dust Road* for an extensive analysis of family interaction in storytelling practices.

[75] Bohanek et al.'s study (2009, 39) examines the role of family narrative for "preadolescents' sense of self both as an individual and as a member of a unified family" and looks at the correlation between perspective style in family narrative and children's self-esteem.

[76] Following Carola Surkamp (2003, 38), a book character's model of reality involves eight aspects: biographical background information, psychic and physical disposition, values and norms, experience and actions, their culturally formed patterns of perception and meaning

family therefore depends on the respective perspectives of its members. Just how far families may go in creating a coordinated perspective on the past, present, and future may say much about their capability to deal with change and to integrate a growing diversity of norms, values, needs, and aspirations within the family unit.[77]

In conclusion, family memory as collective memory ties in with family myth as a central dimension of the family imaginary in Gillis's sense (cf. chapter 2.1). It highlights the role of narrative in the construction of family identity, both with regard to the idea of making sense of the family's trajectory and development through time as well as with regard to the use of storytelling and reminiscing as key family practices for creating and affirming family cohesion and continuity. Within family memory and the vast host of stories circulated in a family, Jane Jorgenson and Arthur Bochner (2003, 525; see also Koenig Kellas and Trees 2013, 394–396) identify such narratives that are particularly meaningful for family identity as "canonical stories". Canonical stories typically encompass 'creation stories', such as 'marital origin stories' and 'birth narratives', which pivot on the nexus between individual and collective identity construction within families.[78] The 'marital origin story', or 'courtship story', is of particular importance as it "functions as the creation myth for a particular family's collective memory" (Jorgenson and Bochner 2003, 526), and as such transmits central themes, values, and ideals regarding relationships and love. Birth stories are concerned with establishing each child's place in the (changing) family constellation and carry strong messages of love, care, and role distribution in the family. Other canonical stories are concerned with shared experiences and the forms of social interaction in the family, and often recount family rituals or routines, such as yearly vacations or family traditions. The telling of such canonical stories often becomes a family routine in its own right with a high degree of "ritualized interaction" (Koenig Kellas and Trees 2013, 396). In this way, family reminiscing has a performative function: "family storytelling ritually and routinely enacts a family" (Langellier and Peterson 2004, 34).

---

making, their level of knowledge and information, their motivations, their needs and intentions, and context.

77 For an example, see the analysis of *Maps for Lost Lovers* in chapter 4.1.

78 Seeing that family memory is "situated against the backdrop of cultural master narratives about family that shape and reflect our narrative practices" (Koenig Kellas and Trees 2013, 392), such stories are 'canonical' in that they not only constitute an intra-familial canon of 'sanctified' stories, but that they also conform to culture-specific normative scripts that delineate family identities and the life course of families. On the canon and processes of canonisation, see A. Assmann (2008).

3) Family as a link between individual and collective memory

Just as individual memory is not formed in isolation but within social frameworks, the family as a mnemonic community is interlinked with other, larger formations of collective memory, such as national memory or the memory of a community. According to Aleida and Jan Assmann, family memory as 'communicative memory' is set off against the myths and narratives of 'cultural memory' (cf. A. Assmann 2006, 213; see also J. Assmann 2008). Cultural memory, in contrast with communicative memory, is understood as disembodied – relying not on personal transmission and interaction but on institutions and different forms of material symbolisation to formalise and stabilise it. However, as Jay Winter (2006, 5) emphasises, any 'collective memory' "lies in the acts of remembrance, small and large, of different collectives at different times". In the family "framework of communicative remembering" (Erll 2011a, 312), such forms of institutionalised memory, as, for example, national memory, are (re-)connected to the personal experience and transmitted intergenerationally. The family provides the link between the individual and the collective, the private and the public, and is, in the words of Anne Fuchs (2008, 4), "a meeting point of competing ideas of what it means to be embedded in tradition." It is in the family that the larger narratives and topoi of the nation and society intersect with private and subjective forms of remembering, thereby connecting personal, family, and cultural memory.[79] In this way, family memory and transmission may yield access for later-born generations to a (sometimes silenced) historical past that they did not live through themselves. This form of transference is characterised by an immediacy of experience specific to the closeness of family interaction (cf. Weigel 2005).

The family is thus not only embedded in culture and a significant place for the transmission of traditions, norms, and values; it is also a realm of historical experience and a vehicle for its communication. Memories in the family are informed by and often narrated along the lines of historical events, and references to different formations of collective memory are important sources of meaning making in the family narrative. Overall, family memory is intertwined with historical narratives and other forms of collective memory in multifarious ways. In the words of Astrid Erll (2011a, 310), "the complex interplay between family and national memory" works both ways, and in analysing the interrelations of these different frameworks of memory one needs to ask "how national memory feeds into family memory, and, in turn, how family memory contrib-

---

[79] Anne Fuchs (2008, 4) here speaks of the family as both *lieu de mémoire* (shaping and reflecting cultural memory) and *lieu de souvenir* (as site of remembrance).

utes to and consolidates national sites of memory (or fails to do so and leads to their obsolescence)" (Erll 2011a, 310). The narratives and images of official and national memory are "continually refracted" (Erll 2011a, 312) in family remembrance; moreover, they are reshaped and adapted to fit new meanings as each new generation takes on (or rejects) these memories as part of their own narrative. Erll, however, rightly points out that family memories if viewed as "memories from below" (Erll 2011a, 310) are not necessarily more authentic or truer to the lived experience than more formalised, official narratives of the past. Family memory may nevertheless be in conflict with the official narrative and provide a realm for re-interpretations of past events by adding different voices and perspectives, as "[h]istory and memory overlap, infuse each other, and create vigorous and occasionally fruitful incompatibilities." (J. Winter 2006, 5–6) Accordingly, memory and history are not opposed, but "braided together" (J. Winter 2006, 6), in a way in which the family serves as "an intersection of the private and the public, a site where official representations of the past are contested by alternative memories from below" (Fuchs 2008, 4).

It is not only important to look at how history is more or less consciously 'transported' within families and how family memory intersects with national memory, it is also necessary to examine how family is a site for the transmission of memories and narratives that "may explicitly or silently challenge official versions of history" (Carsten 2007, 3). In the context of British migration literature, two aspects in particular come to mind: First of all, the family is a crucial framework in which counter-narratives of Empire may be preserved and passed on which act to subvert and unsettle colonialist master narratives.[80] As the novels in this study will reveal, the impact of colonialism and its ramifications on families is severe, and family narratives and identities may be profoundly and persistently shaped by their (often traumatic) experience of colonial exploitation and the subsequent disruption of family structures.[81] Narrative, as a powerful tool for worldmaking, offers diverse forms of dealing with such experiences, which may, for example, be transformed into stories of resistance that carry a

---

[80] See Brunow (2015, 10ff.) for an elaboration of the complexities of and problems with the concept of 'counter memory' as challenging hegemonic master narratives. As Harald Welzer reveals in his studies of post-World War II family memory in Germany, "[n]on-official memory is not always more emancipatory than official memories" (Brunow 2015, 10).

[81] The disruptive force of colonialism and imperialism on family structure and family memory is dealt with in many of the novels analysed in this thesis; the historical grounds may lie in slavery (*Fruit of the Lemon*), or, more commonly, in the wars and forced migrations that followed independence, but whose seeds were planted during colonialism (*Maps for Lost Lovers*, *My Ear at His Heart*, *Anita and Me*).

more self-affirmative and empowering quality.⁸² Alternatively, however, family narratives may also retain damaging and disruptive elements that complicate or obstruct the construction of family identity and the cohesiveness of family relationships.⁸³ In each case, family memory, as a significant site of 'post-colonial memory', adds different perspectives to "the complicated dynamics of the memories of coloniser and colonised, and of their respective descendants in multicultural societies" (Erll 2006, 177). In this way, previously silenced episodes of and perspectives on colonial history return to the 'mother country' along with the migrant families that carry them, with the result that different voices are added to the collective memory of the British Empire. This is the second important aspect of family memory in multicultural Britain, as it offers ways of questioning discrete or exclusive national narratives by foregrounding entangled histories and connectivities that also have a bearing on ethnic, national, and racial constructions of identity. "The study of family memory can thus serve as an important corrective to the top-down approach taken by those who chart 'purist' sites of national memory." (Erll 2011a, 310)⁸⁴ Literary and other media representations of family memory take on an important role in putting forward alternative narratives of the past forward into the public discourse on national memory and history.⁸⁵ As will be demonstrated through a closer analysis of the novels discussed in later chapters, the emphasis on entangled rather than purist national histories may serve as a basis for refiguring concepts of identity,⁸⁶ or for a new understanding of power relations and structures of discrimination and racism.⁸⁷

Secrets and Silences

The family as a framework for memory is not a closed space, and therefore deeply enmeshed with public narratives and images that feed into family memory,

---

82 Examples can be found in *Anita and Me* or *White Teeth*; see chapter 3.
83 See, e.g., the analysis of *Maps for Lost Lovers* in chapter 4.1.
84 Erll is particularly wary of approaches in memory studies that derive from a concept of culture as one that is "constructed upon the assumption of an isomorphy between territory, social formation, mentalities, and memories" (2011b, 7).
85 The boom of family and generational novels in German literature since the 1970s can be generally seen in this light. As Harald Welzer (2004, 53) explains, these novels have attracted so much interest and attention because of the fact that they are closer to people's experience of history than its usual depiction in the authoritative narratives of the state. Cf. Agazzi 2008, 190.
86 See *Fruit of the Lemon*, and *White Teeth*.
87 See *Anita and Me* and *Maps for Lost Lovers*.

connecting it to larger social issues and historical events. Family memory not only transmits seminal episodes of family history but is often impacted in the aftermath of a historic trauma. Such a traumatic family legacy may take the shape of silences and secrets that perplex the younger generation and confront them with unsolved mysteries. Marianne Hirsch's concept of 'postmemory' denotes "a *structure* of inter- and trans-generational transmission of traumatic knowledge and experience" to a degree that for the descendants of survivors these experiences "*seem* to constitute memories in their own right" (Hirsch 2008, 106–107; emphases in the original). Postmemory describes how the lines of transmission and the appropriation of 'inherited memory' in the family framework are complicated through the rupture of traumatic events, causing a break that "necessitates forms of remembrance that reconnect and reembody an intergenerational memorial fabric that has been severed by catastrophe" (Hirsch 2008, 110). Postmemorial work is characterised by "imaginative investment, projection, and creation" (Hirsch 2008, 106), through which an affective and bodily connection to the past is established. The concept of postmemory thus highlights the way in which memory in the family is transmitted in subliminal ways: "The language of family, the language of the body: nonverbal and non-cognitive acts of transfer occur most clearly within a familial space, often in the form of symptoms." (Hirsch 2008, 112)

The children of Holocaust survivors, who discovered in the 1970s that they were burdened with a very specific parental legacy, constituted the paradigmatic context in which the postmemory syndrome became manifest. Hirsch analysed these symptoms, and, with a special focus on artistic responses, also extended her concept to the impact of the Holocaust on non-Jewish survivor families and other post-traumatic situations (Hirsch 2012b). She introduced the term 'generation of postmemory' to describe a condition that is overburdened with 'inherited memories' and dominated by the narratives of the previous generation. This condition is a consequence of symbiosis, of sharing a long-lived "close proximity to the pain, depression, and dissociation" of the parents as opposed to more direct forms of transmission through storytelling or the sharing of memories. It is this on-going impact of trauma that Misztal (2003, 141) describes as "corporeal memory", inscribed directly into the body in a way that makes its recall "particularly vivid, intrusive, uncontrollable, persistent and somatic" (Misztal 2003, 142).[88]

---

[88] Body memory is a vast topic in different disciplines, and covers a range of aspects that tie in with trauma studies and family memory, both conjointly and separately. For an introduction to and an overview of the different facets of body memory from pain memory, bodily risks of

Hirsch speaks of the "language of family" to highlight the way in which the family constitutes a framework that specifically fosters tacit, unvoiced, and subliminal forms of intra-, inter- or trans-generational transmission. These are grounded not only in the close and frequent interaction within families, but also in the powerful metaphors of inheritance and heredity, which produce long-lasting and complex ties and entanglements. It is therefore crucial to not only look at the stories that are told but also at the silences that nestle in the blind spots of family communication.[89] What is told and what is omitted from the story are two sides of the same coin that cannot be separated: Silences are deeply embedded into the well-rehearsed stories of the family and transmitted from generation to generation along with them (cf. Smart 2011a, 543). According to Jay Winter (2013, 245), silences can be conceived as "depots below the surface" that add a further dimension to the "framework of how we think about memory and forgetting". J. Winter further defines silence as "a socially constructed space", demarcated by the "difference between the sayable and the unsayable, or the spoken and the unspoken" (J. Winter 2010, 4).[90] Traumatic experiences, in particular, often create such spaces of the unsayable and the unspoken that result in gaps and fissures in the family narrative, and in the narratives of selves within the family. Postmemory thrives on voids, gaps, and silences, as it "cannot rely on experience but builds on images, stories and documents that have been passed down from the witness to the child" (Seemann 2013, 37).

Silences may be the typical response to an overpowering external impact, but they are also a powerful instrument to back up the "normative nature of collective memory aimed at defending a group identity" (Misztal 2003, 141).[91] In this role, silences assume the quality of taboos or secrets that can be characterised as a 'purposeful hiding' of information (cf. Vangelisti 1994, 114). In either

---

stress and depression, the effects of trauma on genes and brain structure, through to epigenetics, etc. see Bauer ([2004] 2014).

89 Esther Rashkin (1992, 28) uses the image of the ventriloquist to illustrate how the "silence, gap, or secret in the speech of someone else 'speaks' [...] through the words and acts (readable as words) of the subject". In her psychoanalytic study of secrets in literature based on Nicolas Abraham and Maria Torok's concept of the phantom (1979) she defines family secrets as "a situation or drama that is transmitted without being stated and without the sender's or receiver's awareness of its transmission" (Abraham and Torok 1979, 4).

90 See also Fivush (2010, 89), who posits the social construction of voice and silence in conversational interactions, which in turn are determined by cultural frameworks.

91 "Studies suggest that forgetting and silence is a very frequent reaction as groups organize forgetting, reconstruction and positive distortion of the past in order to defend group values and their own image" (Misztal 2003, 141).

way, silences can be seen as a way of negotiating the culturally provided "canonical narratives that are both normative and prescriptive about lives and about selves, and the ways in which specific experiences conform or deviate from these narratives create spaces for voice and silence" (Fivush 2010, 89). As David Morgan (2011, 29) asserts, "[i]t would be difficult to imagine families without secrets". Family secrets work in different ways: they both reproduce larger structures in the society and they serve to build up the internal structure of the family as an autonomous sub-system. One may distinguish between collectively held 'family secrets' and 'internal' or 'intra-family secrets', depending on who shares the information and who is excluded from the secret knowledge.[92] In both cases, secrets create boundaries between the in-group of those who share the information and the out-group that is being excluded. Collectively held family secrets may be a 'vehicle for bonding', as they mark "boundaries [that] function as a relational anchor" (Petronio 2002, 87). In this context, disclosure is associated with intimacy through the co-ownership and co-management of private information (cf. Petronio 2002, 87), as secrets shared between two or more people "can contribute to their sense of bonding and trust" (Caughlin and Petronio 2003, 379).[93] Partially shared secrets within the family will, however, also create "interior boundaries" and barriers of communication around "internal family collectivities" such as marital couples, siblings, etc. (Petronio 2002, 151); of course, secrets may also be kept by a single person from the rest of the family. It is important to note that the functions and forms of internal and external family secrets may be very different although the exterior and interior boundary spheres are likely to intersect.[94] Alongside the question of form or dissemination (who shares the secret), the content or topic (type of information that is concealed or withheld) and the function of family secrets are also important aspects to be considered (cf. Vangelisti 1994, 114–115), while it is often the case that they are closely connected. Secrets surround-

---

92 Given the naming of these sub-groups, one can assume that the secrets that are shielded from non-family members are seen as the default case. The following analyses, however, will concentrate more on internal family secrets.
93 With regard to intimacy, "[t]he development of private 'languages' [...] and personal idioms [...] represents one often-cited form of secrecy used to increase or maintain a sense of closeness" (Vangelisti 1994, 116). This function of secrets in the family context is not to be underestimated, as is that of building and maintaining group cohesiveness (cf. Vangelisti 1994, 117). In both cases, secrets serve as markers of inclusion (and exclusion of outsiders).
94 Cf. Vangelisti 1994, 114; Petronio 2002, 151. For an extensive and systematic elaboration on boundary and privacy management in families see Petronio 2002, or Caughlin and Petronio 2003.

ing taboo topics, such as reproductive secrets, or forms of violence or abuse in families, may be hidden to protect the public image of the family and are consequently externally oriented in their manner; however, their concealment may also serve to protect the internal structure of the family and prevent it "from falling apart" (Vangelisti 1994, 117). These secrets may be "buried and forgotten", but are often "kept alive by innuendo, palpable silences, evasions and rumour" (Smart 2011a, 543) and form an integral part of family memory. In the words of Annette Kuhn (2002, 2), "secrets inhabit the borderlands of memory".

In the context of this study, we are primarily interested in the way that silences and secrets act in disturbing and unsettling family memory. Secrets and silences have much more of a role than simply being gaps of information in family stories. They point to neuralgic nodes in the family network and thus to the fragility of family identity. For this analysis, they act not only as important keys and clues within family narratives but also within the structure of the novels. Although "not all of these secrets will be the basis of explosive or tragic outcomes" (Smart 2011a, 543), many family secrets are potentially disruptive as they may necessitate re-workings and reconstructions of the family narrative (accompanied by whatever adjustments this might entail for the self-narrative of individuals in the family). In the matter of secrets that develop around certain taboo topics and the silences that emerge from traumatic experiences, the divergence of perspectives on, and versions of, the family narrative becomes manifest, in addition to the fissures in the fabric of family memory.

Family Memory and Migration
Apart from the great wars and the major political transitions that came in the wake of colonialism and decolonisation, the twentieth century has witnessed a plethora of large-scale migratory movements, particularly in the first half of the century and in the decades following World War II and following the decline of the British Empire. In the following section, I want to investigate how migration leaves its imprint on the private sphere of family memory, and how family memory, in turn, offers up alternative perspectives for the transformation of the public discourse on national and ethnic identity, belonging, and cultural memory. Or, alternatively, "[i]n the face of the dislocations of modernity and postmodernity, how does memory's role change?" (Landsberg 2004, 1)

Alongside the great waves of migration and the effects of an increasing globalisation, the voices and mnemonic communities that interact with the framework of national memory constructs have multiplied and become increasingly fragmented in the late twentieth century. The frameworks of national memory have consequently come under pressure to become more diverse and to represent more accurately the actual configuration of social groups. This development has led to two transformations: the internal pluralisation of voices within society, and the formation of new memory communities beyond the nation state. New trends in memory studies have paid special attention to these transformations, while recent research has shifted the focus away from "the master narrative of nations to the episodic narrative of groups" (Misztal 2003, 18). According to Astrid Erll (cf. 2011b, 8), the turn of the twenty-first century has seen the notion whereby the nation-state acts as a grid for the analysis of collective memory increasingly lose its pre-eminence.[95] The rapidly expanding field of global history is following a similar trajectory, as Sebastian Conrad (2016, 2) states: "In many places, in particular in immigrant societies, global history is also a response to social challenges and to the demand for a more inclusive, less narrowly national perspective on the past."

Barbara Misztal (2003, 18) also notes that with respect to memory, the national framework has lost much of its cohesive force. She argues that "with [today's societies'] diversity of cultures, ethnicities, religions and traditions, we are witnessing the fragmentation of national memory". Instead of looking at transformations beyond the national framework, however, her research is directed at the micro-level of society, shifting the focus from "the master narrative of nations to the episodic narrative of groups" (Misztal 2003, 18). The result of this shift of attention means that the family now gains prominence as an important site wherein the larger transformations and challenges of memory constructions are reflected. In contrast with the more or less homogeneous constructs of national memory, the family as a framework of memory and a mnemonic community brings to the fore cross-cultural connectivities and the multifaceted and entangled processes of embodied memory (cf. Erll 2011a, 310).[96] Furthermore, the family is a site where different strands of (family and

---

[95] As a result, transcultural memory studies has increasingly gained prominence as an expanding field of research and, more specifically, "a certain *research perspective*" (Erll 2011b, 9) within memory studies that is based on the concept of transculturality as "phenomena which reach *across* and – eventually, as a result of the contemporary process of globalization – also *beyond* cultures" (Erll 2011b, 8, with reference to Welsch 1999; emphasis in the original). Mnemonic practices and acts of remembrance might nevertheless – depending on their context – propagate a different concept of culture. See Erll (2011b) for an overview of the field of transcultural studies in general (8–9) and transcultural memory studies in particular (9ff.).

[96] As Astrid Erll (2011b, 10) points out, Halbwachs's notion of frameworks "implies a certain 'framed-ness' connected with all memory" that needs to be transcended in order to see memory as unbounded and "continually moving across and beyond such territorial and social borders".

other) narrative converge. Family memory is thus an inherently eclectic site of remembrance that relates to a multiplicity of social frameworks and contexts – a condition that is enhanced through migration: "It is through the study of family memory (especially of cross-cultural, transnational and immigrant families [...]) that the actual, multivoiced processes of remembering the nation become discernible." (Erll 2011a, 310)

Migration emphasises the element of movement, which, according to Astrid Erll (2011b, 12), is intrinsic to the logic of (cultural) memory: be it movement between individual people as part of a social interaction, between groups of different sizes, or as part of larger scale political, social, and cultural phenomena that can span the globe (cf. Erll 2011b, 11). Roots are not necessarily cut off in the process of migration, but the routes of migration clearly complicate the structure of family memory, forcing a reworking of the social frameworks of memory with a pluralisation of national, cultural, ethnic, social, or religious narratives that each hold different and often oppositional claims on people's lives. As a result of previous external pressures of isolation or assimilation, and the growing desire to accommodate the "complex set of loyalties and iron necessities" that dominate the lives of today's immigrants, the path "chosen by millions of people, [is] to have plural identities, to live lives in two countries at the same time, not in a physical sense, but in a cultural sense" (J. Winter 2012, x). Migratory movements thus directly impact on the memory frames of family, society, and nation, which have to be conceived of as shifting, and subject to processes of translation and transformation. Diasporic family memory is consequently an important locus of transcultural memory, which Nadia Butt (2015, 19) defines "as 'shared' or 'intertwined memory' – a memory of overlapping 'territorial', 'personal' and 'political histories'".

In this study I want to trace how these larger-scale, global processes become visible in the family and how they affect family memory and narrative as an important site of identity construction and negotiations of belonging. In this process, "memories are a key route into revealing and understanding the processes, adjustments, and negotiations of migrants, of the mobile and liminal

---

The family is not only always in flux (with regard to members and their roles), but also at any given moment in time comprises of a group of people who each have "multiple memberships" and different social, (sub-)cultural, religious, etc. affiliations as well as differing historical experiences. These various realms of collective memory not only intersect in the mind of the individual, but also in the family memory (cf. Erll 2011b, 10–11, particularly with regard to a more differentiated view on the transcultural intersecting of different formations of collective memory and an elaboration of the concept of 'travelling memory' with regard to Aby Warburg's *Mnemosyne*-atlas).

worlds they inhabit, of the connections with and the longings for home" (Chamberlain 2009, 186). The focus therefore is less on the 'politics of memory' surrounding the debates around multiculturalism, integration, and the incorporation of immigrants (cf. Glynn and Kleist 2012), and more on the complex ways in which migration informs family dynamics, subjectivities, and personal as well as collective formulations of identity. Today, the multi-generational family is dramatically ruptured through migration to which the mass of Black and Asian British novels written in the last decade acts as testimony. These texts describe, in concrete detail, the faultlines of family memory in migrant groups, demonstrating the ways in which they are formed, manifested, and stabilised along the generational divide, and illustrating the dramatic ethnic and cultural tensions that play out within the framework of family memory.

2.2.2 Genes and Genealogies

Family memory and narrative play a crucial role in positioning the self within a temporal frame that extends the life span of an individual. A closer look at the interlacing of individual and collective memory in the family highlights the way in which we are embedded in supra-individual structures, constellations, and meanings that have a synchronic as well as a diachronic dimension.[97] Memory creates a trans-generational family identity that is not only based on interactive communication and transmission, but is additionally substantiated by the idea of "biological continuity" (Zerubavel 2003, 56). This idea of a biological link between past and present generations is particularly powerful, as it creates a sense of "organic belonging" (Zerubavel 2012, 10) that is assumed to be natural: "The role of biology in the social construction of historical continuity is most strikingly evident in essentialist narratives that portray blood 'connections' as somehow more real." (Zerubavel 2003, 56) Like the age-old metaphor of blood ties, DNA has become a similarly powerful signifier for the 'substance of kinship' (cf. Zerubavel 2012, 54).

As part of the recent boom in genealogy, the offer of DNA ethnicity testing has become widely popular. A global travel agency went viral in 2016 with an online commercial that featured DNA tests against the backdrop of global migration and tourism. The ad puts across a confusing message of anti-racism and

---

[97] Cf. A. Assmann (2007, 70; emphasis in the original): "Das individuelle Leben ist *immer schon* eingegliedert in Überindividuelles, ohne das es gar nicht entstehen und sich entwickeln könnte."

essentialism that is typical of the current hype around genealogical DNA testing.⁹⁸ As the probands hand in their saliva sample, a man tells them, "The story of you is in that tube". The way nature and culture merge and become indistinctive here proves once more that there is a social construction of relatedness, and highlights the cultural foundations of the ideas of genealogy. In the words of Eviatar Zerubavel (2012, 10; emphasis in the original), "[r]ather than simply passively documenting who our ancestors were, [genealogies] are the narratives we construct to actually *make* them our ancestors". The ad also highlights the way in which ethnicity is generally seen as a form of kinship, materialised in the idea of shared 'blood' (in the sense of consanguinity) or, as in this case, DNA.⁹⁹ The idea of 'national' DNA puts forward the notion of 'scientific evidence' and an "essentialized vision of peoplehood" (Zerubavel 2012, 57) which are paradoxically merged.

The international website, MyHeritage, one of a vast number of online sites for private genealogical research that has popped up over the last number of years,¹⁰⁰ offers its registrants two options: one is the basic DNA test, to "uncover your unique ethnic origins and find new relatives", while the other proposes a family tree tool, to "explore the lives of your ancestors and discover your family's fascinating history". Genetic and genealogical research into the past thus come together to promise its wide and varied membership base easy access to new modes of historical belonging that had traditionally been reserved for the social elites (cf. Castañeda 2002, 75). Genealogy has emerged as a successful phenomenon in the world of pop culture where TV shows such as *Who Do You Think You Are?*, or Henry Louis Gates Jr.'s *African American Lives*, have thoroughly democratised and even commoditised the research of a family's pedigree, an area that was once exclusively the privilege of aristocracy. Family his-

---

98 The storyline of the ad runs along the lines that people are first encouraged to express their stereotypes of and bias against other nationalities or ethnicities, only to be then confronted with the fact that their DNA test results reveal a common ancestry. So the English man finds out he is not 100 % English as he thought, but is actually also 5 % German; and the Kurdish woman discovers that she has roots in Turkey. The idea expressed in the clip is that "there would be no extremism in the world if people knew their heritage like that". The tag line is "An Open World Begins with an Open Mind". Cf. LetsOpenOurWorld 2016.
99 This aspect is emphasised in the video through a 'cousin' who is (somewhat randomly) found through a DNA test and later presented with much emotional effect; cf. LetsOpenOurWorld 2016.
100 Some examples are familysearch.org, ancestry.com, progenealogists.com, afrigeneas.com, archives.gov/research/genealogy, familytreemagazine.com, findmypast.com, genesreunited.com, heritagequestonline.com.

tory is 'sold' "as an identity-affirming cultural practice" (Erll 2014, 397) and a promise of finding one's distant origins for the purpose of "the production of individuality and uniqueness in the West" (Kramer 2011, 382).[101] It is in the very process of carving out such uniqueness, a "process of recognition and dis/identification", that genealogy evolves into a "technology of belonging" (Kramer 2015, 80). Genealogy is thus a constructive tool in the process of meaning-making and identity-building, in which the "ties considered to be 'given in nature' are intrinsically bound up with what people *make of* those ties" (Lawler 2014, 48; emphasis in the original).

The most common image of genealogical relatedness is that of the chain, as can be seen in the long genealogical lists of the book of Genesis in the Hebrew Bible. In such a chain, the most basic relations of parenthood and filiation are ordered in a line of succession that can be indefinitely prolonged with each generation forming a new link in the chain. As Eviatar Zerubavel has established, this image of the chain already contains the basic logic of genealogical relatedness, as "[o]ur entire notions of ancestry and descent are but extensions of these elemental ties" (Zerubavel 2012, 16). Thus the chain links us, via our parents, to our grandparents, so that "intergenerational contact need not be confined to adjacent generations" (Zerubavel 2003, 59). Zerubavel points out that the link to our grandparents is special in that not only is it experienced indirectly through our parents, in their position as our parents' parents, but also as a (generally) directly lived relationship in its own right. In this way, a link in the genealogical chain is skipped as we "mentally compound [two parental-filial ties] into a single, seemingly direct grandparental-grandfilial tie" (Zerubavel 2012, 17). Zerubavel therefore establishes 'grandparenthood' as another central concept in our genealogical imagination: it allows us to conceive direct links between non-consecutive generations. "[I]t is the concept (and thus the idea) of grandparenthood that enables us to mentally transcend such strictly dyadic as well as direct forms of ancestry and descent, and also gives ancestry its distinctly human character" (Zerubavel 2012, 16).

The idea of embeddedness in a chain of descent entails a fundamentally different perspective on intergenerational family relations than the dyadic constel-

---

101 Steph Lawler (2014, 52) points out with reference to Marilyn Strathern (1992) that there are contradictions between individuality and collectivism in this understanding of self: "Strathern's analysis of the ways in which Westerners understand their identities as inherited while that inheritance leads to individuality is crucial in addressing what looks like a fundamental contradiction in Western kinship: that persons are seen as unique, bounded individuals *at the same time* that they are understood as being placed within systems of kin ties."

lation of the 'nuclear family'. While the image of the chain represents long-term continuity and continuance, dyadic generational relations are more often than not marked by confrontation and rupture (A. Assmann 2007, 70ff.). In the words of Claudia Lenz (2011, 326), intergenerational relations are marked by distinct lines of affiliation, either "tradition lines-based or experience-based-generation affiliation". These basic modes of generational and genealogical positioning govern the forms in which we set ourselves in relation to our family, through the processes of identification and dis-identification, connection and distinction. In the case of tradition-oriented genealogical affiliation, "the symbolically maintained connection with inheritance and its carriers" (Lenz 2011, 326) is crucial. In the case of experience-based generations, however, affiliation is created synchronically rather than diachronically, while intergenerational relations are marked by dissociation and "symbolically performed rupture" (Lenz 2011, 323).

These intergenerational dynamics in the family also apply to the relationship between social generations. The sociological concept of generation focuses on demographic cohorts and thus stresses the synchronic similarity and identity-construction of age-groups in the wider context of society and history. The norms of Western culture encourage social generations to react against each other by creating their similarity by seeking to distinguish themselves, which emphasises the idea of successive replacement and renewal rather than continuity. Family generations are both embedded in and a part of social generations, as the individual lives of family members are often heavily affected by historical events that impinge on their values and views.

In the counting of family generations, both strands of the generation concept, the sociological and the genealogical, intersect. The counting of generations is often affected by events that are of particular historical and social significance, such as historical ruptures, traumas, and other incisive episodes or occurrences (cf. Weigel 2002, 162). In a similar way, migration is a key experience and a founding event within families that repositions family members within the chain of generations, thereby creating both a genealogical link between the individual and their family history, and a generational link to a sociohistorical experience. In such constellations of first, second, and third generations, intergenerational dynamics evolve in specific ways, reflecting how experience (or trauma) has been transmitted across generations, from old to young, and, conversely, how the narrative of that experience and the family identity is re-constructed and changed with every new generation.[102]

The term 'first generation', however, also brings with it the promise of new beginnings: The arrival of the *Empire Windrush* in June 1948, with the corresponding label of the 'Windrush Generation', is now widely regarded as the "founding event of postwar migration" (Rupp 2010, 139), and the starting point of a multicultural Britain. Despite the fact that such founding events are vitally important for the formation of retrospective acts of self-definition and the construction of 'imagined communities',[103] this emphasis on a myth of origin often eclipses whatever narrative that came before it.[104] The same pertains to the counting of generations, which suggests that the chain is broken, and that there are no preceding generations to the first. In light of this transgenerational significance of the founding event of the new genealogy, other forms of "genealogical remembering" (Lenz 2011, 326) are easily neglected. This is the reason why, in the context of migration, the idea of grandparenthood as the key to a broader genealogical imaginary takes on a special significance for the second generation. In a way, the concept of grandparenthood has to be re-discovered and the link that was severed in the family genealogy at the point of migration needs to be imaginatively re-established.

The re-established link to the grandparents incorporates the idea of ancestry. Grandparenthood, being "an inherently expandable concept" (Zerubavel 2012, 19), implies that the same logic that allows us to imagine the ties to our grandparents as direct also applies to great-grandparents and great-great-grandparents, and so on. This continuous line of succession that connects someone link by link with temporally distant relatives promotes "a sense of vicarious participation in history 'through' their various ancestors." (Zerubavel 2012, 21) The idea that through the connection we share with our ancestors we can "figuratively touch the past" (Zerubavel 2012, 21) is what makes the family such a significant realm for the transmission of historical experience; the tangibility of the genealogical link conveys a sense of immediacy, proximity, and

---

102 The terms first and second generation have a specific meaning in the context of Holocaust remembrance, the transgenerational transmission of trauma, and the condition of postmemory. See Hirsch 2012a [1997].
103 See also Erll 2014, 402.
104 There is an undisputable tendency to focus on post-World-War II migration in discussions of migration literature in Britain, for instance, that this study is also guilty of. The *Cambridge Companion to British Black and Asian Literature*, for example, deals with the years 1945–2010. Other publications decidedly go beyond this caesura and incorporate older writings; see, e.g., Arana and Ramey 2004.

inescapability that is very different from the way in which we relate to public narratives of the past. The 'vicarious' historical experience requires later generations to have a broader perspective and increased empathy, as they experience augmented cognitive and emotional dissonance vis à vis their ancestors (A. Assmann 2007, 90–91). The family thus functions "as a kind of switchboard" (Erll 2011, 315) between the personal and individual modes of remembering and the larger frames of collective remembrance. The genealogical perspective locates the "specificity of an individual's life experiences in relation to the historical life experiences of family members" (Kramer 2011, 385).

The idea that we are linked in complex ways to the lives of our ancestors, including their experiences and emotional states, has informed new directions in biogenetic research and in psychotherapy. Epigenetic research has demonstrated how external factors can also influence the genetic makeup of a person in a way that they may pass such phenotypic changes on to later generations.[105] We use the broader term 'inheritance' to make sense of the interconnections of our present life with related lives that went before us. The concept of inheritance blurs the boundaries between 'natural' and 'cultural' forms of intergenerational transmission; it is located at the intersection of reproductive processes that are described in biological terms on the one hand and in the handing down of 'tradition', understood as culture, on the other (Weigel 2002, 163).[106] The idea of inheritance comprises of all kinds of transmission from one generation to the next, from the obvious to the not so obvious. It covers, for example, material as well as immaterial goods, ranging from the bequeathing of property to the communication of family memories and stories, the passing on of values, traditions, norms, etc., or the handing down of a family 'legacy'. Inheritance, furthermore, may refer either directly to the transferral of genetic material, or to subconscious 'traces of memory', transgenerational trauma, or behavioural patterns, attitudes, and relationship dynamics (cf. Willer et al. 2013, 7–8; see also Plahl 2016). The idea of inheritance is not simply unidirectional, but may involve (inter)active processes of (dis)identification and meaning-making on the receiving end in which past, present, and the future seem to converge. In another form of doing family, inheritance has to be actively recovered; it can be experienced as enriching, but may also be challenging, and problematic.

Aside from the image of the chain, there is another visualisation that refers to the lineal concept of descent as the pedigree or family tree. This tree enables us to envision more complex ancestral connections that may also involve collat-

---

105 See Plahl 2016; Bauer 2014 [2002].
106 On the complex concept of inheritance see Willer, Weigel and Jussen 2013.

eral ties. With its horizontal as well as vertical axes, it more closely captures the "multidirectional nature of relatedness" (Zerubavel 2012, 32). The family tree is the most widely used form of representing genealogical relations; it constitutes an epistemological figure that enables us to depict movements that happen over time on the breadth of a page (Castañeda 2002, 78). Its spatial layout is highly suggestive to the genealogical imagination because it visualises not only ancestral ties but also the collateral ties that link us to our relatives. For migrant or transnational families the evocations of such a "virtual family reunion" (Zerubavel 2012, 34) are particularly powerful. Moreover, the family tree, even in its neutral representation as a genealogical chart, carries rich metaphorical connotations connected with its arborescent imagery. There are two basic formal layouts of the family tree that each convey different aspects of the tree-metaphor (cf. Zerubavel 2012, 66). The first follows in its logic the basic form of the tree, and indeed stems from traditional formats such as Ernst Haeckel's *Tree of Life* (1866) and other tree-related models of evolutionary theories and systems of descent (cf. Macho 2002). The tree's trunk, encapsulated in the German word *Stammbaum*, represents the notion of co-descent as a basis of kinship: It positions the ancestor at its base, and all of the different generations of offspring branch out from this stem. In the simplified version of the genealogical chart, the tree is mostly flipped on its crown so that it produces a cone-shape in which the reading direction runs from top to bottom with the ancestor at the top. In contrast with this traditional 'ancestor-centric' model, "modern genealogical awareness" finds expression in a 'descendant-centric' model (Zerubavel 2012, 66; cf. also Weigel 2006, 45). This genealogical model arises from an individual at the bottom of the chart and builds up an ancestry from this point; it is similar to the idea of lineage except for the fact that each generation multiplies from the previous line, producing a fan-like shape. In this model, the network of relations resembles the tree's roots, implying permanence and immutability (cf. Zerubavel 2012, 54). The first model represents "a predominantly group-centered" and the second a "predominantly person-centered conception of genealogy" (Zerubavel 2012, 66–67). While the first is useful for the construction of "genealogical *communities*" and collective group identities, particularly with regard to family identities, the second is geared towards enhancing individual identity through "genealogical capital" (Zerubavel 2012, 24), as the heritage industry promises.

2.3 Doing Family as a New Field for Literary Analysis

The concept of 'doing family' offers us a broad and useful frame within which different aspects and dimensions of family can be more closely examined. Indeed, the study of the family is not a new subject for literature; it is and always has been a very prominent and popular theme. In literary studies, however, the concept of family is generally taken for granted while the focus tends to be directed to other specific research questions such as, for example, the problems of narrative and genre. A new perspective on the specific social structure and emotional network of the family has been opened up by the phrase 'doing family'. While the meaning of the English phrase is transparent and conveys an immediate understanding, its German translation: "Familie als Herstellungsleistung" (Schier 2009, 55; Schier and Jurczyk 2008) sounds rather abstract and peculiar. The technicality of the German term jars with basic associations such as care, proximity and emotional bonds. In spite of its awkwardness, though, the term has much cognitive potential, as it prevents us from assuming that the family is an entity that is implicit, natural and self-evident. If the family is no longer taken for granted in an essentialist way, new questions and perspectives are opened up for the benefit of a literary analysis of family matters. In addition, it becomes evident that there is a considerable overlap between concerns introduced in the concept of 'doing family' and approaches to narrative that can be specified in the following three aspects:

1) Emphasis on inter-action
As the term 'doing family' indicates, this concept is used to highlight how family is lived and realised in communication and interaction, and how a sense of family is created and evoked in relationships. Literary texts offer a rich basis for the exploration of such questions, as they not only represent the characters' actions and dialogue, but can also provide insight into their reflections and emotions. Therefore, it is possible to examine different levels of verbal and nonverbal communication, and to get a better understanding of the intricacies and complexities of family relationships. Within the larger frame of the overall narrative, even small scenes and details may yield rich and illustrative material for the analysis of how and to what end family is 'produced'. How a family communicates and interacts reveals much about the level of intimacy and understanding (or lack thereof) between its members, and about the general quality of the relationships within the family. In addition, literary texts generally invite the reader to explore the characters' inner lives, their affective states and their cognitive processes. In families, as in novels, different perspectives come to-

gether, or, as Jerome Bruner (1991, 68) puts it, different 'psychic realities' impinge upon each other. Analysing their relationship with one another can open up interesting pathways in order to gain a deeper understanding of the inner workings of the family. This may prove fruitful on two levels: the level of the family story, as rendered through family communication and storytelling in the text, and the superordinate level of the perspective structure of the overall narrative. The characters' interaction can reveal much of their respective norms and value systems, primarily with regard to their idea of family, which, in turn, also profoundly shapes family memory and narrative. Also a total or near absence of a certain perspective in the text may reveal much about a family and its conflicts, as confirmed by the marginalisation of the perspectives of the second-generation characters in *Maps for Lost Lovers*.

2) Emphasis on temporal dynamics

The concept of 'doing' family is based on a dynamic understanding of family that allows for both change and continuity. This "sense of motion" (Smart 2007, 29) is applied to the transitions and socially and culturally established stages in a person's lifetime such as children leaving home and entering adult life,[107] but also takes into account other changes and challenges that profoundly affect and transform family life. Smart's examples are those of unemployment and divorce; migration can also falls into this category – as an event that might, in retrospect, be constructed as one of the 'turning points' in a life story, or in a family narrative. I mention the "genuinely narratological phenomenon" (A. Nünning 2012, 31) of turning points here in order to emphasise how this aspect of doing family ties in with the idea of plot in literature and the element of "disruption or 'disequilibrium'" as a constitutive feature of narrative (V. Nünning 2013, 9). In general, one might say that the concept of doing family brings the temporal axes of family life and family identity to the forefront. While the term 'doing family' seems to emphasise the synchronic aspect in terms of the continuous process of creating family through actions and practices (cf. N. Schneider 2015, 30, as expressed by the present participle of 'doing'), the concept also covers aspects of the diachronic family that impinge on family matters in the present. Doing family thus interconnects the synchronic and the diachronic level in families. Family history and memory affects family relationships, structures, and meanings in ways that often remain half-conscious, subliminal, or hidden. Novels provide rich examples that relate to both of these time dimensions of the

---

[107] This element of change in family is considered in the life course perspective.

family. For this reason, the concept of doing family can easily be combined with current narratological theories and approaches that link memory, narrative and identity – which leads us to the third and most important point:

3) Emphasis on meaning
As with literature and narrative, the concept of doing family is concerned with the production of meaning. Rather than dealing with the question of what constitutes a family, the concept pertains to the construction of identity and the processes of meaning-making in a group that understands itself as a family. As narrative plays an important role in shaping processes of meaning-making in general (cf. Bruner 1991a; Bruner 1991b), it is not surprising that the production of narrative(s) is also a prominent feature of families. In this regard, acts of interpretation are as equally central for assessing and shaping family relationships as they are in literary analysis. The process of meaning production naturally involves these other two aspects introduced above, as meaning is generated interactively, inter-subjectively, and over time. In literary texts, the meaning produced overall in the text is distinct from the meaning produced at the level of the story. David Morgan describes a very similar concept of family with the term 'practices', which are "both constructed by the observer and lived by the actual practitioners" (Morgan 1996, 199). In his understanding, the concept itself thus holds the level of observation and analysis by the researcher as distinct from, and yet also interlinked with, the perspectives and understandings held by those under investigation (cf. Morgan 2011, 5). This can be related to the different levels of communication and of meaning-production in a literary text. This focus on meaning considerably broadens the realm of what might be potentially relevant for the analysis of how family is produced at the intersection between collective and individual identity construction. Meaning created around the idea of 'family' may reach a normative or consensual form as family myths, or can be contended as nodes of conflict between individual members or between generations. The family practice of meaning-making is thus directly related to issues of hierarchy and authority, bonding and individuation.

What makes 'doing family' attractive for this study is that, as a concept, it is on the one hand both broad and flexible, providing scope for a great "variety of ways in which family life is lived and experienced" (Morgan 2011, 6), while, on the other hand, it is specific and concrete, allowing for detailed case study analyses. The following analyses of family writing take their cue from Morgan's statement about family as "a way of looking at, and describing, practices which might also be described in a variety of other ways" (Morgan 1996, 199). This proposition corresponds with the plurality of meaning as a basic characteristic of literature – the novels and memoirs selected here could also be read in different ways and with other questions guiding the analysis. However, as I hope to demonstrate in the next chapter, the idea of 'family' as an approach, and as a way of looking and describing, will yield fruitful and interesting readings of these novels precisely because it is an open and connectible approach that ties in with a variety of other perspectives, such as genre-related questions, methods of narratological text analysis, and concepts and theories such as memory, identity and narrative.

3 Uncovering Family History: The Intergenerational Construction of Identity through Family Memory

Over the past twenty years, the field of 'fictions of migration' has seen considerable expansion and has gained a distinct profile in contemporary literature. At the beginning of the twentieth century, Roy Sommer (2001, 1–8) called for new concepts, approaches and criteria for the analysis of the 'intercultural novel' that moved beyond the concerns of postcolonial studies. Instead, these novels required a reading that was more closely tailored to the actual conditions, the historical experiences, and the themes of the authors living and writing in Great Britain but who had family relations that reached beyond its national borders. Through their respective studies, Sommer (2001) and Mark Stein (2004) paved the way for ensuing publications that picked up on the Black British *bildungsroman* as an evolving new genre in second-generation Black and Asian British writing.[1] The transformation of the traditional *bildungsroman* genre in the context of cultural changes occurring in twentieth and twenty-first century Britain has already been extensively discussed (cf. Stein 2004). This chapter, however, focuses on the way that the genre is transformed as a result of a new genealogical perspective on the family. While it has been acknowledged that "the conflict of generations is part and parcel of the novel of transformation, and it is of particular importance in that different generations correspond to different cultural and social affiliations" (Stein 2004, 25), little attention has as yet been given to the way in which intergenerational dynamics change in these novels when the temporal and spatial scope is expanded to include family relationships that lie beyond the dyadic model of the nuclear family. As the traditional 'identity quest narrative' of the *bildungsroman* is supplemented and transformed by the genealogical search motif, the concept of the relational (and related) self is seen to replace traditional Western notions of autonomous individuality. With this broadened scope, the possible functions of the family that can affect the process of the protagonists' self-development are also significantly diversified. When read in this way, *Anita and Me* and *Fruit of the Lemon*, two novels that are often categorised as prototypical Black British *bildungsromane*, will reveal aspects

---

1 See also Stein 2002, Stein 1998, Frank 2010, Gunning 2010, Upstone 2010, 127ff.

that are characteristic of the multigenerational family novel, of which *White Teeth* is probably the most prominent recent example in British fiction.

3.1 "Divided loyalties": In-Betweenness and British-Asian Identity in Meera Syal's *Anita and Me* (1996)

Told in the fictional autobiography style, *Anita and Me* is the story of Meena Kumar's transition from childhood to adolescence in the fictional Midlands village of Tollington in the late 1960s.[2] The book also tells the story of her friendship with Anita Rutter, who is three years her senior and a dubious role model. The novel combines the classic coming-of-age narrative with questions of cultural identity, home, and belonging in a British-Asian family. Meena's struggle to grow up is interlinked with her desire to fit in with the local community on the one hand and her "growing sociocultural awareness" (Campbell-Hall 2009, 296) on the other. Besides the issue of ethnic and cultural identity, Syal focuses on class as being a major factor in the lives of the villagers and in Meena's development (cf. Frank 2010, 138). Underneath the rural idyll, the former miners' village is a place of social decay, with large unemployment numbers. The lack of a future or of any hope for the next generation is exemplified when the local primary school is demolished in order to make way for a new motorway.

As the daughter of the only Indian (as well as the only non-white) family in the village, Meena's life is governed by the impression of difference; her world is marked by a "conspicuously dichotomous segmentation" (Frank 2010, 139; my translation) into Indianness and Englishness. This dichotomy is represented most strongly in a spatial division, in which Indianness is confined to the home and inside spaces, while the public and outside spaces are defined as being English:[3]

> Whenever we [the family] went 'out', out meaning wherever English people were, as opposed to Indian friends' houses which in any case was always 'in' as all we would do was

---

[2] The fictional setting is based on the author's own childhood in Essington, a village north of Wolverhampton.

[3] The spatial segregation works both ways, and Meena at one point realises that "in the thirteen years we lived there, during which every weekend was taken up with visiting Indian families or being invaded by them, only once had any of our neighbours been invited in further than the step of our back door" (*Anita* 29).

sit in each others' lounges, eat each others' food and watch each others' televisions, my parents always wore their smartest clothes. (*Anita* 25)[4]

As this passage suggests, the dichotomy between Englishness and Indianness pervades all areas of life, including relationships, clothes, behaviour, food, and language. The difference is so strong that Meena sometimes wonders "if the very act of shutting our front door transported us onto another planet" (165). Meena, with her Indian family on one side and her English peers on the other, finds herself in between two worlds where each has a completely contradictory set of rules and values, "living in the grey area between all the categories" (149–150). This position between being 'in' and 'out' corresponds to a feeling of unbelonging that lies at the heart of Meena's identity construction process.[5]

3.1.1 Family Cultures and Differences

The "system of semiotic oppositions English vs. Indian" (Reichl 2002, 174), which the novel establishes, is most noticeable in its depiction of family life. Family practices and their meaning with regard to family relationships and family values are shown as being very different in the Kumar household as compared to their English neighbours. Desirous of social acceptance, Meena is keenly aware of the dissimilarity and the conspicuousness that her family and their home represent: "It was a constant source of embarrassment to me that our front garden was the odd one out in the village" (*Anita* 15).

In contrast with the rest of the neighbourhood, the Kumars keep a very sociable house, where other British-Indian families from the area come for frequent visits. In the absence of their own extended families, the Kumars adopt this circle of Indian friends as family and Meena calls them Auntie and Uncle. Although this is the general term of politeness used for addressing elders in India, as Meena explains to her confused neighbour (cf. 29), the use of this terminology of 'pretend' relation (which differs from the very complex nomenclature for real relations) still signifies a special bond: "I knew how intensely my

---

[4] *Anita* refers to Syal 2004 [1996]. Hereafter all references to the novel will use only page number, and, where necessary, *Anita* for disambiguation.
[5] Meena's in-betweenness goes beyond the realm of ethnic identity; it is something that very much defines her social position at the onset of the novel. "In the village I was stuck in between the various gangs, too young for Anita's consideration, too old to hang around the cloud of toddlers that would settle on me like a rash every time I set foot outside my front door." (*Anita* 25; see also Frank 2010, 149)

parents valued these people they so readily renamed as family, faced with the loss of their own blood relations" (31).[6]

While the English neighbours seem to marvel at the apparent size of Indian families, Meena's parents, in turn, are completely perplexed by the lack of family cohesion that exists among the English. Their neighbour Mrs Worrall never sees her children and grandchildren, because, although they only live a few miles away, they never come to visit. The lack of "social snacks" in Mrs Worrall's house is particularly emblematic, and is in direct contrast with the Kumars' cupboard full of "nibbles [...] which would be handed round as pre-starter starters to our visitors" (217). Relationships are shown to be similarly deficient amongst the families that still live together. Meena wonders about how the English husbands and wives of the neighbourhood seem to lead separate lives that are in contrast with her parents' "almost claustrophobic connection" (86). Parent-child relationships are depicted as no better in English families, with the most extreme example of neglect, dysfunction, and even abuse to be observed in Anita's family.[7] For Meena's parents, this difference in family relationships is an important aspect of self-definition as a family in opposition to what they regard as the English model. In a passionate tirade, Mrs Kumar sums up the behaviour of their neighbours as "It's My Life, I Want My Space stupidness, You Can't Tell Me What To Do cheekiness, I Have To Go To Bingo selfishness and You Kids Eat Crisps Instead Of Hot Food nonsense" (59), to which she adds, "What is this My Life business anyway? We all have obligations, no one is born on their own, are they?" (59).

Mrs Kumar's speech echoes the idea of the decline of the family in Western societies. In this view, the interest of the individual and the construction of individualist identities are ranked higher than those of communal values and group cohesion, resulting in the disruption of traditional relationship structures. Mrs Kumar, by way of contrast, upholds the oppositional model of collectivism that is generally associated with Asian societies.[8] This model prioritises

---

[6] There is a very strong sense of community among the group, built on storytelling and "anecdotes that reinforced their shared histories" (*Anita* 31). Moreover, these friendships, although they are not based on blood relation, are founded on a link that is created by having extended blood relations, as the story of the beginning of one of these friendships illustrates: "And we found out our cousins had gone to the same college! So we went back to my home and that was that!" (31)

[7] This is hinted at only briefly when Meena notices the signs of physical abuse on Tracey's thighs during a peeing contest (*Anita* 142).

[8] There is a generally accepted "narrative of the historical evolution of self-conceptions" in the 'West', that is based on the assumption of a 'development' that runs from a collectivist concep-

(extended or joint) family relationships and the traditional family values of obligation and caring. In this model, identities are seen as relational, and life stories are shaped by the needs of the community.⁹ The subtext of her mother's sermon is not lost on Meena, who enjoys these "Capital Letter speeches" because "[t]hey made me feel special, as if our destiny, our legacy, was a much more interesting journey than the apparent dead ends facing our neighbours" (59). Alongside their function of transmitting family values and a specific 'family culture',¹⁰ these speeches clearly serve to strengthen a collective family identity, not only with regard to content but also in their apparent recurrence as part of a ritualised family routine. In this context of conscious identity construction, difference is evaluated as an asset by Meena, rather than as a deficit: identity is created through distinction from others. Nevertheless, the sense of family identity transmitted in these speeches remains vague, and does not put forward a story for Meena to live up to. "I just wished whatever my destiny was would hurry up and introduce itself to me" (59). At this point, her own vision of the future and of her life trajectory is focused on her dream of making it big on the popular television show *Opportunity Knocks*, her "most realistic escape route from Tollington, from ordinary girl to major personality in one easy step" (65). This vision is more closely aligned with the values and the narrative schema of an individualist identity construction that is aimed at singularity, autonomy, and success – or, more precisely, at achieving success through singularity and individuality.

3.1.2 The Past Is a Foreign Country: Memory and Longing in the Diasporic Family

As illustrated by the reference to the family legacy and destiny, a strong family identity links past and future in a continuous narrative. Yet, it is precisely this

---

tion of the self to an individual one (Kashima and Foddy 2002, 182). Cf. also Kashima (2002); for the value of collectivism in Indian families see Chadha (n.y.) or Sinha (2010).

9 Fivush (2008, 51), for example, shows how such models of the self are culturally defined through "cultural life scripts", in relation to which an individual life narrative can be seen as either deviating or conforming. In this regard she basically discerns two definitions of the self, the "autonomous agent who controls one's own destiny" that exists in Western cultures, and the "interpersonal agent in relation to a family or community" in Eastern cultures. These correspond closely with the concepts of the individualist and the relational self.

10 Through her emphasis on self-other differentiation, Mrs Kumar highlights the culture-specificity of family values and practices.

continuity of the family narrative and of familial interrelationships that is at stake in the Kumar family. Over the course of the novel, it becomes more and more evident that the circle of 'pretend relations' cannot adequately compensate for the disruption of the joint family due to migration.[11] The parents' heartache and longing in this regard is expressed through family practices that are heavily invested with memory and a nostalgic idea of home: they are oriented towards the past and towards sustaining a connection with the distant family. At the same time, this invocation of the past creates intergenerational differences between Meena and her parents, who, she feels, fail to make her thoroughly familiar with their experiences of the past. This results in the emergence of a conflict in the family culture between its Indian past and its English future, which evolves in the different realms of the Kumars' family life.

As a central tenet of family life, the culture that surrounds food plays a crucial role in this conflict. Cooking and eating are powerful ways of "performing cultural identity" (Mannur 2010, x), and as such carry highly charged emotions that are related to home and nostalgia in diasporic communities. Furthermore, food is at the centre of family interaction and is not only an important means of creating family identity but is also vital for the management of family relationships and roles. In contrast with English family tradition, the Kumars do not eat their meals together, but separately and in shifts. It is therefore not so much the collective family activity of sharing dinner conversations over a meal that is of the utmost importance but the food itself that has a special meaning for them. Her mother's cooking is described by Meena as being "soul food, it was the food their far-away mothers had made and came seasoned with memory and longing, this was the nearest way they would get for many years, to home." (*Anita* 61) It is through the food ritual that the diasporic experience of displacement from the place of belonging (home), as opposed to the place of residence, becomes most manifest.[12] In citing the "far-away mothers", Mrs Kumar's food production also functions as an intergenerational link that creates family connectedness and continuity across geographical distance.

Against this background, mealtimes become an important site for Meena to act out her struggle with cultural identity within the family. With her own

---

11 For an introduction to Indian family culture see Chadha (n.y.). As described by him, the 'joint family', which is the "traditional, ideal and desired family" model in India, requires actually living in the network of the extended family and involves cultivating strong bonds of "cooperation, harmony and interdependence".
12 Cf. Gilroy's (1997, 10) concept of diaspora as "an historical and experiential rift between the location of residence and the location of belonging".

choice of favourite food – fish fingers and chips – she aligns herself with the other neighbourhood children and with their family practices of eating, where food has the purely pragmatic function of being "something to fill a hole" (61). Moreover, Meena fends off her "mother's attempts to teach me the rudiments of Indian cuisine" (61), thus disregarding the cultural (and family) tradition. Yearning to be more like her friends, Meena uses the opportunity of Anita's visit to impose English eating practices on her family: "I want us to sit and talk, you know, like you're supposed to do at dinners." (252)[13] With its strong cultural signification, food acts as an ideal medium for intergenerational (and intercultural) conflict and for Meena's rebellion against her parents (cf. 60).[14] More significantly, for Meena, who does not share her parents' memories and nostalgia, Indian food does not carry this extra layer of meaning and therefore does not hold any particular emotional quality for her. In her eyes, it is primarily a marker of difference that singles their family out from the other families in Tollington, as her visit to Mrs Worrall's kitchen illustrates (cf. 60–62).

Meena's complicated relationship with her family's Indianness and her troubled consciousness of her own differences with regard to their surroundings reveal the divide that has grown between her parents' sense of family identity and her own views. The novel demonstrates that in the diasporic condition of displacement from the family network and its larger cultural context, there is an observable risk that the meaning and emotional substance that lie behind family practices or relationships are not being transported from one generation to the next. This becomes evident in the ritualised 'family lessons', when Meena is

> sat down in front of photos from India and forced to memorise my parents' many brothers and sisters by name, occupation, and personality quirks [...] as if committing them to memory would make up for not being with them (30).

As a result, Meena can reproduce the "litany" of who is who in the family. However, she only *knows about* her relatives in India, but does not actually *know*

---

[13] Her "romantic idea" of "witty stories over the dinner table" is quickly shattered when Anita starts eating and it becomes evident that, in addition to cultural differences in eating practices, class differences that govern table manners also function as markers of distinction between the two friends. This is emphasised in Meena's remark to Anita, who is just as disgusted by the Kumars eating habits as they are by hers, a situation that Meena manages to adeptly turn to her advantage: "We always eat our food with our fingers [...]. Like in all the top restaurants. Bet you didn't know that, did you?" (254)

[14] The motif regarding food and eating practices in families as being markers of cultural and ethnic identification is popular in Black and Asian British novels and films; cf. for example the pertinent scenes from *Pressure* (1975) and *Bend It like Beckham* (2002).

them; her *semantic* memory of them holds very little emotional content and does not match the place that they have in her parents' *episodic* (autobiographical) memory (cf. Nelson 2003, 11).[15] Significantly, she is only given single facts without a narrative to add meaning to the details and to connect these family members with her own life and reality. In contrast to the very present and emotionally significant surrogate family of friends in England, the extended biological family belongs to a past that is distant – a mystery like everything else that connects her family to India. The element of mystery is symbolised by suitcases full of relics stored away on top of the wardrobes that perplex Meena:

> I had noticed that everything in those cases had something to do with India, the clothes, the albums, the letters from various cousins, and wondered why they were kept apart from the rest of the household jumble, allotted their own place and prominence, the nearest thing in our house that we had to a shrine. (266)

By being externalised in these relics, a large part of the Kumars' family memory is shut away and removed from everyday family life to be taken out only on special occasions. These suitcases, in plain view but remaining out of reach (at least for Meena), epitomise the air of secrecy and mystery that surrounds her parents' past. While a few stories are readily shared by her parents, others, which are much more exciting and interesting in Meena's eyes, are held back and actively shielded from her, which only contributes further to their mystification. The transmission of family memory through the sharing of stories is complicated due to the trauma of Partition, which disrupts the narrativisation of family history. Not only are these memories painful,[16] they are, more significantly, non-narratable in the context of intergenerational family storytelling between parent and child: Her parents cannot share the violence implied in these stories with Meena, *because* she is a child.[17] However, by shielding Meena from these stories, they not only emphasise her status as a child, a status that she

---

[15] For more on the distinction between the different types of memory see, e.g., Schacter and Tulving (1982), Nelson (2003, 11), A. Assmann (2006, 212), Eakin (1999, 106).
[16] Mrs Kumar's memory of "see[ing] someone stabbed to death" serves as an example here, a memory that "seemed to upset her [Mrs Kumar] greatly". Although this is her daughter's favourite story, "she would not repeat it more than twice" and Mrs Kumar reacts with shock to Meena's wish to hear the story again (which for Meena has now become capitalised as "the Rickshaw Story", 36).
[17] The grown-up narrator ultimately concedes that her parents were right to protect her from many of their stories as a child: "Later on, when mama had begun to treat me like a grown-up [she …] released nuggets of information about her and papa's experiences in India that would have given me nightmares as a child" (181).

longs to outgrow, they also deny her an important part of their lives and thus create a distance between her and them. Within the family then, the memories of Partition take on the form of a secret that produces gaps and blank spots in the narrative and results in creating a rift between the family generations. Meena is fascinated by this secret, which radiates danger and adventure, and when on one occasion she happens to overhear the elders recounting their memories of Partition, she stays and listens, "terrified", but not due to the horrific and extremely violent stories that she hears, but that "I would be discovered and they would clam up and deny me more" (74).[18]

While the evening parties that are devoted to communal storytelling and revelling in memories of home play an important role in binding the circle of Indian friends together by "reinforce[ing] their shared histories" (31), they also intensify Meena's feeling of exclusion from the community of grown-ups. During the musical evenings hosted by the Kumars, when Meena's father and the others perform their "favourite Urdu *ghazals* and Punjabi folk songs" (71), she finds that

> my elders became strangers to me [...], tragedy and memory illuminating their features [...]. I did not often stay for these mournful *ghazals*, preferring to creep off to bed unnoticed whilst my younger cousins slept in milky heaps like an abandoned litter. There was no point in my being there; when I looked at my elders, in these moments, they were all far, far away. (72)

As the older generation becomes more and more wrapped up in memories of home, Meena increasingly loses her connection with them. They have moved on to a past that is as distant and foreign to her as the setting where that past occured, their home country of India. This shared Indian past, which for the grown-ups functions as an important social glue, alienates Meena. Through the mirror of her elders' stories and memories, India remains a foreign and strange

---

[18] At the heart of the secret of Partition lies the secret of death, which is a common theme in initiation stories and also holds a great fascination for Meena even apart from her parents' stories. Meena's description of her clandestine attempts to listen in on the grown-ups' conversation is reminiscent of Ruth Klüger's famous beginning to her memoir *Still Alive* (2001 [1992], 15): "Their secret was death, not sex. That's what the grown-ups were talking about, sitting up late around the table. I had pretended that I couldn't fall asleep in my bed and begged them to let me sleep on the sofa in the living room, which we called by the fancier French word *salon*. Of course, I didn't intend to fall asleep. I wanted to get in on the forbidden news, the horror stories, fascinating though incomplete as they always were – or perhaps even more fascinating for their opaqueness, that whiff of fantasy they had about them, though one knew they were true. Some were about strangers, others were about relatives, all were about Jews."

country to her, onto which she has superimposed her own fantasy of tigers, elephants, and other orientalist images informed by the media (cf. 82, 118). The musical evenings highlight how migration and the resultant pain of loss and longing create a gap of experience between the generations that runs the risk of damaging family relationships.

The result of her parents' caution towards Meena is that their stories of India ultimately form an incomplete picture in her head where they never lose their unfamiliarity and foreignness. Thus, the single stories fail to connect together to form a larger narrative that can also encompass her own life. Her feelings towards her parents' Indian past consequently remain ambivalent, oscillating between a fascination for the exotic and the dramatic on the one hand and an estrangement and resentment for feeling that she has been excluded on the other (cf. Frank 2010, 148):

> At first I would listen entranced to this litany of love [her mother's mantra about her ancestral home, 34], imagining my mother as I had seen her in those crumpled black and white photographs hoarded in a shiny suitcase on top of her wardrobe. [...] But gradually I got bored, and then jealous of this past that excluded me (*Anita* 35–36).

Meena' feeling of exclusion from a whole realm of experience that her parents share also recurs with regard to language whenever her parents speak Punjabi, which is always "a sign that something was a secret" (24–25) and that she is being deliberately left out (cf. 27). Meena's feelings of unbelonging, exclusion, and insecurity can thus, at least partly, be related back to her lack of knowledge about India and her parents' past. Her awkward identity finds expression in her propensity for lying, which her parents observe with growing concern, and which is directly connected to the gaps in her family history. As the narrator explains in the preface, "I'm really not a liar, I just learned very early on that those of us deprived of history sometimes need to turn to mythology to feel complete, to belong." (10)

3.1.3 Anita Rutter: Meena's "passport to acceptance"

Besides death, there is another secret connected with adulthood and growing up that fascinates Meena and which revolves around love and sex.[19] She associ-

---

[19] Meena not only feels "both fascinated and embarrassed" (83) by her parents' open show of affection, she is also completely transfixed and "unsettled" (84) by the flirtations and intima-

ates this "secret which I worried I might never discover" (84) most closely with Anita Rutter, who is a few years older than Meena. She is the neighbourhood bully and also the undisputed boss of the village children. Meena is fascinated by the way that "sex [...] hung round her [...] like a faint perfume, what she gave off by the tilt of her thin hips, in the quizzical arc of an eyebrow, in her constant unhurried monologues about the boys in her school" (139). At nine years old, Meena finds herself in an in-between stage that does not quite fit in with any of the social groups of the neighbourhood. She hopes that through forming a friendship with Anita she can not only improve her social standing, but also break free from her childhood (cf. 25). Meena sees in Anita the promise of social integration and acceptance, and of a gateway to her own future in the adult world of secrets and knowledge.[20] The realm that Anita represents is consequently characterised by "exclusivity and the forbidden" (17), and the air of being "something unfamiliar [...], something forbidden and new" (104) that Meena perceives from Anita's girl clique is a principal stimulant of her fascination with Anita. Moreover, Anita repeatedly makes use of Meena's ignorance in the field of sexuality to make fun of her and to embarrass her in front of the others, while Meena in her naiveté misreads these instances as her being finally let in on a secret (cf. 106).[21]

The novel begins with an episode that initiates Meena's relationship with Anita when the two end up sharing the candy that Meena has bought with money stolen from her mother's purse. From then on, a friendship slowly evolves along the lines of a clear pattern: it is one where every action that brings Meena closer to Anita's world distances her from her family and the world of her parents. For Meena, these two worlds are irreconcilable, and as she focuses more

---

cies of "Sam Lowbridge's gang and their interchangeable girlfriends" (83), who she secretly watches from the distance.

20 Secrets, as well as the discrepancy of knowledge, and their role in managing power relations and social hierarchies are a key element of Meena's and Anita's friendship. Consequently, the change in their relationship that occurs later on in the novel can be seen most clearly when Meena uses her superior class knowledge against her friend in a reversal of their previous roles over the Kumar family dinner where Anita is invited (cf. 254).

21 Significantly, these instances always backfire on Meena in the context of her family, when her inappropriate use of half-truths gathered from her conversations with Anita cause major conflicts at home (see, for example, her inappropriate use of the phrase 'shag the arse of sth/sb' with which she tries to express appreciation at her parents' Diwali party, 115; or her question to her parents of whether or not she is a virgin, 248–249). In these situations, the two incompatible worlds collide, which is very vividly illustrated during the Diwali fest, when Anita's image slowly starts to superimpose itself on Meena's mind and thereby disrupts the world that she shares with her family (114–115).

on Anita, her family moves more and more to the background: Told off by her mother, she finds that "mama's voice did not have its usual resonance today, [...] everything was fuzzy and unformed except for Anita, what she looked like, what she did, the way she made me feel, taller and sharper and ready to try anything." (53) For Meena, her friendship with Anita through her idolisation of her brings with it the promise of empowerment, and her whole sense of self, her relationships and her behaviour change under this new influence. The relationship slowly evolves as Anita challenges and tests Meena, who gradually has to earn her position in Anita's clique. As she gains ground with Anita, she feels quite clear about "where my divided loyalties really lay", and gives expression to this feeling through the terms of an 'in vs. out'-dichotomy that marks her perception of their family home: "Now I only thought of myself, a hurried visitor to our dinner table, [...] and where I wanted to belong. My life was outside the home, with Anita, my passport to acceptance." (148)

This self-assessment whereby she thinks only of herself and her own wants echoes her mother's speech on individualism and family obligations. The fact that Meena expressly betrays her parents' family values here shows up exactly how deliberately she has changed sides. As Sara Ahmed (2010, 149) asserts, "growing up is usually narrated as generational conflict", which, in turn, finds expression in a conflict of want between the parents and the child: "the child wants what the parents do not want for the child" (Ahmed 2010, 149). Meena herself makes this connection with growing up explicit when she dismisses her 'cousins' Pinky and Baby as suitable company, because "[e]ven their names reeked of childhood, something I was desperate to wrap in rags and leave on someone's doorstep with a note, Take It Away." (*Anita* 148) Conversely, in Anita, Meena sees a chance to move forward, viewing her as a vehicle to vault her from childhood and its condition of ignorance and lack of agency, power, and identity. In her friendship with Anita, Meena's various desires are conflated: growing up, belonging, and acceptance. The intergenerational conflict is intertwined with questions of cultural identity and is hence overdetermined, "such that the parents' wants are associated with the culture of origin [...], and the child's want is associated with the culture of destination" (Ahmed 2010, 149). Herein lies a typical dilemma (in representations) that is faced by second-generation immigrants who grow up between the two cultures and have to deal with the corresponding demands of their families on the one hand and of the host society on the other.

However, Meena soon realises that the question of belonging is not simply one of desire and choice. It is precisely through her friendship with Anita that the promise of acceptance is broken and that she has to experience exclusion and difference. When Anita's girl clique flirt with boys at the village fair, she suddenly ends up being the odd one out: "I knew, I knew that it was not because I was too young or badly dressed, it was something else, something about me so offputting, so unimaginable, that I made Fat Sally look like the glittering star prize" (*Anita* 105). In the adolescent mating ritual that follows, Meena is excluded to the point where she feels invisible, and is not being let in on the secret that is shared by the others (cf. 105–106). However, it is not only her lack of knowledge and the age difference that exclude her. In her desire to emulate Anita, she becomes aware that no matter how well she can put on an "authentic Yard accent" (122) she will never be regarded as being the same. In consequence, Meena turns against her own body, which stands in her way of acceptance and social success:[22]

> I had never wanted to be anyone else except myself only older and famous. But now, for some reason, I wanted to shed my body like a snake slithering out of its skin and emerge reborn, pink and unrecognisable. I began avoiding mirrors, I refused to put on the Indian suits my mother laid out for me [...], I took to walking several spaces behind or in front of my parents when we went out on a shopping trip, checking my reflection in shop windows, bitterly disappointed it was still there. (146)

This alienation from herself and her ethnic identity also involves disassociation from her family as the link to that identity. Meena's "visibly racialised body" (Neti 2008, 99) starkly contrasts with her performative understanding of identity, and repeatedly obstructs her attempts to 'pass' as being truly English and a "real Wench" (*Anita* 154). The main device that she uses in her performance of Midland Englishness is language, which she strategically employs to foster alliances and to create sameness (or difference).[23] In scenes of crisis, such as, for instance, the incident when she tries to appease the other drivers in a traffic jam that her mother has caused on their way to the *gurudwara* (Sikh temple) in Birmingham, she puts on a "deliberately exaggerated Tollington accent" in order to prove that she "was very much one of them [...], that I belonged" (*Anita* 97). Being confronted by a racist slur as an answer in this situation consequently crushes Meena all the more severely. In scenes like these, "Meena constantly draws attention to her Tollington accent as a token of identity [... because] she believes, ultimately erroneously, that her accent will [...] help her achieve the

---

[22] The pressing question at this point for Meena is whether "any boy would ever notice me, the way that they always noticed Anita" (145).
[23] For an instance of the latter, cf. Meena's use of her Midland speech on her cousin Pinky (cf. 152)

sense of belonging that her body cannot assume." (Neti 2008, 104, 106) Against this background, her wish to be friends with Anita reproduces and thereby reinforces the unhappiness that she initially wanted to lose through the friendship (cf. Ahmed 2010, 152), because it positions her in a social context that demonstrates the discrepancy between her attempts to blend in through her performance of identity on the one hand and other people's perception of her on the other.

Whereas her perfect linguistic assimilation does not grant her the sense of belonging to the English working-class community that she desires, her lack of fluency in her parents' native language presents a barrier to belonging in the context of her family and Indian relatives. Here, Meena feels excluded because she cannot understand Punjabi, a language that also holds the promise of belonging, a promise that remains as yet unfulfilled. In her ears, the language that she "could not recognise but felt I could speak in my sleep" feels "unfamiliar and instinctive at the same time" (*Anita* 112; cf. Reichl 2002, 169ff.). Moreover, Meena's situation of unbelonging and her position of in-betweenness is intensified by the fact that not only does she fail to "belong definitively in the category British" (Neti 2008, 104), but her body and physicality have the effect of making her a misfit in the Indian community as well: "I knew I was a freak of some kind, too mouthy, clumsy and scabby to be a real Indian girl, too Indian to be a real Tollington wench" (149–150).[24] In contrast with her Indian cousins Pinky and Baby, who Meena sees as the epitome of the quiet and obedient Indian daughter, she senses "a kindred spirit, another mad bad girl" (150) in Anita, and ultimately regards their potential friendship as an option for identity formation that promises authenticity.[25] Through her identification with Anita and her concomitant attempt to assume an English identity, she becomes increasingly removed from her Indian one (Neti 2008, 99).

However, Meena's hopes for sameness and acceptance are dashed by the experience of rejection and exclusion. As the former rural childhood idyll that

---

[24] When Meena steals money from the charity can in the local shop, the accolades that she earns from Anita emphasise her "Wench potential" (150): "Yow'm a real wench. That was bostin what yow did. Yow can be joint leader with me now if yow want, you know, of our gang." (154)

[25] In the end, Meena feels used by Anita as a "convenient diversion, a practice run", when she finds out that Sam Lowbridge is Anita's boyfriend but her friend never bothered to tell her (cf. 277). Meena's vision of Anita as a "passport to acceptance", however, reveals a similarly functional approach to their friendship; as Ahmed (2010, 152) points out, "[s]he wants not simply to be friends with Anita but to be Anita". Anita is both a mirror and a projection screen for Meena, who predominantly sees her "own questioning reflection" (*Anita* 150) in her friend's eyes.

was Tollington faces social upheaval due to the building of the motorway, she is soon increasingly confronted with racism in her own village, which "marks the second stage of her double estrangement: first from family [...], now from her 'elected' community" (Bromley 2000, 147). When the Sam Lowbridge led youth gang suddenly crashes the village Spring Fete appearing "as skinheads [and] armed with a new-found racist discourse" (Bromley 2000, 147), Meena again feels "punched in the stomach" and stands up to Anita for the first time, as a result of her uncritical admiration for Sam. Her loyalties clearly start to shift as Meena, after speaking her mind, turns away from Anita and does "not look back until I had reached the haven of papa's arms" (*Anita* 195). From this point on, the experience sets off a slow process of identification with her own ethnic group. After the racist incident on the way to Birmingham, Meena comes to recognise in her father "something I had never seen before, a million of these encounters written in the lines around his warm, hopeful eyes" (*Anita* 98). The experience that had made her feel "hurt, angry, confused, and horribly powerless" (98) thus also creates a bond of shared experience between herself and her father.

3.1.4 "Help from overseas": Meena's Initiation into Family History

The experience at the village fete, "which had made strangers out of friends, labelled friendly passers-by as possible enemies" (196), sets off a process of maturation in Meena, who is lying in bed that evening, thinking about how

> tonight I had finally made the connection that change always strolled hand in hand with loss, with upheaval, and that I would always feel it keenly because in the end, I did not live under the same sky as most other people. I did not need a bra or some blue eyeshadow to appear older, not tonight. (196)[26]

The idea of growing up is disconnected here from her relationship with Anita and from the idea of external markers of physical maturity as opposed to the idea of transformation through experience. The recognition that change is tied up with loss aligns Meena's experience more closely with her mother's, who she

---

[26] Later, Meena reflects clearly on how the incident at the village fete has affected her process of growing up when she says that in "that one moment [...] Sam [...] had taken away my innocence" (227). This phrasing also hints at the vague sense of an ambivalent attraction that had been building up between Sam and Meena and which reinforces the effect of the betrayal as a result of Sam's words and his relationship with Anita (cf. also 311).

heard lamenting that night before she was going to bed. Mrs Kumar, depressed and overburdened after the birth of her overly attached baby son, looks into the sky that night, "as if she was counting the stars in her head. 'I can't cope any more, Shyam. Back home I would have sisters, mothers, servants...' The stars were her family, his family, she was crossing them off one by one, naming them to keep them alive." (196) The starry night sky that builds a bridge to India is the same sky that Meena does not share with her English peers in the village, but which, at this moment, emphasises her connection with her family.

Meena's identity struggle takes a new turn with the transformation of the family from a two-generational to a three-generational unit. Help comes "from over the seas", as predicted by the fortune teller at the village fete (184), in the form of Meena's maternal grandmother, her Nanima. Her arrival marks a crucial turning point in Meena's development and in the narrative. Just as Meena starts to turn away from Anita, Nanima appears on the stage to fill the role of guardian figure (cf. Frank 2010, 151). When they first meet each other, Meena is surprised by how natural and instinctive her own emotions are, when "the tears I was praying would come to prove I was a dutiful granddaughter, came spilling out with no effort at all" (*Anita* 200). The spontaneity of her reaction renders her planned performance unnecessary. From the start, there is a mutual sense of recognition and a great familiarity between Meena and her grandmother, who immediately sees her granddaughter as a 'Junglee' – "a wild girl, uncivilised", as Meena's father translates (200). Nanima thus offers her an identity model that is located within Indian culture that Meena can truly and affirmatively embrace. Meena, in turn, sees a kindred spirit in her grandmother, and she can relate to her in ways that she cannot do with her mother, who is "the epitome of grace, dignity and unthreatening charm" (28), and thus embodies qualities that Meena could never aim for.[27] In contrast, however, Meena directly spots a trace of mischief in her grandmother's eyes and instantly knows that "Nanima was going to be fun" (200). And indeed, there is an understanding between the two that transcends language (cf. 201).

When, after Nanima's arrival, the three generations of women in the family are "lined [...] up for a photograph, daughter, mother, and grandmother, all of

---

[27] Earlier in the novel, Meena "realised what part of my problem was – I had been born to the wrong type of Indian woman. If I had been given a mother like Auntie Shaila, the fat loud type who didn't mind the patches of sweat forming under their sari blouses after a good dance, I would not have to feel so angry at my body, the way it betrayed me by making me stand with my legs akimbo, hands on hips, the way it tripped me up into the dirt, skinning my knees – it was never meant to behave like the body of a lady. But next to mama, I would always feel lumbering and clumsy." (111)

us the product of each other, linked like Russian dolls" (201–202), Meena suddenly feels a strong connection with her family through this visual reconstruction of the intergenerational family bond that was severed by her parents' migration. "[I]t struck me how difficult it must have been for mama to leave Nanima and how lonely she must have been. [...] I vowed then that I would never leave her, this wrenching of daughter from mother would never happen again." This 'Family Constellation'[28] of three generations realigns Meena at an implicit emotional level with the family values of relationality and interdependence.[29] In this pose of the family photo, "[s]he is relocated, reconfigured along an 'Asian' continuum" (Bromley 2000, 148). Meena later describes Nanima's power of re-organising and re-adjusting the constellation of family relationships in almost magical terms, particularly when her grandmother manages to break the baby Sunil's fixation with his mother (207). As a result, Meena not only loses her resentment towards her baby brother, she even starts helping her mother with his meals and in doing the laundry (cf. 209).

Most importantly, however, Nanima turns out to be the missing link between Meena on the one hand and India and her parents' past on the other (cf. Frank 2010, 151). What Meena enjoys most of all are her grandmother's stories about the past and about various members of her family. Through storytelling, both her world and that of her grandmother slowly move closer together. Unlike Meena's parents, Nanima offers her memories readily and without constraint, and without stopping to think about what is appropriate for a child.

> At first, these remembrances seemed so far fetched, so far removed from anything I recognised as reality [...]. But gradually I got used to Nanima's world, a world made up of old and bitter family feuds in which the Land was revered and jealously guarded like a god, in which supernatural and epic events, murder, betrayal, disappearances and premonitions seemed commonplace [...]. They all put mama's rickshaw story and papa's unexploded bomb tale into some kind of context for me; my parents' near brushes with death were not one-off happenings, they were simply two more incidents in a country that seemed full to bursting with excitement, drama and passion, history in the making, and for the first time I desperately wanted to visit India and claim some of this magic as mine. (210–211)

---

[28] This refers to the practice of "Familienaufstellungen" in the sense of Bert Hellinger.
[29] However, Meena, at this point, immediately qualifies her commitment to her mother and the family: "Of course, this would not stop me having all the adult adventures I had been planning for myself; [...] I would just have to make sure mama came with me, that was all." (202) This view still hints at the possible disparity between the individual want and the collective want of the family.

Meena minutely describes the movement of approximation here which turns the unfamiliar and strange into something that is recognisable and which has its own meaning and is something that she wants to discover more about. Nanima's stories also enable Meena to feel closer to her parents' stories and memories by giving her a more complete idea of the setting and of India as an actual location, however fascinating and magical that it may still seem. In this way, the disparate memories in the family eventually form a comprehensive narrative that Meena can connect to her own life; the family stories are no longer exclusively about the past, but now also include the future of herself and her family. Nanima's storytelling serves as a cue for Meena's parents to talk about their reasons for migration, and thus answer the question that had been formed in Meena's mind for quite some time. When her mother explains that there were superior opportunities for building a future and for attaining a good education in Britain, Meena becomes aware of just how closely her own life is tied up with these stories of a century of political and social upheaval in India that has shaped her family history and the lives of her ancestors. This perspective of continuity sheds a new light on her eleven-plus exams that are due in the following year, and gives her an understanding of the family legacy and the destiny that has been hinted at earlier in her mother's sermons. "[T]his was no longer a mere exam. If I failed, my parents' five thousand mile journey would have all been for nothing." (213)

Nanima's stories, moreover, construct a positive counter-image of India for Meena to posit against the racist and deprecating version that is transmitted by the education system and through the media. She comes to realise that her "continual compulsion to fabricate, this ever-present desire to be someone else in some other place far from Tollington [...], this urge to reinvent myself [...] was driven purely by shame, the shame I felt when we 'did' India at school" (211). In the photographs from the "tatty textbooks", Meena used to recognise "my uncles and aunties in period clothes", represented either as downtrodden servants or as part "of teeming unruly mobs, howling like animals" (211), both common stereotypical racist renditions that show how intricately the British school system is still caught up in a colonialist discourse. Meena, in retrospect, identifies her lies as an attempt, in line with postcolonial critique, to gain authority over her own story (cf. Reichl 2002, 162–163).[30] With the introduction of Nanima's version of India however, there is no need to continue to distance herself from India, which she now feels confident enough to embrace as part of her own

---

30 This self-reflexivity as well as knowledge and understanding of previous stages of the self indicate that Meena has undergone a significant development here.

identity. Consequently, she can forget her lies, as is now typified by Meena's resolution to "always tell the truth" (284).

Through Nanima's presence and the practice of storytelling with a simultaneous translation being provided by her father, Meena quickly improves her Punjabi. Nanima, moreover, has an "amazing gift of communication" (Reichl 2002, 171) with almost magical traits; her language "seems to work as a trance and gives both children a feeling of safety and home" (Reichl 2002, 172). With Nanima, Punjabi is no longer a language of exclusion and unbelonging for Meena; on the contrary, with her acquisition of her parents' native tongue she gains access to a whole area of the family identity that was previously closed to her. When Nanima eventually tells her own story, Meena needs no translation. In a mysterious, feverish dream-like scene, the language barrier between Meena and her grandmother is magically transcended, so that "although I am almost sure that she spoke in Punjabi, I understood every word" (230). The understanding emerges slowly, first from sounds, then through the words and phrases that are formed, until Meena finally hears "all the stories I had been waiting to hear, the stories I knew Nanima owned and kept to herself, but I had never owned enough Punjabi myself to ever ask her if she would share them with me" (230). Understanding here is propelled by the process of the imagination, which gains momentum exactly through the half-knowledge and partial comprehension. This scene can thus be read in line with the postmemorial perspective that is employed by Daphne Seemann (2013, 39), who sees in "the re-imagination of a lost family tradition in contemporary narratives [...] an empathic attempt of imaginative recuperation". In this view, the gaps (due to the parents' silence) and only half-understood stories (due to the language barrier) also bear a particular potential for inciting the imagination and for creating empathy.

This time, Meena not only sees a vision of India in these stories that she can understand and embrace; she is also able to relate more directly and emotionally to Nanima's stories, finding her own experiences implicated in those of her grandmother: "I knew this feeling, I had felt it too, but did not know why." (231) She thus puts her own experiences of racism, social exclusion and the denial of self-identity in the same category as her grandmother's story about expropriation by the British, when suddenly "nothing we owned was ours anymore, not even our names, our breath" (231). Against this background, Meena is also open to the wisdom that Nanima's story has to offer about overcoming hardships and crises by starting a new life. From this, Meena acquires a definite understanding that she herself has to assume agency in order to effect change (cf. 250).[31]

Empowered by this feeling of family continuity and cultural inheritance, Meena gains a new self-confidence and the strength to finally completely break free from her fixation with Anita. In a radical and "deliberate act" (184) of defiance and rebellion on hearing that Anita has joined the ranks of the skinhead gang in the village and participated in a brutal beating of a man of Indian origin, Meena provokes an accident while out horse riding which puts her in hospital for three months with a complicated leg fracture. Three months – a time she decides to use for self-healing, for 'erasing' Anita from her mind and for studying for her eleven-plus exam (282), which will eventually enable her to be the first Tollington child in decades to go to grammar school. She subsequently has to deal with the loss of her grandmother, who goes back to India, as well as with that of her hospital friend Robert who dies of cancer, which both prove to be experiences that complete Meena's maturation. Although this experience of severe loss is painful, she absorbs it

> like rain on parched earth, drew it in deep and drank from it. I now knew I was not a bad girl, a mixed-up girl, a girl with no name or no place. The place in which I belonged was wherever I stood and there was nothing stopping me simply moving forward and claiming each resting place as home. This sense of displacement I had always carried round like a curse shrivelled into insignificance. (303)

Meena's confrontation with racism and the experiences of identifying herself both with the victim of the racist assault as well as with her grandmother's story of how her family was treated under British rule in India have settled the question in a very decisive way as to where her loyalties lie. This self-confident assertion of successful identity formation and its overly optimistic outlook on belonging as "ultimately a product of one's own creation" (Neti 2008, 115) have often been read, somewhat too readily, as an example of having overcome the system of cultural dichotomy.[32] Tobias Frank (2010, 158–159) rightly states that Meena's process of identity formation does not point towards a concept of iden-

---

31 When Meena's parents start to talk about moving, Meena feels scared, because she senses that she is not ready yet for that change. "Leaving Tollington was something I had planned on my own terms, in my own fantasies so many times. But not like this, [...] leaving behind people whom I had yet to outgrow" (250).
32 Neti (2008, 116), for example states that „Meena's future will be characterised by a constant manoeuvring through the dual – even if now less fixed – perspectives of being both Indian and English", while Helff (2013, 123), even more confidently, ascribes Meena a "newfound cosmopolitan ethnicity". Cf. Stein (2004, 52).

tity that transgresses cultural boundaries, but is a clear method of positioning her within the existing system that allows her to stand her ground as an autonomous and powerful self. Her experiences lead to a widening of her "scope of options" (Stein 2004, 40), and a "furthering of subject positions" (Stein 2004, 38), which allow her to "enter a more mature stage" (Stein 2004, 40). In the end, Meena, "believ[ing] utterly now in the possibilities of change" (*Anita* 326), passes the exam as if it were "a mere formality" (326), thus taking an important personal step and, at the same time, playing her part in the larger family narrative.

The novel shares key structural features with modern Western narratives of adolescence, growing up and maturation. Within the framework of this narrative pattern, the protagonist comes into contact with some of the mysteries of the adult world such as sex and death which act to crack up the child's world like an egg shell. Another factor that propels her process of maturation is a deep disillusionment with life that challenges and shatters the self-constructed fantasies of the child. Encounters with such incidents usher in a crisis that stands for the process of maturing. Maturing, according to this narrative pattern, is a necessarily painful process that acquaints the child with experiences of frustration and isolation. Syal's novel seems to follow this pattern up to the point of crisis, but deviates significantly from it later as a result of the introduction of the migration theme as an additional element that transforms the whole construction.

In line with the *bildungsroman* plot structure, we may distinguish separate relevant phases in Meena's development: Firstly, there are the estrangement from her parents and the simultaneous attempts at integration into the host society. A strong will to change and the revolutionary potential of adolescence are deployed to rebel against parents, home, and past in order to become a fully-fledged member of the peer group. This is exacerbated by the experience of displacement due to the family's history of migration. Gaps that appear in the language and communication within the family lead to a fragmentation of the past and a resulting weakening of family cohesion. Secondly, there is a severe crisis that results in total isolation. This crisis is induced by a growing awareness of the irreconcilable difference between her and the group she tries to gain entrance to, as well as by her previous endeavours at distancing herself from her family. As a consequence, she is completely set adrift. Thirdly, there is the process of reconnecting with her family, her home, and the past. The decisive turning point in the narrative that boosts Meena's ability to construct a sense of identity that is not based on emulation and performance but on a more stable sense of belonging occurs with the introduction of her grandmother. As a benign ancestral figure and a benevolent spirit of the past, she helps to suture the torn fabric of the family and restores a sense of identity by opening up a way for Meena to access the past and the family stories that had been previously out of bounds for her. It is from this decisive self-positioning as "a British girl with a Punjabi background" (Stein 2004, 52) that she derives agency and the power to initiate change in her own life. Agency and change emerge from her new sense of extended identity as she learns to see herself as part of her family and her family as a part of British colonial history. As Roger Bromley elaborates, "her conflicted and contested belonging involves a process of conceptualising her parents' place of origin in both a temporal and spatial sense, and of translating, rerouting, that 'origin' into the 'vernacular' of her own split location as a British-born Asian" (Bromley 2000, 143).

3.2 "Everyone should know where they come from": Genealogical Identity in Andrea Levy's *Fruit of the Lemon* (1999)

Andrea Levy's third novel entitled *Fruit of the Lemon* (1999) has often been read, in addition to her two previous novels, as a paradigmatic example of the Black British *bildungsroman*.[33] It features an autodiegetic narrator, Faith, whose parents came from Jamaica to England as part of the first wave of immigrants from the West Indies to the UK in 1948. Set in 1980s London, the novel traces Faith's attempt to start an independent life after moving out of her parents' house. In line with the genre conventions of the *bildungsroman*, the narration primarily focuses on the protagonist's search for agency and a firm place in society. The novel consists of three parts, the first part and second parts, entitled respectively 'England' and 'Jamaica', are about equal in length and follow a clear structure, with the first part building towards a crisis moment and the second part dealing with the resolution of this crisis. Part III is once again entitled 'England', and only reaches half a page in length. This humorous meta-narrative way of unsettling the readers' expectations points towards an open ending and a continuation of the story that has yet to be written.

---

[33] Cf. Frank 2010, Stein 2004, Meyer 2013. See also Gunning (2014, 9) for a differentiation between Levy's third novel and both of her previous works as regards the *bildungsroman* genre. In his comparison, *Fruit of the Lemon* is "more at ease with the transformations of personal identity captured within the form" (Gunning 2014, 9–10) of the *bildungsroman*, while his analysis goes on to demonstrate that a reading of the first two novels along the lines of this genre is more problematic and complicated – hence his use of the term "unhappy *bildungsromane*".

Far from being a straightforward *bildungsroman*, however, the novel represents an interesting take on the genre that demonstrates both its 'transformative qualities' in the context of Black British literature (cf. Stein 2004) as well as the transformation of the genre itself. The first point in the novel where it deviates from the genre conventions is at the beginning of the book, where Faith seems to have already arrived at the place that she aspires to reach: In the first chapter, she moves out of the family home and into a shared apartment with friends and gets a job with the costume department of the BBC. Her detachment from her parents is marked as an important step in her development towards autonomy, adulthood, and self-determination. Faith is, at this point in time, where and who she wants to be. However, this situation is not without its drawbacks: Her new surroundings not only correspond with her understanding of herself and her place in society, they also happen to be exclusively white. In the first half of the novel, her whole understanding of herself, of her social life, and of society in general is ultimately shattered as she gradually becomes aware of this discrepancy. In order to re-construct her collapsed identity, she embarks on a journey that eventually gives her a new sense of self-assurance and a new sense of solidity. In a similar manner to *Anita and Me*, the constructivist notion of identity as a basis for the creation of the autonomous individual is complicated and thrown into crisis, only to be rebuilt under different conditions that are open to an idea of diasporic identities and transnational belonging that transcend the multicultural sphere of the novels' settings.

3.2.1 The Family Tree Stub: Migration as a Narrative of Arrival and Beginning

The first part of the novel covers Faith's development of an individual self that is created not through violent break and rupture, but on the premise of a continuously growing independence. The beginning of Faith's individual story in the first chapter of Part I is preceded by a reiteration of the family narrative that she has constructed at this point. This prelude is opened by a small family tree diagram, which, in combination with the changing typeset that is introduced by the illustration of a lemon when her parents' narrative begins (recounted by Faith), aligns this chapter with later chapters in the novel in which Faith's Jamaican family history is narrated. This opening chapter and its version of the family narrative form the basis on which Faith's story unfolds in the first part of the novel. Pieced together from the "little scraps" of information that her parents reveal of their past before Faith and her brother were born, Faith has constructed a "story that seemed to make sense" as she says (*Fruit* 4):[34] it covers how her mother grew up in Kingston, Jamaica, met Faith's father, how the two married and moved to England, and eventually, after initial setbacks and disappointments, how they slowly worked their way up through society and settled down. The story presents a fairly straightforward, linear narrative of struggle and of overcoming hardships, of growing independence and success, where each move from one place of accommodation to the next marks a stage in their steady progress until, at the end, they purchase their own house – "[w]e finally arrive home", as quoted by Faith (11).[35] When Faith begins the first chapter with her own experience of moving out, she aligns her story with this family narrative: Her move is the natural next step in her individual development that builds on her parents' process, and she finds out how to make good use of their hobby of "collecting empty boxes" (15).[36]

What is left behind and edited out of the family story as a narrative of migration, arrival, and coming home is the family's past in Jamaica, which is reduced down to the most basic information. This corresponds with her parents' apparent unwillingness to talk about this past. As Faith says, "[m]y mum and dad never talked about their lives before my brother Carl and I were born. They didn't sit us in front of the fire and tell long tales of life in Jamaica [...]. There was no 'oral tradition' in our family" (4), at least none that goes beyond the

---

34 *Fruit* refers to Levy 2004 [1999]. Hereafter all references to the novel will use only page number, and, where necessary, *Fruit* for disambiguation.
35 Toplu (2005, 2) reads this exclamation by the parents as one of irony, which seems a bit strong, in my opnion, although the story does contain comic elements (such as, for instance, the misunderstanding about the Guy Fawkes fireworks at their arrival). Nevertheless, whatever irony there is in her parents' phrasing, I would argue that Faith herself does not recognise it at this point because her version of the family narrative shares this strong teleological orientation. The disparity between her understanding of home and that of her parents only dawns on her later in the novel.
36 The collection of empty boxes is reminiscent of the often used image of suitcases being stored on top of wardrobes that is employed in migrant fiction, "a metaphor of the parents' immigrant selves" (Toplu 2005, 2; see, e.g., *Anita and Me*), which points to the parents' belief that they will return home (cf. Frank 2010, 118). Faith only sees this 'hobby' as a strange quirk of her parents, which ties in with her version of the family narrative and its closed ending of finding a 'home'. Her parents' understanding of home, however, is quite different from hers, as becomes apparent when they announce their plan "of going back home" (*Fruit* 40), an announcement that completely throws Faith off balance, and confronts her with the question that makes her think "why Jamaica? Why is Jamaica home?" (45).

point of arrival:[37] "We came on a banana boat to England" is how the core narrative starts. The story of arrival is shaped and enriched as an anecdote of intercultural misunderstanding, as Faith's parents initially mistake the fireworks of Guy Fawkes' night as a sign of welcome. The way this anecdote is fleshed out highlights this particular moment in the narrative of arrival and gives it emphasis. Furthermore, the anecdote encapsulates the disillusionment experienced by Faith's parents and thousands of others who came from the Caribbean, expecting to be "travelling to the centre of [their] country", where they "would slip-in and fit-in immediately" (Levy 2000, n.p.).

Faith and her parents[38] use the story of the banana boat to set a starting point for their family history that is synchronised with their migration to Britain. The act of migration thus becomes a new point of origin that is linked to the 'fiction of a new beginning'.[39] It connects the family history with the goal of a new life, and directs it exclusively towards the future. In doing so, the new foundational narrative may wipe the slate clean, yet it can also erase the past along with its ties to an extended family history. This cutting off of the past and the establishing of a new beginning is symbolised in the two-generation family tree that is juxtaposed with the novel's beginning. It posits the parents, Wade and Mildred, at the head of a new genealogy of (future) generations. Furthermore, this emphasis on new beginnings highlights the way the parents' story is aligned with that of the Windrush Generation. This generation label, which designates the first large group of immigrants who came to the UK from the West Indies in the wake of the British Nationality Act in 1948, marks the arrival of the *Empire Windrush* as the "founding event of postwar migration" (Rupp 2010, 139). The usage of the term 'Windrush' as a generation label testifies to the broader historical significance that was later ascribed to the event, not only for the group itself but also with regard to British history and the national narrative.

---

[37] Cf. 45: "Dad would never talk about Jamaica, just telling me it was a long time ago when I asked him about his growing up – his mum and dad, his tooth fairy." Later, she also tells her aunt Coral that "Mum and Dad didn't really talk about Jamaica." (183)

[38] Faith's meta-narrative comment preceding this version of the family story draws attention to the construction of meaning through the use of narrative (what she offers the readers is a story that, first of all, "seem[s] to make sense") and suggests that she has to be seen to be at least on an equal footing alongside her parents as regards the authorship of this family narrative.

[39] Cf. A. Assmann (2013, 149ff.). The construction of a new beginning is a trope for the modern concept of 'revolution, innovation and individuality' (A. Assmann 2013, 158). The idea of having a 'clean slate' carries with it the possibility of self-invention that is independent of history and tradition.

The moment is "seen as symbolic of the rise of multicultural, multiracial Britain" (Ellis 2012, 70), which translates into the counting of immigrant generations from this point on, and the implicit gesture of wiping out any history that lies before the event, which accompanies it.

The myth surrounding this new beginning ties in with Faith's self-understanding and the image that she has constructed of herself. Being, as she writes "born and bred in [the London suburb] Haringey" (30), she assumes an unproblematic and natural sense of Englishness, which implies, however, a certain dissociation from her Jamaican 'origins'.[40] In line with this self-image, the act of moving out of the family home is a way of distancing herself from her ethnic identity and her Caribbean heritage that is represented by her family.[41] This is shown vividly in two visits to her new home, firstly by her father and later by her brother. Her father's visit is, in Faith's view, initially a confirmation of her newly established independence and cultural self-determination (cf. Frank 2010, 117): "He looked smaller. He used to take up so much space in my childhood." (*Fruit* 26) Being "in my own house now" (28) grants her a new sense of autonomy and confidence to ward off her father's parental advice. There is no need for teenage rebellion and defiance anymore, no need "to respond to the stricture as I always had in the past" (27). When her roommate Simon arrives home and instinctively mistakes Faith's father for a burglar, she does not even recognise her friend's behaviour as a typical instance of everyday racism. Her complete identification with Englishness that at this point in the novel makes her blind to the xenophobia that surrounds her (cf. Frank 2010, 117).[42] Her colour-blindness is in line with British society and "the racist logic organizing the public sphere" (Sáez 2006, n.p.). She feels as distant from her family's racial identity as she is in the eyes of her friend, who takes another second to realise

---

[40] In contrast to the famous opening lines of Hanif Kureishi's *The Buddha of Suburbia*, the lack of any qualification of her statement (like Karim's postposed 'almost') is conspicuous here; Faith's lack of awareness that anyone might question her natural claim to Englishness also demonstrates a lack of awareness of the reality of racism in 1980s Britain.

[41] This concerns ethnic/racial as well as cultural identity, as illustrated by Faith's relief to finally be able to free herself from her parents' expectations and "Caribbean strictures" (16). As Frank (2010, 116) elaborates: "Neben diesem klassischen Generationenkonflikt wird damit gleich zu Beginn deutlich, dass Faith die elterlichen Erwartungen mit einem kulturellen Hintergrund verbindet, dem sie für die eigene Selbstkonzeption keine Bedeutung beimisst und den sie eher als Einschränkung versteht".

[42] See also Sáez (2006, n.p.): "Faith rejects the negative terms of racial identity and otherness to the extent she is also disassociated from all ethnic and cultural markers, and cannot read social interactions through any of these lenses."

that the black man in the house is, of course, Faith's father – implying that he eventually makes the connection between his blackness and Faith's. When her father asks her after the incident, "your friends, any of them your own kind?", Faith "isn't sure what he meant" (28) and thinks that he is asking whether they went to college with her. This reveals the deep gulf of understanding, experience, and self-image that exists between Faith and her father with regard to race.[43] Her dismissal of the factor of race and ethnicity for her own life, and her dis-identification with her family in the company of her friends, becomes clearer yet when her brother Carl visits. "For a brief moment as he stood looking around the room at my friends I saw my brother as a stranger." (53) He seems to her "large and dark", a "tall man", a "big man – with a brown complexion", and, finally, a "black man with a round head of afro hair" – "out of context" (53) in her new surroundings of whiteness. This sudden awareness of his blackness reveals her complete obliviousness of her own colour.

However, in the same way that her family members begin to become strangers in her eyes and their skin colour becomes conspicuous in her new environment, her own difference slowly surfaces as she is increasingly confronted with the fact that she is black and with a sense of not belonging that isolates her from her friends and the 'White' majority population. Like Meena in *Anita and Me*, Faith comes face to face with the situation that her own naturally assumed Englishness is not recognised by a society that is permeated by racism and xenophobia. Her sense of sameness and her feeling of belonging do not change the fact that she still remains "visibly different" to the others (Mirza 1997, 3). An important incident which adds to Faith's growing awareness of racial differences is the night when her roommate Simon plays a small gig at a pub that she and some friends accompany him to. There are different acts on

---

[43] The issue of racial awareness and self-understanding is an interesting one in families that often highlights generational differences. Although Faith's brother, Carl, shows a sense of racial awareness and identity construction that is completely different from hers, his self-positioning could be read as an alternative response to their familial upbringing. In this way, the family constellation is reminiscent of the two brothers (and their parents) in Horace Ove's film *Pressure* (1976). Caro's overt and political racial identification – illustrated by his name: "Carl, he decided, had a certain Superfly, Shaft, don't-mess-with-me-I'm-a-black-man message" (18) – is the other extreme to Faith's racial blindness, but is similarly different from their parents' stance, which is determined by their wish for social acceptance in Britain, and therefore, the feeling that they have to remain as inconspicuous as possible, which also regards their past (cf. 4). Carl's political blackness could be said to be reflected in his even more activist girlfriend Ruth, whose white family (she has no contact with her biological Guyanese father) would then function as a 'mirror' to the way Faith's parents wipe out the past.

that night, and as the last performer, a poet, comes on stage, Faith is completely unsettled by the fact that he is black:

> Marion looked at me and winked. Suddenly, as I looked up at this black poet I became aware that the poet and me were the only black people in the room. I looked around again – it was now a room of white people.
> I became nervous waiting for the poet to start. I was thinking, 'Please be good, please.' The poet became my dad, my brother, he was the unknown black faces in our photo album, he was the old man on the bus who called me sister, the man in the bank with the strong Trinidadian accent [...]. He was every black man – ever. (*Fruit* 91–92)

In contrast with the scene of her brother's visit, Faith here feels included in the poet's difference; her feeling of being singled out by virtue of her skin colour and or being put in opposition to everyone else elicits a strong affinity with the poet from within her. This time she feels a complete identification with the poet based on their shared difference, whereas her awareness of her brother's difference had led to a feeling of dis-identification. Just as her brother became a 'stranger' to her, this stranger now becomes kin to her. Her vision of kinship moves from her immediate family such as her father and her brother to the extended family in Jamaica that she is disconnected from.[44] In an expansion of the idea of kinship to the global brotherhood of black identity politics, the poet becomes a 'black everyman', whose poems are representative of the black experience. The scene initiates Faith's growing identification as being 'black' and helps to form a stronger solidarity with the black community and the oppression of it, which results in a simultaneous distancing from 'white' English society. The imposition of a black identity that Faith now experiences closely follows Heidi Mirza's (1997, 3) description of racialisation:

> being 'black' in Britain is about a state of 'becoming' (racialized); a process of consciousness, when colour becomes the defining factor about who you are. Located through your 'otherness' a 'conscious coalition' emerges: a self-consciously constructed space where identity is not inscribed by a natural identification but a political kinship [...]. Now living submerged in whiteness, physical difference becomes a defining issue, a signifier, a mark of whether or not you belong.

---

[44] The "unknown black faces in our photo album" in her reference to her family in Jamaica indicate how little her parents have talked to her about the family that they left behind. An album of family photos exists; however, due to the fact that knowledge about the people in the pictures is not simultaneously transmitted, the photos become mere "depersonalized signifiers of a distant place and a bygone era" (Hirsch 2012a [1997], xi) with no personal meaning for the next generation.

Faith had previously been witness to a varying array of everyday racism and discrimination, however, after having left the family home and having lost the safety net of being surrounded with people of 'her own kind' on a daily basis, she is now fully and deeply confronted, for the first time, by questions of ethnicity, race, and cultural identity. While the recognition of her brother's blackness makes her feel remote to him – with the implication that the act of setting herself apart from him moves her even closer to her friends –, Faith herself feels increasingly distant from her friends through similar confrontations with her own racial identity. As a consequence, she experiences a painful sense of difference that isolates her from her White surroundings.

Faith's incomplete family history cuts her off from any positive sense of heritage or blackness that can be used as a source of self-empowerment. The image of the banana boat, which forms the beginning of Faith's self-narrative, carries with it negative connotations for her as it is closely connected with the racist remarks that she had experienced from the other children at her school after they had learnt the Banana Boat song in music class.[45] Her parents' failure to offer an alternative story as a positive counter narrative leaves her with no other context for this story than "the illustrations of slave ships from my history lessons" (4). "[H]er rootlessness produces a lack of self-awareness" (Sáez 2006, n.p.) as her idea of cultural and ethnic origin is limited to an image of black history imposed on her in school, where she

> drew diagrams of how the triangular trade in slaves worked, like we drew diagrams of sheep farming in Australia. I hated those lessons. Although there were no small boys laughing and pointing, I felt them. 'Your mum and dad came on a slave ship,' they would say. 'They are slaves.' (4)

Faith at this time has internalised the racist comments from the bullies at her primary school in a way that indelibly links her family history with slavery. Faith contrasts this focus on slave history as has been transmitted through school directly with her parents' failure to talk about Jamaica and to adequately answer her "childhood questions" (4) about their past.[46] This lack of a family

---

[45] The novel actually begins not with her own (family's) version, but with the version imposed on her by others: "'Your mum and dad came on a banana boat,' that was what the bully boys at my primary school used to say." (3) Faith has internalised this other-perception and incorporated it into her own narrative in a way that is similar to her adoption of the othering gaze of white society when she begins to move more exclusively in white circles.

[46] There is a close interconnection between the history of slavery and cultural amnesia. Mary Chamberlain (2009, 178) reveals to us that through the deliberate dehumanisation of slaves and the destruction of "any vestiges of culture and family organization, [...] slave memories

history leaves her without a positive reference point to oppose the racist slights that she is confronted with. Similar to Meena's lack of knowledge of her Indian heritage, Faith's Jamaican heritage is "something she does not know about but is always associated with" (Reichl 2002, 162). When her tutor in art college describes her work as having "an ethnicity which shines through, [... a] sort of African or South American feel which is obviously part of you", Faith does not find this factor quite as "exciting" as her teacher, and can "only suppose that I had some sort of collective unconscious that was coming through from my slave ancestry" (31).[47]

Faith's moment of recognition that formed an affinity between her and the dub poet opens up the possibility of a new historical narrative, one of resistance against oppression and injustice. Her apprehension and nervousness before the poet starts his act not only shows her identification with him but also the way in which her sense of origin is dominated by a feeling of shame that derives from its association with slave history. This shame is countered in his performance and his poetry of resistance: "His first poem was about his fantasy of kicking a policeman back after the policeman had kicked him. People started to laugh and clap. [...] And I slowly began to look up." (91) At this moment, it is his acceptance by the crowd that makes her feel re-assured and confident. However, the incident indicates the start of a change inside her, as "the unknown black faces" in the family photo album are re-invested with meaning through the sense of 'political kinship'.

3.2.2 Models of 'Rooted' Englishness: Genealogies, Family Traditions and Cultural Identity

The close interconnection between cultural identity and family heritage, or the lack thereof, is emphasised in the way in which Faith sees her white friends and

---

became bifurcated" and transmitted only "at the 'deeper' levels of values and attitudes and in the ways language, music, proverbs, food, and families, especially, became creolized". For an account of the history of British slavery and the complexities of the memory cultures that are set around this topic, see Korte and Pirker (2011), who also refer to Levy's novel *The Long Song* (2010), set during the era of British slavery in Jamaica.

47 This incident is the first in a series of racisms rows that she encounters in the job sphere. While there is a certain degree of sarcasm in Faith's response to having the quality of her work disavowed, as the tutor does not seem to account for the fact that "perhaps it was that I was just better than everyone else" (31). For an elaboration on how the tutor here "reduces race to a market(able) category" see Sáez (2006, 5).

the implicit comparison that she draws between them and her own family. Faith's own truncated family tree symbolises the uprooting of her parents through migration and the perceived deficit of history that the nuclear family subsequently suffered. This idea of the immigrant without a history that is present in Faith's family story echoes the colonialist trope of historylessness, which refers to the "lack of a 'dense' past as one discursive feature [...] typical of settler colonial ideological formations" (Veracini 2007). The formerly colonised immigrants, on arrival to the 'mother country', are cast once more into a fictional state of historical oblivion. "The nexus between memories and migrant incorporation is a typical, widespread and significant feature of any country with immigration." (Glynn and Kleist 2012, 3) In the case of Faith's parents, their silence about the past has two main sources. First of all, it expresses a concern with the present and the future, with the hardships of building a new life in a new country and the hopes and wishes that are connected to that dream. While secondly, they seem to have internalised an imperative to practice forced forgetting as a pre-condition for their assimilation and integration into the majority society. Thus, when her mother lets a detail slip about their past in Jamaica, Faith is explicitly told "not to go blabbing it about to my friends, not to repeat it to anyone" (4). Migrant memories are signifiers of difference, and the act of standing out, in whatever manner, will become an obstacle to integration and social participation.

The Jackson family narrative that is directed towards the future but lacks the backing of a past thus feels somewhat incomplete in contrast with the situatedness and 'inherited' identity that Faith's friends have that is derived from their family history, and which gives them a sense of belonging that Faith lacks:

> Whenever Marion talked about her white working-class origins – her extended family who had all lived in the same street for generations – everything they said, everything they did was a cultural thing. Something that belonged to their way of life – like an instinct. (93)

With this notion of tradition and of being rooted in place, the white working class identity of her best friend's family is distinctly different from Faith's own non-white working class background, which is marked by frequently having to relocate. In her own family narrative, 'home' is something that had to be acquired by her parents through hard work and perseverance as opposed to something that was handed down to them by previous generations. Marion's family, conversely, sign their greeting cards as "the Coopers of Holloway" (93), demonstrating that the family name is tied to the place through a long history of settlement in that district, and their identity, due to its being derived from this connection, conspicuously contrasts with Faith's background. The connotations of this idea of inherited identity are made explicit in the concept of equating this 'cultural thing' with instinct. Marion thus inadvertently reveals the essentialism that underlies this concept of culture as being intrinsically tied to family and place and therefore as something innate and unchanging.[48] She takes a certain pride in this family background, and goes on to educate Faith on how her "family are very close. Working-class families in this country have traditionally been close." (93) Not surprisingly, Marion's family, with her "gran and grandad and aunts and uncles and sisters and cousins" (93) is a source of envy for Faith, who, in comparison, lacks any extended family, on both the diachronic and the synchronic level. However, she is doubly cut off from this model of family, firstly, through her family's migration, and, secondly, because it is presented as a racial model of family. Not coincidentally, Marion gives this "lecture" (93) on British working class culture to Faith in order to explain and ultimately excuse her father's racism.

As an alternative to Marion's urban working-class version of Englishness, Faith's other flatmate Simon is an embodiment of the rural upper class English gentry. This form of identity is, however, similarly exclusive and closed to Faith. When he takes her on a visit to his home village, Simon describes the place as "[q]uintessentially English" (115). On seeing it, Faith is reminded of "a model village that used to be in our park in London" where she used to go with her brother, "lean over the railing and point out the shop and the church and the village green" (116). Their careful intrusion over the fence and walks "among the little thatched houses, feeling like giants" (116) are a prelude to their later drives in Carl's van to the English countryside and their dream of entering into "that green and pleasant land" (56).[49] On these trips, however, they discover that the country, which from the van "always looked so charming [..., m]iles and miles of picture-book pretty", turns out to be inaccessible once they step outside the car: "we were always greeted with fences and gates and barbed wire" (56). The pastoral landscape, which initially seems to be welcoming but ultimately rejects Faith and her brother Carl, stands as a symbol of nostalgic Englishness that they both desire but from which they are excluded (cf. Frank 2010, 134).

---

48 The two concepts of family and place are dangerously close here to the Nazi 'blood and soil'-ideology.
49 Faith's quote from William Blake's hymn *Jerusalem* evokes the Romantic topos of nostalgia for the idyllic English landscape and its 'pleasant pastures' (cf. Barfoot 2004; see also Frank 2010, 134). The phrase itself, more than being an intertextual reference perhaps, has come to be used as shorthand for a nostalgic concept of Englishness (see, for example, Ray Davies' use of the term in song lyrics: "I close my eyes and lay back and I think of England. / I dream about that green and pleasant land we knew as England." in "Yours Truly, Confused N10", 2005).

This pastoral Englishness is connected to conservatism and traditionalism; it represents a closed and stable concept that is, essentially, historical and past. In Simon's home village, everything is "steeped in history", from the pub that "goes back to Tudor times" (129) to Simon's own family. Their house is described as a shrine of family memory, replete with an ancestral portrait gallery, which Simon presents to Faith as if he was a museum guide:

> 'This is my great-grandfather who designed the house, that's on my mother's side... The paintings there, there and there are of my father's parents' parents and their grandparents and interestingly enough they were painted by my great-great – I lose count to be honest – but an old uncle anyway who became quite famous – we sometimes have to lend the pictures out for exhibitions. (121)

The house is thus filled with references to family and genealogy: "Everything seemed to have been someone else's once." (121) Apart from the portraits, there are things like "[o]ld furniture passed down from generation to generation", "model ships" in cases "made by my maternal grandfather", and a "model train engine [...] made by his [the maternal grandfather's] father" (121). Family history is materialised here in the house itself, and in the objects and heirlooms that make up its furnishings, which ensure the comprehensive intergenerational transmission of tradition and family memory. Simon's ability to connect each object to a specific relative shows how the knowledge of family history is passed on and kept alive in the house, in addition to its personal relevance for the family members. Apart from this personal relevance, Simon seems to derive a certain amount of pride from the broader significance of these heirlooms as objects of a more general cultural history.[50] As Faith learns, the model train engine, for example, is "a replica of the first engine on the Carlisle to Settle railway" (121). This link between family history and national or cultural history is accentuated in a – somewhat grotesque way – by the drawing of a royal family tree on Simon's bedroom wall. "It goes back to Ethelred the Unready" (122), as Simon points out, not without pride.

In addition, their walk in the countryside and the subsequent visit to the town pub make her feel alien and different, due to being not acquainted with the customs of the place, and not equipped to move freely, with people staring

---

[50] This is not only true with regard to Simon's impressive family history, but applies to his parents as well, who are linked to English history: While his mother was in intelligence during the war (cf. 120), his father looks like a colonial officer from the past century (133).

at her.⁵¹ Even the pub itself is "terribly old" and displays its history in photographs hung on the wall, which Simon is able to explain to Faith in a similar way to his guided tour through his family home. In the pub, a friend of Simon's parents comes over to tell Faith of his recent holiday to Jamaica, where he met a man with the same last name as his own, Bunyan. What seems like a funny story for the man actually makes perfect sense to Faith, who explains that "that would have been his slave name" and "[y]our family probably owned his family once" (131). The man is shocked at this inference; while before it had seemed funny to him to have taken a photograph of "[m]e and my brother Winston", he now claims that his "family never had connections like that in Jamaica. My family were not in that sort of business." (131) This incident reveals the mechanisms of silence and silencing in British society with regard to colonial history and its legacy. It moreover points to the fact that the family is a realm for the transference of history that can add to or challenge the "official version of the truth" (133).⁵²

Against the background of the proud display of lineage and Englishness in Simon's family, Faith becomes increasingly aware of her own lack of cultural belonging. Simon's detailed knowledge of his family history and its complex genealogical network is contrasted with Faith's own ignorance about her own family when Simon's mother quizzes her about her relations in Jamaica (132–133). What is more, the consistency and reliable sense of 'home' that Simon's family house conveys jars with Faith's own imminent loss of home due to her parents' plan to return to Jamaica. For her, every visit home to her parents seems to bring her face to face with a new set of changes. In Simon's house, not only is the multi-generational history of the family preserved but it extends right up to the more recent events of his family life. "Simon's bedroom still had the musty sweaty smell of adolescent boys." He admits that he is "just not ready" (122) for his mother to redecorate the room. Faith's frequent visits home to her

---

51 Cf. Frank (2010, 134–135) for an insightful reading of Faith's attempts to enter the "green and pretty" (125) countryside as a metaphor for her inability to transgress the boundaries of national identity and claim the Englishness that is represented by the land. Her increasing difficulty to move in this way demonstrates a great "Skepsis gegenüber der Vorstellung permeabler (kultureller) Identitätskreise" (Frank 2010, 135). For a more encompassing and highly interesting analysis of the novel's treatment of body and space, see Bromley (2000, 135–138).

52 Simon's mother later tells Faith that she thinks her response was "very brave" (134). Just previously, she had been telling Faith of her work in intelligence during World War II, a largely forgotten story in official historiography. Frank (2010, 133) reads this whole passage with regard to its proleptic function in the novel, whose ending suggests that after her return from Jamaica Faith is ready to tell her own story.

parents, where she rummages in the cupboards for Fondant Fancies and enjoys her Mum's dinner of chicken and rice, reveal that she, too, is 'not ready' to live entirely independently from her parents (cf. 40–41).[53] When her parents announced their plan of "going back home" (44), it comes as a double shock to Faith: firstly, due to the prospect of her losing her parents and their support,[54] and secondly, because her parents refer to Jamaica as 'home'.[55] The idea that her parents see Jamaica as home and wish to return there completely undermines her version of the family narrative, and thus "calls into question the small hold Faith thought she had on understanding her family" (Sáez 2006, n.p.). When, one day, Faith finds her Mum clearing up the house by getting rid of all of her children's remaining belongings, she tries to intervene. "'Don't throw this away [...] It's our history,' I told her. She laughed and kept repeating, 'history' under her breath whilst shaking her head and stuffing more things into the bin liner." (96)[56] There is a stark difference here between the increasing fragility of Faith's sense of family history and home and Simon's family's firm rootedness in history.

While her understanding of home collapses and her family and her self-narrative unravel in the face of her parents' return to Jamaica, Faith also becomes more and more disillusioned with her new-found home, with her friends, and with the life that she has built for herself. Her growing sense of racial awareness distances her both from her friends and from "[t]he public systems of

---

[53] Her brother Carl teases her that he does not understand "how you've meant to have left home, right. But how you seem to be back here every minute looking for something to eat?" (40). The narrator justifies herself to the reader that she can only arrange her mealtimes around her housemates' eating habits, "if I knew that I could go home to my mum and dad's, binge on chicken and eat a Fondant Fancy whole whenever I got desperate" (41).

[54] Faith's first thought after finally having understood what her parents mean by "going back home" is of Fondant Fancies and whether she can afford them on her own. Her parents justify their wish by indicating that "you and Carl are grown-up, so we can go home and ..." (45). Faith's parents here raise the interesting issue of when the parents' obligation towards their children ends, and whether there is also such a thing as an emancipation of parents from their children when the latter are grown up.

[55] Faith's first association at hearing 'home' is the family's council flat in Stoke Newington, where the family had lived for the first ten years of her life, and which she still "thought of as home" (44). In her desolation at hearing her parents' news, Faith's desire for home is expressed in her wish to "go sit in my bedroom. The bedroom with council-pink walls" in Stoke Newington (47).

[56] Cf. Smart (2007, 167): "As with homes, possessions too become invested with meanings as parts of relationships". Faith's mother's treatment of her daughter's possessions, when compared with Simon's artefact filled house, plays a significant role in demonstrating the importance of filling a house with the meaning of 'home'.

erasure" and British society's "regime of color-blindness" (Sáez 2006, n.p.). As a result, Faith increasingly loses her sense of self and belonging. This process is propelled even further by a racist assault on a black feminist bookshop by members of the National Front that is witnessed by Faith and Simon, and which painfully reveals the deep-seated "racist logic organizing the public sphere" (Sáez 2006, n.p.) to Faith. Despite an abundance of evidence for the racist motive of the attack, the policemen reject the obvious facts: "All these leftie bookshops are getting done [...]. They say they're National Front but they're not, they're just a bunch of thugs."[57] (154) Faith, who identifies with Yemi, the black woman who was attacked, suffers profoundly from the shock caused by the incident. When she and Simon get home to their friends and retell the story however, everyone's sympathy is directed exclusively at Simon, who tried to chase the thugs and, in a distortion of the events, comes out not only as the story's hero but also as the potential victim. Faith realises that the attack holds a different reality for her than it does for her friends.[58] While they refer to the bookshop owner in general terms, thereby implicating themselves in the system of colour-blindness, Faith repeatedly emphasises the fact that "[s]he was a black woman", and that "the woman that was struck on the head was black like me" (156). Her friends, after having gotten over the initial shock, eventually laugh the story off, but Faith is more profoundly shaken and becomes aware of how comprehensive the difference between herself and her friends actually is: "Mick put four mugs of tea on the table and three white hands and one black stretched forward to take them." (157)

In the end, Faith feels painfully alienated and excluded from both her family and her circle of friends, and has nowhere else to turn to. Her awareness of her own 'blackness' not only isolates her, it also unhinges her concept of self and tests her sense of belonging (cf. Frank 2010, 121). At the culmination of her identity crisis, she suffers a serious nervous breakdown. She stays in bed for days, without eating or speaking to anyone. Her paralysis, in the same way as the act of covering up the mirrors in her room, is a negation of her sense of self: "I didn't want to be black any more." (160) Faith's desire for self-erasure in conjuncture with her denial of racial identity can once more be connected to the

---

57 The policemen's repeated use of the phrase 'getting done' (cf. 153–154) additionally blocks out the actual violence of the attack, making it seem unexceptional and harmless.

58 Cf. Simon's impression that "this is surreal" (154) and Faith's assertion that "It was real" (155). To her, when they tell the story, the whole reality of the incident sinks into her consciousness and is "[n]ot something skipped over in the local paper or tutted about at the dinner table" (155). Her experience of the event has brought her face to face with the reality of racism in Britain.

emotion of shame as part of a collective trauma of slavery: "For resonating in individual, African Caribbean memories are the echoes of collective trauma and the persistence of shame which present themselves in compulsive and often compelling ways." (Chamberlain 2009, 180)[59] Her parents' suggestion to go on a trip to Jamaica, because, as her mother says, "everyone should know where they come from" (*Fruit* 162), is a very conscious move to take Faith away from the 'othering' gaze of her white circles to an environment that will enable her to form an affirmative self-image.

3.2.3 The Fruit of the Family Tree: Appropriating Family History and Reclaiming Englishness

Faith's trip to Kingston is, from the very start, not cast as a 'return' to her origins and to her ancestral homeland;[60] to begin with, her feeling of culture shock and overwhelming strangeness dominates. She completely lacks any sense of innate belonging or cultural knowledge that she feels should be hers, "[i]f not by experience then in my genes" (173). Through the act of making connections with the members of her family, however, she partly loses this sense of alienation and a feeling of recognition and familiarity sets in (cf. 174ff.). While upon her arrival at the airport Faith feels that "[a]ny Jamaican family could have claimed me and taken me home" (175) because everyone looks so similar to her and shares roughly the same experience of having a transnational family, when she does meet her aunt Coral, there is an instant sense of family identity: "I recognised her but not from any photograph. [... S]he was unmistakably my mother's sister." (176)[61] The feeling of home in her aunt Coral's house contrasts with her obvious foreignness, which is betrayed by her stereotype-based expectations and prejudices. There is even a chaise longue that can rightfully be granted the status of a family piece; as Coral explains, it "used to be in our house at home. That's how old this seat is." (183)

---

[59] See Eyerman (2003 [2001]) for an exploration of the role of cultural trauma in the formation of black identity in the African American context.
[60] See Brähler (2013) for an extensive analysis of the 'myth of return' in the Caribbean migration novel. Brähler (2013, 139), moreover, introduces a typology that distinguishes between a 'return to origins' and the 'travel', in which the latter is characterised by its 'cyclical character' and the idea of "reinventing a culture".
[61] The first man to approach her to help her with her bag at the airport "looked like my brother Carl" (169).

In Jamaica, Faith becomes "Miss-want-to-know-everything-from-England" (195) and questions her relatives, aunt Coral in particular, about her family history. These stories are set off from the main narrative through the use of a different typeset and the illustration of a cut lemon. The family stories are re-told in the novel by Faith, but their narration is interspersed with many direct quotes from the original situation of family storytelling. These reveal the dialogic nature, in which these stories are told, with Faith taking an active part as a questioner. The sometimes lengthy quotes, reproduced in the dialect and diction of the original narrator, also introduce the previously absent element of oral storytelling into Faith's narrative. The fact that these stories are rendered through Faith's narrative voice, instead of entirely through her aunt Coral's,[62] indicates that she has appropriated them as her own stories, which she can now retell. The element of conflicting versions, which is typical of family stories due to the fact that everyone has their specific angle, is still present in Faith's rendition and in the interspersed little dialogues that she shared with Coral and the other narrators.[63]

With each story, the little stub of a family tree that was in place at the beginning of the novel slowly grows and branches out, incorporating each member of the family referred to in the stories. In this way, the diagram embodies how stories function as "the badge of *connectivity*" (Chamberlain 2009, 185) in families. The repeated indications and specifications of relational connections ("her sister – 'That's your great-grandmother, Faith'"; "Eunice's mum 'your grandmother, Faith'", etc., *Fruit* 213, 215) not only enable Faith to draw the lines in the diagram, they also highlight Faith's own position in it and add a subjective perspective that the diagram itself cannot have.[64] The novel illustrates how the passing on of stories in family communication serves a similar function to the drawing of connecting lines in a family tree diagram. Both create "historical contact chains" that imply the idea of "intergenerational transitivity" and thus

---

[62] The family stories are inserted in between the counted chapters and have titles such as "Coral's Story told to me by Coral" (189), or, "Eunice's Story told to me by Coral" (211).
[63] See, e.g., this little exchange: "James's family was evicted from their house and land. 'I don't know why.' They were evicted so that the landowner could graze more sheep in the area. 'Sheep! Are you sure that is why, Faith? They teach you that at school, that it was for sheep? Cha.'" (239)
[64] The perspective has changed: while the tree at the beginning implied a promising future, it is now oriented towards uncovering the past, and also now branches out on a synchronic level. The expansion of the family tree diagram does "not follow any particular genealogical order. Rather, the stories are organized by Faith's errantry, her journey on the island and the family members she speaks to." (Sáez 2006, n.p.)

serve to "compress[...] historical distances experientially" (Zerubavel 2003, 58).⁶⁵ The family tree represents Faith's self-positioning within the connective schema of the family. The expanding web offers her a number of new familial affiliations. The continuously 'growing' tree illustrates the way in which these different stories that are circulated by the family come together to form a unified narrative for Faith, which in the end bears the perfect shape of a lemon. The family tree in its final shape represents two aspects of Faith's family narrative: 1) as a fruit it is part of a larger system of historical ramifications in that it connects to a larger tree; 2) as a tree it resonates with the notion of 'roots' and 'rootedness' – the tree visualises a "spiritual home [...] located in the family" (Chamberlain 2009, 185).⁶⁶

Through her exploration of family history, Faith acquires the past that she had been lacking, which she describes in an imagery of "birthing/rebirthing" (Bromley 2000, 138): Her Jamaican relatives "laid a past out in front of me. They wrapped me in a family history and swaddled me tight in its stories. And I was taking back that family to England. [...] I was smuggling it home." (*Fruit* 326) The frequent references to degrees of kinship, which work as a verbal equivalent to the connecting lines in the family tree diagram, emphasise the way in which all these stories are tied to Faith's own story, and, in a way, serve as a commentary for her identity crisis and her experience of racialisation. The stories of the different family members "reveal a socially stratified and pigmentocratic Jamaica" (Frank 2010, 126; my translation), where status is directly based on tone of skin, but the classification and evaluation of them changes with historical processes. Against this background, her ancestors' life stories resonate with Faith's own experience in England, and with themes of race, racism, and the struggle associated with identity construction (cf. Frank 2010, 126–127).⁶⁷

---

65 The term transitivity stems from the field of mathematics and expresses the relationships between A-B-C. If A is related to B and B is related to C, then A is also related to C. The parallel to storytelling is exemplified by Zerubavel (2003, 58) in his reference to the children's book *Pink and Say*, in which the story of an ancestor having shaken the hand of Lincoln is transmitted from generation to generation in a family, along with the shaking of "the hand that has touched the hand ... that shook the hand" and so on.

66 In its original context, this phrase is employed by Mary Chamberlain to describe the meaning of family in the diasporic memories of Caribbean communities.

67 Most obviously, the story of her distant aunt Constance/Afria serves as a "mirror image of Faith's identity crisis, foreshadowing Faith's own complex and ambivalent negotiation of her Caribbean diasporic identity" (Sáez 2006, n.p.). Constance is at first admired for her "fair hair, her blue eyes, her pale skin" (316), but after World War II she is discriminated against and excluded because of her whiteness; as a result she places greater emphasis on her blackness, saying that "she was proud of her black race" and "letting her black inside out" (317). She even

Most importantly, this newly acquired family history not only gives Faith a sense of rootedness and belonging, and hence a firm foundation on which to return, it is also the basis of a new concept of Englishness that she brings home with her. In the family story, the private and the public narrative intersect: "the succession of family trees graphically represent 'the regeneration of generations' (Ricoeur), the story of the living and the dead, made up both of anecdotes and genealogies, and slavery and colonisation: the meeting point of private time and public time" (Bromley 2000, 138). Highlighting the entanglements of her Jamaican legacy with British history, her own lineage shows that both aspects of her identity are closely interconnected and supplement each another. As her aunt Coral says, "we are all the Mother Country's children" (*Fruit* 326). By uncovering this "shared past" (326) from both England and Jamaica, Faith resolves the contradiction of being 'black' and English:

> I am the granddaughter of Grace and William Campbell, I am the great-grandchild of Cecelia Hilton. I am descended from Katherine whose mother was a slave. I am the cousin of Afria. I am the nice of Coral Thompson and the daughter of Wade and Mildred Jackson. Let them say what they like. Because I am the bastard child of Empire and I will have my day. (327)

Her own family narrative is just as rooted in British history as those of her white friends'. From her English ancestor, "Mr Livingstone (plantation owner)", two branches lead to his "his other children in England" and his "other children in Jamaica" respectively.

The central symbol of the family tree in the novel also underscores the culture-specificity of family identity and the way that it is narrated. The pedigree chart, the diagrammatic schema of genealogical research, initially relies on documented history, on records and bureaucratic archives of dates and facts; it is deeply embedded in a culture of writing. Faith adapts this schema for the contrasting model of her own family tradition of oral history and communicative memory, there are no birth or death dates given in her version, only the

---

joins a group of people "who wanted to visit Africa to trace their ancestry" (318) and returns with the wish to be called Afria. Her story, which, like Faith's, is also about self-denial and the wish to be different, shows how the "Black West Indian experience [...] is twice diasporic": "The narrative of slavery – and its denial and silencing – is not the direct diasporic memory [...]. But it is what drives it. Understanding the shame of slavery makes sense of the subsequent stories which families told – whether of the white ancestor or the closeness of families through the links of consanguinity. [...] The stories celebrate family and affirm survival" (Chamberlain 2009, 185).

lines that tie the family together. Faith employs the family tree as a way to open up the concept of Englishness to include new forms of hybrid identities. Unlike Marion and Simon, whose family identities are based on (exclusive notions of) locality and place on the one hand, and objects that symbolise the material dimension of memory on the other, Faith builds her family identity on narrative. The stories transmitted through her family are the glue that binds the familial web together. In contrast with both of her friends' comparative models, these stories have the advantage of being mobile; through the medium of narrative, Faith can take her family back home with her. Faith's appropriation of the family tree diagram represents family connectedness across time and space and thus becomes an emblem of diasporic memory: "What links the family is kinship and lineage, neither of which rely on place for meaning." (Chamberlain 2009, 184). Moreover, when it is transferred to the related concept of Englishness, her model of narrative is not exclusive, but allows for different perspectives on national and imperial history, and consequently provides an open and inclusive frame that emphasises intersections and entanglements. At the end, Faith revises her own narrative: "I had thought my history started when the ship carrying my parents sailed from Jamaica and docked in England on Guy Fawkes' night. But I was wrong." (325) At the end of the novel, she also arrives back in England on Guy Fawkes' night, as if in a way reliving her parents' arrival and "coming home to tell everyone ... My mum and dad came to England on a banana boat." (339) The novel ends as it began, with the exception that this time the family tree fills the whole page, and the banana boat is no longer the beginning of a story that shuts off a past, but is now a door that opens out onto this past that is abundantly filled with family stories.

3.3 "Past tense, future imperfect": Breaking Free from Tangled Family Roots in Zadie Smith's *White Teeth* (2000)

When *White Teeth* was published in 2000, it was hailed as a literary sensation, "the outstanding début of the new millennium", as the *Observer* is quoted as saying on the cover of the paperback edition. The great public attention and extensive marketing campaign that accompanied its release was testimony to the fact that Black British writing had indeed reached the centre of the cultural mainstream.[68] However, it is not only "its unprecedented success and excessive

---

[68] See Pérez (2009, 144–148) for an overview of the novel's critical reception as "a landmark in the contemporary British literary panorama" (Pérez 2009, 144); Pérez also points out the more

media coverage" that make Smith's novel stand out as a "significant moment in Black British writing" (M. Thompson 2005, 122). The novel takes a decisive step away from the formal layout of the *bildungsroman*, which had by then been established as the most prolific and established genre of second-generation Black and Asian British literature (cf. Stein 2004; see also Stein 2002, 34). Although *White Teeth* shares its central themes with the issues raised in the Black British *bildungsroman*,[69] it does so along the lines of a different genre – that of the family novel –,[70] and accordingly promises a different perspective on the topic of migration and identity construction in contemporary Britain.

The choice of genre alone attests to the growing significance of family histories and extended family networks in second-generation writing and emphasises the relational aspect of identity construction. The family novel genre shifts the focus from a more linear type of narrative and an individually-centred approach to the life story, to a more rhizomatic structure displaying a transgenerational network of family relations and a first-hand experience of complex cultural constellations, thereby pursuing a tendency that was already present in the two novels previously dealt with in this chapter, albeit to different degrees. As Erll (2007, 117–122) elaborates, *White Teeth* features a number of formal aspects of the family novel genre, such as the complex constellation of characters covering multiple generations, a wider temporal horizon and the introduction of multiple perspectives. *White Teeth* thus clearly differs from the structure of the novels discussed so far. Instead of putting a single protagonist at its centre, it follows the entangled histories of three families with three different ethnic and cultural backgrounds in multicultural London from the 1970s through to the '90s: The Iqbals (who are Bangladeshi), the Jones family (who are Jamaican-English) and, a little less prominently, the Chalfens (a white English family with

---

negative voices among the reviewers and places the novel's critical success in relation to the excessive marketing campaign that accompanied its publication. See also Stein (2004, 180–181), and Walters (2005, 315), who notes that the "literary establishment has elected to define *White Teeth* as British" rather than Black British, a clear promotion of the novel's mainstream distribution.

69 Cf. Stein 2004, xii. Stein begins his study on the Black British 'novel of transformation' with a quote from *White Teeth*.

70 The distinctions between the terms *bildungsroman* and 'family novel' are rarely clearly defined. The lack of a consistent terminology is reflected in the coexistence of a variety of genre terms. Besides 'family novel', the terms 'family chronicle' and 'family saga' are also widely used. While Hirsch (1979) discusses the question as to whether the *bildungsroman* can be considered "a European, rather than a purely German genre" (Hirsch 1979, 294), Erll doubts that the term 'family novel' has already been elaborated enough to serve as a critical term in the discussion of English literature (2007, 117).

a Polish Jewish background). At the thematic level, the novel puts forward many genre-typical issues such as a perspective on history through the private lens of family history, intergenerational conflict, as well as a critical reflection on generationality, genealogy, and on questions of the differences between genetic and social determinants of identity. These topics are dealt with in various ways and on many levels, including the use of digressions and commentaries by the authorial narrator, the insertion of different text types, and, on the diegetic level, through story and focalisation. This multiplicity of registers and voices allows for a great variety of perspectives and (often opposing) stances and models of identity construction. The various characters with diverse backgrounds and from different generations, moreover, represent divergent concepts of identity, ethnic heritage and cultural belonging. There is, at the same time, a special focus on second-generation characters, through which the novel explores questions of nature versus nurture and different concepts of hybrid identities (cf. Erll 2007, 121). For the sake of comparability, this analysis will concentrate primarily, but not exclusively, on one strand of this complex novel and will focus on the character of Irie, the daughter of Archie Jones and Clara Bowden.

3.3.1 Root Canals: The Inescapability of (Family) History

The main plot line covers a longer time span in order to not only depict the younger (second) generation growing up in the 1980s and '90s, but also their parents' generation in the 1970s. There are four parts in the novel, each of which has a clear focus on one branch of the narrative and a temporal setting, which is indicated in the chapter overview. Each of these parts also has a temporal reference that lies outside the time frame of the main narrative and concerns a specific episode of particular importance to that narrative thread, which is also referenced in the table of contents: "Archie 1974, 1945", "Samad 1984, 1857", "Irie 1990, 1907", "Magid, Millat and Marcus 1992, 1999". While the year 1999 is only briefly hinted at in a short flash forward to the future, the other three chapters are concerned with specific episodes in the prehistory of the families: The first is set at the end of World War II, when Archie Jones and Samad Iqbal meet as soldiers of the British Empire, an event which forms the founding narrative of their friendship,[71] the second deals with the Indian Mutiny in 1857 as the found-

---

71 The act of going back in history is made explicit at the beginning of the chapter, "The Root Canals of Alfred Archibald Jones and Samad Miah Iqbal" (*Teeth* 83–122), when the narrator

ing myth of Samad Iqbal's family history,[72] while the third of these chapters takes the reader back to the great earthquake in Kingston, Jamaica in 1907, the setting for a decisive anecdote in the Bowdens' family history.[73] These chapters are entitled "Root Canals", evoking, as part of the dental imagery that pervades the novel, the idea of (sometimes hidden or invisible) sources of present actions and identities that reach well into the past. These historical chapters disrupt the chronology of the main narrative in order to connect the post-imperial multicultural London with its imperial prehistory (Erll 2007, 124). One of the many convictions expressed in the novel is that "old history will come out like wisdom teeth" (*Teeth* 304)[74] – and that the characters are bound to the past through their family heritage and descent. The metaphor of 'wisdom teeth' carries ambivalent connotations: Although the name is linked to the positive idea of gaining maturity and self-knowledge in the process of growing up, these teeth are an archaic rudiment that is not only dispensable but is also often the cause of painful infections or disease, and are more often than not required to be removed. Root canals, similarly, are mostly associated with painful inflammations and infections, as well as with complicated dental treatment.

The root-canal chapters counter the image of the 'historyless' immigrant, which the narrator explicitly takes up in a longer comment. She critically reflects on the assumed resourcefulness of immigrants who, according to the early twentieth century British assimilationist immigration policy, often referred to as the 'melting pot', were made to shed their pasts like a snake sheds its skin:

> Because we often imagine that immigrants are constantly on the move, footloose, able to change course at any moment, able to employ their legendary resourcefulness at every turn. We have been told of the resourcefulness of Mr Schmutters, or the footloosity of Mr Banajii, who sail into Ellis Island or Dover or Calais and step into their foreign lands as *blank people*, free of any kind of baggage, happy and willing to leave their difference at

---

announces "a meticulous inspection that would go beyond the heart of the matter to its marrow, beyond the marrow to the root – but the question is how far back do you want? How far will *do*? [...] Back, back *back*. Well, all right, then. Back to Archie spit-clean, pink-faced and polished" (83). This introduction to the leap in diegetic time gives an impression of the critical meta-discourse in the novel about questions of narrative and origins.

72 The chapter "The Root Canals of Mangal Pande" (244–261) is not set in 1857 but deals with Samad Iqbal's memorialisation and narrativisation of Mangal Pande's role in the mutiny.
73 "The Root Canals of Hortense Bowden" (356–364).
74 *Teeth* refers to Smith 2001 [2000]. Hereafter all references to the novel will use only page number, and, where necessary, *Teeth* for disambiguation.

the docks and take their chances in this new place, merging with the oneness of this greenandpleasantlibertarianlandofthefree. (465)[75]

Samad Iqbal, in particular, who traces his family history back to Mangal Pande, a key figure in the 1857 Indian Rebellion (especially from an Indian revisionary historiographical perspective),[76] employs this story as a usable past and a key element both for his own self-positioning and for the construction of a collective family identity (cf. Erll 2007, 125). In the face of this history, his twin sons Millat and Magid are the very opposite of being baggage-free and a blank slate. They feel "weighed down, burdened, unable to waver from their course or in any way change their separate, dangerous trajectories. They seem to make no progress [...], occupying a space equal to themselves and, what is scarier, equal to Mangal Pande's, equal to Samad Iqbal's. Two brothers trapped in the temporal instant." (*Teeth* 465) In this logic of lineage and genetic determination, which leaves no room for the freedom of individual space or the possibility of something new, space and time are contracted into a single space and a single instant, and thus, ultimately, become meaningless. In this view, there are no new beginnings, not even for immigrants, and there is no way to leave history behind, neither in space, nor in time. "This is the other thing about immigrants ('fugees, émigrés, travellers): they cannot escape their history any more than you yourself can lose your shadow." (466)

The two principles of destiny, determination, and fate on the one hand, and chance and indeterminacy on the other are respectively linked to the Iqbal and the Jones/Bowden family. While Millat and Magid seem trapped in a circular fatalism (507),[77] and are controlled by an "imperative secreted in the genes" (525) that determines their lives and actions, Irie's family is dictated by chaos and contingency. The "Root Canals" connected to Irie trace her family history back to her grandmother Hortense's birth during the earthquake in 1907, an episode that her mother Clara interprets as "luck. Luck and faith." (227) Irie's father Archie has similarly built his life on the principle of chance, symbolised by his habit of coin-tossing for every decision he has to make. The story of the

---

[75] As in *Fruit of the Lemon*, 'green and pleasant' is employed here as shorthand for Englishness (cf. footnote 180), just as 'libertarian land of the free' stands for the USA. See also 3.2.2 for an elaboration on the trope of historylessness.
[76] See also Erll 2006.
[77] Cf. also Samad's insight that he shares with Archie when they are soldiers: "the generations [...] speak to each other, Jones. It's not a line, life is not a line [...] it's a circle" (119). In the case of the Iqbal family, this circular model of family history feels so constrictive that it resembles a single dot.

earthquake is introduced as a "family memory" (356) that is shared by the chain of generations through a strong bodily link:

> Her [Clara's] own mother, when inside *her* mother (for if this story is to be told, we will have to put them all back inside each other like Russian dolls, Irie back in Clara, Clara back in Hortense, Hortense back in Ambrosia), was silent witness to what happens when all of a sudden an Englishman decides you need an education. (356)

The image of the Russian dolls for the transference of family memory follows a similar logic to the spatial and temporal contraction experienced by Millat and Magid; it hints at the inescapable cohesiveness of genealogical bonds and the contiguity of transmission in families.

3.3.2 Families of Choice: Irie's Search for 'Pure' Englishness

The two subject families, the Iqbals and the Jones, are linked to a third family called the Chalfens when Millat and Irie, a pair of rather unruly adolescents, are ordered by their school to join a "conduct management" (303) programme that sets them up with Joshua and his family for a twice-a-week study group. For Irie, who is going through a phase of self-hatred and total rejection of her Afro-Jamaican heritage, the Chalfens become her ideal image of an English middle-class family. Aged fifteen, she is at the peak of an identity crisis that becomes manifest in her rejection of her own body. Like Faith, she "lacks black referents, apart from her mother, to value the significance of her hybrid identity; she needs a complete family structure, she is looking for a genealogy and a past, roots to support her" (Pérez Fernández 2009, 149).[78] Her desire for physical transformation, it turns out, is a desire for Englishness, belonging and recognition: "There was England, a gigantic mirror, and there was Irie, without reflection. A stranger in a stranger land." (266) When she meets the Chalfens, her former wish to somehow rid herself of her "genetic fate" (266) and transform

---

78 Cf. 328: "From Irie's bedroom shrine of green-eyed Hollywood idols to the gaggle of white friends who regularly trooped in and out of her bedroom, Clara saw an ocean of pink skins surrounding her daughter". Irie's mother Clara tries to reassure her that she is "just built like an honest-to-God Bowden – don't you know you're fine?" (266). However, Clara herself is tall and slender; to Irie's chagrin "[t]he European proportions of Clara's figure had skipped a generation, and she [Irie] was landed instead with Hortense's substantial Jamaican frame" (265). Hortense, the grandmother, does not serve as a reference point as Irie's "sense of an extended family is made impossible due to her mother's neglect of Irie's relationship with her grandmother" (Pérez Fernández 2009, 149).

"her *wrongness*" (268) to meet the English standards of beauty turns into the strong wish to appropriate the Chalfens' identity.[79] "She [...] wanted to, well, kind of, *merge* with them. She wanted their Englishness. Their Chalfishness. The *purity* of it." (328, emphases in the original) Her exploration of the Chalfens is described with the colonialist imagery of an expedition voyage that becomes a leitmotiv in her identity formation process. "She was crossing borders, sneaking into England; it felt like some terribly mutinous act, wearing somebody else's uniform or somebody else's skin." (328) The mutiny hinted at here is not only a rebellion against her parents and her family of origin; her desire to be like the Chalfens is also an act of mutiny against her own self, because in adopting the Chalfens as her family of choice, she denies and gives up her birth family and heritage.

Irie's fantasy of exploration is also mutinous in that it upsets the Imperial world order in reversing the perspective of the coloniser and the colonised.[80] Irie, "assessing the Chalfens like a romantic anthropologist" (322) and intrigued by the "strange and wondrous" (321), adds an ironic twist to the Chalfen's obtrusively patronising behaviour, which reveals a clearly colonial imperialist mindset.[81] Their exoticising gaze, along with their stereotyped generalisations and ready-made opinions (cf. 319ff.), are thus returned by Irie, who, having "never been so close to this strange and beautiful thing, the middle class, [...] felt like Columbus meeting the exposed arawaks, not knowing where to look."

---

[79] Irie, "intent upon transformation, intent upon fighting her genes" (273) decides upon undergoing a physical make-over, which turns out to be a complete disaster and is covered in the chapter "The Miseducation of Irie Jones".

[80] This role reversal is constructed to great comic effect primarily through the level of discourse put forward by the overt narrator. Although Irie is described here as *feeling* like Columbus meeting with the exposed Arawaks, the feeling might be Irie's but the comparison does not necessarily have to be. Later, when Irie delves deeper into her family history, the narrator, speaking about the Arawaks, the indigenous people of Jamaica, clarifies things further: "Not that Irie had heard of those little sweet-tempered pot-bellied victims of their own sweet-tempers. Those were some *other* Jamaicans, fallen short of the attention-span of history." (400; emphasis in the original) In this way, the narrator's voice and the representation of the characters' thoughts and feelings are interfused throughout, and difficult to disentangle.

[81] The sense of border-crossing is very present on both sides, the Chalfens' and Millat and Irie's – all parties involved very aggressively want something from the other side and proceed to take it, an attitude reflected in the chapter's title "Canines: The Ripping Teeth". Along with the border-crossing, "boundaries among the three families begin to fade away and new social networks and alternative space(s) of interaction are created" (Pérez Fernández 2009, 149). See Pérez Fernández (2009, 149ff.) for a more extensive analysis of the production and meaning of space in *White Teeth*.

(321) The Chalfens, like "[p]ilgrims and prophets with no strange land" feel destined to spread civilisation and education,[82] and all tasks are delegated between Joyce and her husband Marcus tasks are delegated "[a]s on any missionary vessel" (323), with Marcus, as the biologist, experimenting with genetic engineering, and Joyce, as the botanist, in charge of the field of nurture.

One aspect of the Chalfens that fascinates Irie is the sense of scientific organisation, regularity and order – in short, what she sees as their 'purity'. The contrast to her own family background becomes most striking when she visits "Marcus's study at the very top of the house, by far her favourite room" (335). This room is unlike any place that Irie knows, a room that is solely devoted to the work that is being done in it, and not to the objects that it holds: "It wasn't like Clara's attic space, a Xanadu of crap, all carefully stored in boxes and labelled just in case she should ever need to flee this land for another one." (335–336) Unlike the packed "spare rooms of immigrants", in which all their possessions are stowed away to reassure them "that they *have* things now, where before they had nothing" (336), Marcus' study attests to the Chalfens' purity – a cleanliness that enables them to engage fully with the future instead of being held back by the past, as his FutureMouse© project shows. In Irie's eyes, Marcus stands in stark contrast to the other parents that she knows, her own father Archie and Millat's father Samad: "So there existed fathers who dealt in the present, who didn't drag ancient history around like a chain and ball. So there were men who were not neck-high and sinking in the quagmire of the past." (326)

However, the Chalfens are not completely devoid of history; on the contrary, the walls of the study are scattered with "photos of the Chalfen clan" (336). Among the "larger framed centrepieces" is a "map of the Chalfen family tree" as well as the portraits of pioneers in the study of genetics such as Mendel, Watson and Crick, and of his mentor (336–337). Marcus's work is thus framed by a coalescence of family and scientific ancestry – a relational network of the past and present that follows clear patterns of linearity, coherence, and causal order.[83] Irie is fascinated by the family tree, which is so intricately drawn that she can

---

[82] Irie's mother Clara feels reminded of her grandfather Captain Charlie Durham, an English colonial officer posted to Jamaica, who, after impregnating her grandmother Ambrosia, feels the need to infuse her with "a little English education" (356), as the phrase is passed down in the Bowden family. Part of this English education is, besides swinging a cricket bat, a recital of Blake's poem "Jerusalem", which again appears here as an epitome of Englishness (cf. 357).

[83] The combination of family photos and pictures representing Marcus's intellectual heritage suggests that Marcus sees himself as being part of a direct succession of these scientists in the sense of having a "spiritual pedigree" (Zerubavel 2003, 56).

only study "a small slice" of the "elaborate illustrated oak that stretched back into the 1600s and forward into the present day" (337). To Irie, the family tree exposes all of the differences between the Chalfens and her own family:

> For starters, in the Chalfen family everybody seemed to have a normal number of children. More to the point, everybody knew whose children were whose. [...] The marriages were singular and long lasting. Dates of birth and death were concrete. And the Chalfens actually *knew* who they were in 1675. Archie Jones could give no longer record of his family than his father's own haphazard appearance on the planet in the back-room of a Bromley public house circa 1895 or 1896 or quite possibly 1897, depending on which nonagenarian ex-barmaid you spoke to. Clara Bowden knew a little about her grandmother, and half believed the story that her famed and prolific Uncle P. had thirty-four children, but could only state definitively that her own mother was born at 2.45 p.m. 14 January 1907, in a Catholic church in the middle of the Kingston earthquake. The rest was rumour, folk-tale and myth (337–338).

The Chalfen family tree is characterised by facts, exact knowledge, regularity, and order. The concreteness of historical facts and dates and their foundation in written documentation of the past underpins the 'truth' value of the Chalfen family history in contrast to Irie's own, which follows "more of an oral tradition" (339) and which is marked by unreliability and indeterminacy.[84] Irie's idea of her family history is visualised by an inserted genealogical chart, which differs decidedly from the Chalfen's traditional illustration of a family tree in its original arborescent shape, and thus draws our attention to the level of form and the historical variance in genealogical representations. The depiction of an oak tree as a basis for mapping genealogical succession invokes a specifically European tradition of "domestic family trees" (Bouquet 1996, 45) that can be traced to the sacred genealogies of the Bible and a long tradition of illustration of Christ's line of descent, as well as pointing to a tradition of relying on lineage as a central source of political legitimacy (cf. Bouquet 1996, 48; see also Macho 2002).[85] This kind of family tree conveys a certain degree of 'snobbishness':

---

[84] The question of truth vs. fiction is raised by Marcus, who advises Irie not to take the Iqbal family history seriously: "One part truth to three parts fiction in that family, I fancy." (339) He implies that due to the fact that "the Chalfens have always written things down" (339) naturally makes their account of history more trustworthy. This hierarchy of prioritising written over oral history and tradition is indebted to the Eurocentric world view that the Chalfens represent.

[85] The Chalfens' genealogical oak tree is reminiscent of zoologist Ernst Haeckel's "Pedigree of Man" from 1874, which, while also formed in the shape of an oak, constructs a "genealogical narrative of evolutionary history" (Zerubavel 2012, 41) based on the concept of co-descent, and thus presents another piece of scientific prehistory to Marcus Chalfen's own work in genetic engineering.

"Like animal breeders, families use *pedigree* as their key to nobility." (Zerubavel 2003, 62; cf. Castañeda 2002, 75)[86] In contrast, Irie's family tree is based on oral history rather than written documentation, and thereby represents, particularly in the colonial context of the Caribbean, "the hidden and sometimes secret histories of those disenfranchised from the historical record by class, race or gender" (Chamberlain 2006, 7). Unlike the Chalfens' tree, a typical example of "middle-class intellectuals' borrowing of the pedigree" (Bouquet 1996, 45), Irie's mental image of her genealogy follows more recent models developed for scientific use, and combines elements of anthropological family tree diagrams with representations of genetic trees (cf. Mitchell 2014, 267ff.). While the illustration of the tree suggests the traditional form of an *ahnentafel*, which positions the progenitor at the bottom (in the tree's stem) and traces his or her descendants in an ascending line over several generations following the direction of the tree's branches (cf. Weigel 2006, 45), the more modern "anthropological design of family trees typically orients the direction of time from the top to the bottom of a page" (Mitchell 2014, 267). This form of genealogical tree is "descendant-centric" (Zerubavel 2012, 66), which means that, following Irie's point of view, the chart represents a past-oriented deduction of origin that progresses from the living to the dead (cf. Weigel 2006, 45).

In its use of symbols, which draws on the scientific use of tree diagrams in the study of heredity and the passing on of genetic traits (cf. Castañeda 2002, 61–64; Mitchell 2014, 268ff.), Irie's family tree emphasises the difference between written and oral tradition and form: The scientific precision of the genealogical chart clashes absurdly with the vagueness of the information and the conversational tone in which her own family tree is delivered. Rather than yielding information with the accuracy of scientific evidence, the symbols mark irregularities in the various family relationships and expose gaps in the transmitted history: "& = copulated with [outside of marriage] / % = paternity unsure / ? = child's name unknown / G = brought up by grandmother" (338). The tree thus reveals the very elements that dominate Irie's idea of family history – chaos, chance, and indeterminacy – as patterns of descent and inheritance in her family (where the combination "%?G" recurs remarkably often). Dates and time specification are given as "Way Back When-Lord Knows" or "Hol Heap of Time" (338). Some information on certain individuals is just as sketchy, for example, the "God knows how many women" that Great Uncle P. produced his 34 chil-

---

[86] As Bouquet (1996, 47) elaborates, the connotations of snobbishness and animal breeding "include the control of procreation through keeping written records that enable the careful channelling of 'blood' as a key to nobility".

dren with, Great Auntie Patricia's liaisons with "some no-good ragamuffins", or "Great-great-great-Grandma (Lady T?)". Importantly, Irie's tree indicates the degrees of kinship with reference to herself (all relatives carry relationship titles such as Grandmother, Auntie, etc.), and thus defies the objectivity of the genealogical chart, which, as a diagrammatic representation, is normally devoid of perspective. The added element of perspective brings the pedigree closer to the realm of narrative, as do the colloquialisms used in it, which indicate how details of family history have become preserved in fixed phrasal units through the repetitions of family storytelling.

Chance and coincidence are the controlling principles of her family history, which strikingly contrasts with the concept of order, linearity, and continuity as represented by the family tree schemata. The incongruity of the diagram thus expresses the disparity between Irie's sense of unease and inadequacy with regard to her perception of herself and her family as being ill-fitting and flawed on the one hand, and her desire to be like the Chalfens on the other. Under Marcus's influence, she already senses that "her brain changed from something mushy to something hard and defined, as she slowly gained a familiarity with the Chalfen way of thinking" (335). Here, the family tree is not inserted on a paratextual level, but is seamlessly inserted into a passage that is focalised through Irie, and therefore might be read as representing the imposition of the hard systematics of the 'Chalfen way of thinking' over the 'mushiness' of her mind. This family tree reveals "genealogical chaos" (Erll 2007, 128) instead of clarity and knowledge, more gossip than history, more gaps than facts; and clearly, most of the information is missing.

3.3.3 "The perfect blankness of the past": Claiming Family History as a Chance for New Beginnings

As Irie's family tree indicates, there are a lot of incoherent details that are circulating in her family, but there seems to be no clear narrative or knowledge about the past. In contrast with Samad Iqbal's obsession with family history, Irie's parents seem to be less bound up with the past. After the experiences of his failed first marriage and a failed suicide attempt, Archie, "tiny and rootless" (11), undergoes the freedom of a new beginning, revering men's "ancient ability to leave a family and a past. They just unhook themselves, like removing a fake beard, and skulk discreetly back into society, changed men. Unrecognizable. In this manner, a new Archie is about to emerge." (18). On the first morning of his new life, while telling himself to never "for gawd's sake look back" (19), he randomly and fittingly turns up at the remnants of an "End of the World" party organised by Jehovah's Witnesses. When Archie meets Clara at this party, "her world had just disappeared" (45), partly due to the unfulfilled prophecy, and partly as a consequence of a scooter accident, in which she had knocked her upper teeth out. While previously, "Clara was from somewhere. She had *roots*." (27), her knocked-out teeth and the loss of her faith signal that these roots have been shaken. Irie's family tree through its gaps and imprecisions illustrates the lack of a coherent tradition and transmission of family history. With its hints and allusions, it reflects what Irie calls "the Jones/Bowden gift for secret histories, stories you never got told, history you never entirely uncovered, rumour you never unravelled" (379).

Irie thus grows up in a family of "open secrets" (Zerubavel 2003, ix). In a similar manner to the protagonists in *Anita and Me* and *Fruit of the Lemon*, she feels that her parents hold back information and deny her access to their past, thereby piquing her curiosity all the more. Irie's description of her family vividly illustrates the way in which secrets in families are embedded within the family stories that are told and sewn into the very fabric of family communication (cf. Smart 2011a, 543). The "End of the World" party where Irie's parents have met symbolises both their wish to close this chapter of their respective pasts, which leads to them having incoherent life narratives and produces the feeling of ignorance and incomprehension regarding her parents' lives in Irie. Their secrecy and reticence regarding the family past is epitomised by Clara's false teeth. This is a secret that Irie stumbles over by chance one night when she "embarked upon a late-night attack" (*Teeth* 376) on her mother in order to finally get permission to take a year off after her A-levels to travel around the Indian subcontinent and Africa – an issue that has completely divided the family over the previous months because neither party is willing to concede ground on the issue.[87] Irie knows "from experience that her mother was most vulnerable when in bed; late at night she spoke softly like a child, her fatigue gave her a pronounced lisp; it was at this point that you were most likely to get whatever it was you'd been pining for" (376). This time, however, she accidentally kicks over the glass in which Clara keeps her teeth at night. Irie feels betrayed by this

---

[87] Clara mistrusts the persistence of colonial thinking that is evident in the idea of 'a year off', whether organised privately or with a volunteer programme, and which, she feels, serve to perpetuate the structures of inequality as based on the idea of 'development' that reifies the Global North-South Divide: "Permishon for *what*? Koo go and share and ogle at poor black folk? Dr Livingshone, I prejume? Iz dat waht you leant from da Shalfenz? Because if thash what you want, you can do dat here. Jush sit and look at me for shix munfs!" (378)

"disguise" (378) and the secrecy that it implies,[88] which, she feels, adds to "a long list of parental hypocrisies and untruths" (379). To her, family life is "littered with clues, and suggestions" about her own and her parents' past, and is reduced to faint memories and snatches of information picked up from somewhere, which make no sense to her and are never explained, such as "shrapnel in Archie's leg ... photo of strange white Grandpa Durham ... the name 'Ophelia' and the word 'madhouse' ... a cycling helmet and an ancient mudguard [...] faint memory of a late night car journey, waving to a boy on a plane", and so on (379).[89] Irie's inventory of clues lists stories that can neither be forgotten, nor actively remembered, and, in particular, cannot be narrated and shared; as they are not incorporated into a coherent family narrative. As she cannot dispose of them, they get in her way, cluttering the house like litter lying about randomly. She decides that "Millat was right: these parents were damaged people, missing hands, missing teeth. These parents were full of information you wanted to know but were too scared to hear. But she didn't want it any more, she was tired of it. She was sick of never getting the whole truth." (379)

The act of tipping over of the glass containing the false teeth thus symbolises Irie's revolt against family secrecy. Her list of clues shows how family secrets exist at the fringes of the family narrative; they are attached to every story that is told, and to every object that holds memories of the past.[90] The false teeth image recurs throughout the novel and is connected to the (more or less deliberate) suppression of information in families, and the way in which information is controlled in the process of constructing family (and individual) narratives. Secrets are a by-product of family communication – in the same way that forgetting is a necessary by-product of remembering, and selection is a part of narrativisation. The metaphor of the false teeth, however, suggests that there are limits to controlling the narrative, because there are elements in life, and in families, that can neither be smoothed over by a coherent narrative, nor simply submitted to the realm of forgetting, and so they persist in the form of secrets, which eventually re-surface. When Samad brings his son Magid to the airport to send him to Bangladesh – an episode that also appears in Irie's list –, he already feels the burden of his decision: "Years from now, even hours after that

---

[88] Clara claims that this secrecy was not intended on her part: "It wasn't that she had deliberately not told her. There just never seemed a good time." (378–379)
[89] This list covers details of her parents' lives from before she was born in addition to details from her own childhood (Magid being sent to Bangladesh) that have not been transformed into an understandable memory in the form of narrative.
[90] In line with the dental imagery of the novel, family secrets could be said to be deposits that gather in the periodontal pockets.

plane leaves, this will be history that Samad tries not to remember. That his memory makes no effort to retain. A sudden stone submerged. False teeth floating silently to the bottom of a glass." (209)[91]

After her chance discovery of the set of false teeth, Irie decides to "return[...] to sender" (379):[92] Instead of flying to Jamaica as Faith did in *Fruit of the Lemon*, Irie's return journey through London takes her "deep into the heart of it, where only the N17 would take her at this time of night" (379), to her grandmother Hortense Bowden. Here, Irie experiences something that is not so much a culture shock, but a "shock of sameness" (381). Her grandmother's insistence on calling her by her full name, Irie Ambrosia, indicates that Irie can connect with a past through her that was cut off from her as a result of the argument between Clara and her mother.[93] To Irie, who once more takes on the role of explorer, Hortense's house turns into an "*adventure*. In cupboards and neglected drawers and in grimy frames were the secrets that had been hoarded for so long" (399): pictures of her great-grandmother Ambrosia and of her great-grandfather Charlie 'Whitey' Durham, photos of her mother in her schooldays, "grinning maniacally, the true horror of the teeth revealed" (399),[94] and other documents from the family's Jamaican past ("birth certificates, maps, army reports, news articles", 400). Left to rummage through these documents on her own, Irie "laid claim to the past – her version of the past – aggressively, as if retrieving misdi-

---

[91] The image is used earlier in the novel with regard to the selectiveness of the official memory of history: "a day that History has not remembered. That Memory has made no effort to retain. A sudden stone submerged. False teeth floating silently to the bottom of a glass. 6 May 1945." (90–91)

[92] Despite her father's attempt to play things down by declaring that "It's just some bloody teeth. So now you know. It's not the end of the world." (379) This incident invokes both his and Clara's own respective ends of their worlds before they met at the eponymous party and suggests that this might be a similar turning point in Irie's life, because for her, "it was, in a way" (379).

[93] Clara has radically turned her back on her family and her past as a consequence of the "convivial relationship" (40) that her high-school boyfriend Ryan Topps strikes up with her mother, which excludes her and eventually leads to their break-up and to Clara's disaffection with the Jehovah's Witnesses, as Ryan becomes a believer and teams up with her mother, who is "now trying to save *her*" (41; emphasis in the original). As a child, her father took Irie to her grandparents, but Clara stopped these secret visits as soon as she found out about them (cf. 381).

[94] The "true horror" hints at the set of buck teeth that Clara used to share with her daughter when she still had her own front teeth (cf. 28, 268). This revelation of the physical sameness between daughter and mother establishes a first link to the matrilineal past.

rected mail. So *this* was where she came from. This all *belonged* to her, her birthright" (400; emphasis in the original).

Unlike Faith, whose exploration of her family's history is a way of acquiring 'a past' (*Fruit* 325–326) that she had been lacking through her conversations with relatives, Irie, in constructing her own version of the past, creates something new that she can see entirely as her own. Family history is not transmitted here through oral storytelling; it is a story that she writes herself, based on the stray documents that she finds in rummaging through the items in her grandmother's house. These documents leave much room for interpretation. In her eyes, Captain Durham is "dashing" in the picture, "handsome and melancholy, [...] looking worldy-wise despite his youth, looking every inch the Englishman, looking like he could tell someone or another a thing or two about something. Maybe Irie herself." (*Teeth* 400) Her reading of the photo thus goes strictly against the family lore, which refers to him as a "[d]jam fool bwoy [who] taut he owned everyting he touched" (354) and approves of Ambrosia's ultimate rejection of him and his offer of education for her. Other than being pre-assembled stories, these documents leave much room for interpretation, as does Irie's ignorance. In this fashion, she imagines herself "back to somewhere, somewhere quite fictional, for she'd never been there. Somewhere Columbus called St Jago but the arawaks stubbornly re-named Xaymaca, the name lasting longer than they did. *Well-wooded and Watered.*" (400) Thus newly discovering Jamaica and her family background, Irie turns back time and history itself.

This newfound territory frees Irie from the influence of the Chalfens and her desire for pure Englishness: "It just seemed tiring and unnecessary all of a sudden, that struggle to force something out of the recalcitrant English soil. Why bother when there was now this other place? (For Jamaica appeared to Irie as if it were newly made. Like Columbus himself, just by discovering it she had brought it into existence.)" (402) Her previous desire to "merge with the Chalfens, to be of one flesh" had emerged from the wish to be "separated from the chaotic, random flesh of her own family and transgenically fused with another. A unique animal. A new breed." (342) This desire was therefore driven not so much by the aim of acquiring a different past or a more elaborate family history, and thus a stronger sense of rootedness or belonging; on the contrary, Irie saw the chance for renewal in genetic hybridity. Now, the discovery of her family history is described in terms of the discovery of Jamaica, "fresh and untainted and without past or dictated future – a place where things simply *were*. No fiction, no myths, no lies, no tangled webs – this is how Irie imagined her homeland." (402) The journey to the past takes Irie back to the beginning not only of her own family history, a place where "a young white captain could meet a young black girl with no complications" (402); the discovery of Jamaica is also the start of colonialism and the Imperialist project, it is the foundation point for the 'Happy Multicultural Land', of the great migration movements during and after colonialism, of "the century of strangers, brown, yellow and white [...] the century of the great immigrant experiment" (326).

This image of the freshly discovered Jamaica presents itself as a possible homeland for Irie, who is attracted by its quality of sounding "like a beginning. The beginningest of beginnings. [...] A blank page." (402) Her desire for "the perfect blankness of the past" (402) – which is just as paradoxical as her vision of the blank homeland – invokes the dehistoricisation of the land and its people carried out by the settlers and colonialists (cf. Janmohamed 1995, 22). In this context, Irie's vision of a homeland also has a self-empowering side, giving voice to the subaltern through "the resources of deconstruction" (Parry 1995, 37),[95] for Irie's gesture of going back and back can easily be read as an act of deconstruction. This idea of homeland thus offers her the chance to escape the confining bonds of her family with its baggage of pasts and entangled roots. Irie's vision of going back to the beginning, "back to the source of the river, to the start of the story, to the homeland..." (407) is a counter fantasy to Samad Iqbal's deterministic view of family history and legacy. The myths of family history offer up bottom-up counter-narratives to the official colonialist historiography and focus on intercultural encounters and transactions, thereby bringing to the fore the long-standing entanglement of histories to the fore as being a basis for the creation of a multicultural society (cf. Erll 2007, 125).

This involvement finds its most pertinent form through families and intergenerational transmission, just as the act of getting involved with one another (as the euphemistic term for sexual or romantic intimacy indicates) is often the beginning of families (cf. 439). Irie "didn't *want* to be involved in the long story of those lives, but she *was*" (459; emphasis in the original); eventually, she attempts to escape from her involvement in them through the very act of getting involved, first with Millat and shortly afterwards with Magid, the identical twins.[96] As a result, she becomes pregnant with a child whose paternity is impossible to determine: "[a] perfectly plotted thing with no real coordinates. A

---

[95] Benita Parry here quotes Gayatri Chakravorty Spivak's essay on "Imperialism and Sexual Difference" (1986). The colonialist fiction of there being a new beginning makes the reader suspicious of Irie's utopian vision of finding a "neutral place" at the end of the novel.

[96] Magid comments afterwards: "It seems to me [...] that you have tried to love a man as if he were an island and you were shipwrecked and you could mark the land with an X. It seems to me it is too late in the day for all that." (463)

map to an imaginary fatherland." (516).[97] In the end, Irie thus opts for the randomness and contingency that runs in her family, and gives up on the idea of perfect order and purity. It is precisely the openness of such randomness, and the many gaps and blanks in her family transmission that allow her to truly claim the past as her own and to envision it as a chance for new beginnings. "Some secrets are permanent. In a vision, Irie has seen a time, a time not far from now, when roots won't matter any more because they can't because they mustn't because they're too long and they're too tortuous and they're just buried too damn deep. She looks forward to it." (527) Irie envisions a new truly hybrid family that is not confined by the fetters of roots and origin, and "give[s] up the *very idea* of belonging" (407; emphasis in the original).[98]

'Root' has increasingly become a dead metaphor that has lost its quality as an image and has become a fixed term. In *White Teeth*, Zadie Smith brings the metaphor back to life, using it as a tool to explore the complexity of legacies and genealogies. By shifting the attention from 'roots' to 'root canals', she reinvests a cliché word with a new sensuous energy, reminding us of the hiddenness of roots, their intimate connection with the body and their high degree of sensitivity. Speaking of root canals invokes something extremely delicate and which brings with it an imminent sense of pain. Her use of the word 'roots' is highly ambivalent: it conveys positive connotations of belonging and self-positioning as a source of self-empowerment ("tradition was culture, and culture led to roots, and these were good, these were untainted principles [...] roots were roots and roots were good", 193);[99] but roots can also obstruct free personal development, "not allowing anything else to grow" (195). The logic of roots with its claim to heritage, its sense of pride and its emphasis on belonging, as represented by Samad Iqbal, is clearly too rigid. Towards the end of the novel, Irie in particular becomes more and more apprehensive of the way in which roots

---

97 To know for sure would "require[...] her to go back, back, back to the root, to the fundamental moment when sperm met egg, when egg met sperm – so early in this history it cannot be traced. Irie's child can never be mapped exactly nor spoken of with any certainty. Some secrets are permanent. In a vision, Irie has seen a time, a time not far from now, when roots won't matter any more because they can't because they mustn't because they're too long and they're too tortuous and they're just buried too damn deep. She looks forward to it." (527)

98 Samad's nightmare of unbelonging and the complete loss of his belief system, when "birthplaces are accidents, [...] everything is an *accident*" (407) is attractive rather than terrifying for Irie; "the land of accidents sounded like *paradise* to her. Sounded like freedom." (408)

99 Cf. Erll (2007, 125): Samad Iqbal's "imaginierte Genealogie verweist jedoch auf die Funktion des Erinnerns an Familiengeschichte: Die Rückwendung zu den – realen oder nur vorgestellten – Vorfahren ermöglicht Selbstverortung und Identitätsstiftung". See also Schäfer (2009).

branch out and become unmanageable. The general entanglement of everything is reflected in the word "involvement", which is described by Alsana Iqbal as "a consequence of living, a consequence of occupation and immigration, of empires and expansion, of living in each other's pockets" (439). The pervasive dental imagery of the novel allows for a series of extensions of the metaphor, such as Clara's false teeth and Irie's "thick metal retainer" (268), to discuss the different ways of losing, restoring, or reconstructing one's tradition.[100] Like a dentist, the novel's narrator also uncovers the root canals and lays bare the sensitive hidden bonds that connect the main plot line, set in post-imperial London, with its imperial prehistory, thus revealing the intricate intertwining of contemporary multicultural Britain with its colonial past. Smith's novel thus deconstructs the essentialising rhetoric and (delusional) fantasy of roots and creates ample creative space for their reconstruction through imagination.

3.4 Concluding Thoughts: Family History and Genealogy as a Framework for Narratives of the Self

The novels analysed in this chapter illustrate how migration often involves a rupture of family transmission, which leads to serious feelings of a deficit among their second-generation protagonists. Meena, Faith, and Irie all share the sentiment of having inadequate material for their identity construction, which they overcome – each in their own way – by appropriating a family past and constructing a sense of family origin. Taking "family and kinship as a significant means of framing and understanding the self" (Lawler 2014, 47), each of the protagonists embarks on a genealogical search. *Fruit of the Lemon* and *Anita and Me* both show the importance of coherence and continuity as a basis for an integrative life narrative not only for one's own story of the self, but also beyond it. A continuous family narrative that transcends the protagonist's life span places them into the wider context of family relationships and meanings. The genealogical search for identity illustrates the importance that an intergenerational family narrative has for the creation of a meaningful self. The concept of "family as a framework for understanding one's self" (Fivush 2008, 55) not only embeds one's story "in the story of others in the past and in the present" (Fivush 2008, 55), but also links the individual life to the larger setting of transnational history. The uncovering and re-appropriation of family history in the

---

[100] Very fittingly, Marcus envisions that dentistry would be an ideal profession for Irie (cf. 368).

three novels produces stories and memories that explicitly challenge the authority and legacy of colonial discourse and myths, and thus provides for a means of empowerment through a counter-narrative. The novels' protagonists thus also find a basis for countering the continuities of racism and discrimination in present-day Britain, and for calling purist notions of culture and identity into question.

In focusing on the search for origins, the novels emphasise the diachronic as well as the synchronic dimension of the relational self. The growing concern with the significance of the 'intergenerational self' in second-generation novels also affects their formal layout. *Anita and Me* remains close in structure to the coming-of-age narrative, which is, however, supplemented and enhanced by the element of reconnection with family, home, and the past. While Meena's maturation process is set off by a severe crisis resulting in total isolation, it is overcome only with the help of her grandmother as a benign ancestral figure with the result that, at the end, Meena is seen to rejoin the family circle.[101] Even more so than in *Anita and Me*, Faith's 'education' (in the sense of the *bildungsroman*) in *Fruit of the Lemon* is a lesson in family history. The novel does not ultimately promote individuality as the classical *bildungsroman* narrative does, but, on the contrary, emphasises relationality by highlighting the connections of Faith's own story with the other stories in her family. In the end, this connectivity, which is symbolised in the image of the family tree, is the key to her successful identity formation. At the discourse level, Faith's autodiegetic narration makes more and more room for other narratives and voices once she travels to Jamaica; the stories that are shared in the family intersect with her own story in a similar manner to the way in which her narrative voice becomes suffused with the voices of her family's oral history. The linear chronology of Faith's story of development is thus opened up and expanded into the past, and the formal and thematic layout of the *bildungsroman* is transformed to additionally include the genealogical and historical preoccupations of the family novel. Only through this perspective of family history is Faith able to regain the agency she lost over the first part of the novel, having become "increasingly passive and spectatorial, reduced ultimately to the confines of her room" (Bromley 2000, 135). This

---

[101] She even becomes, at least for a while, "a walking cliché of the good Indian daughter" (302). She has taken a new pride in her family's origins that now allows her to strategically play up her Indianness for her own advantage, as indicated in the Preface. Meena thus still represents a performative notion of cultural identity, but her options have decisively expanded. Moreover, her positive identification with her ethnicity gives her the backbone to self-confidently deal with everyday forms of racism in British society, such as in her confrontation with Sam Lowbridge.

tendency to open up the novel's story line towards both the individual and the collective past, which can be observed in both *Anita and Me* and *Fruit of the Lemon*, is taken up in *White Teeth*, raised to a meta-level and given a self-critical and ironic twist. In this novel, the shift from the paradigmatic Black British *bildungsroman* to the transcultural multigenerational novel is made complete. The multi-perspective narration critically compares and contrasts the different discourses on migration, genealogy, and identity construction between determinism and constructionism. With the character of Irie, the novel questions a simple 'rootedness' in the past, and demonstrates another form of empowerment and self-advancement that lies in the overcoming of "dysfunctional family trees" (Erll 2014, 403). Read optimistically, Irie's act of claiming a past puts into positive use the parent generation's reticence, as it creates new possibilities for the imagination and therefore holds great potential for identity construction. In the end, the parents' silence, in all three novels, becomes "the motor of the fictional imagination" (Hirsch 1996, 661; see also Bromley 2000, 134).

4 Family Secrets and Religious Conflict in the Muslim Diaspora

In the field of Black and Asian British literature the issue of Islam and the representation of Muslim identities has become a growing concern and a topic of debate that has gained much public attention and recognition. Over the last two decades, writers of Muslim descent have become increasingly visible in British literature, their work helping to give off the impression of a great diversity under the umbrella term of British Islam. Importantly, 'Muslim writing'[1] has brought attention to the axis of religion in migrant identity constructions and to the importance of recognising religious affiliation as a crucial factor for intersectional approaches to contemporary British literature. As the importance of the issue of representation with regard to Muslim writing indicates, religious belief is much more than a question of personal and private choice. Rather, it is a system of cultural practices and values that are transmitted down through the family. It heavily affects an individual's relationships with other family members, the family's connection with their community, and the ways in which people are perceived from the outside, or how they perceive the outside world. The following chapter deals with the more general theme of family secrets and silences through the perspective of (incongruous) belief systems and values and the impact that they have on family relationships and the family narrative.

In the context of migration then, Muslim identity is no longer seen to be confined to the domain of a family's cultural heritage but has now almost in-

---

[1] The way in which the term 'Muslim writing' is used will always provoke further discussion. It is important to not, therefore, that its use here is meant to be synonymous with 'writing by authors of Muslim heritage', regardless of the individual author's personal belief or faith. This understanding of 'Muslim writing' excludes books featuring Muslim characters written by writers who are non-Muslim and who do not have a Muslim family background (as in Zadie Smith's *White Teeth*). For a more elaborate discussion of what constitutes 'Muslim writing' see Claire Chambers (2011, 5–10), who takes "a broad view of the category 'Muslim'" as denoting a "civilizational heritage" (C. Chambers 2011, 10). This chapter will compare and contrast a South Asian British writer with an Arab British writer to illustrate the variety of angles that can be considered in any discussion of Muslim representation in present-day Britain. It thus transcends a narrower grouping along the lines of regional categories (as in R. Ahmed's book on *Writing British Muslims*, 2005, which deals with "contemporary fiction authored by writers of South Asian Muslim heritage", 16). For an overview of contemporary South Asian Muslim writing in Britain see R. Ahmed (2005, 16–20).

stantly become a public issue. With regard to the positioning of British Muslim identities and the representational politics of British Islam, one can make out two defining moments in recent history.[2] The first concerns the public book burning of Salman Rushdie's novel *The Satanic Verses* in Bradford in January 1989. This protest by Muslim groups threw multicultural Britain into a fundamental crisis, as it highlighted what were seen to be irreconcilable differences between East and West. More importantly, however, the book burning marked "the breakdown of traditional alliances within and between Britain's various non-white communities" (Procter 2006, 102), and highlighted the fact that the comprehensive concept of 'Black British' did no longer align itself with the self-conceptions of British Muslims. Significantly, it was questions of representation and recognition that ignited the book burning protests, as large groups of British Asians in particular (cf. C. Chambers 2011, 9) felt that their specific history and experiences in Britain were silenced and denied. In retrospect, this instance of agency has been framed as *the* defining factor in forging Muslim identity and presence in Britain, and has been regarded as having "paradigm-shifting centrality [... for] contemporary representations of British Muslims" (C. Chambers 2011, 9). In this light, the Rushdie Affair can be seen as exemplary of what Stuart Hall describes in his seminal essay "New Ethnicities" (1996b [1988]) as a shift in 'Black' British culture: the scattering of one single difference into a variety of differences that include, among others, the axis of religion as an axis along which identity may be formed. Thus it has raised awareness of the fact that multicultural Britain encompasses various "groups and communities with, in fact, very different histories, traditions, and ethnic identities" (Hall 1996b [1988], 163).

In a different vein, the Rushdie Affair has also largely been cast as a starting point for attempts to construct a genealogy of Islamism in Britain and Europe,[3] and as an event that paved the way to the second watershed moment in British Muslim writing, the 9/11 terrorist attacks. Since the onset of the "War-On-Terror Decade" (Falkenhayner 2014) and the rise of Islamophobia, the issue of how Muslims are represented has become highly contested and politicised, but has had the effect of drawing more attention to Muslim writing (cf. C. Chambers

---

[2] For the following, cf. also Childs and Green (2013, 95–97), who expound on the connection between the Rushdie Affair and 9/11, and its legacy for contemporary British Muslim writers.
[3] Cf. Falkenhayner (2014, 3): "For many [the Rushdie affair of 1989] had become an event of inauguration either for Islamism in the West or for the emergence of an assertive European Islam." See Falkenhayner (2014) for an extensive overview and analysis of the cultural impact of the Rushdie Affair on British culture and identities.

2011, 13). The two books discussed in this chapter are regarded as post-9/11 novels as they both, in very different ways, deal with religious fundamentalism and the political and social climate that fosters it.⁴ In *The Road from Damascus*, the plot is set at some point around the time of the 2001 terrorist attacks, which heavily influence the novel's discussion of Muslim identities and its perspective of the second generation's attraction to a politicised Islam, whereas *Maps for Lost Lovers* is set in the late 1990s and therefore recalls a pre-9/11 Britain. Nevertheless, its investigation into "the routes/roots of racial tensions and religious divisions in contemporary British society" (McCulloch 2012, 77) can be read as a commentary on post 9/11 concerns. Both novels focus on the conflict between belief and non-belief as a divisive force both within families and the migrant community itself. Interestingly, the conflict is not reduced to being a simple generational clash as the two texts delve into the complexities and diversities inherent in the topics of religious belief, secularism, and identities of Muslim heritage.⁵

Although the two novels differ widely, they share a similar theme in that religion and fundamentalism are alienating forces that tear families apart when ideology and unbending dogma are held higher than family values and the love between people, be it romantic or familial. The disintegration of family becomes palpable in both novels and involves a breakdown of communication. As silences grow, the rift between family members widens and the boundaries harden. Both novels reveal the corrosive effect of family secrets on collective family identity and narrative unity.

4.1 Migration and Loss: Family Relationships under the Burden of Cultural Trauma in Nadeem Aslam's *Maps for Lost Lovers* (2004)

Maps for Lost Lovers, Nadeem Aslam's second novel, offers a rather different perspective on post-migration communities and families in Britain in comparison to the novels dealt with in the previous chapter. He obviously paints a much

---

4 McCulloch (2012, 88), e.g., describes *Maps for Lost Lovers* as "a post-9/11 novel that was written before and after that moment in history, [...] though mention of extremism only exists on the fringes of the narrative". For the novel's linkages to 9/11 see also Aslam's own comments in Brace (2004), and Yaqin (2012, 104).
5 See also Childs and Green (2013, 95–97) for the connection of the Rushdie Affair and 9/11 as a "socio-political backdrop" to *Maps for Lost Lovers*. Cf. also R. Ahmed (2015, 6–7).

bleaker image of multiculturalist society than the previous authors, in that the environment depicted in his novel is marked by all of the severe problems that are faced by modern societies all over the globe: racism and religious fanaticism, parallel societies, enclave cultures, and a deep schism between diverse ethnic and religious groups. As he was born in Pakistan and migrated to England with his family at the age of fourteen, Aslam himself cannot be regarded as a typical second-generation writer and thus defies narrow classifications under groupings such as generational or national affiliation.[6] What is more, he also gives more weight to the point of view of the first generation of immigrants over that of the second generation in his depiction of the tensions that exist within immigrant families and communities.

The novel is set in a Pakistani-British neighbourhood in a Northern English industrial town that the South Asian British community exclusively refers to as *Dasht-e-Tanhaii*, which is alternately translated in the novel as "The Desert of Loneliness" or "The Wilderness of Solitude".[7] The narrative revolves around an honour killing that occurred five months prior to the beginning of the novel. An unmarried couple, Chanda and Jugnu, had moved in together and were consequently murdered by the girl's two brothers.[8] Shaken by this event, the community waits in expectation of the results of the police investigation and court proceedings. The trial against, and the final resolution of the case, which ends in the conviction of Chanda's brothers, constitutes the end of the one-year arc

---

6 Cf. Aslam's comment on the categorisation of his novels so that they appear in different sections of the bookstore (C. Chambers 2011, 151–152). His choice of topics and settings for his other novels illustrates his transnational outlook as a writer. Having spent most of his private and professional life in England, he is, however, widely seen as a British novelist and generally included in the respective lists and overviews. However, the literary prizes awarded for his novels attest to his classification as both South Asian and Asian British (cf. also Weingarten 2014, 147, fn 175).

7 In this setting the novel expresses some autobiographical traits, if less so with regard to story, characters, and perspective. Since the town is not named, critics have speculated that it is modelled on Huddersfield, where Aslam's family moved to after migrating to Britain. He confirms this in an interview with Claire Chambers (2011, 150), in which he also says that "my generation's story has yet to be told", with a promise for a future novel about the 7/7 bombings that will involve a similar setting (C. Chambers 2011, 153). In this comment, his own explicit generational self-positioning that aligns him with the terrorists from Leeds shows an awareness of the significance of the social generations that lie beyond (but are intricately interwoven with) family generations.

8 Chanda's brothers are the primary suspects throughout the novel, but are only convicted in the final pages. Although there is never much doubt as to the motive and the perpetrators of the murder, there is a strong sense of uncertainty that pervades the story due to the unsolved nature of the crime and the fact that the bodies are not found.

that was built up by the narrative. The novel is divided into four parts in accordance with the seasons of the year, running from winter to autumn, which reflects the theme of nature on a structural level and imbues the novel with rich symbolic language and references to the imagery of South Asian poetry.

Located at the centre of the panoramic narrative is the family of Jugnu's elder brother Shamas, and his wife Kaukab, who serve as the main focalisers of the novel. Shamas fled Pakistan as a communist and aspiring poet after the military coup in 1958 (cf. *Maps* 80),[9] and now, at almost 65, awaits his retirement. His liberal views clash with the religious orthodoxy of his wife, who, largely uneducated, and with only a very basic knowledge of English, clings to an extremely rigid form of Islam and its laws and traditions.[10] Her views largely coalesce with those of the tightly-knit Pakistani-British Muslim community into which her family is embedded. While the community shuts itself off from the outside, the internal relationships within the 'enclave' are governed by social control, distrust, suspicion and anxiety. Overall, the community resembles a cage in which the characters seem confined to in their thoughts and in their actions. This claustrophobic atmosphere is conveyed impressively through the focalisation and restricted perspective structure of the novel, which, while it features a heterodiegetic and omniscient narrator, closely follows the viewpoint of the main characters. An outside perspective is only marginally introduced, represented by Shamas' and Kaukab's children, who have turned their backs on their parents' home and the community.[11]

---

9 *Maps* refers to Aslam 2005 [2004]. Hereafter all references to the novel will use only page number, and, where necessary, *Maps* for disambiguation.
10 There are some biographical parallels between Shamas and Nadeem Aslam's own father, who, being also a communist poet and filmmaker, left Pakistan in the 1980s to avoid persecution by the Zia regime. Moreover, there is a similar difference between his father's and his mother's side of the family. As he states in an interview, "when staying with my father's relatives, people were painting, singing, the radio was on, and there were beautiful pictures on the wall. My mother's side of the family was far more austere [... and] in line with Islamic law [...]. Although I found my mother's side difficult, it helped me understand a range of people." (C. Chambers 2011, 146) The diversity he found in his own extended family is thus the basis for his complex view of Pakistani society and of Pakistani-British immigrant communities (cf. also C. Chambers 2011, 153).
11 For a closer analysis of the perspective structure and its implications for a generation-studies informed reading of the novel see Weingarten 2014. While Weingarten's reading highlights "the conflict between orthodox Islam and secular British values" (Weingarten 2014, 147), which she claims is 'overstated' in the novel, I would argue that the more important contrast in the book is that between the constricted thinking of ideological fundamentalisms on the one hand, which is conveyed through the closed perspective structure at the character focalisation

Like the ageing couple, the immigrant community suffers from a double loss through migration – firstly, the loss of the home and the families that they had to leave behind, and secondly, there is the on-going loss of their children, many of whom suffer from the over-restrictive attitudes of the community and its adherence to an excessively orthodox form of Islam (cf. Weedon 2012, 33). The destructive forces converge in the murder of the novel's eponymous lovers and its repercussions on the community and the families affected by it. These 'lost lovers' are at the centre of an array of similar couples who have fallen victim to the strict religious and ethnically based authoritarian boundaries of their community, and whose tragic stories are woven into the fabric of the main story line. In the memories of other characters as well as through the use of leitmotifs, the lovers retain a ghostly presence despite their absence and form a significant part of the theme of loss.[12] Not only is Chanda's and Jugnu's house empty after their disappearance, but Shamas and Kaukab's home also features as a site of emptiness and loss as it has been deserted by their three children for more than eight years. The last to leave was their youngest son, Ujala, who, at the age of sixteen, broke off all contact with his parents. The eldest son, Charag, rarely visits home. He works as a painter in London despite his parents' wish for him to become a doctor. He is 32 and has a 3-year-old son with his ex-wife Stella. Of the three, their daughter Mah-Jabin, 27, is the one who maintains closest contact with her parents, or more precisely, her mother, telephoning once a month and visiting once or twice a year. After a two-year marriage to a first cousin in Pakistan that ended in divorce, she has returned to live and study in London.

Through the perspective of Shamas and Kaukab, the reader gains a profound insight into the inner workings of the community and the fault lines that run through it. The conflicts in the family are shown to be representative of a general breakdown of family structures in the community. An important topic will therefore be the way that the family is embedded in, and interacts with, its

---

level, and a richly-spun web of a transcultural poetic and literary tradition with many interrelated motifs and connections on the other hand, spun by the narrator's commentary, references, and through the memories and associations of the characters.

12 This theme is continuously evoked through the dense use of leitmotifs, among which moths predominantly feature. The ubiquitous moths serve as a constant reminder of Jugnu, who, as a lepidopterist, used to breed, collect, and study various species of moth. They also stand for the element of the mortal danger inherent in lovers' attraction to each other, and are closely connected with the novel's pervasive imagery of light and darkness, which dominates throughout; see, e.g., the naming strategy for characters (with references to the moon or sun being the most prevalent, cf. Chanda = the moon, and Jugnu = firefly; or Shamas = sun, Kaukab = star, Charagh = lamp/light, Ujala = light of the universe/brightness, Mah-Jabeen = moon-faced).

social context. The following analysis will focus mainly on the character of Kaukab, who epitomises the multicultural struggle in a paradigmatic way. As director of the Community Relations Council, her husband Shamas is given a special role and often acts as a connection to the outside world for a largely secluded community. Despite his commitment to his job, he is, as Amina Yaqin (2012, 109) remarks, "a curiously passive character", who observes all the wrongdoings in the community, as well as in his family, but never takes a strong-enough stance to actually change or prevent any of it.[13]

4.1.1 Mapping Loss: Inside and Outside of the 'Desert of Loneliness'

The central theme of loss – of absences and disappearances –, which permeates the whole narrative, is essentially the emotional core of the novel. The opening scene already shows how the main protagonists couch their experience in an overall framework of loss. Stepping out into the year's first snow, Shamas engages in a small personal ritual to commemorate the monsoon season, because, as he states, "[a]mong the innumerable other losses, to come to England was to lose a season" (5). He melts a snowflake in his hand, thus "transform[ing it] into a monsoon raindrop" (5), which ties in with the community's many ways of remembering and protecting the memory of a home that is lost.[14] Loss and memory are thus inseparably linked, and the novel is suffused with palpable absences that are preserved and reactivated through continual remembrance. Like the waft of incense that is cleared away by the snowstorm, what is gone "is there even when absent, drawing attention to its own disappearance" (3).[15]

---

[13] The dominant figure in the family is clearly Kaukab, and Shamas, although rarely sharing her opinions, seldom contradicts her and generally subordinates himself to her. The incident where he does make a stand against her (when he finds out that she has forced her new-born baby to fast during Ramadan to prove his religious devotion), he eventually shirks his real responsibilities by moving out and leaving the children alone with their (now obviously) abusive mother for three years. His affair with Suraya, a younger woman, which runs for a large portion of the plot of the novel, underlines this sense of detachment from his family.

[14] The text itself performs this act of transformation through numerous allusions to the literary tradition of the Indian Subcontinent and its rich imagery (see Aslam's interview with Marianne Brace 2004; cf. also Moore 2009, 7).

[15] This dominant theme of 'present-absence', as well as the spectral role of lost lovers (not only in the case of Chanda and Jugnu but with all the other lost lovers), suggests an interpretation along the lines of the postcolonial concept of 'hauntology' (cf. O'Riley 2007; Davis 2005). Coined by Jacques Derrida, the term evokes "its near-homonym ontology, replacing the priority of being and presence with the figure of the ghost as that which is neither present nor absent,

For the South-Asian community, reality in England is overwritten by their longing for home and a feeling of displacement. This is most strikingly expressed in the immigrants' habit of renaming the streets of their neighbourhood to recall place names from home:

> As in Lahore, a road in this town is named after Goethe. There is a Park Street here as in Calcutta, a Malabar Hill as in Bombay, and a Naag Tolla Hill as in Dhaka. Because it was difficult to pronounce the English names, the men who arrived in this town in the 1950s had re-christened everything they saw before them. They had come from across the Subcontinent, lived together ten to a room, and the name that one of them happened to give to a street or landmark was taken up by the others, regardless of where they themselves were from. But over the decades, as more and more people came, the various nationalities of the Subcontinent have changed the names according to the specific country they themselves are from – Indian, Pakistani, Bangladeshi, Sri Lankan. Only one name has been accepted by every group, remaining unchanged. It's the name of the town itself. Dasht-e-Tanhaii.
> The Wilderness of Solitude.
> The Desert of Loneliness. (29)

Like a palimpsest, the town is thus superimposed with the diasporic experience of the immigrants;[16] the way in which it eludes the longitudes and latitudes of English maps reflects the feeling that they do not belong to the country and illustrates their determination to gain some control over what remains utterly strange to them.[17] This resignification of spaces and surroundings can be accorded with the wish and the "ability to recreate a culture in diverse locations", which James Clifford (1997, 306) regards as characteristic of the South Asian diaspora (cf. Lemke 2008, 173). The translation of Pakistani place names into

---

neither dead nor alive" (Davis 2005, 373). In terms of a hauntologically informed reading, the persistent presence of the community's victims as ghosts and memories connect its traumatic condition with the colonial past. In a way similar to the transformation of the English setting through the narrative voice, the fundamentalism and extremism amongst the community disrupts the social makeup of multicultural Britain as it evokes this colonial history and its legacy as "spectres of the nation's colonial heritage" (O'Riley 2007, 1; cf. Moore 2009, 12). See also Moore (2009, 12ff).

16 The "concept of diasporic dwelling [... as a] stereoscopic notion of place and non-synchronous view of time" (Childs and Green 2013, 101, with reference to Brooker 2002, 21) is similar to the image of the palimpsest.

17 At the same time, this experience is made palpable to the reader, for whom the experience of living England from this 'foreign' perspective conveys a strong sense of disorientation and alienation from that which is familiar. However, the "citational quality of the landscape" (Moore 2009, 7), which is imbued with many allusions to South Asian poetry, also links the two worlds through a net of interrelated references (see also Moore 2009, 7).

the English surroundings functions not only as an act of remembrance; it also entails the transferral of a whole system of values, norms, social relations, and codes of behaviour. It attests to a more general act of world-making: The different place names indicate that life in the immigrant community is organised along a completely different grid of coordinates than that of mainstream British society.

The striking inability of the immigrants to deal with and to adapt to the new situation can be interpreted as a symptom of cultural trauma. As David Waterman (2010, 18) elaborates, "[i]n the face of cultural trauma and the sense of loss it entails, community cohesion and identity are preserved not so much by re-membering as by re-membering, literally using first-generation memories to reconstitute the community, often elsewhere." As defined by Jeffrey Alexander (2004, 1),

> [c]ultural trauma occurs when members of a collectivity feel they have been subjected to a horrendous event that leaves indelible marks upon their group consciousness, marking their memories forever and changing their future identity in fundamental and irrevocable ways.

In this theory, trauma is understood not solely in terms of being a psychic wound, but also as a symbolic, collective and cultural form of coping with and shaping of devastating loss. Cultural trauma can thus be described as "a construction of social meanings, of how the event is transformed and migrates into a grid of significations" (Sundholm 2011, 123–124). In this symbolic shape, trauma organises group dynamics and "is linked to the formation of collective identity and the construction of collective memory" (Eyerman 2004, 60).[18] Ron Eyerman describes cultural trauma in contrast with individual, psychological, or physical trauma as referring to "a dramatic loss of identity and meaning, a tear in the social fabric, affecting a group of people that has achieved some degree of cohesion" (Eyerman 2004, 61).[19] It is evident throughout the novel that

---

18 John Sundholm (2011, 123) points out how Alexander's constructivist notion of trauma (in the sense of how a group chooses to represent themselves in a certain way), albeit controversial, is useful for the description of processes like migration which cannot be traced to the intentional creation of trauma such as, for example, the effect of warfare. Sundholm adopts a "cultural perspective" on collective trauma in contrast with Alexander's "empirical one" (124). He also emphasises the fact that trauma in this context "is used as a metaphor" (125), or as a 'travelling concept', and is therefore distinct from the psychological context of individual trauma.
19 See also Weingarten (2014, 70). Weingarten (2014, 148ff.) ascribes a "doubled cultural trauma of post-Partition migration" to the first generation of immigrants in *Maps for Lost Lov-*

the traumas of both colonialism and Partition have made an impact on the trauma of migration felt by the South Asian immigrants. Both are successively evoked in the re-naming of the neighbourhood, which at first reproduces colonial appropriations of space,[20] and then, after an initial phase of communal living across the ethnic, national and religious divide, reinstates the borders that have been drawn on the Indian Subcontinent since the end of the British Indian Empire.

From this point of view, it is plausible to link the notion of cultural trauma with other forms of meaning-making in the novel that characterise a post-traumatic mind-set. The immigrant protagonists re-enact their trauma in the English neighbourhood, which becomes particularly obvious in Kaukab's deviant behaviour. Her assertion that "[her] religion is not the British legal system, it's Islam" (115) captures the "enclave mindset" (Waterman 2010, 21) of the diasporic community, whose system of values and norms she generally represents. Mary Douglas's grid and group theory helps us to further understand the inner workings of a community that lives under the constraints of a cultural trauma of irreparable loss.[21] According to her analysis, enclave cultures are characterised by a strong emphasis on group identity and cohesion, which goes hand in hand with self-exclusion. The strongly bounded in-group typically locates itself outside of the mainstream of society. It is dominated by a "fear of defection" (Douglas 2007b, 7) and a consequent "closure of boundaries" (Douglas 2007b, 10). Douglas regards the enforcement of boundaries as a reaction to external pressures resulting from cultural contact and interaction (Douglas 2001 [1966], 4), as an attempt to re-establish order in a situation of disorder, the desire to emphasise the familiar in the face of confusion and the loss of identity. The construction of strong boundaries and demarcation lines serves as an affirmation of identity, which is, in turn, based on the strong juxtaposition of us versus them: "that which is not with it, part of it and subject to its laws, is potentially against it. [...I]deas about separating, purifying, demarcating and punishing transgressions have as their main function to impose system on an inherently untidy experience." (Douglas 2001 [1966], 4) The overwritten and re-charted city is a powerful image for a comprehensive process of meaning mak-

---

ers, whose lives are marked by loss and a "feeling of dislocation" (Weingarten 2014, 149; see also Waterman 2010, 18). In this manner, one could even speak of a 'tripled cultural trauma' in order to acknowledge the long-term effects of colonialist ideologies and politics on the colonised and their repercussions for present-day 'multicultural' Britain.

20 The reference to cartographic practices under British imperial rule is explicit in the colonial place names that are re-migrated such as Goethe Road and Park Street (see also Moore 2009, 6).

21 See Douglas (2007a).

ing in a situation of threatened identity. It is both a map of memory, which keeps in the present what is past and absent, i.e. lost, and a map that offers each person an alternative reality that follows more familiar codes. Through the designation of street names, clear boundaries are drawn and order is restored.[22]

In the case of enclave cultures, the borders defining the in-group are intensified and are assigned with moral undertones through the cultural metaphors of purity and pollution. As the out-group is identified with dirt and defilement, the in-group exists under the stress and danger of imminent contagion. In Kaukab's eyes, "England is a dirty, an unsacred country full of people filthy with disgusting habits and practices" (267) that pose a constant threat of contamination. In contrast with "the moral vacuum of this obscene and degraded country" (269), Pakistan, the 'land of the Pure', is seen as "a country of the pious and the devout, a place where boundaries are respected" (63). As Douglas shows in her work on *Purity and Danger* (2001 [1966]), dirt is not an objective phenomenon but a culturally defined category for the organisation and the structuring of the environment: Dirt is an offense that poses a threat against order.[23] With such categories of purity and pollution, "the ideal order of society is guarded by dangers which threaten transgressors" (Douglas 2001 [1966], 3).[24] Such threats are routinely employed as an element of social control in the Pakistani neighbourhood, mostly by the first generation to regulate the second generation's behaviour.[25] Boundaries are thus enforced against external pressures

---

[22] Despite this reassuring effect of structure, the feeling that persists for all of the immigrant community is loneliness – which also serves as the name of the town that everyone agrees on. The town's shared name *Dasht-e Tanhaii* also emphasises the linguistic closeness of Urdu and Hindi and thus reveals threads of relatedness and similarity among the different groups of immigrants from the Indian Subcontinent that lie beneath the surface of inter-religious and inter-ethnic differentiation and dissociation. The underlying affinity and transcultural interconnectedness of groups that appear, on the surface and through their interaction in the novel, as though they were separated by a deep schism of racism and animosity, is a major theme of the novel.
[23] Cf. Douglas (2001 [1966], 2): "dirt is essentially disorder. There is no such thing as absolute dirt: it exists in the eye of the beholder. [...] Dirt offends against order. Eliminating it is not a negative movement, but a positive effort to organise the environment."
[24] The quote continues: "These danger-beliefs are as much threats which one man uses to coerce another as dangers which he himself fears to incur by his own lapses from righteousness. They are a strong language of mutual exhortation." (Douglas 2001 [1966], 3)
[25] A common threat used by Kaukab and other mothers to scare their children into compliance is that of being "handed over to a white person if [they] didn't behave" (72; see also 220). In general, behaviour that deviates from the extremely rigid social codes of the community is sanctioned with cruel severity that includes physical and psychological violence, which ranges from slapping to murder, as evidenced in the case of the 'lost lovers'. In another family, the

as well as against the risk of transgression from insiders, both of which are closely connected.

As the integrity of the group depends on the unity of the family as the bedrock of cultural identity, the private home holds a key function in this spatial organisation. The house is regarded as a protected space for the family as the nucleus of the group, and it is here that the inside/outside division is most strongly manifested. In order to guarantee the purity of this space, "most Muslim men and women of the neighbourhood have a few sets of clothing reserved solely for outdoors, taking them off the moment they get home to put on the ones they know to be clean" (267). Like many others, Kaukab, who feels that she cannot "go from the house to, say, the post office without being confronted by the decay of Western culture" (269), prefers to stay in most of the time, when each outside venture is fraught with danger and pollution.[26] Similarly, the world outside is seen as a threat to the integrity and constancy of the family. Beyond the threshold of her home, her control wanes and her children are subjected to change: "Each time they went out they returned with a new layer of strangerness on them until finally I didn't recognize them any more." (146) For Kaukab, the family home is a sanctuary in an unfamiliar, confusing world, a place where time stands still and change is prevented. In contrast to her children, for her "there's nothing [...] out there in Dasht-e-Tanhaii, to notice or be interested in. Everything is here in this house. Every beloved absence is present here. / An oasis – albeit a haunted one – in the middle of the Desert of Loneliness." (64–65)

Her confinement to the house illustrates the way in which her restricted and rigid world-view aggravates her loneliness and isolation by cutting her off from other people, particularly those who are closest to her heart.[27] Having left the

---

daughter is killed in an exorcism performed by a Muslim "holy man" because they found her to be "not behaving appropriately towards her family and husband" (170).

26 Conversely, an earlier incident where Jugnu transgressed this boundary by bringing home a white girlfriend for dinner with Shamas and Kaukab was experienced by her as a profound danger and a threat to both her and the family's identity. Over dinner, Kaukab observes that "it sounded like a normal family gathering, yes, but she herself – and everything she stood for – was excluded from it" (37). The whole narration of the dinner scene, during which Kaukab acts as the focaliser, is filled with references to her fear of pollution, and it culminates with an ultimate and shocking act of defilement when Kaukab herself, in a desperate act of expressing her repulsion, serves the perfectly cooked *dahl* in shoes instead of plates (40).

27 Her ambivalence towards Jugnu is representative of the excruciating battle that is fought in her heart between love and family cohesion on the one side, and religious duty and ideology on the other.

family home to live in London, the three children have become "lost" to Kaukab, their lives are "beyond her imagining" (129), which, in England at least, is confined to what happens in her house and its immediate vicinity.[28] The space that is the house consequently comes to represent the barriers and constraints that restrain interfamily communication. As the lives of her children become increasingly incommunicable within their mother's restrictive frame, secrets and silences become magnified which in turn corrodes the relationships in the family.[29] "There is so much outside the house that may not be brought into the house" (93), Mah-Jabin observes during a visit home. As a result, she has to constantly check her behaviour and speech, missing the freedom to act openly and unreservedly with her mother. Kaukab, similarly, is careful in her conversation, "concealing everything regarding the Pakistanis that the children might deem objectionable" (110). Communication in the family has thus become a minefield, where any careless step may cause an explosion. This is particularly true of the intergenerational family relationships portrayed in the book. Nevertheless, when the siblings meet at the end of the novel, it becomes apparent that the silences in the family also affect their relationships. Similarly, communication between Shamas and Kaukab is disturbed as talking has become, "for both of them, frequently another way of being alone, the conversation highlighting the separate loneliness of each" (156).

The description of the family home as "a narrow house where all the doors disappear into the walls, except for the two that give on to the outside world at the front and back" (7) emphasises the inside/outside dichotomy. The spatial confinement that is described in the novel reflects the impression of social constriction within the family. The fundamental belief system that dominates life in the house (as it does in the neighbourhood that has been mapped out by the immigrant community) allows no room for the development of the family mem-

---

28 Her daughter's marriage in Pakistan, by contrast, used to deeply satisfy Kaukab because it meant that her daughter would live "against a background she had thorough knowledge of" (129). However – and somehow tragically – it is precisely her knowledge of Pakistan, as well as of the part of her husband's family into which her daughter married (although the patrilateral cousin marriage is prescribed), that should have helped her to save Mah-Jabin from entering a disastrous and abusive marriage. As a result, this marriage fails to bring mother and daughter closer; on the contrary, it becomes the source of silence in their conversations, having planted a secret between them that disrupts their communication and substantially harms their relationship.
29 Charag, for example, initially keeps his first girlfriend Stella "a secret from everyone at home" (129) for fear of his mother's reaction. He cannot even confide in his uncle or father because he does not want to implicate them in his "sinning".

bers. The sense of regulation is supported by the image of the disappearing doors, which suggests that while boundaries to the outside are carefully guarded, internal boundaries dissolve to the extent that personal space and individuality are annihilated. Consequently, Mah-Jabin, while at home, feels "anxious not to hurt Kaukab by presenting herself to her in any capacity other than a daughter, *her* daughter" (93; emphasis in the original). Inside the house, there is no room for any form of orientation beyond the fixity of the family constellation. The narrowness of the house, moreover, conveys the sense of closeness and intimacy that is also present between the family members. In their regular everyday habits of living together, Shamas and Kaukab communicate almost telepathically, their words resembling "a thought being passed into her head from his" (60; cf. also 55). A similar connection born out of intimate knowledge of the other exists between Kaukab and her daughter Mah-Jabin, whose relationship is seen to oscillate between closeness and estrangement, between love and hurt, their profound familiarity paving the way for their mutual offences. Consequently, their communication is extremely fragile: "It wouldn't tip the scales on a pin, the amount by which a comment has to fall short from the ideal in the listener's head for it to be regarded an affront, an offence – a crime." (101) The view of the family house as a closed space illustrates the way that Kaukab, "[t]rapped within the cage of permitted thinking" (110), loses touch with her family in spite of all of her love for them, and falls deeper and deeper into loneliness.

4.1.2 A House "full of disappearances": Memories and Silences

As the pervasiveness of the theme of loss indicates, it is not simply a 'cage of permitted thinking' where its codes and laws bind life in the community together but it is also a form of preoccupation with the past. The dominance of the past – which includes the normative system of religion and tradition – is shown to restrain the immigrant community by narrowing their agency and perspective. As Shamas notes, "[m]ost people live in the past because it's easy [sic] to remember than to think. Most of us don't know *how* to think – we've been taught *what* to think instead." (282; emphasis in the original)[30]

---

[30] The non-religious Shamas almost seems to be serving as a mouthpiece for the author here, as he made a very similar statement in an interview, saying that "turning to religion means we don't have to think anymore, we don't have to make decisions anymore – we are told what to think, what to eat, what to wear, who to meet, who to talk to" (qtd. in McCulloch 2012, 86). The

Kaukab, again, embodies this issue, as she appears trapped in the spiral repetitions of traumatic memory. She tells her daughter that "[e]very day – wishing I could rewrite the past – I relive the day I came to this country where I have known nothing but pain" (101). The cultural trauma of the community is thus borne by, and finds expression in, the various individual traumas of the migrants.[31] Kaukab's orientation towards the past becomes manifest in the house itself. "[F]ull of disappearances for so long" (289), it has acquired a ghost-like quality. Moreover, it has been actively stylised as a site of memory, painted by Shamas in "the colours of the three rooms in the olive-green house in Sohni Dharti" (5), their native village in Pakistan, and is thus transformed into a reproduction of the family home as a constant memory while living "in the years of exile and banishment" (6).[32] The house harbours both "reminder[s] of home" (21) from a pre-migration past and the traces of more recent family life.[33] Thus, it has come to represent the double loss of migration. After "the move to England had deprived her of the glowing warmth that people who are born of each other give out, the heat and light of an extended family", Kaukab had tried to rebuild her life around her own family, moving on from the family of origin to the family of procreation (cf. 296). However, it becomes clear that migration has caused a rupture in the social fabric of the (formerly extended) family that cannot be restored nor can its values of mutual obligation and care be passed down to the next generation. The intergenerational link that has already been damaged through migration remains indelibly scarred. In view of the loss of her own children, Kaukab wonders whether "Allah is punishing us for leaving behind our own parents in Pakistan and moving to England all those years ago" (146). It is in the house that the pervasive motif of present absences has its densest quality. It also shows how the two defining coordinates in the lives of the immi-

---

similarity of expression indicates that Aslam addresses more or less the same issue in the two quotations, and the novel in general treats 'tradition', 'religion' and 'past', in this context, as referring to a single semantic field.

31 Symptoms related to trauma are fairly common among immigrants (see Schouler-Ocak 2015). At each stage of the migration process, "possible factors affecting vulnerability include the individual personality features of the immigrants and experiences of loss, bereavement, depression, post-traumatic stress disorder and cultural shock" (Küey 2015, 62).

32 This is in line with the patrilineal logic of Pakistani kinship structure, according to which Kaukab's parents' house in Pakistan has lost the significance and qualities of 'home' that it once had as she entered into her husband's family after marriage.

33 These reminders of home are also a constant reminder of loss and displacement, as, for example, the vase that Shamas had brought in the 1950s: "the fine layer of dust he had picked the vase out of all those years ago continuing to cry out across the years with an agonised O for it to be put back exactly where it had been set by his mother's hand" (21).

grant Muslim community – memory and religion – converge to produce this state of hauntedness.

For the adult children returning home, the house is similarly charged with memories, particularly ones that bear witness to family conflict. As Mah-Jabin observes, the "house is almost not a building but an emotion; every last surface here bears scars of war" (120). Indeed, it is not only the surfaces of the house that show memory traces, the dark corners and hidden places are also keepers of memory. In the bathroom, she discards a letter from her ex-husband, throwing it away, unread, into "the narrow angular cupboard in the corner that houses the immersion heater", like "toxic waste to be dumped into some distant black hole" (109). It is the same 'blind spot' where years previously she had hidden a knitting needle that she intended to use as an abortion instrument on finding out that she was pregnant after returning from Pakistan. Her body makes the connection before her mind can process what is happening:

> [A]s though acting on a will and independent memory of their own, the fingers of her hand open the door to the immersion heater once again, reach around the belly of the quilted water-drum and grope in the darkness there: when they find what they are seeking she too remembers it suddenly, as though a jolting electric current has passed from the object to her brain.
> The knitting needle she had dropped there nearly nine years ago [...] is still there, undissolved by the passage of time and the lack of light. (109)

In this scene, Mah-Jabin's haptic and bodily perception of her spatial surroundings in the bathroom triggers a body memory that is only gradually followed by cognitive understanding. Her hiding away these remnants of her marriage in the darkest corner of the house parallels her psychological detachment from this part of her life. While she has tried to ban the memory from her mind, her body has kept it stored in the same way as the house still holds the knitting needle.[34] The experience of her marriage in Pakistan has caused a traumatic disruption in Mah-Jabin's life that is expressed in her disassociation from that particular part of her life: "The two-year marriage is strange to her as though someone is telling

---

[34] A later scene in the novel once more shows the close link between this particular room in the house, the bathroom, and her traumatic memory of her marriage and of her abortion, when "Mah-Jabin goes upstairs to the bathroom (where all those years ago she had sat with a knitting needle, not knowing how to proceed)" (299). Mah-Jabin did not go through with the knitting-needle procedure at the time, but instead "induced a miscarriage by taking quinine tablets for a fortnight" (109). Nevertheless, the knitting needle still stands for her desperation at the time, when her pregnancy made her feel "as though chains to bind her were being forged within her" (109) – a child would have made it nearly impossible for her to leave her husband.

her a story." (91) Her failure to integrate this episode into her own self-narrative can be understood as a dissociative symptom that was triggered by a traumatic experience.[35]

The marriage not only harms Mah-Jabin's own sense of a coherent and integrative self, it is also a disruptive factor in her inter-family communication and relationships.[36] The bathroom is a significant space to store her memory: not only does it tend to be the only room in the house that can be locked (making it a likely place for family secrets), it is also a room that is shared by everyone in the family, which stresses the way that the secret impacts on the family as a whole, just as the whole family can equally be implicated in her silence and suppression.[37] The concept of the family home as a place for the storage of memories and secrets alike shows how closely "family secrets [are] tied into the workings of family memories" (Smart 2011a, 540) and constitute a major part of the family imaginary, or 'the family we live by'. Silences and secrets are often a response to threats against family identity: while concealment is generally intended to support family relationships, the disclosure of a secret may cause division in the family (cf. Smart 2011a, 543). Accordingly, Mah-Jabin's secret, on the one hand, is meant to protect her mother: "She knows the truth that her daughter had suffered would cause Kaukab more pain than the lie that she had selfishly and scandalously abandoned someone loving. How Kaukab would react to the truth would be a proof of her love, that she is being spared it is proof of Mah-Jabin's." (97) On the other hand, however, wrapped up inside her silence is also a deep-seated reproach against her parents. Although she entered into the marriage voluntarily, she was only sixteen at the time and therefore holds her parents responsible for this disastrous episode in her life. She cannot understand how her mother in particular, in full knowledge of the horrors that might await her daughter, could have sent her off to Pakistan to marry someone she did not know: "why didn't you make sure I avoided such a life? Answer me

---

[35] For an elaboration of the idea of dissociation and memory lacunae acting as a symptom of post-traumatic stress, see Staniloiu and Markowitsch (2012).

[36] In the end, the reader learns that Mah-Jabin's move to Pakistan did not only considerably alter her own life course, but also heavily affected her younger brother Ujala, who was twelve at the time and suffered severely from the loss of his sister, "his only *friend*, his *only* friend" (300) at the time, and a possible 'guidance figure' for him in the family. From this, the reader can only guess at the psychological consequences of this experience of emotional and social loss. It is very likely to have been a crucial factor in his repudiation of his parents.

[37] In the novel *Guapa* (2016) by Arab writer Saleem Haddad, the bathroom plays a similar role. As a place of retreat within the family home, it is here that the protagonist can reflect on his homosexuality, thereby marking the room as keeper of his secret.

... Answer me ... Why do you people keep doing the same things over and over again expecting a different result?" (113) Mah-Jabin sees the older generation as being caught up in a compulsory circle of repetition that they cannot escape from and into which they try to drag their children.[38] Similar to Kaukab's recurrent memory of the day of her arrival in Britain, this obsessive adherence to the past, tradition and to normative values allows for no change or transformation, and consequently no future. Jutta Weingarten (2012, 167) makes the point that this form of "transmission, in this case a repetition of experience," from the first to the second generation stifles the latter's potential for development.[39]

Interestingly, the language of defilement is also invoked by Mah-Jabin when she expresses her contempt for "your laws and codes, the so-called traditions that you have dragged into this country with you like shit on your shoes" (114). In the logic of purity and pollution, these traditions threaten the structure of law and order in British society. After closer inspection, however, Mah-Jabin's inverted image is much more concerned with the way that the rigid system of social control within the community leads to the corrosion of the group from within rather than acting to strengthen its cohesion. The community has turned on itself, and the honour killing is the clearest sign of its disintegration as it testifies to the terrible truth "that a family can kill one of its own" (114).

---

[38] See also Mah-Jabin's comment after being hit by her mother: "[I]t's not the first beating I've taken from you. Your husband beats you and you beat your children in return." (116)

[39] Weingarten (2014) cogently parallels this suppression of the second generation's freedom to make their own choices and experiences with a silencing of their voice in a way that is reflected in the novel's closed perspective structure: "the generationality that refuses to be dominated by their parents' trauma of migration is marginalized to the point of being denied representation in the novel" (Weingarten 2014, 148). Weingarten, furthermore, deduces from this that there is an inhibition of "the formation of a generational identity in the succeeding generation" (Weingarten 2014, 148). I feel slightly uncomfortable with this reading because, firstly, it overstates the intergenerational conflict and smoothens out a number of aspects of the novel that go against a very clear separation of the generations, as, for example, characters whose age falls in-between the generations (such as Suraya or Jugnu; moreover, Chanda and Jugnu share an intergenerational relationship), or characters who do not fit into a generational division of characters along the lines of fundamental Islam vs. liberal secularism (like Chanda's brothers, Kiran and Kaukab's brother, and Shamas and his parents). Secondly, this reading rules out the fact that practices and beliefs that adhere to Islamic fundamentalism or cultural traditionalism can be understood as pertaining to specific generational identities of second or third generation immigrants.

4.1.3 Body and Self: The Disintegration of Family

Perhaps one of the most interesting aspects of *Maps for Lost Lovers* is the way in which the novel puts forward the notion of the body being a carrier of meaning in the struggle for identity, belonging, and connectedness. The body is central to the themes of relatedness and family ties on a diachronic and synchronic level: it is closely connected to questions of origin and descent (as often expressed in the metaphors of shared 'blood' or 'flesh') as well as with everyday family practices related with feeding, intimacy, and nurture in general. Analysing family relations through the perspective of family practices has been increasingly recognised in family studies as a way of "making sense of the body, embodiment and bodily interactions in families" (Morgan 2011, 3.8). Furthermore, it can be seen in the novel that the materiality of the body takes on more of a metaphorical meaning whereby the disintegration of the family is expressed in physical terms. While the body's potential for familial continuity is also highlighted, the fabric of family connectedness dissolves as the cracks of religious disagreement and the pressure of social constraint become apparent in instances of disease, violence, abuse, and the severing of family bonds.

Kaukab's self-image is decidedly relational, revolving around two familial roles: as daughter and as mother.[40] The first pertains to the family of origin and orientation, the second to the family of procreation. Her idea of a meaningful life (and her success as a mother) relies on the continuity between these two roles – a continuity that is disrupted by migration. Her sense of self is based on the conjunction of familial and religious roots, which is evoked repeatedly in the formula of her story of origin as "daughter of a cleric, born and raised in the shadow of a minaret" (62).[41] Her religious orthodoxy, practiced in a number of rituals and physical routines, links her back into her origins and serves as a confirmation of her identity. Her role as a mother and a housewife performs the similar function of maintaining this weakened family link as it connects her to a

---

[40] Her role as a wife is clearly secondary to these and is limited to household chores and taking care of Shamas when he is ill. She denies him all forms of physical intimacy at this stage in life, since it does not comply with her religious upbringing (cf. 56). All in all, husband and wife lead largely separate lives in their shared house, and although they used to be close, the wedge of religion now divides them. In a sad twist, Kaukab thinks of their pre-marital love story within the pattern that "everyone loved someone before marriage" (64), which implies that marriage itself does not allow for this kind of love. This attitude may also explain her disdain the marriage of her husband's parents.
[41] I call this story of origin formulaic because the phrase is invoked repeatedly, as, for example, on pages 42, 56, 64, 140.

particular gendered space both within the family household and within family history. When she is cooking,

> [t]here is a sense of consolation to the activity her fingers are engaged in, almost as though contact is being made with the dead: as a child she had seen her mother and grandmothers, and the other women in the house, similarly bent over the myriad daily tasks of the day, and sometimes – but not today, not now – the feeling is close to celebration, a remembrance and a praising of those now dead and absent but still living in her mind, unsung elsewhere and otherwise. Gone so thoroughly it is as though she had dreamed them. (116)

The intergenerational connection is continuously re-established through specific activities that are performed through the body; in this way, a strong sense of kinship is transmitted in the matrilineal line, which also includes a broader understanding of relatedness and affiliation based on gender. In the absence of these women, family ties are preserved through the living memory of the mind and of the body. On this day, however, Kaukab's celebratory feelings are in check due to a violent dispute that she just had with her daughter, which points to the disruption of this sense of intergenerational continuity, and which is also hinted at through Kaukab's remark that her daughter might have picked up new ways of cooking outside of home (cf. 95).[42]

Kaukab's expectations of her children are subordinated to her sense of familial obligation and connectedness to the same degree that she feels responsible for the continuation of culture and kinship among her family. Her plan for the family was, in short, that Charag, her eldest, endowed with the weight of "the family's betterment" (122) would study medicine, and his professional success would then enable the family to move back to Pakistan. Mah-Jabin was expected to strengthen family connections via a first-cousin-marriage and move ('back') into the house in Sohni Dharti. Ujala was expected to be very religious. All of her children eventually flout these expectations. When Ujala is born without a foreskin, a rare condition that is seen as a particular blessing in the Muslim community, Kaukab is elevated by the attention and admiration from the neighbourhood, and the affirmation of self that she sees therein: "Who else but a cleric's daughter would have been blessed by such an event!" (140) She subsequently tries to forcefully assert her belief that Ujala is "destined to be an especially pious Muslim" (139), first by forcing him to fast as a new-born during

---

[42] Before the violent quarrel, which erupted over the issue of Mah-Jabin's marriage, mother and daughter were sharing an intimate moment of communion while cooking together, whereby Kaukab was sharing an anecdote from her own childhood and from her mother (cf. 94–95).

Ramadan, and later, by mixing a 'holy salt' into his food in order to make the sixteen-year old more compliant. When Ujala notices this and has the salt examined, it turns out to be a sedative that curbs his libido, a discovery that causes him to leave home and to break off all contact with his parents. Both instances of perverted feeding can be considered as acts of physical abuse.[43] The way in which such acts of violence and of exerting control are interwoven with essential practices of maternal nurture and care is indicative of the inextricability of kinship, culture, and the social constrictions of family roles. Kaukab's own contradictory behaviour can be seen as a "product[...] of tensions and dynamics that are internal to the *birādāri* [kinship] structure" (Shaw 2000, 7).[44] Her wish to control her children is expressed in her endeavour to lay a claim on their bodies, thereby asserting her sense of self and seeking to fulfil her legacy of being a cleric's daughter. Consequently, after her children have moved out, "she feels as bewildered as a child whose dolls have been stolen" (70). This feeling shows the extent to which she is blind to her children's own needs and feelings and denies them any agency or independence. On the other hand, their breaches of religious law and unwillingness to submit to what they consider to be an oppressive system threaten her very sense of identity based on the legacy of religion and culture. What makes her a "selfish monster" (302) in the eyes of her children is thus ultimately her own subjugation to the system, her role in the generation contract. She feels just as obligated to the system of family as she feels that her children are to her, through the "the debt they incurred by drinking her milk" (146). The "debt of milk" (146) is passed on from generation to generation and implies that there is a more general debt to the system that the family is tied up with. Consequently, when her daughter confronts her about her arranged marriage, Kaukab answers: "I did not have the freedom to give you that freedom" (115).[45]

---

[43] While Kaukab herself regards her actions as harmless, their seriousness is in both cases revealed through the perspectives of other characters, Shamas in the first event and Ujala in the second (cf. 141; 304).

[44] In her anthropological long-term study of Pakistani immigrants to Britain, Alison Shaw (2000, 5) introduces two Urdu words that she finds are central to the organisation of life and social relationships amongst the Pakistani community: *birādāri* (kinship group, extended family, patrilineage) and *lenā-denā* ("the principle of 'taking-giving'").

[45] Before, she comments on Mah-Jabin's divorce in a way that reveals her own bitterness about her constricted role: "Not everyone has the freedom to walk away from a way of life" (115). However, this is a highly ambivalent feeling. When she talks to Charag about child rearing, she endorses strict discipline, stating that "[t]oo much freedom isn't good for anyone or anything" (58).

The second generation's attempts to break free from familial and religious constraints are similarly performed or fashioned through the body. While still living at home, Ujala expresses his contempt for his parents in a graphic scene. As his mother and father find him masturbating in his room, which they entered without knocking, he not only remains unabashed in their presence, but even flicks his discharge at them in an ultimate gesture of defiance (cf. 73). In Mah-Jabin's case, she expresses her desire for change with a new haircut that prompts her mother to "examine[...] the girl's face for signs of forgetting" (92) when she comes home. The hair's history – Kaukab nostalgically comments that it "was nearly eighteen-years' worth of growth" – was for Mah-Jabin only "[a]ll the more reason" to cut it off. The daughter's desire to forget is in direct contrast with Kaukab's wish to preserve the past by holding on to a memory: Preparing to dye her daughter's hair with henna, "she draws the comb of her fingers along the length and when it ends suddenly – shockingly, as in the dream in which the dreamer stumbles off a kerb – her fingers groping the empty air are an illustration of what is now missing from her life, what was once so palpably there – so palpably *here*" (104). This sensation perfectly captures the way in which memories are retained in the body through simple habit, and how change and loss create a perceived void and emptiness that cannot be thoroughly cognitively processed. Mah-Jabin's self-performed abortion that follows her divorce is a more radical act of re-gaining control over her own body and freedom – both from her abusive husband and from the constraints of the *birādāri*/kinship system. At the same time and despite its emancipatory value, the abortion is a strong act of violence against her own body that is in line with the (both physical and psychological) violence of the system (that does not shrink from terrible acts of brutality within the family).[46] Her act of self-inflicted violence demonstrates how it takes radical measures to interrupt the cycle of repetition. Charag's vasectomy sends out a similarly extreme message of discontinuation.[47] In contrast with these physical acts of corporeal self-determination, Charag

---

[46] The novel emphasises the way in which religious and cultural norms and traditions are enforced brutally either by the family members themselves, or on behalf of them (often parents). There are manifold examples in the novel, most of which are of incomprehensible cruelty.

[47] Charag confesses to his mother that he once hit his small son, who had interfered with his work; this incident ultimately led to his decision not to have any more children. Kaukab's response that "[p]arents are *supposed* to hit children, disciplining them" (58) and Charag's dry comment, "I remember" suggest that his desire for familial discontinuation is a desire to break free from the cycle of violence, in which each generation passes on the violence that they had to endure from their parents.

explores yet another form of re-claiming control over his life and body through his art. His painting *The Uncut Self-Portrait* conveys a powerful image of self-healing, in which he reverses his circumcision, "the first act of violence done to me in the name of a religious or social system" (320).

The violence of the religious and social system did not enter the family on their migration into England; rather, the transgenerational history of the family is suffused with division and religious difference.[48] Most crucially, the story of Shamas's father, Chakor, shows how deeply the history of religious conflict, ethnic discrimination and communal violence on the Subcontinent is inscribed into the family genealogy, in a similar way to how this history constitutes the background for division among the immigrant community in Britain. As a child Chakor, who was born as Deepak and as a Hindu, was injured a British airstrike in in the aftermath of the Amritsar massacre in 1919, losing not only his memory, but also his sister who was with him at the time. Lost to his family, the injured boy was found by strangers at a Muslim shrine, given a new identity and raised as a Muslim. When, during the early years of his marriage, memories of his past life slowly return, he at first hides them from his family, not knowing what else to do. After Partition and the rise of communal violence, this "truth about his true identity [...] that he hid from his family for as long as possible" (76) turns into an increasingly explosive secret. While his wife Mahtaab shows great compassion when he eventually reveals the truth, knowing "*how much he must've suffered with that secret gnawing at his innards*" (77; italics in the original), their community is less tolerant and Chakor becomes the victim of harassment and discrimination. Their oldest son, Shamas's brother, turns against his father and "accuse[s] the man of betraying them all by concealing the secret from them, prolonging the sin he was committing by living with a Muslim woman" (83).

Chakor's life story is thus closely intertwined with the traumas of British imperialism, Partition, and civil war, and the way in which these events of the recent history of India and Pakistan have torn families apart – through external

---

[48] Even before their marriage, Shamas's disregard of social etiquette and religious tradition caused distress to Kaukab (cf. 66), as did the liberal attitude of his parents (cf. 56). Moreover, Kaukab's brother had wanted to marry a Sikh woman, which "horrified her entire family" (39). Also in Pakistan, religion estranges the elder brother of Shamas and Jugnu from the rest of the family, as he becomes "increasingly religious" and drawn "towards the austere and volatile form of the faith that was alien to his parents and brothers" (83). Before moving on to a stricter form of Islam, he attended the mosque of Kaukab's father, who in this context appears to be more moderate than his daughter. This supports the view that her own radicalisation of views might have come about as a consequence of migration.

as well as internal pressures.⁴⁹ His disease and death illustrates the corrosive effect of trauma and silence as he falls ill with pancreatic cancer during the Indo-Pakistani War in 1971. The last stages of his illness are paralleled with the events of the civil war and the division of the country.

> On the day in December that Chakor vomited [...] blood – the aorta had ruptured and spilled its contents into the stomach so that now his body was consuming itself – the Indian army moved into East Pakistan, and Pakistan surrendered after a two-week long war: East Pakistan was now Bangladesh – India had not only defeated Pakistan, it had helped cut it in two. (82)

The corrosion of the body relates to both the disintegration of the divided country due to interfaith conflict between Muslims and Hindus, as well as to his own split identity. The repressed secret of his Hindu heritage rises to the surface as death draws near and claims his body. One night, Chakor leaves his sickbed and walks to the ruined Hindu temple, deserted since 1947, where he sets himself on fire. The fact that his corpse is repeatedly dug up and has to be re-buried after having received a Muslim burial hints at the haunting legacy of this story for the family.⁵⁰

The disruption of the family can thus be traced back to a history of violence on the war-torn Indian Subcontinent. The issues of racism, inter-religious strife, belief and identity are sewn into the family history and erode its cohesion from the inside. The family secret of having a mixed Hindu/Muslim lineage poses an immediate threat to an integral part of the family identity.⁵¹ It also profoundly questions any readily assumed or 'natural' correlation between family origin and religious affiliation. Jugnu's statement – "I was born into a Muslim household, but I object to the idea that that automatically makes me a Muslim" (38) –

---

49 Shamas' elder brother prevents the family from trying to locate Chakor's Hindu sister, although the enmity between Pakistan and India would have made it impossible for her to attend her lost brother's funeral anyway. The description of the complicated logistics of sending tamarind foliage from India to Pakistan via England illustrates the chasm between the two countries that also divides families: "Countless thousands of families wait for the news of their loved ones from the other side of the border – a wall that also effectively cuts the whole of Asia in half – but what they feel is less important than nationalistic ideals." (74).
50 Although he desires a Hindu cremation, Chakor is buried in the Muslim tradition as his family fear social exclusion. Nevertheless, the desecration of his grave is very likely to be an act of vandalism from the people within the community (in Kaukab's words, the "filthy infidel's corpse was spat out repeatedly by the earth no matter how deep they buried it the next day", 59).
51 From the perspective of religious law, the children of the union of Chakor and Mahtaab are "all illegitimate" (83), as Shamas' elder brother claims.

directly contradicts Kaukab's concept of identity as determined by the close interconnection of religious laws and family obligations. His non-deterministic concept of having a choice can be read as an alternative option for understanding the relationship between family origin and identity. For Kaukab, however, her children, in trying to break free from the chains of family embeddedness that automatically bind them to an authoritarian system, become lost to her. Her suffering from this loss is, once more, expressed in physical terms as she experiences post-menopausal uterine prolapse, "[h]er womb [...] a constant source of pain these days" (260), which can be read as a physical reaction to the strain put on the 'ties of the womb' by her children's estrangement (cf. also 331).

It is the most recent trauma suffered by the family, namely the murder of Jugnu, their beloved uncle, brother, and brother-in-law that, eventually transforms the smouldering conflicts in the family into an open flame. As the children gather at home towards the end of the novel on the occasion of the court trial, the buried secrets and long-kept silences are brought out into the open. The evening culminates in a fierce argument between the generations, fuelled by their contrasting views on religion that becomes manifest in the children's suspicion that their mother condones the honour killing. Kaukab senses the rift in the family, "a wall-like hate in whose foundations lie the bloody cut-up bodies of the two lovers" (295). Finally confronted with the truth (directly by Ujala, and indirectly by Mah-Jabin, whose hidden letter from her ex-husband she finds by chance in the bathroom), Kaukab finds herself faced with an outside perspective that questions the very foundations of her life and identity:

> She sits there, wondering if that's who she is, if that's what her image looks like in the mirror: a mother who feeds poisons to her son, and a mother who jumps to conclusions and holds her daughter responsible for the fact that her marriage ended disastrously? The realizations are still new and she is not sure what effect they will have on her soul after she has lived with them for an hour, a day, a month. (308)

Her later attempted suicide through poisoning herself after the children have left is indicative of how completely her identity is challenged by this revelation. Her own perspective and value system clash with those of her children in such a way that one side, if given validity, completely wipes out the other. Consequently, to recognise her children's desires, values, and choices in life would mean that she would have to cast away her own value system and negate her own sense of identity. The family gathering, which in Kaukab's eyes should have reunited the family, makes it painfully apparent that the cracks that run through it have become too wide to be mended, and the accusations and hurt now cut too deep.

4.2 Discovering Secrets, Unsettling Scripts: (Family) Identity and Islam in Robin Yassin-Kassab's *The Road from Damascus* (2008)

Yassin-Kassab's novel paints a complex image of Muslim identity politics in 'post-Rushdie Affair' contemporary Britain, one which takes into account the complicated intersections of post-colonial British identity constructions with national as well as international politics. Yassin-Kassab's focus on Arab Muslims in Britain also offers an interesting counterweight to the more widely represented and discussed South Asian British Muslim identities and concerns. For, as the novel's protagonist Sami asserts, "[i]n Britain Muslims meant Pakis, which meant crumbling mills and corner shops" (*Road* 61).[52] Sami, however, "wasn't a Paki. But there were so few of what he was that it barely qualified as a community" (61). There is no straightforward or simple way of pinning down his identity by connecting him to a larger group neatly delineated through stereotype.

The novel's main narrative detailing Sami's 'conversion' from atheism to a tentative acceptance of religious ideas and practices is presented on a larger canvas that depicts a variety of backgrounds, meanings, and interpretations of Muslim religiosity as represented by some of the other members of his family. In this regard, the novel remains consistent with the aim of many novels that deal with migration and which seek to present, reflect on, and de- or re-construct images of collective identities from within in order to allow for new perceptions, understanding, and interactions within the immigrant society. Clearly aiming to add more layers to the often homogeneous image of British Muslims, Yassin-Kassab is very consciously aware of the "delicate issue of a writer's responsibility in an Islamophobic climate" (Yassin-Kassab 2008, n.p.; cf. Rashid 2012, 94).[53] The author's conscious strategy of a multiperspective, heterodiegetic narration allows for different perspectives, so that it not only follows Sami's development, but also recounts the experiences of his wife, Muntaha, offering glimpses into the histories of both of their families as well as their parents' backgrounds and

---

[52] *Road* refers to Yassin-Kassab 2009 [2008]. Hereafter all references to the novel will use only page number, and, where necessary, *Road* for disambiguation.

[53] Nadeem Aslam was criticised for the anti-Islamic undertones of his novel. Yassin-Kassab's comment, however, although from a review of *Maps for Lost Lovers*, is directed more at Salman Rushdie than at Aslam, whom Yassin-Kassab refers to as being „undoubtedly a better, more serious writer who confronts real issues rather than making a virtue of insults for their own sake and an ultimately unchallenging iconoclasm" (Yassin-Kassab 2008, n.p.).

the details of their migration to Britain.[54] In addition, characters such as Sami's mentor Tom Field, a survivalist and successful academic, or Muntaha's colleague at school, Gabor Vronsk, a science and art teacher, reflect a variety of further identities and ideologies, which extend the range of viewpoints represented in this "novel of ideas" (C. Chambers 2012, 121). Questions of religious/political affiliation and of personal faith are presented as being closely connected with the individual concerns of identity construction and belonging, as well as with the abroader issues of Muslim identity politics in a multicultural Britain. The theme of identity, both individual and collective, lies at the heart of the novel, which shares an affinity with the *bildungsroman* genre,[55] and forms a continuous thread that runs through all of the layers and strands of the narrative, revealing the different ways in which it shapes family relationships and dynamics.

Sami's conversion, as hinted at in the novel's title, is more than just a simple revision of his stance on religion; it encompasses a complete transformation in terms of his personal development. The plotline follows the main indicators of the *bildungsroman* genre as defined by Marianne Hirsch (1979), as demonstrated by, in particular, Sami's comprehensive "self-cultivation" (Hirsch 1979, 295), which leads him from his initial state of immaturity to "*growth and development*" (Hirsch 1979, 296; emphasis in the original). Elements of the "quest story" are also quite apparent, with clearly defined stages that mark the protagonist's development and several characters who, in one way or another, serve to educate Sami and to further his progress. All in all, the novel has a clearly didactic undertone, which can already be deduced from the author's comment on the Muslim writer's responsibility as quoted above. In the first half of the novel we find Sami, at thirty-one years old, spiralling towards the climax of a life crisis that has been building up for several years. At this point he has to confront the reality that, after ten years of collecting material and writing notes for a PhD project, he actually has very little to show for his work, and is compelled to consider other career options. At the same time, he is faced with the consequences of his wife's gradual turn towards Islam. Since his opposition to reli-

---

54 While it concentrates on describing Sami's struggle with his faith, the novel also delineates his wife Muntaha's gradual turn towards an intellectual and personal religiosity, and contrasts this with her brother Ammar's growing fanaticism, in addition to their father's practice of Islam in exile whereby he uses it in the form of a physical and mental routine to give himself something to hold on to.
55 See Rashid (2012) for a more extensive analysis of the novel's "reappropriated *Bildungsroman* form" (Rashid 2012, 92). Rashid, moreover, offers an interesting insight into the novel's incorporation of Sufi narrative to transform the structure of the *bildungsroman*.

gion, as well as what he considers as his academic vocation, had been assiduously cultivated building blocks of his identity, he is forced to fundamentally reassess how he sees himself and who he wants to be at this stage of his life. He is becoming more and more aware of the danger that he might be re-enacting the basic conflict of his parents' marriage in his personal life. While growing up, he experienced their mutual hostility as a domestic war that was reflected by the political conflict under the Ba'athist government in their homeland of Syria. Sami recognises that his atheism and his academic aspirations are the result of his father's legacy, and how these blindly assumed principles have led him to repeat his parents' estrangement in his own domestic struggle over Islam versus secularism. When Sami's marriage and all of the other pillars of his existence fall apart, he is compelled to confront his relationship with his parents and the ramifications of the extended familial and political history in order to reposition himself in his life and within his family. Sami manages to overcome the crumbling of his carefully constructed self-image not just by replacing it with another, but by entirely transforming his perspective and, in this process, by acquiring a new understanding of (his own and others') identities. In moving away from the unbending standpoint of identity politics towards a more open concept of identity that allows for change and inconsistencies, Sami also comes to re-evaluate the meaning of family.

4.2.1 Self-Fashioning and Postmodern Identities in the Multicultural Sphere

Through its account of a variety of multicultural identities, the novel puts forward a constructivist view of identity as a process of meaning making through signs and scripts, symbols and narratives. It emphasises the way in which genealogical, political, national, ethnic, religious and other allegiances constitute more or less conscious forms of self-fashioning and self-positioning in the process of identity construction, which open up different forms of belonging. In his desire for integration and to understand his cultural and ethnic affiliations, Sami first turns to his father's secularist Arab nationalism as a scaffold for constructing an assertive narrative of the self. In his childhood and early adolescence, his world is explained to him by his father, Mustafa Traifi, an intellectual, whose magnum opus, *The Secular Arab Consciousness*, still serves as guidebook for Sami after his father's death. Sami is thus raised under the terms of his father's "secularist repudiation of Islam" (R. Ahmed 2015, 218), an allegiance that explicitly rejects and excludes the position of his religious mother, Nur. "Sami learnt early on to separate these two narratives" (53) of secularist

Arabism and Islam, which he experienced as strictly incompatible in his parents' house:[56] "There were conflicting worlds in this scene, worlds which could never be reconciled." (59) In this scenario of irreconcilable world-views, Sami finds it easy to "choose his side" (56; cf. 60) – thereby internalising and reproducing this opposition.

After having experienced his own Arab ethnicity as an empty signifier in the context of late twentieth century multicultural Britain,[57] Sami "refigured Mustafa's Arabism as his own" (60), turning it into something "to be proud of" (60), an image that he loves to see reflected in mirrors or "in the [...] eyes of women" (13). His identity formation during his adolescence and young adulthood relies heavily on an assemblage of signifiers in the shape of props and objects pointing to different aspects of the message of self that he wants to transmit. One clear example of this type of self-fashioning is the *kuffiyeh* that Sami wears, a traditional Middle Eastern headdress, which is not only something that "[a] member of his class in Syria would never wear" but which, moreover, he wears "in a Kurdish style" (13). Stripped of its complexity and the variety of meanings that can be attached to it, the *kuffiyeh* stands for "a transplanted nationalism in which the significance of signs had swivelled away from their original focus" (13). It becomes no more than a fashion article that underlines his individualistic and hedonistic "sexy version of the Arab world", through which Sami finds a way to "come to terms with what he now described as his heritage" (13). In the summer of 1991, when he at 21-years-old, he meets Muntaha, in whom he sees a reflection of himself (cf. 18) and a "confirmation of the difference he flaunted" (12): "A proper Arab. Baghdad-born, she had an accent. [...] She was every bit as Arab as the kuffiyeh he checked in the mirror before leaving his flat." (13)[58]

---

56 His mother's attempts to "mix[...] Islamic language with that of nationalism and modernity, not understanding how they could exclude each other" in the early phases of her religiosity eventually fail.

57 Other ethnicities that had more 'schoolyard credibility' during Sami's youth in the 1980s were the white English, simply "through strength of numbers, and because it was the normal standard", black, which "even made converts", the Sikhs, who "had bhangra", the Irish, and the Jews (60). Muslim identity is considered as being weak in this context by Sami (before the Rushdie Affair), and Arabism as being even more so. "This was before the Iraqis arrived. The visible Arabs were Gulf Arabs, tourists and princelings, obese, wealthy, stupid." (61) Asked about his origins, he tries to evade pre-determined and fixed definitions, explaining that he is "a kind of Arab" (61), or that Syria is "a Mediterranean country" and not necessarily "a Muslim country", as his teachers suggest (60).

58 Given the doubtful authenticity of Sami's *kuffiyeh*, this statement carries a strong irony that reveals the stance the narrator takes vis à vis his protagonist, whom he lightly derides here and in other places for his arrogance and feeling of superiority. The comparison of Muntaha with

Thus in "claiming allegiances", Sami, "in memory of his father" (13), carves out an idea of Arabness that stifles other, parallel or competing, narratives of national, ethnic or religious identity. When Muntaha, on one of their early dates, quotes Imam Ali and thus hints at a partly Shii heritage, Sami frowns, deploring "the drawback of an Arab woman, the shackle-weight of history" (18). While Sami wishes to discard history because it entails complexities that challenge his idea of Arab identity, Muntaha, by contrast, sees her own identity construction enhanced by history and the better understanding that it offers her. In school, her interest in history is sparked by her teacher's unconventional lessons and his approach that succeeds in unravelling the present day continuities of (imperial) history so that it highlights its entanglements and ramifications (cf. 85). Muntaha, "because she came from somewhere else, because she couldn't take her present position for granted" (85), feels that her biography is particularly closely tied up with history: "She knew she came from ancient depths" (85). As a teenager, Muntaha felt her world to be "especially awkward", and yearned to somehow "fit in" (83) and belong. This is exacerbated not only by the act of her migration from Iraq at the age of nine, but also by the loss of her mother, who was brutally killed by the henchmen who took her father to prison, either for the act of copying and distributing communist poetry, or, perhaps, due to "a false report" (71). Even her father, physically and mentally broken after six months of torture in prison, is not the same as she remembered him, and his disillusionment, his smallness and sense of failure (cf. 84), only adds to the awkwardness of her life. The attempt to understand and link her life story to the larger context of history serves to embellish its awkwardness with "mystery" and "strangeness" (84), and thus gives it a positive turn. History thus offers a sense of belonging to Muntaha by providing a framework that gives meaning to her own narrative: "There was no dividing line between her personal circumstances and what was discussed in Mr Sorrel's class. Beyond the beauty clique, she fitted, jaggedly, into historical narrative." (86)[59]

The fact that Muntaha does not fit in with Sami's self-image and his understanding of Arabness as neatly as he initially assumed increasingly becomes a challenge for him and for their relationship. In light of his externalised under-

---

his *kuffiyeh*, moreover, hints at his view of her, which is similarly blind to history and the contradictions within Arabism as his appropriation of the *kuffiyeh*.

59 The "beauty clique" is Muntaha's way of 'fitting in' at school – a group based on the "exotic charms" of their members, regardless of their ethnic affiliation other than their "being brown" (84). The whole idea of the group is: "Just to be cool. To fit together by being a bit different." (84)

standing of the identity that he has constructed with semiotically charged objects, Muntaha, in "threatening to wear the hijab" (3), becomes a threat to Sami's whole concept of self.[60] While her recently established routine of prayer is something he manages to more or less ignore, the hijab, in his perception, is predominantly a symbol that is overdetermined by meaning. As such, the hijab challenges his carefully assembled world-view and the very underpinnings of his identity. Identity, for Sami, is a product of conscious self-construction, "a position to hold, a reputation, loyalty to a certain image" (101) – an image that is carefully modelled on his own vision of his father. In his eyes, the symbolism of the hijab eclipses Muntaha's individuality, and he fears that his own loss of identity and individuality would follow suit: "[W]hat did it mean for him, being the husband of such a sign? What was he now? What was he a symbol of?" (102) On his first "public showing" alongside Muntaha who was wearing the hijab on the way to visit her family, he feels alienated from himself – merely through being associated with her:

> Sami supposed they must look like a proper Muslim couple, what with the hijab, Muslims out on dark business, their trauma children and a string of austere relatives left behind in an unfurnished overcrowded room. Four or five children already, that's what it probably looked like. These two Muslims at large. (110)[61]

Although he projects this perception of Muntaha and himself onto the other passengers on the tube – "[t]here were four viewers to see them in the carriage"

---

60 In a dispute with his wife over the issue, he becomes "increasingly desperate, the ground shifting beneath his feet" (98).
61 His subsequent reflections on his own view of himself as opposed to how others see him make it obvious, at least to the reader if not yet to Sami himself at this point, that his self-image is in desperate need of a thorough revision and adjustment. Interestingly, he imagines himself "[i]n his mind's eager eye" as looking like he is "twenty, at a stretch twenty-two" (110), roughly the age when he first met Muntaha. Although his outer appearance has definitely changed in the ten years since then (Sami's body is "ageing quickly [and] increasingly swell-bellied", with "climbing baldness", 1), Sami's inner development seems to be in a state of stagnation since his early twenties. In the same chapter, his father-in-law, Marwan, will later expose Sami as someone who is "always too young to have children, to take responsibility" (114). The chapter's eponymous "Family Visit" also shows up Sami's inability to take up his responsibilities regarding the older generation (in this case, it is his father-in-law, who he obviously very rarely visits despite his illness, and whose ta'ziya/wake he will miss later on in the novel; the same is even more true with regard to his mother, with whom he has no contact). The distorted reflection of "trauma children and a string of austere relatives" that complete his image of the generic multigenerational Muslim family can thus be read as a commentary on his failure to start his own family and maintain a connection with his relations.

(110) – his heightened awareness of the disparity that he feels in Muntaha's company and his overall feeling of conspicuousness reveal his own deep-seated bias. This bias, implanted in him by his father, is predicated on the opposition between Islam and nationalism, and the backwardness of religion on the one hand and the modernity of secularism on the other. For Sami, the multiplicity of religions and confessions of faith that he encounters on his route to school alone, can all be boiled down to a simple equation: "Belief X cancels belief Y. Leaving zero belief." (57) Claiming a religion, in his eyes, means to claim to have "found the exclusive answer" (57), and consequently, to "ha[ve] to deny all the others" (56). Over the course of the novel, Sami has to learn that his idea of secularism is no less dogmatic than the "one-and-only truths jostling for attention", and is in no way more accepting of pluralism or difference. Having built a surrogate religion around the "sepulchre" (10, 153) of his father, Sami is just as defensive of his single narrative, with its meanings and truths, as, for example, the religious fundamentalists he encounters in his brother-in-law's mosque. It is a simplistic and reductionist world-view, in which, "issues [always] returned to hijabs and beards" (116) as signifiers of backwardness and superstition.

The reductionism of such an image-oriented understanding of identity is deeply enmeshed in the "often crude identity politics of contemporary British Islam" (Rashid 2012, 93), and similarly revolves around questions of representation and recognition.[62] His final plea to Muntaha, after all attempts at discussion have proven fruitless, reveals his central and actual concern: "I thought that we stood for something else" (109).[63] As a result of his personal agenda of secular Arabness, he fears the disintegration of their identity as a couple in light of his wife's adoption of a new identity that is itself tied in with the collective identity of British Muslims (cf. 98). While Muntaha claims that her desire to "belong" has "nothing to do with the Arabs" (98), for Sami, the two identities form an

---

[62] The novel's story is set around the September 11 attacks and has to be considered in the context of the anti-Muslim backlash in the UK and elsewhere. Sami's anti-Muslim position and his fixation on superficial markers of religiosity can be read as comment to the widespread post-9/11 Islamophobia and the inherent suspicion of people with hijabs and beards that accompanied it. This becomes most evident when Sami himself is arrested towards the end of the novel on exiting a mosque while wearing a beard.

[63] His idea that the two of them, as a couple, have to represent a certain idea or ideology, is refuted by Muntaha in a similar way to her reaction to his understanding of vocation based on familial legacy or heritage earlier in the novel. Her simple answer that "We don't stand for anything" (109) invokes her previous attempt to deflate Sami's sense of mission and innate predetermination ("you weren't born for any job. Nobody is", 47).

irreconcilable divergence that evokes his parents' conflict. In their relationship two different concerns of identity formation clash, due to the fact that they seem to exclude each other: his political and outwardly oriented focus on representation on the one hand, and her inwardly directed need for belonging on the other.

4.2.2 Family Legacy as Life Script: Setting a 'Straight Path'

Sami's postmodernist construction of self is a playful, yet problematic one. His wariness of grand narratives, reflected in the "high frequency of Re and Post among the titles" (33) in his bookshelf, clashes with his own understanding of ancestral roots and family legacy, which converge to form his idea of 'Arabism'. "Sami's identity is pulled between the two contradictory poles of postmodernism and Arabism" (C. Chambers 2012, 119) – a contradiction that eventually leads to and is resolved by his identity crisis. The novel, although mainly set in London, opens in Syria, where Sami has gone for the summer – his final attempt in a series of endeavours to get back on track with his PhD thesis in the field of Arab literature. After a sabbatical spent travelling the world and a research stay in Paris, the trip to Syria, from where his parents emigrated, is his hoped for "talismanic last-chance cure" (44). For Paul (Acts 9, 1–31), Damascus is the symbolic place for an ultimate identity test, crisis and conversion; for Sami it is equally charged with meaning: "Damascus was supposed to offer him answers. He'd been here for a month, in order to (he listed): reconnect with his roots; remember who he was; find an idea." (1) At this point, he is already quite deep into a crisis, living off his wife's income as a schoolteacher while having spent all of his own money on his fruitless studies (cf. 37). He hopes that the trip to Syria will somehow get him back on course to recover the 'right path'. The three objectives of his trip – "to reconnect with his roots, remember who he was, find an idea. In that causal order" (38)[64] – are not only closely interconnected, but are all linked to his father Mustafa, who, despite his death 19 years previously, still acts as the main 'guiding figure' in Sami's life.[65] In Syria, although alienated

---

[64] This mental list of "reasons for going" seems to have become a kind of mantra for Sami, since it is repeated verbatim in the novel (cf. 1, 38). This indicates that on the one hand he has a slight obsession that is connected with his desperation and "the sense of a last chance" (38), while on the other hand it shows Sami's desire for control and his fixation on this particular life script, which connects his own narrative with his father's.

[65] Their close connection exists despite his father's early death, but is at the same time also furthered by it, because, "dead, embalmed and mummified" (10), Mustafa becomes the object

in many ways and "feeling foreign now" (1), Sami tries to re-assure himself that "it was his country too. His father's country." (2) The connection to place and roots is thus clearly conceived from a patrilineal perspective that elides his mother's line – a one-sidedness in his perception of the roles of family member and their importance that registers in the fact that Sami still talks to his dead father while having simultaneously broken off all contact with his mother, despite the fact that she lives nearby in London. Sami's relationship with his parents is based on a reduced and simplified narrative that he follows and trusts: the story of his mother's betrayal of his father by choosing religion – desecrating the domestic space through prayer during his father's lifetime, and disrespecting his memory after his death by wearing a hijab. His perspective on family also blatantly disregards living (and lived) connections, as the people he actually visits in Syria are his mother's relatives, but his interest in them is merely professional. Seeking to follow the legacy of his father, a renowned scholar in Arab literature, Sami sees the coveted doctorate as his (supposedly self-fulfilling) destiny: "It had seemed inevitable, and it had never happened." (2) His image of himself is narrowly aligned with that of his father, and his life script is sketched out accordingly, with the result that he feels that the attainment of his PhD will be the only way to set all other things right that are off in his life: "So he was here to find a new idea, gather material – and then return home, write the thesis, become Dr Sami Traifi. As a proper academic, like his father before him, he'd be able to get it all back on course, his place in the world, his marriage, his mother. So he believed." (2)

Damascus is not only the "home of his ancestors" (1) but it is also a renowned place of cultural memory and tradition, "[w]here Ibn Arabi wrote his last mystical poetry, where Nizar Qabbani wrote 'Bread, Hashish and Moon'." (2) It is through this conflation of the concepts of legacy and heritage with his object of study, Arab literature and the Syrian poet Qabbani,[66] that his dissertation project becomes overly charged with (personal) weight and meaning, and therefore his failure to finish the work drastically calls his self-conception into question. His doctorate is designed to confirm his own position in "the Great Arab Nation narrative. A story told in Mustafa's voice, with Qabbani's words"

---

of his son's nostalgic and unconstrained idolisation, a "porcelain sepulchre. Mustafa Traifi, enshrined in Sami's head." (10) Moreover, the fact that he experienced his father's death at the age of twelve is, for Sami, a central aspect of his self-narrative and a defining factor of his identity – "this most important fact about Sami" (18).

66 His initial topic for his PhD project is Qabbani's influence on the Arabic language, and "to show how poetry improved language and therefore the world" (33).

(33). Sami's father takes the inspiration for this narrative from the stars in the sky, across which, "joining the dots, [he] found lines and arcs in the chaos" (50). With Mustafa's guidance, Sami learns to see the stars as "[s]hapes with meanings, histories" (51), which, in his father's reading, tell an alternative story of origin and beginning to that of Islamic tradition. In this light, the epic of Gilgamesh, "our great ancestor" (51), which Mustafa teaches to Sami with reference to the stellar constellation,[67] becomes a founding myth for the Arab nation. His delineation of Arab history is thus based on a literary and cultural tradition rather than the canonised religious text of the Qur'an. As told by his father, the Gilgamesh epic is the beginning of a straight line that can be drawn from the "first sky stories" narrated by Arabs through centuries of Arab secular culture and literature right down to the Traifi family. "Mustafa could map genetics and geography on to the sky. Sami half expected to find the map of Syria up there. He expected to find himself." (51) The "different mythology" (53) of Islam that Sami hears from his mother is tolerated by his father only insofar as "[t]hese Semitic myths, after all, were essential to the literary traditions Sami would study" (55).[68] Thus, his father's education, which he enjoyed as a child, is targeted to lead directly to his later studies at university, in a single predetermined 'Straight Path'.[69] The sense of destiny that Sami feels with regard to his doctorate is articulated in a quarrel with his wife after his return home, when he counters her suggestion for him to get a job with the claim that he "wasn't born to work in a cab office" (47). Clearly he feels a strong sense of legacy and filial duty; his PhD project is what he was 'born to do'.

Sami has compelled himself to follow the life script of his father, eschewing any possible alternative route. His doctorate is deeply informed by this world-

---

[67] The epic of Gilgamesh is connected with what is now widely known as the constellation of Orion, which is host to a number of narratives with different origins. Among these, the Gilgamesh epic is not only the most extensive, but also the earliest – as Mustafa does not fail to point out: "It was us who named him first" (51).

[68] As this passage indicates, the idea to study Arab literature, as both his parents did before him (they met at university) was implanted in Sami at an early age by his father.

[69] Cf. 38. The metaphor of the 'Straight Path' is an allusion to the conversion of Paul as told in the Acts of the Apostles, in which the disciple Ananias is told by the Lord to find the blinded Paul in "the house of Judas on Straight Street" (Acts 9; 11). The prescribed path of his life is underlined by Sami and his father's regular visits to the cinema, "a ritual as educative, as acculturing, as a Friday mosque visit. It anticipated the shape of life to come." (32) The teleological narrative pattern of the films and their happy endings map out his own life for him as a story of success, at the end of which he would "write about Arabic literature, and become famous [...], like his father. But better than his father. Leaping forth from the giant's shoulders, he'd go further." (32)

view and by his father's ideology – "a kind of secular fundamentalism that can, [the novel] suggests, be as blinding as [religious] dogma" (Jaggi 2008, n.p.).[70] It is the unbending dogmatism of his views that eventually leads to his academic failure, because his research is steeped in pre-determined conceptions and biased beliefs that narrow his scope, cancelling out all perspectives and topics "that he'd been brought up to despise" (34). The different theses that he comes up with are all construed to support, in one way or another, "the Great Arab Nation narrative" (33) as told by his father, and to uphold his intellectual legacy. As his supervisor, Dr Schimmer, observes, in Sami's work there is "always the big idea looming behind. Always you have wanted to map the details on the big idea." (154) Sami himself becomes increasingly insecure in his work, hopping from one topic to the next with a feeling that "reality wouldn't quite submit to his vision" (33). The metaphor of 'the path of life' reveals Sami's simplistic notion of roots and vocation as binding constants – an image that, like the idea of the Arab grand narrative, stands as a contradiction to his postmodern construction of self as a collage of de- and reconstructed signs and meanings.[71]

Sami's trip to Syria, instead of yielding the hoped for self-affirmation and confirmation of his 'chosen path',[72] discloses "roots he didn't want to dig up" (39). These unwanted roots, instead of confirming his ideas, open up new questions and alternative truths. The crisis that ensues reveals how, for Sami, his counter-narratives to the grand narratives of history and religion have themselves taken the shape of unshakeable truths, and how, in an attempt to escape religion, he has built a surrogate religion around his father's 'sepulchre'. Sami experiences a moment of *epiphany* at the end of his trip in which he anticipates the development and formation that he will undergo in the course of the novel:

> he lucidly conceded that things were complex, that nothing was simple. There were paths other than the one his father had trodden. Other, but not necessarily mistaken. Paths taken, for instance, by his wife, or by his mother. Other, valid paths. He conceded it just for a

---

[70] Cf. the novel's epigraph: "unbelief itself is a religion with its own form of belief" (Ahmad Yasavi).
[71] He takes note of this contradiction himself, conceding that "[t]he roots are shallow, and mythical; we all come from everywhere at once, and we are floating creatures. Sami as much as anyone was inheritor of the great postmodern division." (38)
[72] The first chapter is titled „The Other Path", pointing to the possibility of other options and life decisions.

few moments. It would take a summertime for the realization to sink into his core, corrosively, like salt into snow. (10–11)[73]

4.2.3 Memory, Narrative, and Family Secrets

Sami's moment of epiphany occurs after his visit to his aunt's house in Damascus, where the hint at a family secret suggests that his parents' conflict is interwoven with the larger context of his family history. His notion that there might be other valid paths to this includes the recognition that there might also be other versions of the past, different narratives other than his own idea of family roots and legacy. An understanding and recognition of these alternatives requires a thorough rerouting of his family narrative, and his memory, which has been devoted to paying tribute to his father. Sami's study, the location for his academic endeavour, emphasises the way in which his sense of legacy is interconnected with family memory.[74] The room is decorated as a shrine to the remembrance of his father, and contains inherited furniture and the 'stink of nostalgia' (cf. 44). At the heart of his study is a drawer with well-chosen memorabilia and relics: a constellation map, an Arabic edition of the Gilgamesh epic with a personal dedication from father to son, a signed first edition of his father's book, a miniature whiskey bottle that they shared in hospital before his father's death, and a selection of photographs. In their deliberate selection, these objects tell a clear and definitive story:

> Sami had one collection of Mustafa relics in his head and another in his desk drawer. The desk-drawer collection was more satisfying. He could handle it when he liked, each item fully present to his touch, unlike his vapourish memories which burst on him at odd moments and disappeared again into the insect whirring of his thoughts.
> Anyway, as time progressed the internal pieces came more and more to resemble the external, so that he considered the external, the empirically verifiable, the trustworthy, to be the originals. (49)

---

[73] The snow is a recurrent image that recalls the state of emotional frigidity that Sami entered into after his father's death (cf. 172ff.; for the leitmotivic use of snow and coldness vs. heat and fire see pages 253 and 348).

[74] Sami and Muntaha's shared house in London is "divided into spheres of influence" (41), with the study being the room that is most completely Sami's own. The absence of shared spaces ("[t]he kitchen and bedroom and upstairs bathroom belonged to her. and since he'd been away she'd reclaimed the hall and stairway", 41) hints at the lack of a shared narrative and life script of husband and wife. Moreover, Sami's furnishing of his study as a 'male' space emphasises his focus on patrilineal family history, from which Muntaha is just as equally excluded as his mother.

The conscientious collection of heirlooms thus reveals Sami's strong desire to control his memory. The carefully chosen objects enable him to fix his memories in a coherent, unified and convenient narrative that fits his idea of the past and of the family narrative. His memory thus works exactly like his construction of identity through objects that bolster his self-image, "a definite, deliberated image, constructed of solid elements" (13). Sami's memory objects, however, tell a very biased and partial story; one that neglects whole parts of the family history and reduces his familial identity to his close relationship with his father. The assuring stability and fixity of these memorial objects gives Sami control over the family (and thus also his own) narrative – a narrative that conforms to his father's version of the truth. This is most prominently represented by the "wad of photographs – of him and Mustafa only, no mother, no uncles – curling at the edges" (49). The 'family photographs' underline Sami's vision of a patrilineal family identity, and write his mother out of the family narrative. Moreover, in blocking his mother from his consciousness, he represses any indication that there might be other versions or other truths besides that of his father.

The 'missing uncles' in the photographs hint at another blind spot in his family narrative that Sami comes across in Syria during a visit to his maternal aunt in Damascus. Here, in "the darker interior of the house" (4), he discovers a man who turns out to be Faris, his mother's brother, and who, apparently deranged, sits in a darkened room doing nothing but clicking his prayer beads. Although Sami does not consciously remember this uncle, he senses "[s]omething […] stirring […] in the inner chambers of his memory" (4). His memory is now tormented by a story, hidden in "the gloom of the house" (4), which Sami views as challenging his narrative in a way that he does not yet understand. Sami initially tries to distance himself from the matter, casting it as part of the conventional narrative of a family secret and misreading his aunt's family's behaviour as shame: "This was the skeleton in the backroom, then: a loonish relative. This is what they were ashamed of." (5)[75] His "inward smile" on returning from the dark room emphasises his feeling of detachment and superiority towards his family, which at this point only interests him from an ethnographic standpoint as a representation of "ordinary Syrian Arabs" (4), but to

---

[75] In Sami's view, this case seems typical and falls into the category of "shameful illness", one of "five broad types" of family secrets that Carol Smart (2011a, 542) lists. In his perception, the case of his uncle presents an issue that is shielded from the outside because it touches on a topic that is stigmatised by society (cf. Segrin and Flora 2011, 63). As part of the family, this type of "*[w]hole or shared family secret*" (Segrin and Flora 2011, 62; emphasis in the original) would now include him in the group of those who are privy to the knowledge.

which he has no emotional or personal attachment. At the same time, his own lack of knowledge underlines his outsider's position in his (maternal) family and hints at the isolation of his perspective: "There was a secret here which Sami alone had not penetrated." (5) Before Sami's aunt tells him the story of how Faris had joined the Muslim Brotherhood during the Islamic uprising in Syria in the early 1980s and, without yet having done anything, was arrested, tortured, and imprisoned for decades, she tells him to put away his notebook. Even so, Sami's attitude remains distant, and he refuses to see himself connected to it, instead preferring to remark on his aunt's "foreignness" (6). At the end of the story, his first reaction is to feel betrayed by his mother, who had "humiliated her son" (8) in front of the family by letting "him grow up without telling him this essential piece of family information, about her brother" (9). For Sami, the element of shame that is so closely connected with the family secret here shifts from his aunt to himself as the one to be singled out, as the boundaries delineated by the secret run right directly through the heart of the family. His feeling of betrayal, which he immediately blames on his mother, shows the fixity of these boundaries. The actual question of betrayal in this story, however, is "who informed on Uncle Faris" (9), whose involvement with the Brotherhood was only known to his immediate family. Sami is confused by the manner in which his aunt and cousins ask him this, apparently implicating Sami in the guilt, "[s]taring at me, as if it was me" (341).

This new piece of family information, the realisation that 'reconnecting with his roots' might uncover a family history that does not fit into and therefore challenges his carefully constructed story forces Sami to reconsider the identity that he has constructed – and the truths that this identity is based on. Although indecipherable to him at first, the story continues to haunt him and unsettles his controlled memory. After the visit to his aunt, the image of his uncle – "A man in a gloomy room worrying prayer beads. Click, click. Cause and effect." (44)[76] – forms a returning memory that he is unable to repress. His attempts to push the incident from his mind, or to silence it, fail.[77] "It was too much infor-

---

[76] Cf. also the passage in which Sami enters his father-in-law's room, where, "in a rush of dizziness, [he] was reminded of a hotter, dryer, but equally gloomy room, in Damascus" (111).
[77] At home with Muntaha, Sami alludes to the incident with his uncle, saying that he had "a bad time in Syria" and wishes that he had not gone, but refuses to talk about it: "That was Sami, opening doors only to slam them shut again." (42) The story has thus added to "the list of forced silences they now had: his work, her ideas. Her feelings. Important subjects" (36), which indicate the deterioration in their relationship. These forced silences are also the result of Sami's state of emotional coldness: "A coldness descended when Muntaha tried to talk seriously about it [the fact that Sami didn't talk to his mother]." (87)

mation of the wrong sort, this Faris story. Nothing that would help his thesis or his fraying life in London." (9) It does not help because it does not confirm what he already knows, and instead opens up new questions and suggests alternative versions to his narrative, which he was heretofore able to ignore. The indication of 'cause and effect' resonates as a distant warning, demanding his attention; it hints at the long-term ramifications of family silences and their transgenerational potential to disrupt relationships. His cousin's question – "*I wonder who informed on Uncle Faris?*" (262; emphasis in the original) – remains with Sami and suggests that his own story is in some way connected with the betrayal of his uncle. The incident at his aunt's house thus becomes an involuntary and uncontrollable memory that obtrudes the fixity and manageability of the narrative that he has built around his adoration of his father as made tangible in his collection of memory objects. On a more subconscious level, the story triggers a recurring nightmare in which Sami, in panic, tries to run from a galloping horse, "becoming entangled in the newly sprouted undergrowth" (9). When the horse collapses dead on the ground, Sami recognises that it wears his father's face, "elongated to fit the equine muzzle" (10), and wakes up with a shock.[78] The nightmarish vision of the acceleration of hooves galloping behind him and the collapsing horse invokes paintings of the Pauline conversion as well as images of the horsemen of the Apocalypse.[79] The vision thus directly relates to Sami's conversion and epiphany, putting an increasingly pressing claim on him to reassess the image that he has of his father and to face the implications of what he has learnt in Damascus: his father's guilt, and his own 'entanglement' in it.[80]

In line with the *bildungsroman* form of the novel, the Damascene incident does not in itself lead to recognition, but the revelation is prolonged by a difficult process of understanding and self-reinvention, urged on by the "apocalypse horse" (166).[81] The narrator makes the connection between Sami's epiph-

---

[78] The horse is later described as a centaur (281); its exact form, however, is not quite clear as in most scenes it is described as a horse with only the "leering, fish-eyed face of Mustafa Traifi" (166) where its head would have been.

[79] In many paintings of the Pauline conversion on his way to Damascus a horse is part of the scene, often dramatically collapsing along with its rider in shocked reaction to the epiphany.

[80] The nightmare replaces his hitherto "nostalgic dreams" of his father (10). When Sami reviews his relationship with his father at this point, he assesses that "[t]here was nothing wrong in the father-son relationship, nothing except the fact that the father was dead [...]. Not until now. Bubbles were rising" (10). The vision, often pushed away by Sami and only perceived as the clacking of hooves, also haunts him during the day.

[81] Sami, at one point, feels "he was being on the verge of something. The lifting of a veil. The Greek word for it is apocalypse." (181)

any and his nightmarish vision explicit by mentioning the Greek etymology of 'apocalypse': "The lifting of a veil" (181). The veil that is slowly lifted by the force of the horse that haunts him is the one that covers the great family secret. The 'Faris story', although incomprehensible to him at first, functions as a "catalyst" (Rashid 2012, 95) that precipitates Sami's 'conversion'. When he returns home from Syria after the visit to his aunt's house, he rushes headlong into a crisis: "Whatever he was accustomed to was falling away beneath his feet" (39). As his beliefs start to become unravelled, he tumbles into a self-destructive cascade of alcohol, drugs and parties, bringing his whole world crushing down around him in a grand gesture of iconoclasm. In the chapter entitled "Evolutionary Loss", Sami, after having been arrested for doing cocaine, wakes up in prison to the realisation that there is literally nothing left of his previous life.[82] It is at this point that he "glimpsed the unvarnished truth: that he had betrayed everybody, in various ways. Mustafa. Marwan. His mother, of course. Now Muntaha. Not just now, but for a decade." (201) Failing each member of his family in his relationship with them or in their expectations of him, by not being a successful academic, a Muslim, a father, a son, or a husband. His list of betrayals continues from there, and finally tumbles "deeper into obscurity, [to include] his broken uncle Faris, in Damascus. Why was Sami responsible for that? The question posed itself in bright clarity, and Sami at once forgot it. Forgetful Sami." (201)

Once released from prison, he is kicked out by Muntaha and has to take up lodgings in a student dormitory, living off of a small bank loan. "[L]osing the past and his natural habitat, losing context, losing any stable definition of himself" (203), he takes the opportunity to stablish new beginnings. Sami enters a stage of nihilism, during which "his sense of standards, and so much else, seemed to have melted" (176) until nothing remains: "Like his Big Idea decon-

---

[82] In a dazed frenzy of alcohol and drugs, during which Sami loses all sense of time and orientation, he shatters the remnants of his deteriorating marriage, first by neglecting the message informing him of his father-in-law's death (and subsequently by failing to attend the gathering of mourners at the deceased's house), then by having sex with a stranger at a party. Although he is completely beside himself most of the time, his conscience is still present in decisive moments for him to take note of his wrong-doing. The two acts of betrayal towards his wife act as a microcosm for his general failure as a husband over the course of their marriage: "Sami by his absence and betrayal had abdicated all pretence to husbandhood." (198) Similarly, his excessive use of alcohol and drugs in this night, as an escapist reaction to his supervisor's rejection of his idea, reflects his usual inability to face reality and act responsibly.

structed: nothing." (179) In a thorough process of 'cleansing',[83] Sami subsequently dismantles his prior self, taking it apart and abolishing all aspects of it: the godlike image of his father, his concepts and beliefs ("the expensive isms which he'd previously taken as sacred text", 202), his vanity ("Sami's curls came sprinkling downwards" in his decision "to come to terms with [his bald bit]", 209, cf. also 218), his "secular" appearance (he discontinues his excessive shaving habits, 209), his opinions and "illusions" (particularly those on secularism vs. religiosity, cf. 222, 244), "his pleasures" (successively giving up alcohol, marijuana, tobacco, 254). He radically changes his diet, repudiating all food that is not organic, regional, seasonal, vegetarian, in an attempt at self-purification and re-programming. "Sami aimed for self-control. The body, he reasoned – and the self is what he meant – was a monster that could be weakened through lack of sustenance." (255) This desire for self-chastisement stems from a feeling of disgust at his former inflated self and, less consciously, at the betrayal that lies at its foundation: "All those associated slow-vomit words [...]: 'spill' and 'spew', 'purge' and 'purify'. Somehow they brought him to Syrian detention chambers. Hanging parties. The detergent of bombs. Liquidation" (255).[84]

Sami has his crucial revelation during an experiment as part of a neuropsychological study on the inheritability of religious belief conducted by a character called Professor Fencestoat.[85] Fitted with a helmet that causes transcranial stimulation, he has a vision that begins with a childhood memory of his mother, who finger-combs his curls to the sound of Qur'anic singing on the radio. The memory triggers strong emotions of comfort, tranquillity, and, most significantly, unity between mother and son, which translates to a feeling that the boundary between their bodies dissolves in the shared after-bath routine of motherly

---

[83] This is preceded by a passage of utter debasement and defilement, of Sami's intoxicated journey through London's party scene which ends in a prison cell full of "stink. It was thick and heavy and full of horror. It prised open dark areas of his brain." (179)

[84] See also 262: "There it was again. Purge, purify, imprison, torture. *I wonder who informed on Uncle Faris?*"

[85] Prof. Fencestoat's thesis is that a tendency towards belief can be inherited, as opposed to the object of belief, likening the "spiritual experience" to the "experience of orgasm, in which we seem to overspill the boundary of ourselves for a moment, to become one with the other, this experience so useful to building close familial bonds and loyalties..." (277). According to this reasoning, a person's spirituality thus enhances their interpersonal (especially familial) relationships (cf. 278). The name Fencestoat reads very much like Pentecost, drawing a (perhaps slightly ironic) parallel between Sami's vision and the descent of the Holy Spirit and the birth of the Church.

care: "He ends not at his scalp but at the top of her hand, [...] he ends where she does" (280). When the harmonious scene is violently crashed by his father, who enters the vision, Sami feels a "constriction [... and t]he force of [his] adult body bearing down on him" (281): The sense of childish innocence and security is lost. Along with the vision of his father, the images that Sami has tried hard to repress re-enter: "Black and bloody walls. Detention chamber. Screams. [...] The looming secret, Mustafa looming." (281) Instead of running away, Sami this time confronts his father and the secret that he has come to embody; while savagely stabbing the centaur with a sword suddenly found in his hands, Sami draws an admission of guilt and an explanation from him: "I thought it was worth it." (281) Mustafa thus reveals the murderous potential of his secularist ideology, for which he was willing to betray and disavow his family, a behaviour that Sami has repeated unquestioningly in the past.[86] With Sami's 'sacrifice' (cf. 281) of his father, the peaceful atmosphere returns to his vision as the body of the horse dissolves and "Mustafa raises a palm in farewell", leaving "lightly, in human form" (281).

Returning the father from his idolised status to human form not only allows Sami to finally say goodbye to his father (an opportunity that he was deprived of earlier, due to not being present at his father's final moments, cf. 245), it also enables Sami to emancipate himself from his obsession with his father, making room for new forms of meaning to enter his world.[87] When he ventures to pray in a mosque, he enters a meditation-like state, in which he feels the dissolution of his self and at the same time senses its connectedness and 'oneness' with the world – a sense of wholeness that is conveyed in the idea of the sky, which, "containing stars" (330) but emptied of the image of his father, seems to him to be "overarching and complete" (330). In the end, Sami is able to reconnect with Muntaha and even joins her in prayer, having "developed a trembling, contingent faith" (348). Moreover, he seeks reconciliation with his mother, asking her for her side of the story, and acknowledging her pain. While she is hesitant to speak about her brother and her husband's betrayal, Sami is eager to voice what happened and to break the silence. As a condition for taking him back, Muntaha

---

[86] Through his betrayal, Mustafa is implicated in the crimes and guilt of the Ba'ath Party, which killed several thousand people in the Hama massacre in 1982, the terrible culmination of the conflict between the Arab nationalist and secular government and the Muslim Brotherhood. He had always downplayed this massacre for the greater political aim of ending the civil war "[a]t any cost", as well as "[f]or the sake of the future, of progress" (169).

[87] By the end of the summer, which ends with the 9/11 terrorist attacks, Sami has no more fixed opinions and certainties, instead he now sees the contradictory nature and contingency of world events: "Nothing is simple. Everything is always changing" (323; cf. also 314, 318).

had demanded that he talk to his mother, stressing the importance of family values and relationships in contrast with his previous individualistic self-absorption.[88] While his previous solipsistic idea of family was focused on (one-sided patrilineal) lineage and descent, this reconnection with his wife and mother indicates a clear conversion to a different view of family as lived through the interaction with present relations, and by carrying out mutual obligations and responsibilities.[89] Sami ultimately re-formulates his sense of identity accordingly, moving away from his individualistic and "unbearably lonely sense of being special" (329) to a relational understanding of self that stresses his commitment to the living family rather than to an abstract idea of lineage and descent: "For what is he, now? [...] Not Mustafa's son, nor Marwan's son-in-law. Not the child of corpse dust. [...] He's Nur's son. Muntaha's husband." (348) In this relational understanding of self, Sami already primarily casts himself as "an attribute, a descriptor, not a subject" (338); a change that his mother Nur envisions to happen with a child, because "[a] child would mean Sami was a link in a chain, would make Mustafa a grandfather (deceased), and Sami a father, not the inheritor" (338).

Although Sami's previous concept of self as the inheritor of his father's ideas and legacy is also basically relational, it is oriented towards a dead father, a father who has become an unchanging, stable image that is, moreover, prone to fictionalisation and idealisation. At the beginning of the novel, Sami aligned himself and his life with a certain vision of his father quite literally in the way that a traveller in ancient times would have used the stars for navigation. The idea that his father is among the stars that offer orientation (cf. 49) reveals the one-sidedness of this relationship, in which his father is a screen onto which Sami only projects what he wants to see. Sami's idealisation of his father is refracted in Gabor Vronk, Muntaha's school colleague, whose function in the novel is to act as a commentary on and a counter-figure to Sami in a number of ways. Gabor also focuses on lineage as the main building block of his identity. However, as he is disenchanted with his "unexceptional" (135) parents, Gabor crafts a "personal history" for himself, in which he "[a]voids his parents" and "as much of muddy contemporary England as he can and focuses instead on his Russian grandfather, Vronsky" (132), who, in his eyes, is the embodiment of

---

[88] Muntaha's desire for a more responsible husband evokes her father Manwar's assessment of Sami as lacking the responsibility to have children (cf. 115).

[89] As Sami reconciles with Muntaha, he senses "the abyss of himself – his ancestors falling infinitely away inside him – and his shallowness, just a skin's thickness of conscious time between the deeps of past and future" (321).

"the strange and exotic" (186) which he desires for himself.[90] With little factual information about or any personal experience of his grandfather, Gabor has all the more freedom to make up his ancestral myth and narrative of origin to serve his self-fashioning. He "had to imagine it into shape. And what you're looking for, and how you look, determines what you see." (135; cf. also 132) The issue of the questionability of objective truth, which is so prevalent with regard to the ideology and religion in the novel, is transferred here to the context of family history. As such, it is also a comment on Sami's idea of family identity as a 'single story' and his failure to reflect on the perspectivity and stance of his family narrative.[91] Likewise, in his complete rejection of religion as being typical of the claim to truth and singularity of grand narratives, Sami disregarded the personal aspect to individual faith, which is represented through his wife Muntaha. As Muntaha's father states, "[b]elief is a duty. It isn't a choice. It isn't something you pick up in the market because you like the colour or you have enough coins in your pocket." (115) This allusion to the postmodern 'supermarket of identities' also relates to families and to the lived dimension of relationships, as they are upheld by family duties, mutual obligations, responsibilities, and respect for each other's differences. As he moves away from his previous understanding of family as a statement of identity, Sami opens up to an idea of family that is – much like identity – contingent, processual, interactive, and allows for multiple perspectives and meanings.

4.3 Concluding Thoughts: Trauma and Silence

Despite their great differences in theme and form, *Maps for Lost Lovers* and *The Road from Damascus* present some striking similarities. Both novels feature traumatised families and analyse the breakdown of communication in them.

---

90 The irrationality of his attempt to evade his synchronic family through association with his diachronic family is made explicit in a conversation with his parents, in which he claims not to have anything to do with them as they are "not my kind of people". When they tell him that "We're you're parents. You can't escape your past" he counters: "My ancestor is my grandfather" (188). This conversation also illustrates the fact that there are no predetermined meanings of family for the self; relatedness is always negotiated in interpersonal contact and constructed through forms of meaning-making such as narrative or family photographs.
91 V. Nünning (2013, 9) includes 'perspectivity' and 'morality' in her list of key characteristics of narrative, but points out that these two aspects are less likely to be generally agreed upon than the other four (situatedness, world-creation, disruption as a vehicle for the plot, and the conveyance of experience).

The secrets and silences that dominate the families attest to a clash of perspectives and meanings that affects the very foundations of the family identity. One can say that trauma, in these novels, becomes manifest in the silences that obstruct the construction of a meaningful and coherent family narrative. These gaps in communication reveal the fissures that run through the fabric of relationships in these families; the boundaries that they demarcate are hardened through ideological fundamentalisms that negate the possibility of other perspectives, alternative versions, and contingency. As a result, the idea and meaning of family itself becomes ideologised.

For Kaukab – the "cleric's daughter" (42) – in *Maps for Lost Lovers*, family is so closely intertwined with religion and cultural tradition that her past-oriented family ideology subordinates to it and cancels out all other aspects of family life and family love. Whatever does not fit in with it has to be silenced. At the same time, her sense of self is so indivisibly connected to her understanding of family that her children's and her husband's unbelief cuts to the very heart of who she is. In a similar way, Sami in *The Road from Damascus* has developed an idea of family that is both ideologically charged and fundamental to his identity. Over the course of the novel he comes to realise that he cannot uphold his understanding of patrilineal descent as the basis for his narrative of self without also taking on his father's guilt. The betrayal that lies at the heart of the family forecloses the communication within it; here also there is one side of the story that silences the other. The meta-narrative of Arab secularism turns out to be just as excluding and fundamentalist as orthodox religion can be. In both families, the obstruction of a pluralistic or multi-perspectival narrative is indicative of the way in which individual identity construction is dominated by the coercive imperative of familial inheritance and the legacy of a particular understanding of tradition. The result is that in both families the adherence to a belief system, be it religious or secular, overrides and cancels out familial loyalty and love. As Kaukab realises, "[t]he only way, it seems, that she can convince the others of her loss regarding Jugnu [and therefore also her love for him] is by renouncing Allah and His injunctions" (146). The great strength and beauty of Aslam's novel is that it features many small scenes and poetic details that convey a profound idea of the many nuances of love and interpersonal relationships as a counterweight to the sense of loss entailed in Kaukab's predicament. The secrets that haunt these families are connected to the voids that imply incompatible and unnegotiable views that not only question the collective family identity but also the identity of its individual members.

Secrets and silences are both a source and a symptom of family disintegration. Both novels show how the historical conflicts of the societies that they belong to affect the families and bleed into the family narrative, creating chasms between family members that can be traced via the silences in family communication. The family thus functions as an image of the barriers of communication in society. In *The Road from Damascus*, it is the trauma of the 1982 Hama massacre and the brutal quelling of the Muslim Brotherhood uprising by the forces of the al-Assad controlled Syrian army that is personalised in the form of a family secret which begins to haunt Sami.[92] *Maps for Lost Lovers* goes back even further into history in order to detail the complex entanglement resulting from a traumatic history of British rule, including the Amritsar massacre and the Gujranwala bombing, Partition, the 1971 Civil War, and, finally, migration and the difficulties of living in a society marked by a racism that is rooted – on both sides – in former colonial structures. The troubled history of Pakistan in the twentieth century is seen to come together in the person of Chakor/Deepak and his story of amnesia (the people's unity in rioting against the British), regained memory (Partition), and reclaimed identity and death (Bangladeshi independence) – a story that haunts the family and disrupts its narrative unity. The repeated desecration of his grave points to the haunting effects of this violence on future generations that splits the nation, community, and family. Sami's hauntedness in *The Road from Damascus* comes in the form of involuntary memories, the clicking of prayer beads and the apocalypse horse, which unsettle his carefully controlled narrative of self. The lost lovers Jugnu and Chanda best capture the spectral effect of trauma in families: Having gone missing, their bodies remain undiscovered, giving no rest to the living. "Where are they? They are nowhere and yet he [Shamas] feels as though he is handcuffed to their corpses." (79) The lost lovers have gone off the grid, and therefore find no meaningful place in the family narrative. While Sami is able to reunite with his family in the end through a change of perspective and a willingness to break the silence, this form of resolution and reconciliation is now beyond the reach of Kaukab and her family.

---

[92] This concerns Sami's Syrian family; Muntaha's Iraqi family is similarly unsettled by the trauma of political persecution and torture under a tyrannous regime.

5 Family Memoirs: Relational Life Writing

This last chapter expands on the previous chapters and moves from novels to autobiographical writing. All of the novels studied so far have focused on families and migration, yet the previous analyses of them deals only superficially with the question of overlapping aspects of the writing with facets of the authors' own lives. Nevertheless, both modes of literature, whether they are predominantly fictional or autobiographical, share an interest in the examination of identity constructions and place an emphasis on the relational self. Life writing, in recent decades, has seen a noticeable rise in production, popularity, and critical acclaim; it is also a field of writing that has increasingly brought attention to the importance of the relational self – so much so in fact, that one can even speak of a trending genre of 'relational autobiographies' (cf. Rüggemeier 2014).[1] Indeed, "[o]ne of the most consequential insights in auto/biography theory in the last two decades has been that identity – for both men and women – is essentially relational, defined and represented intersubjectively" (Davis 2009, 229). Relational autobiographies discuss the basic question of 'what makes us who we are' in favour of an understanding of the self that focuses on the relationships, interaction, and social frameworks that fundamentally shape and influence one's life and the narratives of the self. In presenting the self in its social embeddedness and interconnectedness this new form differs significantly from the classical genre of autobiography that had been committed to the 'Western' notion of an autonomous, independent individual (Rüggemeier 2014, 2).[2]

Relational life writing, in focusing on the individual in relationships, oscillates between the genres of autobiography and biography, which results in a conflation and blurring of genres that is often expressed in the innovative spelling 'auto/biography'.[3] In *How Our Lives Become Stories* (1999, 69), Eakin has defined

---

[1] For some of the basic elements of autobiographical genres, whether referred to as auto/biography or memoir, see, e.g. Couser (2012, 37), or Rüggemeier (2014, 19ff.).

[2] Anne Rüggemeier (2014, 2) registers an increase in relational autobiographies since the 1970s and through the 1980s, with an outright 'boom' in the late 1990s. In viewing this through a transnational perspective, it may be added that this development in Anglophone literature runs parallel with the trend of 'Väterliteratur' in German literature and its follow-up genre of 'Familienromane'.

[3] Cf. Egan and Helms (2002, 6–7): The slash is suggestive of "the broad continuum of life writing discourses that range from writing about the self (auto) to writing about another (biography).

these forms of life writing that "feature the decisive impact on the autobiographer of either (1) an entire social environment (a particular family, or a community and its social institutions – schools, churches, and so forth) or (2) key other individuals, usually family members, especially parents". Relational autobiographies offer extensive and profound insights into the construction of the relational self and the meanings that are attached to it. They emphasise the dominance of the family and of family members as 'proximate others' for relational lives and, accordingly, in relational life writing (Eakin 1999, 86, cf. Eakin 1999, 68). In particular, the relationship with one's parents, typically with a focus on either the mother ('matriography') or the father ('patriography'), is often the subject of such an exploration and brings about a re-evaluation of one's own life as well as the other person under scrutiny (cf. Couser 2005, 148; Couser 2013, 21).

Thomas Couser (2005, 150–151) has termed these texts 'narratives of filiation' based on "the driving impulse [...] to shore up, repair, or compensate for a flawed relationship" that lies behind many such memoirs. Couser's denomination highlights how the narratives themselves become a part of the parent/child relationship as a form of doing family, and how they "enact" the author's engagement with their parent(s) through writing (Couser 2005, 151).[4] The term 'filiation' encompasses both sides that are present in these texts: firstly, it refers to "the condition or fact of being the child [...] of a particular parent" (Couser 2005, 151) and covers the relationship between them; while secondly, in its legal form, it refers to the "judicial determination of paternity" (Couser 2005, 151), and the legal establishment and definition of a parent/child relationship.[5] When it is understood in its more figurative sense, this second meaning can be set in relation to Smart's

---

The slash also acknowledges that today contemporary auto/biographers increasingly practice, and theorists are recognizing, original and creative approaches to these genres, a combining or blending of genres to produce, for example, the collaborative work or the family memoir, the art installation, the film, or the web site". Since the intention here is to focus less on the complex question of life writing genres, I use the term 'memoir' instead of autobiography in these analyses because it has a broader definition than the term autobiography: "*Memoir* can also be used to refer to a narrative that is primarily about someone *other than* the author" (Couser 2012, 18; emphasis in the original). For a more elaborate distinction between the genres and subgenres of life writing see Couser (2012, 18ff.); see also Rüggemeier (2014, 5), who ultimately prefers the term of 'autobiography', to which she attests a broadened meaning in recent usage.

4 As Couser (2005, 152) emphasises, the term 'narratives of filiation' is concerned with what these narratives *do* rather than what they *are* (as the terms 'memoirs of fathers' or 'patriography').

5 Couser bases his etymology on the definition in the *American Heritage Dictionary*. The *OED* offers as its first definition "The process of becoming, or the condition of being, a son."

notion of 'relationality' as being actively established,[6] while the first meaning more closely fits in with her idea of 'embeddedness' as a given 'condition' or 'fact'.[7] The meaning of 'filiation' is primarily determined by the dynamic interrelation between these two aspects. Couser differentiates between two conflicting impulses in these narratives, those of affiliation and disaffiliation. The first is concerned with asserting and strengthening the filial connection, while the second is accusatory and censuring. Affiliation and disaffiliation often appear together in a memoir, usually in a way that expresses the ambivalence of "identification and dis-identification" (Couser 2005, 154) that characterises family relationships.

Since single family relationships (such as, for example, between son and father) are never isolated but are connected to the larger constellation that is the family (on both the synchronic and diachronic level), narratives of filiation necessarily include a wider outlook on family identity and on self-positioning within the family. This is why I classify the two books in this chapter as 'family memoirs'.[8] As the title of Hanif Kureishi's *My Ear at His Heart: Reading My Father* indicates, the book largely details the negotiation of his relationship with his father, and thus fits into the category of 'patriographies'.[9] At the same time, the process of unravelling this father-son-relationship ingnites a more all-encompassing exploration of (intergenerational) embeddedness, relationality, and the meaning of relatedness. In *Red Dust Road*, Jackie Kay tackles these questions against the backdrop of her own adoption and her attempts to re-connect with her birth parents, while at the same time giving a wonderfully rich impression of

---

[6] In *Red Dust Road*, of course, ascertainment and acknowledgement of paternity also play a role on a literal level. This is, however, rather rare, since adoption and other cases of uncertain paternity are an exception.

[7] Cf. Chapter 2.1.2.

[8] Davis (2010, 3; emphasis in the original) defines the 'family memoir' as "*narratives or films that inscribe the story of at least three generations of the same family*". While *My Ear at His Heart* certainly fits this definition, the same cannot be equally said of *Red Dust Road*. Nevertheless, Kay's book is very much about what makes a family, and how it, in turn, shapes its individual members. Both memoirs are not only concerned with specific family relationships, but also with the way in which these relationships reveal certain family patterns.

[9] Kureishi freely admits to the one-sidedness of his project, recognising that "we don't hear enough from the women in the book I am now writing" (*Ear* 132). His view of family history is decidedly patrilineal, "a story of generations, told through the males" (238). Couser, who has followed the great boom in memoir writing in the US that has emerged in recent decades, attests to a much larger number of 'patriographies' than 'matriographies', a predominance that he explains with regard to family roles in patriarchal societies, which "make[...] fathers comparatively inaccessible to their children" (2012, 155). This constellation favours narratives of fathers as these memoirs are often "written out of a certain sense of need or lack" (Couser 2005, 151).

how family culture is created in her adoptive family. Both Kureishi and Kay were almost 50 when they embarked on the project of writing their memoirs, an age when retrospection and the transformation of identity tend to become more of a pressing issue, and which sees them having a changed perspective on family after having had children themselves. As Kureishi notes in the early chapters of his memoir: "Some sort of search is beginning. I guess you don't really go looking for your parents until middle age. For me, this has become a quest for my place in father's history and fantasy, and for the reasons my father lived the semi-broken life he did." (*Ear* 35)[10] Both Kureishi and Kay describe the exploration of their identity through the use of the image of a search for their (and their father's or parents') past, which is performed in Kureishi's memoir via the medium of reading while Kay renders it through the central motif of a journey – as indicated in the titles of their respective memoirs.[11]

5.1 "An ongoing story": Hanif Kureishi's Collective Family Memoir *My Ear at His Heart: Reading My Father* (2004)

Hanif Kureishi's memoir *My Ear at His Heart* was published to great critical acclaim and much attention in 2004. Besides the general curiosity about an author's life – particularly when he is one of the most prominent voices of British second-generation Black and Asian writers[12] – it is the discussions about "the possibly exploitative nature" (Thomas 2006, 186) of the representations of real people in fiction, which have been stirred up from the very beginning by Kureishi's works, that have sparked an interest in this memoir (cf. Al-Shawaf 2010; Thomas 2006).[13] The ethical issue of how artists utilise their lives and experiences as well as the lives of others is indeed a recurring theme in Kureishi's work and has already played a significant role in his first novel, *The Buddha of Suburbia* (1990), in which the protagonist Karim betrays his friend Changez by modelling his stage character on him. This novel shows that the representation of another person is

---

10 *Ear* refers to Kureishi 2005 [2004]. Hereafter all references to the novel will use only page number, and, where necessary, *Ear* for disambiguation.
11 The first edition of *Red Dust Road* bore the subtitle "An Autobiographical Journey". In later editions such as the one used in this study, the term "road" still clearly points to the journey motif.
12 Cf. McCrum (2014), who refers to Kureishi as "a kind of pioneer, the first of many 'writers of colour' to have been born here".
13 For an overview of the controversies and inner-familial tension that have been caused by some of Kureishi's writings, see Brown 2008.

always an act of appropriation. It was also already "explicitly autobiographical" (Brown 2008) and contained many parallels between Kureishi's family background and that of his auto-diegetic narrator. In the later memoir *My Ear at His Heart*, however, there is an even stronger sense of this possibility of betrayal, as Kureishi puts his own life on display alongside the personal lives of his family, particularly with regard to his father. Again he seems to be aware of the danger of appropriation and exploitation and remains uncertain of the boundaries of the relational self; at one point he confesses that "I feel guilty about what I am doing to the family. By what right can I do this? Who does father, or anyone, belong to?" (*Ear* 94)[14]

From a literary quality standpoint, *My Ear at His Heart* is a highly complex, intricately wrought text. It connects the author's reading of three of his father's unpublished novels and his uncle's memoir with his own memories of growing up in the London suburbs of the 1960s and '70s. From these family texts and his own recollections, the author gains a new perspective on his writing career. Although nominally a memoir about his father, the book is conceived to answer the question of what has made Kureishi the man he is and the writer that he has become. As he explains at the beginning of the book, his initial idea was to look back at his life via the books and reading experiences that have shaped him. At first, this concept had been informed by the assumption that it is the intimate relationship with books and the subjective choice of their favourite authors that shape the imagination of an artist and make a writer. Kureishi had thus pondered that "a way of capturing the flavour of my younger self might be to reread the writers I'd liked as a young man" (1), which would then allow him to "reinhabit the worlds they once made in my head, and identify myself in them" (2). As related by Kureishi, it was the chance discovery of an unpublished manuscript by his father entitled "An Indian Adolescence" that shifted the focus of Kureishi's reading from his artistic to his familial legacy. Instead of entering into an imaginative conversation with his former selves through the medium of reading books, he finds himself suddenly re-connected to his father through a different sort of text, one that he has never read before and which fills him with anxious anticipation (cf. 8). What had started as a project aimed at 'reinhabiting' his past and evoking his familiar ghosts becomes a search for new perspectives on his life and for unknown facets of the family past. Hence, the solipsistic view of the individual auto-biography gives way to a broader perspective that re-connects his biography with the family narrative as a way of re-evaluating and understanding his

---

14 On the "ethical dangers of memoir" (Couser 2012, 10) and the memoirist's "obligation to others" (Couser 2012, 11) see Couser (2012, 79ff.).

own life. In putting his father's unpublished writing at the heart of his memoir, Kureishi not only acknowledges literature (in both reading and writing) as being a key factor in his own life but also recognises the fact that it is a core element of the (patrilineal) family tradition.

5.1.1 Affiliation and Disaffiliation: Becoming a Writer in Fulfilment of and through Rebellion against the Family Ideal

For Kureishi, the memoir provides a way to come to terms with the legacy of his family story, his own role in it, and the way in which it has manifested itself and worked to shape his relationship with his father. In this, he constantly moves between the two impulses of affiliation and disaffiliation, identification and disidentification, which are connected through their constant interplay with each other (cf. Rüggemeier 2014, 122). His own writing and the process of becoming a writer is not only closely linked to his father's unfulfilled dream of a living literary life, but is also part of the larger Kureishi family tradition: "Whatever else was going on in my life, through books I was entering a narrative, or myth, which concerned reading, and writers, as a kind of family transaction. Sport – and cricket in particular – was part of this myth." (9) Kureishi recognises cricket and literature (in both reading and writing) as the two motifs from which the family myth is spun. Both activities distinguish the family from the Indian mainstream, and reveal the social and cultural ambitions of the family, linking them with the elite class of the British Empire.[15]

In referring to reading and writing as a 'family transaction', Kureishi hints at the multiple ways in which the engagement with literature and books has managed to shape family interaction and relationships. The use of the word 'transaction' for family practices emphasises the centrality of exchange and the interdependence that exists in family activity, as well as the processual nature of family life. The exchange effect of family relationships is tangible in the more or less explicit expectations that parents impose on their children and in the way in which that shapes their character. The family story itself is elusive and hard to grasp; it becomes manifest mostly in form of the values it transmits, and the claims that it puts on the members of the family. Through the 'family legend', "an important communication was being made about what counted in the family,

---

15 In Poona, the family even has their own cricket team, Colonel Kureishi's XI. Cricket is not simply a sport, it is highly "political; it is where the British can be beaten at their own game" (40).

about how I should live and who I should be" (9). In this way, "every child has their place in the family dream or economy, and the parents have a project for the child, [even though] neither they nor the child can be sure what it is" (9). Despite the difficulty of pinning down the exact ways in which the family myth has influenced him, Kureishi recognises how books and reading are part of a family legacy that has fundamentally shaped his life from the outset.[16]

Over the years, this vague sense of a mission crystallises into Kureishi's wish to become a writer, "according to my father's plan" (10). His career and success as a writer are intricately connected with his father's own literary ambition and sense of failure. Although Hanif Kureishi's first advancements into the field of writing are strongly supported by his father, Kureishi Sr.'s influence on his son's writing and career path is far more complex and ambivalent than by what could be described as merely an act of delegation – in the sense that the son should fulfil what the father could not achieve for himself. "Really, I was to be like him in every way; if we deviated, there would be trouble." (52) This insight is an important hint at the power struggles that are taking place within the family. As Kureishi later understands from his reading of "An Indian Adolescence", his father's childhood and adolescence were profoundly affected by, firstly, his fear of his distant and tyrannous father, the Colonel, who continuously made him feel small and ashamed, and, secondly, by the sibling rivalry between himself and his brother Omar, whose "charm, good looks, intelligence and personality" he envied (43).[17] Both relationships result in a feeling of failure and uselessness, and both are reproduced in the relationship between Shannoo and Hanif Kureishi. The latter consequently wonders "whether this is 'the wound' he seemed to be nursing when I was a child, the feeling of defeat and inferiority he tried to overcome by becoming a writer, and by having me become one" (43). In reading his father's novel, Kureishi realises the deep impact that these family relationships in previous generations had on his own upbringing and on his relationship with

---

[16] Hanif Kureishi describes how their father "made a religion at home out of library books, discontent and literary ambition" (13). Although apparently not worthy of a mention in Kureishi's memoir, Hanif's sister Yasmin Kureishi is also a part-time writer, who, in an article in the *Independent* (2008), concedes that "[i]t is hard to resist the allure of the Biro if you've been brought up by someone like my father". She also mentions a certain degree of sibling rivalry between herself and her brother, feeling that "he can't stand the thought that I might be any good, might be better than him".

[17] In "An Indian Adolescence", the narrator writes of his brother as "the son adored by the parents; he is excellent at sports, his studies and the tango; he can even jive, and adores Fats Waller. He speaks of himself as a future Foreign Secretary of Free India." (43)

his father. Although Shannoo, in teaching him cricket in the backyard, might appear to "be the father he wished he'd had – involved, attentive, guiding, rather than the remote figure he describes Colonel Murad as being" (50), what the son primarily remembers of these lessons are the "arguments and the terrible humiliation he made me feel" (51). Shannoo thus elicits the same emotions in his son as his own father made him feel: "scared, useless and ashamed" (53).[18] When Hanif, as his father did before him, exchanges cricket for writing,[19] it is also a gesture of resistance against the sense of failure and shame transmitted down to him, a "move away from the conflicts that cricket stirred in me" (56).[20] It is through the shared activity of writing, however, that the relationship between Hanif and his father begins to reflect the old sibling rivalry between Omar and Shannoo, as his father apparently feels threatened by his son's accomplishments: "Reading my father's book I am becoming aware that, partly, I was being made to feel as he had felt. He might want me to be successful, as his father had required him to be, but he was afraid of me becoming too powerful or rivalrous." (52)[21]

In his commitment to his writing, Kureishi manages to both align himself with the family myth and to simultaneously break free from the family. The process of becoming a writer, which always occurs in the zone of tension that exists between the power of influence and the desire for distinction and difference, parallels in many ways the conflictual interrelation between autonomy and individuality on the one hand and heteronomy and embeddedness on the other that is typical of family relationships. Kureishi's emancipation from his family is closely linked to his formation as a writer, and his search for his own voice and subject matter is accompanied by a search for father figures from outside of the family. Although his father initially 'introduced' his son into writing – "his thing, the

---

18 Kureishi is well aware of the potentially long-lasting and damaging effects of these emotions: "These failures stay with you, particularly if you don't know the source of their power." (56) The feeling of uselessness being experienced in combination with shame is the central emotion in "The Redundant Man", his father's other novel that features in the memoir.
19 "The idea of being a writer replaced the idea of being a cricketer, for me as for him." (54)
20 However, Kureishi admits in hindsight that "[a] real insurgent would have rebelled properly." (54)
21 While their cricket lessons echo elements that are handed down from Shannoo's relationship with his father, their writing interaction tends to categorise them more in terms of a sibling constellation, a dynamic that, in Kureishi's eyes, was pushed by his father: "He put us on the same level: writers – almost brothers – together, with neither of us more talented than the other." (116) "He [father] lacked support and attempted to find it in me, his prop, confidant, brother." (181)

desire he lived with" (148) – they soon stop working together, unable to circumvent the charged competitiveness that is part of the family story and which is brought out by their shared interests and values.²² The work on his first novel, written at the age of 14, already distances Hanif from his father, whose criticism, which he describes as "brusque and discouraging" (149), only seems to highlight failure and provides no room for potential or learning.²³ Instead, Hanif's uncle Omar puts him in contact with a publishing house, whose editor takes it upon himself to advise Hanif, an act which seems to have "laid the basis for my actual writing" (150). He is the first in a long line of surrogate fathers and guiding figures that Kureishi looks to for orientation in his literary career (see also Rüggemeier 2014, 136–137). Kureishi thus describes writing as simultaneously connecting him with and keeping him apart from his father.

For Hanif, writing and reading becomes a vehicle for his emancipation from the family, and a form of rebellion against the sedateness of his suburban family home. His writing starts as an extension of his teenage revolt against his parents and is symbolic of his alliance with his peer group and generation, "trying to see what sort of stories I could make out of our lives [...]: teenage sex, overdoses, sadistic teachers, the weird lives of parents when perceived by children" (152).²⁴ Writing becomes an outlet for all of the pent-up emotions and energy stemming from the "suburban semi-sleep" (81) of his parents' world, and thereby provides him with an escape from the silences at home, where "[t]here were lots of things I couldn't think about – race, sexuality, my parents – things which I couldn't process but which seemed jammed inside me: another kind of silence, feeling without words" (58). In the same way, his reading at the time focuses on books that "countered the suburban ideal with a more spontaneous life" (165).

---

22 The end of their working relationship coincides with the peak of Hanif's adolescence: "After the age of about sixteen, I didn't read any of his novels and didn't offer him my work to look at. His tough, somewhat sneering criticism was unbearable, and I found myself being too hard on him, too." (15)

23 The complexity of the father/son-relationship and, in particular, his father's feelings towards his writing career is also hinted at in the episode of Hanif Kureishi's first performed play. The play is sent in to the theatre not by Hanif himself but by his father, who "[i]n retrospect, seems more ambitious and confident on behalf of me than he was for himself" (167). When Kureishi's father attends a performance of the play, however, his son knows there is no way that he can be satisfied, because, no matter what happens, "the production would be too little or too much for him" (167).

24 The implicit spurning of his father is emphasised in Kureishi's reference to Chekhov, his father's role model, who "was a great writer, but there is always something shocking and exhilarating about seeing the contemporary world in fiction." (153)

The same forces that propel Kureishi's writing thus also work to pull him away from his family – or at least from his parents. Unlike his father, who "instead of living, [...] began to write about those who lived" (59), Hanif sees writing not as a "parallel life" (102), or a substitute for living, but as a pursuit that is based on life and the lived experience.²⁵ Admiring the "'beat' existence" of his favourite authors, he understands writing as a "life-style" choice (165). Searching for "another form of knowledge" than that represented by his father, he is enticed by his uncle Omar's "idea of sexual awareness, of the force of desire, which was more like a novelist's knowledge" (185–186). Omar, a successful cricket commentator who has "one of the best known [voices] in India and Pakistan on the radio" (Kureishi 2004), and a journalist and political author, serves the young Kureishi as a role model and idol in ways that his father cannot. "As an adolescent, I was enraptured by a black-and-white photograph of my most glamorous uncle Omar on the cover of a collection of his essays" (35). What fascinates Hanif is not only the fact that his uncle is a published writer, it is also the perfect staging of masculinity, wordliness, and self-importance that his uncle embodies in his "Hemingwayesque pose" (36) in the photograph which Hanif associates with the writer as a public figure.²⁶ While visiting Omar in his London apartment where he is introduced to the "city pleasures" (156), seventeen-year old Hanif is enthralled by his uncle's lifestyle and the pervasive air of eroticism that surrounds him, "something that I wanted for myself, over and over" (154).

When seen against the backdrop of the long history of sibling rivalry in the Kureishi family, however, this fascination with his uncle bears the strong hallmarks of "a betrayal" (156; cf. Thomas 2006, 191–192).²⁷ In his memoir, Kureishi reflects on his rendition of a similar family constellation containing a father and an uncle in his screenplay *My Beautiful Laundrette* (1985), which, he concedes,

---

25 The suburbs represent this distance from life and the possibilities that it offers: "The view from the suburbs was that, as the world was terrifying, one should keep as far away from it as possible, hugging the known." (150)
26 The contrast between the two brothers lies not so much in the question of who is a published or unpublished writer (Rafiushan Kureishi did publish two political books on Pakistan, cf. 59) but more on the fact that one remains an insignificant clerk at the Pakistani embassy while the other has gained a certain degree of fame and recognition as a cricket commentator and accordingly lives a completely different lifestyle. Another photo in the memoir shows Omar Kureishi with Bob Hope during his time in the US, and thus casts him as a 'celebrity'. With regard to his father though, Kureishi pays far less attention to his published non-fiction work than he does to his unpublished fiction writing.
27 This gesture of giving precedence to his uncle over his father is repeated in his reading process when Kureishi decides "to put my father's novel aside in order to read Omar's memoir" (37).

was a take on his own situation at the time: "Thinking about it now, I am aware that my film concerns two brothers, one 'useless', the other 'effective', between whom the young hero moves. [...] The story begins to gather speed when the 'effective' brother leads the boy into a sexualised, semi-criminal, dangerous world apart from the father." (86–87) Hanif's identification with his uncle Omar can be seen as his way of following the family vocation of becoming a writer without falling into the trap of becoming his own father (cf. Thomas 2006, 191). Through Omar, he is able to inscribe himself into the patrilineal family tradition while at the same time distancing himself from his father.[28]

Moreover, Kureishi casts his process of becoming a writer in conventional terms as based on the accumulation of life experience. In this regard, the exploration of his sexuality metonymically represents Kureishi's hunger for life and inspiration as an artist, a personal development that actively and necessarily distances him from his father. Sex is characteristically a topic around which boundaries are established in a family setting and an area where silence is formed in families, particularly between parents and child(ren). Just as a child is excluded from their parents' sexual intimacy, the child's sexual development distances them from their parents and family of orientation.[29] Kureishi describes how this

---

[28] Kureishi already links his move from cricket (where he felt humiliation in front of his father) to writing (where he proved to be much more adept than his father) to his uncle Omar, the famous cricket commentator. So, while "[o]bediently" practicing specific cricket moves to improve his hitting accuracy, young Hanif entertains himself with "whispering imaginary radio commentary to myself in Omar's accent and locutions. [...] Being alone in this way, making things up, might, inadvertently, have prepared me for being a writer" (53).

[29] The idea that sexuality sets a person apart from the rest of their family is also present in the description of Shani's first sexual experience, a visit to the brothel, where "[t]here's no father, mother or brother – only him, the woman, and his pleasure without guilt or disgust" (74). At the same time, however, there is a competing scenario which highlights the complex nature of the interrelatedness of closeness and distance in families as the whole visit to the brothel is set up by Shani's father and executed in the company of an older cousin: "If the scene begins with a boy being terrorized by his father, and the father, in turn, being humiliated by another man, Niazi, it concludes with a boy becoming potent and thinking about the world of pleasures ahead of him, away from his family." (74) Hanif Kureishi concludes that in this as well as in his father's other novel, "The Redundant Man", in which the protagonist enters into an adulterous affair, sex "is designed to attack the family. For dad sexual pleasure and the family are incompatible. The family [...] is where the sex stops." (132) Kureishi thus in a way shares this theme of sex with his father, however, they differ widely in their treatment of it. In his father's writing, sex is "split off" (140) and serves as a way of getting away from real desire, whereas he himself is interested in how desire works as a drive that transforms families from within. This not only occurs in in *My Beautiful Laundrette*, but "[i]n *The Buddha of Suburbia*, too, I sexualised the family, turning them on, putting desire at the centre of the family." (86)

step not only created a new way of looking at his own family, but also gave rise to a general broadening of perspective:

> What I also learned in these early relationships was that love and sex, taking you out of your family, led you into the strange field of other families, from which vantage point you could see your own family as an objective item, as just another struggling family in the world, as opposed to it being the entire world, and that this was disconcerting, like questioning a religion while wanting to believe in God. (164)

As this passage indicates, there is something sacrilegious in gaining such a distanced view of one's own family. Kureishi expresses a strong sense of guilt when he compares his own adolescent "vigorous curiosity and sexual enthusiasm" with his father's failing health, his "suffering [... and] loss of power and potency" (15), even going as far as constructing "a causal connection between the events – my absence, having sex – and father's illness (175). This interdependence encapsulates the feeling of guilt that Hanif feels about his general emancipation from his parents (as demonstrated, for example, by his move out of the family home),[30] and the vague sense of unfulfilled duty and obligation that he has towards them (172). At the heart of this inner conflict is the question "How can you live your life when your father is failing to live his?" (15), a question that also worries Kureishi with regard to the shared occupation of writing and the burden he carries with him for having earned a success (quickly and with comparable ease) that his father struggled hard for but failed to achieve.

In a way, the area of sexuality is emblematic of the way in which closeness and distance exist together in families, as either aspects or as whole areas of life that cannot be talked about and thus remain silenced and in the shadows, away from the consciousness of other family members.[31] In a similar vein, "the idea of

---

30 "I felt bad about leaving, as though I might suck all the life out of the family and should protect dad and mum by giving them something significant to do. [...] Nevertheless, if a parent's duties to the child are relatively clear, the child's to the parents are less so, particularly as the child gets older. What exactly do you owe to them now? Why are you being more loyal to your father than you are to yourself?" (172)

31 Of course, a talk about the 'facts of life' is a standard situation in family life in which sex is discussed intergenerationally, while it is also a situation that is typically associated with total awkwardness. Thus, while being a standard family practice, it is also emphatically removed from everyday forms of doing family. The fact that Kureishi's father "went to some trouble to avoid discussing sex with" his son (140) is very telling: "If, mainly to provoke him, I suggested we have 'a little chat about the facts of life', he'd flee, ordering me to do my homework. [...] Of course no parent, whether they talk about storks or about penises and vaginas, can explain the dirty reality of sexual desire to a child; it is always the erotic wildness which is left out, the point is always missed." (140)

dreaming [...] will certainly have a place in each family. We didn't, for instance, tell each other our dreams over breakfast. This said something, of course, about what is hidden." (183–184) Dreaming, desire, and the unconscious are closely related to creativity and the artistic process (cf. 184): "Writing, amongst other things, is a form of extended fantasy; and since fantasy, daydreaming and the imagination are already linked, one cannot be surprised that there is inhibition." (191) With these words Kureishi describes an episode of depression and writer's block, which he feels is complexly connected to his father's ambivalent expectations of him. During this time he takes note of John Stuart Mill's feeling of liberation at his father's death and the "pleasure [he took] in the thought that the father's realm had been attacked" (189), and sympathises with Sartre's "sacrilegious line, 'I loathe my childhood and all that remains of it ...'" (189). For Kureishi, writing both requires and causes a break with the family that is similar to the intergenerational conflict of authority and rebellion. He illustrates this with reference to Philip Roth's novel *The Ghost Writer* (1979), which also features a father and son who are both writers. In a scene from the novel that Kureishi quotes, the father is shocked by his son's writing, whose vision, he feels, betrays his (the father's) understanding of family identity and his image of his son: "This story isn't us, and what is worse, it isn't even you. [...] I've watched you all your life. [...] You are not somebody who writes this kind of story and then pretends it's the truth." (194) Kureishi recognises himself and his own struggle in the fictional son's need to shed the "social inhibition" of the family in order to "be who he was, and wanted to be" (195).

5.1.2 "Dad is speaking to me again": The Memoir as a Multi-voiced (and Multimodal) Transgenerational Family Dialogue

When Kureishi finds his father's manuscript, he anticipates it to be "a legacy of words, a protracted will, perhaps" (1). The fact that the manuscript entitled "An Indian Adolescence" was his father's final text heightens the sense of inheritance and expectation of last words. He divines that the text will open up the chance of a conversation between himself and his father that was not to be had during his father's lifetime. The "object, or gift, made by dad" seems to Kureishi to be "like a letter from the dead, delivered more than ten years late" (12). He not only sees the manuscript as a legacy in itself, in the sense of being a document that was passed down to him by his late father, but as something that might also help him to come to terms with the immaterial legacy that he has already been living with – the way in which his own life was and is being shaped by that of his father. He anticipates that the text will "tell me a lot about my father and my own past" (1). The expectation that this fortuitous access to his father's life promises a new or enhanced understanding of his own past entails the idea of continuity across generations and the transmission of certain themes, constellations, and conflicts that determine family relationships and identities. In this way, the father's manuscript is read as a legacy that contributes to the transgenerational family narrative.

This sets the tone for Kureishi's reading of the text, which goes explicitly against his father's own vision for how it should be read. While Kureishi Sr. insisted on the text's fictional quality and its denomination as a 'novel' (despite the fact that Hanif Kureishi's publishing agent suggested that the manuscript would have had better chances of publication if labelled as a memoir, cf. 19), the son reads the story "as personal truth" (18), trying to eke out its autobiographical content beneath the (apparently often rather thin) veil of fictionalisation.[32] In Shani, the novel's protagonist, Kureishi sees an obvious "self-portrait" (20) of his father, who is called Shannoo, the short version of Rafiushan. It is predominantly through Kureishi's narrative voice – through his re-narration, interpretation and commentary – that the reader of his memoir has access to the text. But the son reads the manuscript, originally written and intended for a general audience, as a personal message to himself: Framing the manuscript as a 'protracted will' or letter, he treats it as a family document and thus appropriates it for his own book and for the sake of unravelling his family history. The memoir's subtitle *Reading My Father* further emphasises the son's process of meaning-making in the present: "[W]hatever my father has made, I will be reconstructing him from these fragments or traces, attempting to locate his 'self' in these imaginings or scatterings" (18). His father's text, having started off this particular kind of memory work, "this reconnection with my family's past" (115), whets Kureishi's appetite for family history: "I spend half a day in my basement, rifling through the damp boxes which constitute my 'archive'. I want more." (115) There, "[a]mong the manuscripts, letters and photographs", he finds another text by his father, "The Redundant Man", a story about an immigrant and father of a family that similarly lends itself to an autobiographical reading. Kureishi's approach, which puts his

---

[32] Kureishi justifies this reading by making it seem inevitable, pointing out, for example, how the narrator of "An Indian Adolescence" occasionally switches as if "by 'mistake'" (18) from the third to the first person. "Whatever sort of book dad has written, there is no denying the trickster's fingerprints are all over it, or that he has done an elemental but traditional thing in trying a self-portrait, an attempt to say something about his life by way of a story with himself at the centre. It is also an invitation to have others see him." (20)

father's fictional writing in a category with records of personal history, is enhanced by the inclusion of further documents of family history, including, most importantly, his uncle Omar Kureishi's published three-volume memoir, as well as a dozen family photographs, all of which move the manuscript closer to the realm of family memorabilia. Kureishi emphasises this by comparing his reading and the sense of excitement that it gives him with the process of exploring the family archives: "this book is like discovering a trove of forgotten photographs which have to be inspected one by one, in detail." (16)

Kureishi's comparison of the book with family photographs as well as his use of photos in the memoir highlights the process of 'memory work' that he engages in.[33] "Family photographs may affect to show us our past but what we do with them – how we use them – is really about today, not yesterday." (Kuhn 2002 [1995], 19) Like a family photograph, his father's writing becomes "a prop, a prompt, a pre-text: it sets the scene for recollection" (Kuhn 2002 [1995], 13). The memoir is richly illustrated with family photographs, of which the first two are directly connected to his father's text, and therefore seem to serve as "marshalling 'evidence' for [Kureishi's] assessment of the manuscript as memoir rather than novel" (Lee-Von 2015, 412) through employing formal elements that are typical of that genre. The first photo is captioned as "My father as a child" (16) and shows Shannoo Kureishi at a much younger age than the protagonist Shani is at the beginning of "An Indian Adolescence", and thus bridges a time span that is not covered in the novel but which would be expected to be included in a memoir.[34] The second photo, captioned "In Poona – Shannoo at left" (22), places Kureishi's father in the setting of the novel's opening scene before the family's imminent move to Mumbai. It shows him as a slightly older child, hugged from behind by another boy of roughly the same age, with a young man and woman behind them, who are apparently a couple. Again, there is no explicit reference to the photo in the text, but the implicit connections are more noticeable. The photo exudes an air of joy, nature, and paradisiac serenity that is in tune with the nostalgia of the novel's opening and its description of impending loss in the face of having to leave the family home to move to an unknown future in Mumbai, a move that is conceptualised in traditional terms by contrasting rural and urban living. The photo illustrates what Shani is leaving behind as he touches the trees

---

33 Introduced by Annette Kuhn (2002, 5), the concept of 'memory work' is explained by Carsten (2007, 16) as being a "restoration of the disjunctures of the past", and as a process that highlights the "creative processes of rearrangement of the past, and of regeneration", that are "[necessarily involved in the] intertwinings of memory and relatedness".

34 Cf. Couser's (2005, 149) distinction between 'single-experience' and 'full-life' narratives.

under which "he had studied, chatted, joked and ate raw mangoes with his friends" (22). While this passage suggests that the second boy in the photo might be a friend, its place in Kureishi's memoir enables another reading of it. On the page opposite the photo, the author questions why a discrepancy exists between the real Kureishi family constellation of twelve siblings and its reduction to a single brother in his father's text: "Perhaps father cleared out the rest of the family in order to concentrate on one particular brother, on one representative tension, and that is why he called it a novel." (23) In this context, the photo could be read as representing Shani and his brother, Mahmood in the novel, whom Kureishi interprets as being his uncle Omar.

The inclusion of these images in his memoir frames them as 'family photos', and thus as a form of memory work and 'doing family'.[35] In being viewed as family pictures, these two photographs are moreover directly linked to a third image that depicts "[t]he twins – Carlo and Sachin – and Kier, the author's sons" (26), who, at about eight and roughly three or four years old, are approximately the same age as the versions of Shannoo that appear in the first two pictures respectively. With the help of these family photos Kureishi builds a link between the generations through synchronisation, managing to weave his own life into the fabric of the family history. Throughout the book, synchronisation between the different time levels serves as an important affiliative device; by continuously connecting events in his father's manuscript and other family documents to his own life and that of his sons, the author inscribes himself into a 'dialogic and multi-voiced' family narrative and shows that in the network of family stories one cannot be told without the other (cf. Rüggemeier 2014, 126).

The device of synchrony offers an artistic way of opening up a conversation between the generations while it is also a tool used to explore their entanglements and interrelations. In this spirit, Kureishi perceives his father's late gift of the manuscript to be an invitation to a belated conversation: "Dad is speaking to me again, and not only from inside my head." (17) Unlike the voice inside his head, the manuscript offers him an "objective access to the past" (17), at least on the face of it and in the sense that it is a voice that differs from his own. Kureishi extends this conversation to his own sons and to other family members such as his uncle Omar, whose memoir he consults in order to complement and verify his

---

[35] Based on its use in the memoir, the picture of Shannoo in Poona suggests reading it as a family photograph despite the fact that the other three persons pictured beside him might not actually be relatives. The photo derives its significance not necessarily from the group constellation that is represented in it, but from the place that it holds in the father's (and, by extension, the son's) biography.

father's narrative. *My Ear at His Heart* thus opens up a temporal space of the imagination within which different time levels converge and where various voices and media of family history intersect. In a way, the memoir manages to accomplish the utopian vision that Kureishi once had for a short story where "a man who goes into a pub on his fiftieth birthday and runs into his father, who is also fifty. The two of them would have a conversation as equals for the first time, the son seeing the father as a man like him." (216) His father's text and his own create this utopian space of the imagination where the two can meet – offering them the chance for a belated conversation through the medium of literature. With his memoir, Kureishi breaks through the asynchrony of living in different generations; in re-visiting his father's life in its different stages, he is able to collect clues for his memory work and for re-evaluating his own life. This inter-generational conversation is not restricted to the past and present; in fact, it also extends itself into the future. Kureishi contemplates how his father still haunts him, "as a ghost, as tangible as ever" (216) – just as he himself will one day become a ghost for his son Carlo, "undead to him, haunting him, and perhaps his children, in ways neither of us can anticipate" (217).

The discovery of the manuscript thus not only promises Kureishi that it will be a key to his own past (and present) but it also serves him as a catalyst for a discussion of family history and heritage with his sons: "I show my boys my father's manuscript and they talk about being a quarter Indian. They ask me if they're Muslim and put their arms next to mine, to compare colours." (26) His sons' response to their father Hanif's suggestive gesture of presenting the manuscript is an affirmative instance of filiation as demonstrated by their curiosity about skin colour and Islam as aspects of their ethnic identity. The manuscript is thus a material as well as a metaphysical link between past, present, and future that symbolically ties the generations together – a step that Kureishi explicitly undertakes with his memoir, where he is "trying to bring everything together" (218). By representing Shannoo's past in India, the manuscript also builds an important bridge to a family history that reaches beyond migration and re-connects the family in Britain with a larger family narrative. "My children are also beginning to learn that they have entered a family story, and are curious to see where, and how, they fit into it." (27) As Kureishi recognises, this initiation to a larger story is an elementary part of growing up in a family:

> Children hear scores of stories, in numerous forms, before they can read them. But at the centre of their education is their introduction into an ongoing story. This is the family legend or tradition, various versions of which their parents and family are keen to impress on them. (9)

5.1.3 "Trying to bring everything together": The Multifarious Voices of the Relational Self

Having written himself out of the family through his screenplays and novels, Kureishi reinscribes himself into the family tradition with his memoir. In his re-negotiation of his relationship with his father, he arrives at an understanding of his father's life and its involvement with a dominating family ideal that also throws a new light on his own life and writing career where he finds himself similarly bound up with the family myth. Untangling the strong "competitiveness, and the feeling of failure which accompanies it" (47) among the men in the Kureishi family helps him to explore the source of his own complicated relationship with his father and the inhibition and shame that it led him to feel within the family. Kureishi describes the difficulty of finding his own voice as an artist, a voice that is very much driven by rebellion against paternal authority, while at the same time taking up a profession that is so closely connected with his father. "Anything my father didn't like was rebellion to me. However, I knew that wherever I went and whatever I did, he was, like God, always watching and condemning." (175) After having cut himself loose from the authority of his father, the son discovers that he is unable to shake off the father that he has internalised. Conscious revolt cannot fully overcome unconscious conformity, and even rebellion happens on his father's terms, eventually presenting just another way of conducting himself in relation to his father's views, values, and expectations. The father's role as a condemning and censuring 'Über-Ich' is a transgenerational phenomenon in the Kureishi family from Colonel Kureishi to Rafiushan. As Kureishi recognises, history is not confined to the realm of the past, it is only "a blink away, the present in another aspect" (240). In a similar vein, the child can never fully shake off his parents, since the dead "take up residence within the living" as ghosts (241). It is a sign of the artistic integrity of the author that he concedes that this family struggle can never be completed. "In the end, of course, you can never leave home. However well you know your parents, children will feel the lives of their parents are a mystery, not only because the desire and sexuality of their parents is beyond them, but because the lesson here is about unknowability." (240)

Kureishi's memoir can be read as a complex and, at times, even contradictory attempt to understand and sort the multifarious voices that make up the relational self:

> Writing this book I wonder what my self consists of. I feel inhabited by others, composed of them. Writers, parents, older men, friends, girlfriends, speak inside me. [...] I think of the essential work of imitation, differentiation and opposition, and how it never stops. Also,

the puzzling thing about rebellion is that the order you wish to defy is so deep and hidden within yourself that you cannot even begin to know it. (55)

In his idea of 'family transactions', the two forces of affiliation and individuation – represented by the authority of father figures and the desire for rebellion against them – are presented as basic factors of family dynamics and determinants of family relationships. This structure, however, extends to relationships that are well beyond the family circle. Kureishi demonstrates this by exploring them with regard to the friends, lovers, surrogate and real fathers, brothers and uncles that accompanied his life, and discovers that the conflict inherent in a search for role models, orientation, knowledge, intimacy, the difficulty of maintaining one's own space, and the danger "of being overwhelmed by the other person, of there not being enough of me and too much of them" (190), is present in all relationships and essentially shapes the construction of identity.

It is telling that the two pictures on the front and back cover of the book are the only ones that position father and son together within the frame of a family photo. The photo used on the cover shows Hanif Kureishi as a boy of nine years old on his father's knee at a party at the Pakistani Embassy. Anne Rüggemeier (2014, 128–129) sees this picture as a 'protonarrative' that captures the essence of the father-son relationship as described in the memoir. With their colour-contrasting suits the two figures epitomise the "relational self-constitution of the one in opposition to and against the background of the life story of the other" (Rüggemeier 2014, 128; my translation). The family photos inside the book can roughly be grouped into two sets; the first group relates to the life narrative and the family history of Kureishi's father, with rather frequent pictures of Shannoo at different life stages of his life (as a child in India, 16, 22; as a young man in England and Paris, 49, 91; and with Kureishi's mother, 49), pictures of Kureishi's uncles (two pictures of Omar, 36, 89; one of Sattoo, 70), and his grand-father (with Kureishi's mother, 39). The photo of Kureishi's own sons (26) as discussed above is clearly at odds with this group. Interestingly, his parents are pictured as a couple in 1953, before their son was even conceived. Apart from the paratextual photographs of father and son on the front and back cover, there are no family photographs that show members of the Kureishi family together, a void that is reflected in the way that the frequent sequence of photographs (one every five to twenty pages) ends after the first half of the book. The only domestic family scene in the whole book can be found in the picture on the back cover, which depicts his father with himself as a six-year-old in their garden, his father in a deck chair in the front of the picture, engrossed in smoking his pipe and in his reading, while his son, further to the back, looks at him as if he is trying to get his attention. This desire to establish contact and to communicate is in line with the affiliative endeavour that is generally represented in Kureishi's text. The second group of photos is remarkably smaller and relates more directly to the author's own life. The first, captioned as "The author, 1970" (at age sixteen; 159) is placed within the context of Kureishi's early process of separating himself from his parents and the family home, including his first advances in writing and his first excursions into the world of drugs and sex. The picture shows a self-confident, even bold young man, wearing a half unbuttoned shirt and holding his hands on his hips, while at the same time sporting a cocky smile. The scene depicted in the photo is clearly a suburban setting and might well be the family's back garden. The photo emphasises the element of rebellion and non-conformity, and the young writer's desire for life, adventure, and knowledge of the world. Finally, the last picture in the memoir highlights the element of transgenerational continuity and connectedness by showing the author with his three sons. It also conveys a sense of closure by shifting the perspective from the past to the present and future.

The memoir, despite being full of betrayals of his father, both small and large, (Kureishi even begins to "like Colonel Murad's authority" by the end, although "[i]t makes me feel guilty to say it", 229), is, however, a very sincere attempt to come closer to his father through a deeper understanding and appreciation of the story of his life. The accompanying awareness of the power of deep-rooted family entanglements also helps him to make sense of his own life. This affiliative impulse involves the recognition and acknowledgement that – however problematic their relationship was –, as a writer, he owes much to his father, who ensured that his children learned the value of books and literature as integral part of the process of transmitting the family ideal and myth.[36] The structure of his book, through which Kureishi very literally 'brings everything together', further emphasises this affiliative gesture that is contained in this memoir. It follows an open form, and in this respect resembles his father's manuscript: "I think I am writing this book in the way he wrote his, as a sort of collage, hoping the thing holds together, divided and split though it may be, like any mind." (21) Although it is an assortment of family documents, including his father's novels, his uncle's memoirs, family photos, and family memories, the book gives prominence to Kureishi in the role of both reader and author; it details his 'quest' of sifting through these documents, from which he draws meaning through selecting, sorting, and interpreting them. The divisions and splits of the mind itself, as referred to by Kureishi, are made evident in the autobiographic process and become visible in

---

[36] Cf. "Of course the puzzle of books, what they did and the satisfaction they provided, had always been at the centre of the family." (103)

a plurality of references to the self in the roles of narrator, reader, family chronicler, author of the memoir, famous writer, and as self-conscious meta-commentator (cf. Rüggemeier 2014, 133).[37] Kureishi thus shows that his father's idea of the novel as being superior to autobiography because "the novel, being a conflictual form, is a natural outlet for drama, for internal dispute and multiple viewpoints" (38), does not necessarily apply in this case, and that the memoir can do something similar.

His collage-like, associative memory text includes a meta-level that exposes the process of its own making, which also mirrors his father's text which is characterised by "inaccurate typing, crossings-out and scribbled additions" (12). The lack of form and cohesion (cf. also 222), which Kureishi perceives as a flaw in his father's novels, is an asset for his own writing and engagement with memory work. The multi-modal and multi-voiced arrangement that he chooses for the memoir resembles his vision of a scrapbook-like form that he has based on his reading of his father's manuscripts:

> Looking at the inaccurate typing, crossings-out and scribbled additions of this one makes me think of the limitations of the mass-produced novel with its impression of impersonality, objectivity and authority. Sometimes I fancy making my own books, hand-written in different colours, including photographs, drawings and alternative versions, which would give an impression of its making or process. (12–13)

My Ear at His Heart, with its associative and essayistic form that has been compared to the methods of "deconstructive psychoanalysis" (King 2005, 89), is indeed a very personal account that never conceals the subjectivity of its author's perspective and perception. The book thus attests to the complex multi-layered, multiperspective, and interactive nature of the telling of family stories, "the unrelialibility of memory and competing versions of the family myth" (Thomas 2006, 187).

The fact that the memoir has two endings also bears this out. Compelled by the discovery of yet another manuscript by his father to re-evaluate his image once again, Kureishi emphasises the fact that a family provides an open and never-ending story that will always continue and transform itself as long as its

---

[37] Most notably, the image captions shift between the first person of the text-internal narrator (cf. "My father as a child", 16) and third-person references to Kureishi as a real-world author (cf. "Author's father and mother, 1953", 49). See Rüggemeier (2014, 132ff.) for a more theory-informed analysis of the autobiographical self and the concept of the author. See also Eakin (1999, 43), who elaborates that "the first person of autobiography is truly plural in its origins and subsequent formation".

members live on, struggle with their family relationships, and imaginatively engage with the family myth. The intrinsic openness of the family narrative also lies in its ultimate 'unknowability'; no matter how far one delves into the depths of family memory and its archives, there will always be things that remain hidden and unseen, and any recovered piece of information (such as the discovery that his father was an 'unwanted child') may give the narrative a new perspective. Although it attests to the openness of the family narrative, the memoir's second ending offers a stronger sense of closure than the first. While the previous chapter ends with a future-oriented outlook, where Kureishi reflects on turning 50 and on the next generation of the Kureishis, the last chapter returns the focus back to his father and their relationship, suggesting that the memoir finally fills a void that was left in his father's life: "Father has at last received from me what he wanted when he sat down to write each morning: his stories have been read, pored over, lived with, become the subject of conversation. They've turned out, in my retelling, to mean more than he thought they meant." (237)[38] The family memoir, in "an act of real generosity" (Couser 2012, 14), thus assumes the form of "giv[ing] something back" (*Ear* 241), of repaying the "debt" (241) incurred by succeeding as a writer, the same goal that Kureishi's father, despite his hard work, never achieved.

Reading his father's text and writing his own work becomes characterised by a struggle to leave home, and for recovering space and distance. His literary projects, although they are in line with his father's own literary ambitions, turn out be a way to escape the trap, "because it had occurred to me that unless I had a project, my daily life could turn into a repetition of my father's" (151). Even more important than fulfilling the theme of revolt and separation, however, is the vision of togetherness that is created in Kureishi's memoir and the space of literary imagination that it provides. He draws lines and connects them up to create imaginary meeting points between the different times and geographical locations of the lives of his father, his other Kureishi relatives, and of himself and his sons. In

---

[38] The conciliatory tone of this thought is a bit deceptive, considering the fact that Kureishi's reading of his father's writing is at times patronising and not devoid of the rival criticism that was a feature of their earlier working relationship. The way in which he cites his uncle Omar's memoirs at length, while at the same time only offering short snippets of quotations from his father's writing, is a clear sign of the literary merit that he assigns to the respective works. It is only in the last chapter that he includes longer passages that are taken directly from his father's manuscript, the last one that he discovered, which, in Kureishi's view, is apparently of a higher literary quality than the others: "This time [...] I think it will be less easy for me to patronise my father." (223)

this way, instances of synchrony emerge through parallels, recurring motifs or experiences, which emphasise connectedness and the idea of an on-going story,

> a story of generations, told through the males, from my grandfather Colonel Murad /Kureishi, via my own father, his brothers, myself and my own sons, three British boys called Kureishi. Out of my reading and others' writing I have made a story of the past, imagining around their imaginations. (238)

5.2 "Made up from a mixture of myth and gene": Family and Relatedness in Jackie Kay's Adoption Memoir *Red Dust Road* (2010)

Known primarily as a poet, Jackie Kay uses the prose form of autobiographical life writing in *Red Dust Road* (2010) to explore the theme of her adoption, which she had previously dealt with in her first collection of poetry, *The Adoption Papers* (1991).[39] The non-linear narration of the memoir traces the author's search for her birth parents, firstly through her imagination, and later in reality, all the while interlacing the steps of this search with significant points in her life, from childhood, through adolescence, to young adulthood. These episodes add a further dimension to the issues of family, identity, and relatedness that are at the centre of Kay's search for and encounter with her biological parents. As John McLeod (2016, 222) perceptively observes, "[t]hese narrative strands are interwoven in a form that refuses the progressive linearity of historical time and displaces the discovery of biogenetic origins as a paradigm of narrative climax, for which the adoptee must quest".[40] The constellation of the adoptive family on the one hand and her birth family on the other separates, at least superficially, the two realms of nurture and nature, and thus gives us ample insight into the different methods used to establish family relatedness and construct a sense of home. Despite the narrative's focus on the search for her birth parents, its underlying theme of love

---

39 In his reading of *The Adoption Papers*, McLeod (2016, 218) concludes that Kay here "poses a question that [she] later in her career will pursue much more productively: how to build new relations between adoptee, birth-mother and adoptive mother that *challenge* those prevailing norms – societal and narrative – that insist upon the primacy of biogenetic genealogy over the vicissitudes of the adoptive experience for all concerned".

40 Significantly, the book begins with Kay's first encounter with her birth father in Nigeria and thereby, from the start, flouts the expectations concerning the narrative arch of more conventional adoption writing (cf. McLeod 2015, 212).

and togetherness as experienced in Jackie's adoptive family emphasises the importance of shared family life and family practices that create a strong sense of connectedness, care, and belonging in the synchronic family that form the basis for an integrated self. The emotional warmth and unconditional support that Kay shares with her adoptive parents is contrasted with the complicated and distant relationship that she builds with her birth parents. The book shows that relatedness need not be based on genealogy and blood relations, and that inheritance can be conceived of in other forms than simply through the transmission of DNA.

Despite the alternative family constellation that is introduced through the adoption issue, the memoir shares central themes with the other second-generation migration novels that are discussed in this study. Born to a mother from the Scottish Highlands and a Nigerian father, Jackie is raised by a white socialist couple in Glasgow, along with an older brother, who is also adopted and also mixed-race. Growing up in the 1960s and '70s in the only multiracial family of the locality, she suffers the everyday racism of her neighbours and schoolmates, which, later at university in the early '80s, becomes an even more threatening pervasive racism associated with the rise of the National Front and other right-wing extremist groups. Her growing racial awareness as a child has a dual aspect to it, besides simply being aware of her compartmentalisation from the majority-white society (as is the case in the novels discussed so far), she also has to deal with the realisation that she is different from her parents. Nevertheless, the way in which she deals with questions of origin, ethnicity, belonging, and identity is similar to the other novels, with the exception that she has a stronger and more explicit interest in the issues of inheritance and family connection in relation to the theme of adoption, which makes the memoir a particularly interesting case of analysis. Kay's memoir of transracial adoption falls into a larger category of Black British writing that John McLeod (2016, 214; emphasis in the original) has grouped under the header of 'adoption aesthetics', in which

> [a]doption has been appropriated *productively* as putting into crisis normative notions of race and culture – as in those 'consanguineous' discourses which construct notions of racial and cultural sameness through metaphors of 'common blood' – as if such matters can be transmitted between people in the same way as biological likeness.[41]

---

[41] In his research, McLeod (2015 and 2016) has very productively developed the notion of adoption aesthetics to approach a surprisingly large and diverse group of texts in the field of Black British writing that cover a variety of different genres. As becomes apparent in his analyses, the topic of adoption is a field of literary study in its own right that cannot be dealt here with due

The main narrative line of the memoir follows Kay's tracing of her birth parents, as is the case with many adopted people who decide to "walk back up the road to their past in search of themselves" (*Red* 47).[42] Kay starts tracing her birth mother when she is herself pregnant at 26, and her curiosity is raised by the standardly posed medical questions about family diseases, as well as, most probably, by her own experience of becoming a mother. She only traces her father much later, when she is in her forties, and her engagement with him triggers a growing curiosity about his home country of Nigeria and its culture. Underlying this search is her desire for recognition that is grounded in numerous experiences of being made to feel different, foreign, and not belonging (cf. 192–193). The memoir also shows, however, that recognition, and the affirmation of identity that it it entails, can be found and created in numerous ways and places; it lies at the heart of varying forms of connection that are fundamental for the relational self. The memoir "presents the adoptive self as a freeing constellation of shifting affiliations" (Fox 2015, 277), less determined by pre-given kinship ties and open to actively shaping relations and relationality. Through the emphasis on the active process of recognition, the memoir highlights the way that family affiliation is interactively constructed and maintained.

5.2.1 Family Storytelling as a Way of Doing Family

"Families, it may be said, are as much collections of memories as they are of actual related people and kin" (Smart 2011a, 543). This statement by Carol Smart may reinforce the assumption that the absence of blood relations in a family can be compensated for by a proliferation of memories. Kay's adoptive family is indeed characterised by very strong emotional bonds and a high degree of intimacy between the family members. These family relationships are shown to be built on a tight framework of memories and stories that all emphasise family ties. The memoir details how the telling of stories and the sharing of memories strengthen family identity on two levels, firstly, in building up a shared family memory, and secondly, in creating situations for family interaction in the form of collective reminiscing. In order to examine ways of establishing family identity and relatedness, it is fruitful to look at both the content matter of the family stories as well

---

complexity. McLeod (2016, 222) highlights *Red Dust Road* as "perhaps the most significant representation of black British adoption aesthetics published to date".

42 *Red* refers to Kay 2011 [2010]. Hereafter all references to the novel will use only page number, and, where necessary, *Red* for disambiguation.

as at the ritualised practices that surround family reminiscing and storytelling. In her memoir, Kay presents the practice of storytelling as the social glue that binds the family together. For this purpose, 'canonical stories' have been fabricated over the years – stories that elaborate classic family episodes that revolve around themes central to the construction of family identity.[43] These stories are canonical in the sense that they comprise of a stock of narratives that are repeatedly re-told and hold a higher meaning and value than other stories that are non-canonical or merely "apocryphal" (24).[44] In line with the typical content of canonical stories, storytelling in the Kay family revolves primarily around 'creation stories' relating to seminal transformative events in the family history such as the marital origin story and, in this case, adoption narratives (in lieu of 'birth stories'). A second sub-category of canonical stories relates to shared experiences such as family rituals or routines, which, in this instance, involves their summer holidays on the isle of Mull. While the first group of stories are concerned with the interconnections of individual and collective identity construction within the family, the second emphasises the role of social interaction involved in doing family.[45]

The following analysis aims to expound on how family storytelling enables the members of the family to build a pool of shared knowledge, which they continuously rely on and emphasise in the practice of collaborative reminiscing. The shared stories strengthen family connections by highlighting similarities and by reinforcing and communicating the underlying themes of family history. Kay's

---

[43] See chapter 2.2.1 in this book, and the passage on family memory as collective memory in particular. Cf. also Jorgenson and Bochner (2003, 525ff.) or Koenig Kellas and Trees (2013, 394ff.) for an elaboration of 'canonical family stories'.

[44] Cf. Kay's classification of a particular story in the following manner: "I don't know if this really happened, the minister on the doorstep, or if it's apocryphal, but my mum used to insist that it did" (24). Although used in a comical sense here, the biblical terminology of canon and apocrypha underlines the way in which family storytelling becomes formalised over time to convey specific messages, values, and images. The equation of canon with 'truth' as taken from the context of the bible hints at the "normative and formative" quality of the canon (cf. A. Assmann 2008, 100). The concepts of canon and apocrypha indicated here also underlines the way in which family storytelling serves to create a certain family 'myth' (cf. chapter 2.1.1 in this book, and John Gillis' concept of 'the families we live by').

[45] The re-tellings of family vacations, in particular, are "usually accompanied by high positive affect" (Fivush et al. 2008, 137); family holidays offer a condensed glimpse of family life that is more memorable and yields more storymaking material than everyday routines can: "Now we sit around the table and play the holidays back: family holidays go quicker into the past than anything else; but also, peculiarly, stay in the land of a permanent present, quickly accessed with their fund of memorabilia and materials." (118)

depiction of joint family reminiscing throughout the memoir demonstrates the process of her appropriation of family stories that are beyond her own life span and how they are incorporated into her self-narrative. The chapter "Christchurch to Glasgow", for instance, traces the 'creation story' of the Kay family, covering the family's trajectory from the parents' first encounter and their wedding to the adoption of their two children, Maxwell and Jackie. The family's point of origin is the story of how Kay's parents, both originally from Scotland, met and fell in love in New Zealand (cf. 14). The chapter title points to movement, travelling and migration as an inherent part of family identity, which is emphasised in the anecdote where Kay's 'dad' John gives her 'mum' Helen[46] a rucksack instead of a wedding ring.[47] New Zealand and the journey-motif signify the couple's open-mindedness and are thus indirectly linked to their later decision for a transracial adoption.[48] In the same vein, it is another journey, her mother's trip to Russia for the World Youth Congress in 1958, that manifests, in Kay's eyes, the "story that leads to my brother and me; in an imaginary way, the train stopped at us. We could have been picked up en route." (33–34) In this manner, for Kay, a major part of the appeal of her parents' story is that it has an immediate connection with her own story, which is enhanced by this pre-history dimension. Kay – in her own narration of it – supplements the family *story* with historical data, thereby framing it as family *history*. The pivotal incidents in the family history (her parents' marriage, her brother's adoption) are set in relation to particular historical events that correspond with specific concerns expressed through her own and the family's story. This technique serves to create links between the different narrative strands in the family, even with those that concern her birth parents, and to underline Jackie's connection with events that had happened before her entry into the family.[49] The "polyvocality" (McLeod 2016, 222) of singing, reminiscing, and

---

46 Jackie refers to her adoptive parents as 'dad' and 'mum' or 'mummy'; in contrast with this, she calls her her birth parents 'father' and 'mother'.

47 The lack of an expensive wedding ring as a symbol of their union is of course also in line with their socialist political views; the rucksack, an item in which only the basic necessities can fit, can be seen as a symbol of their anti-materialist stance.

48 Since Kay's maternal grandparents emigrated to New Zealand to be closer to their daughter, only to see the couple re-migrate to Scotland shortly after their wedding, the family could be referred to as being transnational even before Kay's parents opted for a transracial adoption. See also McLeod (2015, 218–219) on the role of transnational journeys in producing the Kay family's "transcultural disposition".

49 For instance, wen referring to the year of her parents' wedding in 1954, there are also mentions of the Supreme Court's rule against school segregation and McCarthyism; the first citation hints at the family's future as a transracial family, the second relates to the parents' communist politics. The reference to "Billy Graham's Christian revival meetings" (15) builds a bridge to

storytelling in the Kay family also "blueprints the form of *Red Dust Road*, which shifts temporally between tracing tales of roots and routes, while adding Kay's memories of growing up black and lesbian in Glasgow and Stirling" (McLeod 2016, 222).

'Marital origin stories' take a central role in family storytelling as they "set the tone for a foundational family relationship" (Koenig Kellas and Trees 2013, 395). In the book, this is not only true with regard to the kind of relationship that Kay's parents build and how they present it to their children, but also in relation to the actual tone of their narrative, which transports important family-related values and aspects of identity. Kay's parents tell their story with dry humour and a self-irony that cancels out any semblance of sentimentality. Humour is a general feature of communication within the family that also characterises the tone of Kay's own narration in the memoir, as she admits to having "inherited, if inherited is the word, and perhaps it is, her [mum's] gift for exaggeration" (24). The result of the "narrative's tonal levity" (McLeod 2015, 211) is that the author manages to "portray sentiment with absolutely no sentimentality", as Chimamanda Adichie lauds Kay for her "Books of the Year" review in the *Guardian*. The memoir is, as another blurb on the back cover states, "warmed by humour and love",[50] two aspects that also feature dominantly in the way in which family storytelling is presented in the book. Humour, overall, is a complex feature. It is also employed strategically in the memoir "as a redemptive force and a distancing device" (Tournay-Theodotou 2014, 16) particularly in dealing with difficult situations, as seen most importantly in Kay's rendition of her meeting with her father. Its function in the book thus surpasses that of being a mere stylistic device and can be more closely described as a fundamental attitude for encountering life.[51]

Jackie's biological father, who, much later in life, will join the movement of born-again evangelical Christians and become a preacher himself. If one disregards the apparent confessional differences and looks instead at the broader theme of religiosity, the reference to Billy Graham could also be read as hinting at Jackie's biological mother, who turns to Mormonism later in her life. In this way, both of her biological parents are subtly involved in the marital origin story of her adoptive parents, and are thus incorporated into Jackie's family history. Maxwell is adopted on September 18th, 1959, the day of the Auchengleich Colliery disaster, with which the family identifies because Kay's maternal grandfather was a miner who had "twice been buried alive down the pits, and twice survived" (23).

50 This blurb is taken from Miranda Seymour's review in the *Daily Telegraph*. The quote from Adichie's review was also found as a blurb in the front pages of the Picador paperback edition, which feature even more quotes from reviews that refer to humour as a key characteristic of the memoir.

51 With regard to humour, Kay also stresses the role of other, outside family, sources in the transmitting of scripts, narratives, and frames of reference for the story of the self, notably the

In her memoir, Kay also highlights the discursive style in which her parents' communications are transmitted. Their style of reminiscing as a couple can be classified as highly collaborative and mutually supporting, confirming a strong affective family relationship.[52] It is marked by frequent turn-taking and a routine of what seems to have become a well-practised dialogue ("he always will say [...] And she'll say, [...] And he'll say [...]", *Red* 14–15). The dialogic nature of family storytelling is stressed by the way in which Kay's mum and dad frequently include each other in their utterances, and ask for confirmation of their memory ("Isn't that right, John? [...] Do you remember, Ellen?", 14–15). The category pertaining to a collaborative style of narration, in which "[t]he story told conjointly is richer than the one the individuals would have told alone" (Fiese and M. Winter 2009, n.p.) corresponds with the way in which Kay describes her parents' storytelling behaviour, which, in turn, considerably enhances the story's emotional effect on her: "I love hearing these stories, partly because they are familiar to me, and partly because I love the way they tell them in tandem, and both remember slightly different things. I envy the rare thing that my parents have, that they have shared over fifty years together and can keep each other's memories" (*Red* 117).

Through numerous retellings, these memories of the early days of her parents' relationship have become 'storied'. Kay knows these consolidated stories by heart, which means that she is able to partake in her parents' shared memory.[53] These stories, besides strengthening the marital connection and reinforcing "the romance" (15) of Kay's parents, thus also play an important role in linking the generations. In the course of their reminiscing, Kay's parents not only focus on the shared nature of the memories that they have between the two of them, but also look to include Jackie, to whom the memory is extended. Her father draws her into the story by linking their first-date visit to the movies with a shared family activity of seeing the same play in a stage production years later, thereby establishing a connection between the parents' experiences and Kay's own: "Do you remember that, Jackie?" (16) Moreover, Jackie is directly addressed at several

---

media and pop culture. A decisive episode in Kay's childhood is her identification with the TV show *Roots* and its focus on black characters, whose "strength and bravery" is conveyed through their use of humour as "a kind of defence against racism" (186).

52 The narrative style displayed by Kay's parents in the memoir fully corresponds with the category of 'collaborative' style of narration in families as discerned by Fiese and M. Winter (2009). See chapter 2.2.1 for a summary of their findings on the connection of narrative styles in families with family well-being and satisfaction. The 'collaborative' narrative style is at the top of their spectrum and indicates very healthy family relationships and a positive and supportive form of interaction.

53 Cf. 15: "My mum often tells me the story of their first date."

points in the reminiscences and is thus invited to participate in the ritual of family storytelling. The "communicative processes of the story and storytelling interaction" (Koenig Kellas and Trees 2013, 391) are directed overall at producing affirmative responses and conveying positive emotions: "'Good for you,' I say again as I've said when I've heard the story before." (16) Through her active role in the joint activity of family reminiscing, Kay can more strongly identify with her parents' story, which, in spite of the repetitive nature of its telling never loses its particular interest: "Somehow, even though I've been told this story of my parents' meeting in New Zealand many times, each time a new bit surfaces that I hadn't noticed before." (16) Kay's memoir shows that the interactive practices of storytelling and communicative forms of reminiscing play a crucial role in strengthening family connections. In these interactions the stories' themes of family cohesion, love, and commonality are continually invoked and reinforced as collective values (cf. Fiese and M. Winter 2009).

The second important group of family stories in the Kay family – as with other families – revolves around their family holidays to the Isle of Mull, recounted in the 'Mull' chapter, which begins with a long string of memories from these holidays as told by Kay's mum Helen, in conversation with her daughter. The direct form of address (the narration moves mostly between the first and the second person), as well as the frequently repeated invitation to join in the process of remembering ("Remember [...]?", cf. 114ff.)[54] again conjoin the narrator and the listener in these stories, and emphasise the connection that is established through the memories of the shared experiences and through their re-telling. The lack of quotation marks to indicate the change of the narrative voice at the beginning of the chapter, and later during the longer passages where holiday memories are being shared, points to the blurring of boundaries between one's own and others' memories and stories as part of the process of conjoint family reminiscing. Even in her adulthood when has her own family, the ritual of re-telling family stories allows Kay to perform and maintain family ties: "Now when I go home, my parents and I like nothing better than sitting round the table going over past holidays. Or they tell me over and over about their days in New Zealand" (116). Family holidays serve this purpose extremely well, as they transport (usually) positive emotions (cf. Fivush et al. 2008, 137) and a condensed image of the 'family we live by': "Now we sit around the table and play the holidays back; (... they) stay in the land of a permanent present, quickly accessed with their fund of memorabilia and materials." (118)

---

[54] Tournay-Theodotou (2014, 18) counts more than thirty repetitions of the imperative "remember".

5.2.2 "What makes us who we are": Stories as Inheritance

As the family is a unit that moves through time, the family is re-constituted at different points in time (Fivush et al. 2008, 138). Next to marital origin tales, stories about additions to the family form an obviously significant sub-group. These "entrance narratives focus primarily on the identity of one family member" (Koenig Kellas and Trees 2013, 395). In Kay's memoir, the stories of her brother Maxwell's adoption, and of her own two years later, loom large over the collection of often-told family stories; they are "the two first big real stories I heard, and we found both stories fascinating" (44). The importance of these adoption narratives in the Kay family shows how non-traditional families "often must do extra 'narrative work' in order to help children come to terms with the family form and their place in it" (Koenig Kellas and Trees 2013, 394).[55] Such 'birth stories' or 'claiming stories' often "restory their [the adopted children's] personal myths" (Koenig Kellas and Trees 2013, 394) and can thus have a healing effect on children suffering from trauma-attachment problems (e.g. if children are adopted from an orphanage). These entrance stories are foundational for the individual's narrative of self and may compensate for the missing link of genetic inheritance by offering another kind of inheritance through stories. In an interview, Kay explains that "for my mum and me, stories being passed down are as important as blood and genes. *Red Dust Road* is really about what makes us who we are, nature, nurture." (*Bookgroup Info*)

The memoir shows the crucial role of adoption narratives not only in establishing and strengthening family ties but also as a vanishing point for narratives of self. It is significant in this respect that the two adoption stories relating to Maxwell and herself are linked, because Kay's parents, "having one 'coloured child' decided to adopt another" (22). This forges a connection between the two that strengthens the family bond of brother and sister. After they decide to register for adoption, Kay's parents find that due to their communist politics, it takes "ages" for them to get accepted by an agency, let alone find a child. After five years of waiting, Helen, Kay's mum, thinks of telling the agency, in "an almost casual, throw-away remark" (22), that they have no preference regarding the

---

[55] Koenig Kellas and Trees name "[a]doptive, foster, same-sex, and stepfamilies" as examples of 'non-traditional families' (103). Kay's own 'family of procreation' is also non-traditional: Being a lesbian, she finds a sperm donor for her child in the British-Guyanese writer Fred d'Aguiar; her reflections on becoming a mother and her prenatal speculations about this biological inheritance are connected to the 'enigma' of her own genetic and epigenetic mix (cf. chapters '1987' and '1988', 91–92, 110–111).

child's skin colour, whereupon they are taken to the orphanage and introduced to Maxwell that same day. In the same way that Kay's parents have trouble passing "as eligible adoptive parents" (21), Maxwell is considered ineligible for adoption by the agency, as he "wasn't even thought of as a baby" (22).[56] In the story of Maxwell's adoption, the coincidence and the accidental are emphasised: "So much was down to chance and timing" (21).[57] This is contrasted with an emphasis on choice in Jackie's own adoption narrative, which focuses on "the stories of my original parents having no choice, and the stories of my mum and dad having choice. 'We *chose* you; you are special. Other people had to take what they got, but we *chose* you.'" (43; emphasis in the original) The story contrasts her adoptive parents' choice with her birth parents' lack of choice, juxtaposing freedom of action with the impossibility of such agency. Both chance and choice are inherent aspects of adoption.

Due to their decision to adopt "another child the same colour" (25), Kay's parents are involved with her early in the process. "So, months before my birth mother gave birth to me, my mum knew that she was going to have me." (25) These "months of ghost pregnancy" (25) create a connection between the adoptive mother and daughter that transcends the merely social and moves into the realm of the body. As Helen tells her, "[i]t was a real experience. It felt real." (25) After her birth Kay turns out to be ill and the doctors expect her not to live, keeping her in the hospital for five months. However, during these months she unexpectedly thrives, and the story of her adoption stresses how her mum's frequent visits to the hospital, "this interest, this love, is what made me survive against the odds." (26) The physicality of the bond, its 'realness', is thus transferred from the biological to the adoptive mother and her relationship with the baby. Clare Hanson (2015, 439) comments on this transfer in the following way:

> the narrative shaped by Kay and her adoptive mother is sensitive to the multiple factors that shape identity and to the inter-relations between social meanings and somatic experiences.

---

56 See McLeod (2016, 212) for an account of the socio-political circumstances and the "unwarranted racism of social workers" surrounding the "emerging practice of transracial adoption that took off in Britain" in the 1950s and 60s. McLeod (2016, 214–15) also provides an interesting overview of the discussions about transracial adoption in the late twentieth and early twenty-first century.

57 Or, as Kay's mum says, "It's all a lottery [...]. It's all pure luck" (21). Chance reoccurs as a leitmotif in the narrative of Jackie's search for her biological father, in which every decisive turn in the story is triggered by chance, "the coincidences piling up like a stack of wobbly books" (257). The motivic linking of her personal life story with these family stories, such as, in this case, the adoption narrative of her brother and herself, reveals the close interconnection of her own story with that of her family, and thus stresses the importance of family connectedness.

Kay's story of origin can thus be read as a fable that dramatises the way in which nurture becomes embodied; moreover, as a narrative that illuminates the embodied connections forged through an adoptive mother's nurture of her child, it complicates a narrowly genecentric view of biological relatedness.

The 'ghost pregnancy' experience binds the adoptive mother to the baby in a way that enables her to provide the nurture that will help to sustain the new-born baby's health so that it is ultimately she herself who gives life to the baby.[58] The "construction of a symbolic pregnancy and birth" (Hanson 2015, 438)[59] is a frequent topos in adoption narratives; in this case, the story casts the process as being (physically) experienced on both sides, by the mother (as a 'real feeling') and by the daughter (as bodily healing). As nurture becomes embodied in the prolonged stage of birthing, the separation between genetic makeup and environmental influences becomes blurred. Kay's adoption narrative thus endorses the findings of epigenetic research which state that "what makes us 'who we are' is not our DNA but what happens to DNA in the complex contingencies of development" (Hanson 2015, 436).[60]

In the course of the memoir, Kay sums up the complexities of identity formation within the family framework with the formula that "you are made up from a mixture of myth and gene. You are part fable, part porridge" (47). This aphorism puts porridge/nurture and gene/nature on the same level as two aspects of the bodily self – two aspects that converge into one in her own 'adoption entrance

---

[58] Apart from constituting a crucial episode in Kay's adoption story, her period of illness in the hospital after her birth also falls into another key category of family narratives, namely "tales of disease management" (Fiese and M. Winter 2009, n.p.). The way in which families deal with "critical events in their collective lives" through such stories plays a major role in the future health and well-being in the family (Fiese and M. Winter 2009, n.p.).
[59] The stages of pre-pregnancy, pregnancy, and birthing as experienced by adoptive parents are described in detail in Howell and Marre (2006, 302ff). This process of vicarious conception and birth-giving by the adoptive parents is called 'kinning', which aims to "symbolically negate the fact that their children are not their biological children" and is particularly pertinent in transracial adoptions as a means to "reconcile [...] physiological differences" (Howell and Marre 2006, 295; cf. also Howell 2003). Overarching these practices of kinning is "a scenario of fate, or destiny" that connects the parents to the child so that "their child was meant for them in some mysterious way. No other child would have done as well" (Howell and Marre 2006, 301). The same holds true for Kay's adoptive mum, who rejects the doctors' advice to pick up another baby.
[60] This statement is based on empirical studies about the effects of "environmental triggers in periods of rapid growth such as infancy and adolescence" (Hanson 2015, 436) that have demonstrated that physical transformations can occur in response to care as opposed to stress triggers. For more information on epigenetic research see Hanson (2015).

narrative'.⁶¹ In this story, as in her memoir in general, Kay posits myth/fable alongside physical substance as the other key constituent of identity. Since "the experience of adoption confronts us with the question of the unknowability of origins in a particularly acute form" (Hanson 2015, 434), it is a condition that provides particularly fertile ground for practices of storytelling as a way of filling the void.⁶² In this vein, the early circumstances after her birth are transformed into narratives of sustainment in order to make up for Kay's lack of a point of origin. The adoption story itself is enriched with many stories of her birth parents and the circumstances that led to the adoption. Here, the scarcity of information that is passed on by the adoption agency leaves all the more room for fantasy, myth-making and narrative embellishment. Consequently, Helen makes up exotic stories full of the mysterious (through the use of words like "betrothed", 42), the sensational ("I liked this story [...] of betrothal which was also perhaps a story of betrayal", 43), and the extraordinary ("Maybe you are an African princess", 42). These stories, which emphasise her birth parents' sorrow at having to give up their baby, work as a remedy against the feelings of hurt and abandonment that may emerge as a consequence of adoption by making Jackie feel special and wanted (cf. 45–46, 13).⁶³ Moreover, the telling of these stories becomes a specific bonding activity between adoptive mother and daughter that helps to absorb at least a part of the difficult emotions that surround the topic by creating a space for collaborative fabulation, where these emotions can be shared and narratively transformed and dealt with: "It was a heartbreaking story and it was mine. In a way my mum and I loved it, the story of me. It was a big bond, the story." (44)

The emphasis on ownership ("it was *mine*"; my emphasis) in this quote reveals that the adoption story fundamentally provides a way of taking narrative control of an experience that initially denies her any agency. For Jackie and Helen, storytelling presents a powerful method for claiming authorship and to create a positive meaning that supports an affirmative story of self. Kay compares the experience of adoption to the image of a fork in the road that splits the self into two, with an imaginary version of "my other self", the one that followed "The

---

61 The mention of porridge is a reference to the "special diet [... of] porridge and extra vitamins" (26) that Jackie was fed on for weeks as a baby when her parents were allowed to take her home after five months of hospital care.
62 This fundamental unknowability is also the poetological origin of the 'Leerstelle' (translated as 'gap', or 'void'), as introduced by Wolfgang Iser (1974 [1972]), who argued on an anthropological level that humans have to create fictions in order to fill in what they can never know.
63 Via the adoption story, Kay manages to sell adoption as a positive thing on the basis that Jackie was not simply 'had' but that her adoptive parents chose her: "And you are special. You were chosen." (13)

Road Not Taken" (223), always sitting in some corner of her mind.[64] The idea of a split self is underpinned by a double naming as her birth parents gave her the name Joy, and her adoptive parents later chose the name Jackie. This "crossroads [...] between fact and fiction" (151) underlines the way in which adoption creates a rift between the real and the imagined: "Everyone involved in adoption has an imaginary version of everyone else" (71). In this case, reality and imagination are not conceived of as dichotomous or clearly divided; instead, their boundaries are blurred, and the categories seem to be interchangeable. It begins with denominations, when Helen tells seven-year old Jackie that she is "not really your mummy" (12), and Jackie misunderstands her and is "worried she means she is not real and that something is going to happen to her, that she is going to disappear or dissolve" (12). She goes on to wonder whether Helen is making this up, since "[s]he's so good, my mummy, at telling stories" (13). However, stories are not only the realm in which the imagination unfolds, stories also create a reality, and thus take on a decisive role in defining family identity and relationships. The stories that Jackie and Helen tell themselves make sense of the adoption in a way that reinforces the adopted self over that 'other self'. The memoir thus strengthens the adopted self, which "should not be imagined as forever split or fractured, but [that] can circumscribe the multidirectional possibilities born from their past as a mode of clinching a productive futurity" (McLeod 2015, 211). When Kay eventually traces her birth parents, it feels like a "fantastic fiction" (*Red* 134). Her imaginary version of them is a source of so much more of a feeling of truth and reality for her that, after she has found her father and exchanged an email with him, she has to "keep telling people the story to tell myself that it is real. That's the strange thing about being adopted: the story of your own adoption seems like the story of some stranger, or even the story of a fictional character. It's hard to make it real. The furniture of the imagination is flimsy, sometimes, not solid." (134)

Kay uses the same image of the crossroads and the split self to describe a 'turning point' in her life when she is sixteen and suffers a serious moped accident that "changed my life" (227). In this case, both images have their literal correlation: the impulsive decision to take a different turn in the street leads to the accident, and an out-of-body experience makes her feel "as if I was outside myself looking down, as if I had split in two" (228). The accident changes her life

---

[64] When Jackie starts tracing her birth parents, the other version of herself takes on a stronger reality, making the inner split more problematic: "Tracing suddenly asks someone who has had one life to have two; and you can't have two lives, you can only have one." (276)

because over the period of her convalescence, Jackie decides to be a writer, a decision that is described as a complete change of identity.[65] The loneliness and boredom of an extended hospital stay cause her to turn to books, and, again, to a heightened desire for meaning: "I read and read and look for meanings." (235) Her readings of classic books offer her alternative versions of her own story of adoption: "*Wuthering Heights* is an adoption story gone badly wrong. Heathcliff is the dark force the kind family invited home; Heathcliff brings the whole house toppling down. *Jane Eyre* is also an adoption story. Jane is adopted by people that don't understand her fierce intelligence and put her in the red room" (235).[66] These readings build on the earlier practice of storytelling between herself and Helen, and the meaning that she finds in these books is meaning that is directly connected to her own life and story of self. In one interview, Kay concedes that her early experience with stories (including adoption narratives) had an impact on her literary career: "listening to [my mum] tell me stories was one of the things that made me a writer" (*Bookgroup Info*). Writing, for her, thus becomes a way of reuniting the split self after the accident. In the same way as storytelling and the uses of the imagination, it provides her with a tool of rejecting the "doubled self, substantial and spectral at the same time, [...] in favour of a singular plural personhood" (McLeod 2015, 211). Like the alternative worlds offered in literature, Helen's stories are "part of an opportunity to play with a range of fanciful and possible pasts rather than resolve racial belonging", and thus "legitimate[...] a promiscuous approach to narrative, inviting her daughter to maker herself up time and again through cultural creativity" (McLeod 2015, 215).

5.2.3 Searching for "the place I come from": Locating the Diasporic Self

In her search for her self and the story of her origin, Kay assigns a major significance to places. The memoir is arranged in alternating chapters that are titled

---

65 Notably, the decision is not to *become* a writer, but to *be* a writer. In her first endeavours at writing, she starts to think of herself differently. Concomitantly, as if to highlight the metamorphosis, her outer appearance also alters due to a change in her metabolism: "I transformed from a slim but athletic-looking runner to a fat writer practically overnight. Now, this distance away from that accident, I can't imagine my life without it. It was the sudden fork in the road; the road I decided impulsively to take that did it." (236)

66 Previously in the book, Wuthering Heights has served as an image of comparison for Kay's "articulation of adoption in terms of spectrality" (McLeod 2015, 212), as she poetically describes the feeling of fundamental loneliness and hurt inherent in the adoption experience as "a windy place right at the core of my heart" (*Red* 45).

according to their respective spatial or temporal setting, and contrasted through the use of typeset and font. While the chapters referencing a specific year follow a chronological line with an increased density in the years 2003 and 2009 – the periods of her two visits to Nigeria in search of her father –, the place-chapters, which are much longer, trace a different (non-chronological) route that emphasises the dominant theme of the journey and the quest motif.

> Kay's temporal and spatial trajectories are evocatively conveyed by the narrative's non-chronological form, which [...] not only emulates the working of memory but is also meaningful as a reflection of the work's narrative and ideological content in that it captures the fractures and instabilities of a diasporic subjectivity (Tournay-Theodotou 2014, 16).

These 'fractures and instabilities' of the diasporic self correspond with Kay's description of the fragmentation of the adopted self as "liv[ing] in two worlds with only one life" (38).[67] While the chronological narrative thread that follows specific years hints at a biographical coherence of the self, the disconnection of the places in it signifies its fragmentary nature, as the locations referred to offer alternative narratives of belonging and of self. Through this structural device, the memoir highlights the role of places as coordinates for a life story; the places that lend their names to the chapter titles indicate the importance of geographical anchors as emotive reference points for the construction of the self.[68] By disrupting the chronological narrative, the place chapters disrupt the idea of a timeline or teleological journey towards wholeness and instead point to the "polyphonous, fragmented, 'hybrid' identity" (Zielke and Straub 2008, 62) of the diasporic subject.

In Kay's narration of transracial adoption, aspects of the adoptive self and the diasporic self converge in her treatment of place as a referent for identity construction. Notions of home and rootedness are fundamentally place-based, and the absence and remoteness of places may lead into feelings of displacement and alienation. The first information that Jackie is given about her biological parents occurs when her mum explains to her what 'being adopted' means. It means that

---

[67] Kay makes this statement about open adoptions, a form of adoption in which adopted children (and their adoptive parents) have access to personal information about their biological parents and also provide an option to contact them. Jackie, in contrast, has little to no information about her birth parents' lives, yet the imaginative and later actual involvement with her birth parents can be said to have had a similar effect, or, at least, hints towards the potential duplication of the self. The motif of living two lives resurfaces yet again during the Nigerian leg of her search.

[68] The stages of one's life are often marked in one way or another by geographical reference points. Significant biographical places are a pivotal source of affect and meaning in autobiographical memories and as such play into the processes of self-definition and identity formation.

"[y]our real daddy came from Nigeria in Africa and your mummy came from the Highlands" (13). These two places consequently become a primary reference point for Kay in contemplating on her birth parents, and in staking out her identity. Their existence alongside her family home in Glasgow and their imagination-stimulating power is indicative of the duplication of the self that comes about as a consequence of adoption. Her mother's home, Ivy Cottage in Nairn, is for Kay "one of those names that I've known all my life" (155); it has been continuously evoked in numerous stories and has always had an imaginary presence in her life long before she started tracing her birth mother. The same holds true for "Fantasy Africa", which Jackie tries to picture as a child but cannot grasp, in the same way that she fails to form a definite image of her father in her mind:

> Africa itself could only ever be imagined in the way that I imagined my father, with bright picture-book colours and bold outlines. Part of me came from Africa, part of me was foreign to myself, strange to myself since I had never been to the *dark continent* and could only really have it burning away, hot and dusty, in my mind. (38; emphasis in the original)

The strangeness of Africa is linked to her own experience of being different from others and having an internalised feeling of foreignness in growing up in Scotland as a mixed-race child. Having been asked repeatedly where she comes from, she finds that "you are subconsciously caught up in asking that question again and again of yourself, particularly when you are a child" (38). The enigma that is Africa holds the promise of attaining an answer to that question; its unfamiliarity and mysteriousness provide a perfect screen for the projection of her imagination that corresponds with her lack of knowledge about her father.[69]

Since "[c]hildren have an intense need to belong" (38), young Jackie looks to media images of black idols as an orientation for the imagining of her father, such as "the young Sidney Poitier or Nelson Mandela or Martin Luther King or Cassius Clay – the only real images of black men I have at my disposal" (37). When she is nine, she chooses Angela Davis as her role model, emulating her hairstyle and dreaming of becoming a "political heroine" (36). Later, in her early twenties, she engages with the writings of post-colonial critics, civil rights activists and African-American novelists in order to understand her origins and racial heritage: "reading changed the mirror that I held up to myself. [... C]oming across writers like Audre Lorde, Alice Walker, Toni Morrison, Ralph Ellison [...] changed my racial awareness; reading them changed my life." (40–41) At university, she joins

---

[69] The chapter "Fantasy Africa" corresponds with the later chapter "Reality Britain" that details Kay's experience of racism in college and her negotiation of blackness and racial identity in the context of 1980s identity politics.

political and activist groups, "meeting like-minded people" and revelling in "the excitement of being in a place where there were other black people who nodded to me in recognition" (182). Through groups like the Black Lesbian Group,[70] she finds and creates spaces from which she gains a "strong sense of support, belonging and racial and sexual self-validation" (Tournay-Theodotou 2014, 18). Kay learns to fill the absence of her black father and the missing legacy of a racial self-understanding with reading, guiding figures and peers. She thus comes to proudly "acknowledge [her] African heritage" (201) through affiliations and identifications with people from outside of the family, and by building "a knowledge of identity which stretches beyond simple familial ties" (Lumsden 2000, 83, qtd. in Tournay-Theodotou 2014, 18).

The novel builds up a contrast between the vagueness of 'Africa' and the specificity of the Ivy Cottage in Nairn as an image of her mother's home in the Scottish Highlands. While the Ivy Cottage manifests the concreteness of her Scottish heritage, which is stressed throughout the memoir as a major part of growing up in her adoptive family, the idea of 'Africa' represents a void rather than a place. In Jackie's imagination, Africa is condensed into the single image of the "red-dust road" (42), which "serves as the chief emblem for Kay's initial imagined and subsequent 'real' relationship with Africa" (Tournay-Theodotou 2014, 17). This road is not exactly a place as it cannot be pinned down on a map, and has no specificity apart from its qualifiers 'red' and 'dust', "which firmly anchor this image in an African landscape" (Tournay-Theodotou 2014, 17). As an emblem, however, the road adopts the motifs of travel, search and movement, and thus complicates any fixed idea of origin and roots connected with the notion of home, with which her engagement with place also resonates. The road hints at the tension between the idea of 'finding yourself' that involves a finite and essentialist concept of self on the one hand, and the image of the journey as symbolising the

---

70 Kay is a founding member of the BLG, formed as a breakaway group from the Organisation of Women of African and Asian Descent. This group points to the beginnings of intersectional approaches that surfaced in Black and feminist movements at that time, as well as to the importance of an awareness of intersectional identity for self-understanding. Kay acknowledges the guidance of African-American poet Audre Lorde, "who told me that I could be proudly African *and* Scottish and that I should embrace both. [...] I didn't need to choose." (201; emphasis in the original)

self as on-going and open process on the other. Kay uses the image of the jigsaw puzzle to address these contradictions in her search for belonging and origin:[71]

> If we think of ourselves as puzzles, and our birth parents are part of that puzzle, do we think that finding our parents will answer the puzzle? Surely we are not so naive?
> The jigsaw can never, ever be completed. There will always be missing pieces, or the pieces will be too large and clumsy to fit into the delicate puzzle. (47)

Accordingly, the hope that is initially conveyed in the jigsaw image is set up to be disappointed after the actual meetings with her birth parents, which turn out to be "upsetting" (67, 74) and generally difficult experiences for Kay, leaving many of her questions unanswered. She meets her mother three times over the course of a decade, and her father only once, after which he rejects her subsequent attempts at making contact. The spatial setting of their meetings echoes the "forced, constructed nature" (Tournay-Theodotou 2014, 20, fn 4) of these encounters and the fragility of the relationship that she tries to establish. These meetings respectively occur in classical 'non-places': in hotels in the cities of Abuja, Nigeria and Milton Keynes, England. Both cities are newly built, "planned [...], with little history" (165), and in that respect resemble the hotel as a neutral, impersonal and transient place, "a space of fleeting encounters" (Tournay-Theodotou 2014, 20, fn 4).[72] Kay describes Milton Keynes as "associated with loneliness and soullessness" (81), which are also typical characteristics of hotel rooms. Like Milton Keynes, which feels "like a toy town" and has "an air of unreality to it" (81), the meetings themselves seem awkwardly surreal. Sitting with her mother for the first time, Jackie senses an "uncomfortable intimacy" between them that makes her "feel a little like a fraud" (65). There is something "fake" and "fabulously made up" (135) about being adopted and meeting birth parents, when "[a]nybody could be sitting there saying they are your mother or father" (135). This sense of arbitrariness echoes the impersonality of the location.

These *non lieux* (Augé 1995) with no past and "no history except that I'm in it now" (81), reflect the reluctance of her birth parents to talk about the past that

---

[71] The jigsaw puzzle, in all this complexity, is repeatedly evoked in the memoir as a metaphor for identity and the process of tracing birth parents (cf. 136, 193). In Julian Barnes' *England, England* (1998) the jigsaw also appears as a metaphor for autobiographical memory and the narrative construction of the life story.

[72] Hotels are the very opposite of 'home'. To reinforce the point that hotels are sites of dislocation, Kay observes that "[b]oth my birth parents, on first sight, looked like some homeless people look, who carry important papers in carrier bags" (3). Hotels are detached from one's personal (geographical) history, and offer a space for actions or events that can resist integration into the narrative of the self.

connects them to their daughter, who represents, for them, an episode that both have tried to leave behind in building a new life. For them, she has become a secret that they want to hide.[73] Kay describes her encounter with them as "interlopers running into each other in peculiar places like cold-war spies, exchanging strange parcels" (74). Thus, a great part of her curiosity remains unsatisfied. To ask all the questions that she has in her head suddenly "seems worse than inappropriate"; it would mean "to drag [her birth mother] Elizabeth back to a painful time in her past, a time she clearly doesn't want to remember" (66).[74] Also her father Jonathan, when asked "to tell me as much as he can remember [...] seems perplexed about the idea of himself in the past, as if he was so totally somebody else then, he can hardly understand or remember himself, or hardly even believe that that Jonathan actually existed" (96–97). Jackie, as part of the past that he has so thoroughly dismembered from himself, has no place in his present life: "You are my before; this is my after. You are my sin, now I lead this life" (10), he tells her. His acknowledgement of his daughter is "between us and God" (108), and explicitly excludes his family, his other sons that Kay already knows about and would like to meet. To acknowledge his daughter is, for Jonathan, a personal step in his religious "career" (56), while her own interests and needs are completely disregarded in this meeting.[75] The fact that he has become a born again Christian

---

[73] At the last meeting between Kay and her birth mother she is invited to her home, which indicates a significant progression in her mother's attitude towards their relationship. In the living room, there is an (unframed) photograph of Kay and her son among the other (framed) family photographs, and her mother declares: "I'm having you both out now. I've put you out on the table." (76) This does not mean, however, that she intends to inform her family about her eldest daughter. Her parents' "extreme need for secrecy" (80) completely goes against Kay's "natural personality, which is perhaps to be too open, too trusting" (174). As her family stories indicate, this openness is also characteristic of the communication and interaction in her adoptive family (cf. the family holiday story about her first period, which she cannot wait to tell her brother about – but which seems to be too much for her friend, who expects the issue to be treated "like it had to be some big secret", 118). In the case of Kay's birth mother Elizabeth, however, secrecy also seems to be a family trait (cf. 153).

[74] Throughout the years in which she has known her, Kay's biological mother becomes increasingly affected by early-onset Alzheimer's disease, which, in some way, seems to reflect her need for secrecy and forgetting: "I was half thinking that people with Alzheimer's might have things they need to forget, things that they've always kept secret, whole children, whole middle-aged women." (86) At the same time Kay notices that in the case of Alzheimer's, "forgetting gives no peace, no resolution. Forgetting is fraught with a terrible anxiety, the kind that is filled with unknowable and unsayable things, a blazing, burning of everything and finally maybe a complete forgetting of the self." (88)

[75] Instead, the two-hour religious service that her father subjects her to, and the subsequent conversation are presented by Kay as a chain of transgressions of boundaries on his side that

symbolises this incision that he has made in his life-narrative, which has helped him to cut off his past.[76]

Kay counters the disillusionment and strangeness of these encounters in non-places with her search for places that offer her something to connect with and provide her with a sense of family history. The process of 'tracing' is thus accompanied by a literal search for the traces of her birth parents. At the point when she visits Aberdeen for the first time, the 'Granite City', where her parents met and where she was conceived, she has not yet met her father, but having recently found him, is full of anticipation for their future meeting. The few details that she knows of him begin to spark her imagination, and her mind starts to "fill him in a little. Tiny details illuminate, like the sparkle in the stone, tiny glittery details shimmer like mica." (138) When she returns to Aberdeen, however, four and a half years after her disappointing encounter with her father Jonathan in Nigeria, she finds new solace in the city, which now seems to her to be "a city that understands things – loneliness, depression, rejection. The stone makes no judgement." (139) With the city's unchanging granite, Kay "can imagine Jonathan here in the sixties" and perceives "something almost healing about being back in the same city that he studied in" (139). The city connects her with a past that her father is no longer in contact with, it retains the memory that he has repressed. Here, she feels the chance of meeting with the younger version of her father, the man as he was "before he was born again and inaccessible" (139). The city thus offers her "a kind of returning" (140). The stories that he denied her, "stories I would have loved to have heard" (141) are still present here and can be recovered in the University Archive and in the places where her birth parents roamed, such as the dining hall where they met, or the house that her father lived in – as well as in her imagination (cf. 140, 148).

---

feel to her "like a kind of assault" (3), and which leave her deeply disturbed. Kay, scared of extreme religion, had already felt alarmed when he only announced his desire to pray for her (cf. 3). The service then comes as a "shock" (5) to her, when she registers with "horror" Jonathan's view of her is as "the live embodiment of his sin" (6). As she has no way to end the procedure, she repeatedly tries to internally distance herself from what is happening. In the ensuing conversation, her father again violates her boundaries by asking her "perhaps the most un-fatherly question I've ever heard" (105) about her sex life. His transgressive behaviour leaves her feeling utterly overwhelmed in the end: "It is too much" (105).

76 Kay draws an interesting parallel between "the plethora of born-again Christian groups in the east of Nigeria" and the ramifications of the Biafra War, which caused a "double blow of memory and record loss" among many people including her father Jonathan, who says that "[i]t wiped us out. It took everything. All the photographic history, all the other family documents were completely lost during Biafra, everything personal." (145)

Apart from the city of Aberdeen, the respective places of origin of her birth parents play a major role in her idea of her self and in her search for origins. In contrast with the history-less cities of Milton Keynes and Abuja, the Ivy Cottage in Nairn and Jonathan's ancestral village in Ukpor in East Nigeria exude a heavy spirit of quaintness and primordiality.[77] These places embody a very family-specific and family-bound sense of history, tradition, and community. Both are 'generational places' (cf. A. Assmann 2009 [1999]) that not only keep family history alive but also stand for family togetherness in the present.[78] In the face of her birth parents' rejection of memory, these places become meaningful 'sites of memory' for Kay. After her birth mother's death, she visits Nairn and her aunts, whom she had been secretly in touch with. Here she receives from her aunts the recognition that was denied to her by her mother. Jackie is welcomed and accepted as part of the family in a way that her mother could not offer her while insisting on keeping her as a secret from her present family, her divorced husband and her other children.[79] In Nairn, "the cottage my birth mother grew up in" (153) has housed the family for generations; it is a place that "smells of the past, [...] of things hidden and left to rot" (160).[80] Among these, the memory of her own story is preserved, the family secret that had no place in her mother's life lives forth in the house:[81]

---

[77] After Kay's disappointing meeting with Jonathan, what remains for her is a strong desire to visit his 'ancestral village', the village where his family comes from. A Nigerian student of hers tracks down the village quite coincidentally because his uncle happens to know Jonathan professionally.

[78] According to A. Assmann (2009 [1999], 301), 'generational places' ("Generationenorte") are places where the members of a family have lived and died in an uninterrupted chain of generations. The 'ancestral village', where different generations and branches of the family live together as neighbours, plays a key role in Nigerian culture, as Kay finds out in conversation with friends and people who she meets on the road. It is also an important site for the homecoming rituals of Nigerians born abroad (cf. 178, 222). On the Scottish side, the cottage, where Jackie's mother grew up with six sisters and one brother, represents the closeness of the family that is referenced repeatedly by Jackie's aunts (cf. 162).

[79] The visit to the Ivy Cottage offers her another degree of familial recognition and welcoming than that which she experienced with her birth mother. Whereas Jackie had looked in vain for a likeness between her mother and herself when they first met (cf. 63), there is an instant sense of recognition on seeing her aunts, "all looking physically like my aunts" (154). Her aunts have "known me about since I was born, and have often thought of me, and imagined me. They see me so firmly as one of them, coming as they do from a close-knit Catholic Highland family." (163)

[80] In addition to the cottage, Nairn itself, much like Jonathan's village, represents (family) history; it is a place where "people are regarded as incomers even if they've lived there for four generations" (154).

[81] The fact that her birth mother forwarded the picture of Jackie as a baby (sent to her by Kay's adoptive mum) to the Ivy Cottage "for safekeeping" is emblematic of this 'outsourcing' of

"I'm grateful for seeing the timeless wee cottage almost exactly how it would have looked forty-seven years ago when my mother [...] lay in the bed nearest the window pregnant with me" (160). Much as the cottage has always had a place in her imagination despite its physical absence, her 'other self', Joy, as her birth parents named her, has been a part of the life of that cottage, represented by a classic family photo of herself with her son Matthew. When her aunts refer to her as Joy in old stories, Jackie feels "like I always was somebody else after all" (163). Not only is Ivy Cottage a place that is rich with family history, it also houses the sense of a shared past through a complementary imagination: It is here that the two sides of her story meet and converge.

These places emphasise the embeddedness of family relationships on a diachronic as well as synchronic axis. Even more relevant for Kay than the Ivy Cottage in Nairn, Jonathan's ancestral village stands for genealogical continuity and a rootedness (through place-boundedness) of family culture and family relationships. In tracing her father at this point in her life, she is no longer driven by questions of racial identity but rather by ethnic heritage and ancestry – her Igbo descent.[82] After her father denies her further contact, she transfers her desire for knowledge and connection to other sources, focusing her curiosity on the Igbo language and culture on the one hand,[83] and on finding her father's ancestral village on the other. Since the ancestral village is customarily connected with an Igbo ritual of welcome (that Kay feels deprived of by her father), the place itself comes to represent for her the hope of finding something that she can 'relate' to and thereby establish a sense of relatedness.[84] When Kay travels to Ukpor, how-

---

memory (158). Kay's mother is also the only one of the family that left Nairn to live elsewhere, which indicates a strong break with the past. As her sisters say, "She kind of took against the place. Maybe she saw it as the place that made her give up her baby? You just don't know." (158–159)

82 Her curiosity regarding her paternal heritage is initially raised by a stranger on a train in England who recognises her as Igbo (51–52).
83 During her visit to Nigeria, Kay talks to "old Igbo people about their customs and beliefs and how they've changed over their lifetime", and plans to do the same in the Scottish Highlands, and to bring together these oral stories as part of a project, which will also, in a way, re-unite her birth parents through their respective heritages. Before leaving, she goes on a shopping spree in a Lagos bookstore and, although she does not find the Igbo dictionary and "book on Igbo customs and beliefs" that she was looking for, she ends up buying a lot of other things: "retail therapy doesn't come cheap", as Kay drily comments (265).
84 In her conversations with friends and other people that she meets in Nigeria, Kay finds that place plays a major role in the understanding of heritage and identity. When she meets a woman from the same region as her father, this woman at once recognises her and acknowledges her as

ever, it is not the village itself but the road leading up to it, "a red-dust road exactly like the one in my imagination" (213), which suddenly offers her the welcome and acknowledgement that she has been searching for:

> I take off my shoes so the red earth can touch my bare soles. It's as if my footprints were already on the road before I even got there. I walk into them, my waiting footprints. [...] I feel such a strong sense of affinity with the colours and the landscape, a strong sense of recognition. There's a feeling of liberation, and exhilaration, that at last, at last, at last I'm here. It feels a million miles away from Glasgow, [...] but, surprisingly, it also feels like home. I feel shy with the landscape too, like I might be meeting a new blood relation. (213)

Unlike her meetings with her birth parents, Kay's experience of recognition and welcome from the land does not jar with – but, on the contrary, emphatically affirms – her imagination and the stories that constitute the core of her self narrative. In a similar way, Kay manages to get "Jonathan back, the man from my imagination" (148) when she visits Aberdeen a second time, and concedes the fact that imagination, "more than genes or blood, [...] offers the possibility of redemption" (149). It is in these places that represent her birth family's history – be it Aberdeen, the cottage in Nairn, or the ancestral village in South-East Nigeria – that fragments of the split self converge, and where fact and fiction come together rather than drift apart. The memoir thus "charts new bearings of being for the adoptee that intercalate biogenetic and adoptive genealogies to shape subjectivity as more supple than serrated, more holistic than holed" (McLeod 2016, 222). At the same time, the emphasis on the road as a place of recognition and belonging, which is also connected with the pervasive motif of the journey, conveys "the weighty importance of feeling rooted to a route" (McLeod 2016, 222) by underlining the ephemerality of any 'homecoming' and the processual nature of identity.

5.3 Concluding Thoughts: Narratives of Filiation

The family memoirs discussed in this chapter offer complex explorations of the meaning of family and the way in which family relationships and myths shape the relational self. Kay's and Kureishi's texts offer a profound insight into how values and expectations are transmitted through family interaction, both explicitly and subliminally. For both, the family thus constitutes the background not only for their identity formation but also for their writing. Exploring the familial

---

'sister': "When you are from the same place, it means you are automatically my sister. Look at us. We even look like sisters." (249)

foundations of their "identity [...] as both *child* and *writer*" (Davis 2009, 229; emphasis in the original), they both discover how closely these two aspects are interwoven and connected to the values and myths that they grew up with. In Kay's case, it is the void in the family narrative and the narrative of the adoptive self that stimulates the imagination, which unfolds its 'redemptive' power in collaborative family storytelling. For Kureishi, writing is not only an intergenerationally transmitted 'family ideal', it is also a way of constantly re-imagining and re-writing the family, of probing the various constellations that it puts its members into and of trying to get to the heart of its mystery, as his father did before him.[85] Kureishi's and Kay's memoirs reveal both the autobiographical self and the writer as being fundamentally embedded and entangled into the framework of family myths, rituals and storytelling.

Although subsumed here under the category of family memoirs, the two books are very different in form and thus attest to the "increasing diversity" (Couser 2012, 42) and the formal freedom of texts in the life-writing field. Kay's *Red Dust Road*, on the one hand, is more novelistic in form, with many renditions of detailed scenes and long passages of direct dialogue (cf. Couser 2012, 53), a complex spatial-temporal structure (indicated by the chapter titles; driven by the 'plot' rather than the memorial process), and, most importantly, a strong focus on the experiencing I as focaliser (switching occasionally to the present tense, as in the very beginning of the text, cf. 1). Kureishi's memoir, on the other hand, is essayistic and associative in form, and, by shifting the focus to the process of meaning making in the present, it gives shape to the process of remembering. With the insertion of family photographs into the narrative in addition to the reading of documents from the family archive, the book illustrates how "the relational configuration of autobiography even controls the shape of the text" (Davis 2009, 230). The same, however, is also true for *Red Dust Road*, in which the dual structure of two narrative strands, one following a chronological line from 1969 to 2009, and the other detailing significant places of family history and identity, can be said to echo the idea of the duplication of the self as a result of being adopted. For Kureishi, it is the medium of the text itself that, in 'bringing everything together', has the power of reconciliation and compensation; for Kay, the

---

85 After reading his father's third and last manuscript, Kureishi offers another reading of another of his manuscripts, "The Redundant Man", which he previously took to be mainly about his father and their family; yet now, "[t]he pivotal relationship of 'The Redundant Man' seems clearer to me: it is a likeness of [Kureishi's grandparents] Colonel Murad and Bibi, which dad seems to have grafted onto the London suburbs, passing his own children onto his parents for the purpose of this story" (227).

'possibility of redemption' lies in the imagination – a fact which is also emphasised in the form of the text, as the memoir ends with a positive nod to an imagined future.

Both memoirs exemplify the richness and complexity of what Couser describes as 'narratives of filiation'. In Kay's 'autobiographic journey', filiation in its most literal interpretation constitutes the main parts of the memoir's storyline, namely the search for her biological parents and her desire for her father's recognition and his acknowledgement of their connection. The journey towards this goal, however, helps her to discover the more "multidimensional nature of relatedness" (Zerubavel 2012, 32). The sense of the visceral connection that she fails to establish with her birth parents in their few meetings together is something that she gets to feel immediately with some of her other relatives, her Scottish aunts on the one hand and her Nigerian half-brother on the other. In addition, the network of genealogical ties comes to be extended into history, whereby generational places transmit a sense of ancestral memory that connects with Kay's own narrative. Although Kureishi's memoir is very straightforwardly presented as a book about his father (most conspicuously with regard to the title and cover design), it is soon clear that his exploration of the father-son relationship is also posited as the starting-point for reflections on a more ramified network of relationships that are either genealogical (Kureishi's many uncles and his grandfather) or are cast in genealogical terms (surrogate fathers and surrogate, "twin-like" brothers, 218). As Kureishi concedes, "[a]fter leaving home, my propensity to find fathers and brothers [...] seemed to increase. [...] However, if a life can be narrated in terms of identifications, it will have to be told in terms of those you leave as well as find." (173) The identification with his father was one that Kureishi fled from in order to find his own literary voice and to become the writer that his father never managed to be. Identification and disidentification, however, exist side by side throughout the book. Kureishi acknowledges the meaning that his father's inheritance holds for his own life and writing by using the memoir to inscribe himself into a transgenerational family myth in the terms of a homecoming.

6 Four Topoi of 'Doing Family': Food, Home, Photography, and the Body

> It is often said that there are no individuals in this world, only fragments of families. This idea reflects the fact that interactions and experiences in the family shape the course of our entire lives and are forever carried with us. (Segrin and Flora 2011, 3)

Given the centrality that family has in most people's lives and in literature, it seems surprising that the topic has not received a broader treatment in literary and cultural studies. In literary analysis in particular, it is still treated as a marginal subject, with research on the topic lacking concepts, precise terminology, and a more coordinated methodology. A reason for this slow development could be the fact that the role of the family in literature calls for a multi-disciplinary approach, one that is informed by subjects such as psychology, sociology, history, and memory studies, to name only the most prominent fields. This is due to the pervasiveness of family-related issues in each of the various aspects of life and, to borrow the narrator's expression in *White Teeth*, its convoluted *involvement* with everything. In the family, the every-day intersects with superordinate issues of identity in multifarious and complex ways that are not easy to disentangle, just as the private realm intersects with issues of public discourse concerning culture, society, and history. The variety of definitions and concepts concerning the 'family' that are put forward through the different disciplines also challenges any attempts to mould the matter in a manageable way.

In order to circumvent some of these difficulties, this book primarily focused on a concept of family that is sufficiently broad enough to allow overlaps between the diverse disciplines, and also offers a focus which is particularly well suited to the study of literature. The conceptual framework that I have adopted and reworked here for the purpose of literary analysis is that of 'doing family', which has been developed in the field of sociology over the past two decades, and which has proven to be widely influential across the different branches of family studies. The examination of the process of 'doing family' in literature can be linked to a variety of concepts that are well established in the field of literary studies, such as, for example, narrative identity and memory, the generations, the body, cultural/ethnic identity, and even space. As the analyses in the preceding chapters have demonstrated, the act of doing family also includes the practices of undoing and redoing family. Although this study concentrates less on the collective family identity, and more on the impact that family matters have on the individual self and the role that family has as a point of reference in identity formation processes, it is now apparent that the dynamics of both collective and individual identity construction are closely interconnected. The texts selected for this study have confirmed that the 'family imaginary' holds a central place in the constructions of the self, whether it is perceived to be either supportive or constricting, or both.

The novels analysed in this book feature a number of recurring themes and motifs that cut to the very heart of what 'doing family' is about in the face of the challenges and changes that are brought about by the experience of migration. From this we can classify the crucial family practices and meaning-making processes that are carried out against a background of displacement and discontinuity into four main topoi. Although this list could be extended at will, the most significant topoi that have evolved from this reading of the selected novels are: food, home, family photographs, and the body. Each one of these topoi could easily be (and has been) the subject of a full-length study, but they can only be recalled in a brief and cursory way here. The aim of this conclusion is to gather together, with the help of these motifs, some of the threads that run through this study in order to emphasise, in particular, the specific meaning that they acquire under the enormous stresses that migration exerts on the family. As demonstrated in the previous chapters, these topoi are invested with a heightened meaning in the context of migration, and therefore make manifest some of the chances, challenges, ruptures, and tragedies that are presented in the novels.

6.1 Food

The preparation and consumption of food is, as David Morgan (2011a, 101) puts it, "the most fundamental of human activities", or, in Roland Barthes's (2013 [1961], 24) words, "the first need". Although frequently and readily associated with nature as a basic biological need, food is deeply enmeshed in culture (Montanari 2006, 14).[1] Indeed, if we consider how food implies the very basic "transformation of a natural object into a cultural one" (van den Berghe 1984,

---

[1] Cf. Montanari (2006, 14): "The dominant values of the food system in human experience are, to be precise, not defined in terms of 'naturalness,' but result from and represent cultural processes dependent upon the taming, transformation, and reinterpretation of Nature." The idea of nature being connected with food stems from the "biological need" (S. Scott 2009, 92) behind eating; nevertheless, "our decisions about when, what, where, how and with whom we eat are socially shaped" (S. Scott 2009, 92). See also Ott (2017, 13).

387),[2] we may assume that each act of food consumption may reveal certain levels of cultural (and social) meaning. This idea of food as being a decisive factor in the nature/culture continuum is also present in the original meaning of 'culture' as derived from the Latin word *cultura*, which refers to land cultivation and the growing of crops. It is important to emphasise the fact that "food operates not only as physical sustenance, but also as a symbol, as a code, as identity" (Jordan 2014, 37). This cultural aspect of food is apparent in all of the different stages of its production and consumption.[3] Eating habits and culinary practices have a notable capacity to display and exemplify complex semiotic processes within a cultural sign system (cf. Csáky 2014, 26). The concept of the 'semiotics of food' covers two broad aspects, "since food is a sign expressing sociocultural identity and a system of communication" (Stano 2016, 20).[4] In diasporic communities and multicultural societies, the symbolic meaning that is attributed to food – or, the role of food as a sign – is highlighted and attains a new urgency, as cultural markers of difference and otherness gain conspicuousness in the 'contact zone'. In this field where "different culinary semiospheres interact" (Parasecoli 2011, 645) food practices turn into prominent signifiers of identity.[5] The famous English 'national dish' known as Chicken Tikka Massala, which is a hybrid of British and South Asian cuisine, is a case in point, particularly as it was employed by the New Labour government of the late 1990s and early 2000s to refashion and promote a British multicultural identity. Consequently, in diasporic films or literature, "[f]ood is a conspicuously prominent

---

[2] Pierre van den Berghe (1984) here refers to Claude Lévi-Strauss' theorisation of culture, which is based on the ethnographic observations of cooking practices as a formal framework for the more general classifications of dual opposites (such as raw vs. cooked). See Lévi-Strauss (2017 [1968], 334–335).
[3] For an overview of the field of 'food-cultural studies', see Ashley et al. 2004. Dorothee Kimmich and Schamma Schahadat (2012, 8) confirm the idea that food is a 'genuine subject' of cultural theory and analysis, having moved from the fringes of cultural sciences to the centre of attention in recent decades, with the establishment of 'food studies' as an interdisciplinary field in its own right. See Piatti-Farnell and Lee Brien (2018, 1) for a comprehensive overview of the rapidly growing field of 'literary food studies'.
[4] The field of food semiotics is heavily influenced by the structuralist approaches of Roland Barthes, whose essay "Toward a Psychosociology of Contemporary Food Consumption" (2013 [1961]) emphasises the communication aspect of food, and by Claude Lévi-Strauss's essay "The Culinary Triangle" (2013 [1966]).
[5] Food cultures and transcultural food practices have become large areas of interest for crossdisciplinary research. See, e.g. Kershen 2002, Lillge and Meyer 2008, Highmore 2008, Narayan 2010, Lusin 2013, Beushausen et al. 2014; see Ott (2017, 191–290) for an elaboration of national food cultures.

theme [...], functioning not only as an expression of cultural memory but also as a marker of ethnic identity and difference" (Berghahn 2013, 142).⁶ As Christine Ott (2017, 10; my translation) demonstrates, "our food identity is always a cultural identity, determined by social discourses and collective fantasies that we are largely unaware of", they become 'myths' that are 'written into the body' (Ott 2017, 10).

The interlinking of food with identity is encapsulated in the phrase 'we are what we eat', which hints at the powerful connotations that the act of eating can have with self-constitution, embodiment, and appropriation of the world (Meyer 2017, 16–17; cf. Lillge and Meyer 2008, 12).⁷ In this way, concepts of national, ethnic, gender, and religious identity become naturalised through the medium of food (Ott 2017, 24). Consequently, food also plays a major role in constructions of the other, particularly in multicultural societies, where this idea can go either way. On the one hand, "food will identify difference, separate and frequently act as the catalyst for xenophobia" (Kershen 2002, 12) and as a means to reinforce racial/ethnic stereotyping.⁸ On the other hand, the popularity and commodification of 'ethnic food' and 'fusion kitchens' is often used to certify cultural hybridity, based upon the idea of the 'incorporation of the other' through food (cf. Lillge and Meyer 2008, 19), and to serve as an example of the capacity that food has for "diminishing contrasts" and "increasing varieties" (Mennell 1985, 322, qtd. in Kimmich and Schahadat 2012, 8).⁹ This "conjunction of multiculturalism and food" (Gunew 2000, 227) seems natural, as food is not locally fixed but moves with migration and has, over the course of history, always been a key driving force behind the processes of exchange and transculturality.

---

6 Berghahn's observation refers to film, but can well be extended to literature. Nevertheless, the multi-sensory medium of film is likely to more closely capture the "sensuous pleasures [of food and eating] by rendering visible [and audible] the taste, texture and smell of the food" (Berghahn 2013, 144). However, Aslam's lyrical and colourful depictions of the family's cooking procedures, and of spices and meals, in *Maps for Lost Lovers* are similarly evocative and conjure up an abundance of the smells, sounds, and tastes that surround food.
7 See also Scholliers (2001, 3–4) for the different variations and meanings of the phrase. His edited volume explores "the way in which identities were built, interpreted, negotiated, narrated and altered by means of food" (Scholliers 2001, 5) from the perspective of different disciplines.
8 Kershen (2002, 8) speaks of a "dietary xenophobia" in this context. The role that assumptions about food play in the expression of racism is dealt with in detail in *Maps for Lost Lovers*.
9 This focus on the cultural aspects of food should not mask the role of food as a marker of social class. *Anita and Me* illustrates how closely the two aspects of class and culture are intertwined (see below).

The close nexus of food and culture is also connected with the role of food in creating and demarcating a collective unit. At least two levels are involved here, firstly, the important role of food in generating laws, taboos and rules that lie at the heart of the construction of social order (see Douglas 2001 [1966]), and secondly, its functions with regard to the creation of commonality, because "food, and what we do to and with it, is at the very core of sociability" (van den Berghe 1984, 387; cf. Ott 2017, 18). This is also true in the family microcosm; in fact, the family is a prime site where the link between food and sociability is enacted on a daily basis. Locations such as the hearth, the kitchen, the fridge, and the dining table, which act as centres of communal eating and meal preparation, are at the heart of what we associate with family life, and hence at the heart of doing family and of creating, re-creating and displaying a collective group identity. At the same time, food constitutes a highly gendered space and can be closely related to issues of care, which is another important aspect of doing family and the management of (intergenerational) family relationships. More generally speaking, food and methods of feeding are tied up with the most central and meaning-invested family practices because of the basic need for alimentation and "the very routine and regularity of eating" (S. Scott 2009, 93). Located at the intersection of family and culture, food constitutes perhaps the most obvious form of maintaining, displaying and transmitting family and cultural values, beliefs, and norms.[10] Likewise, "feeding provides one of the major ways through which family is constructed and reconstructed" (Morgan 2011a, 101).

Based on the literary analyses in this book, two functions that are associated with food in the context of the family can be emphasised in particular: care and belonging. The care function is connected with the building up and the maintenance of relationships and close familial bonds. In many cases, food, or feeding, may even be used as metonymic shorthand for care, as exemplified by the porridge in *Red Dust Road*. In Jackie Kay's aphorism about the formation of the self – "you are made up from a mixture of myth and gene. You are part fable, part porridge" (*Red* 47) – food beautifully epitomises parental care and love. Viewed as being on the same level as DNA, the nurture received from her adoptive parents is a key constituent of her identity, as the porridge which is given to her as a basic nutrient stands in for the mother's milk. It is 'substance' in the anthropological kinship studies sense of the word. As an important con-

---

10 Cf. Csáky (2014, 12; my translation), who describes the family meal and dinner conversations as an important site for the "transmission of social behaviour and the intergenerational implementing of cultural memory in general". See also Kershen (2002).

cept that underlines the material aspect of relationships, 'substance' may relate to 'biogenetic substance', but may also refer to the feeding practices that can, in some groups, also create a "shared substance" (Carsten 2000, 18).[11]

Besides this basic level of substance, the practices connected to preparing food and to feeding are also significant for the management of family relationships and roles. Much of what 'family culture' is about becomes perceptible in these "most everyday, yet fundamental" activities that have to do with eating (Morgan 2011a, 101). In *Anita and Me*, food consequently becomes a marker for belonging and cultural difference. Meena's desire for sameness with her English friends becomes visible with regard to eating practices (the family gathered around the dining table over a shared meal and conversation) as well as to what is eaten (fish fingers and chips). By making food a site for the acting out of intergenerational conflict, Meena calls attention to "the important signifying functions food-related attitudes, habits and practices generally fulfil" (Lusin 2013, 468). Meena's understanding of food and its powerful cultural meaning is in line with her performative view of identity both in her idea of 'family display'[12] when Anita comes to visit, and in the conflation of her strong wish to *be* Anita (cf. Ahmed 2010, 152) with the desire to *eat like* Anita. Her mimetic desire for fish fingers and chips echoes the phrase 'you are what you eat', a powerful fantasy of both embodiment and incorporation that highlights "culinary symmetries in which culinary tastes isomorphically align with bodies" (Mannur 2010, 7). In this view, the consumption of 'English' or 'white' food corresponds with the desire for an English or white body.[13]

While Meena expresses her cultural and racial affiliation with Britishness through her eating preferenced, food has strong cultural ties to Indianness for her parents. However, the Indian food that Meena's mother cooks is not only a cultural signifier: it is "soul food" that functions as a link to the families that Meena's parents have left behind. Their "immigrant nostalgia for tastes of home" (Mannur 2010, 14; see also 20) is more than an articulation of a "sense of ethnic or national identity" (Mannur 2010, 14), it constitutes a *family* practice: it is a way of evoking and re-establishing a brittle intergenerational connection with their "far-away mothers" (*Anita* 61). A specific food, cooked in a specific

---

11 See also Carsten (1995).
12 On the importance of 'displaying' family in addition to 'doing' family, see Finch (2007). The idea of 'display' always involves the presence of non-family members, as with Anita in this case.
13 See Becher (2008, 55ff.) for a description of performing ethnicity through food consumption practices, particularly in the context of South Asian families in Britain.

way, serves as a powerful symbol of family continuity here; it evokes strong links and memories in its taste and smell. Significantly, Meena is excluded from this meaning of food as a site of memory.

Given its centrality to family life, cooking and eating practices open a doorway to an understanding of how relationships work in a family and highlight the conflicts between its members. In *Maps for Lost Lovers* this can be observed on several levels with regard to Kaukab, for whom cooking and feeding are expressions of maternal care and love, emphasising her large investment into her family relationships. At the same time, they are sites for miscommunication and abuse that reveal the rifts that run through the family. The family meals in this novel erupt in chaos and conflict and leave her shattered and distraught. In both cases, Kaukab's laborious and time-consuming preparations, which are executed with loving care and anticipation, present remarkable instances of 'doing family' only to result in acts of 'undoing family' as the meals are disrupted by scenes of violent arguing. Kaukab's preparation of food for the final family meal is minutely and beautifully described in a long stream-of-consciousness scene that is rendered in free-indirect discourse, in which the different time levels of her life begin to merge as each habitual action carries within it the memory of all of the previous gestures and movements that she and women of previous generations in the family have made in the process of cooking (cf. *Maps* 289ff.). Her meal is a declaration of love,[14] but it fails to transmit the message of love and redemption that she wishes it to convey. Instead, it becomes a bone of contention as her children resent the feast-like nature of the meal, which is completely at odds with the occasion of the trial of Jugnu's murderers. All of the contradictoriness and internal conflicts of Kaukab's character, who simultaneously keeps the family together and tears it apart, become evident in her family meal, an ultimately selfish act performed with the signs of caregiving. Consequently, these age-old practices miss their aim and become dysfunctional in a family that is disjointed by strife and violence.[15]

The space devoted to food practices, particularly in *Maps for Lost Lovers* but also in *Anita and Me*, measures up to the particular importance of food for South Asian families. Both novels show how "the work of feeding the family is part of the process of producing the family" (Smart 2007, 170), while simultaneously stressing the actual workload carried by women in the household. In the area of feeding practices, meanings that are connected to the synchronic family (i.e.

---

14 Cf. the title of the chapter: "How Many Hands Do I Need to Declare My Love to You?".
15 It is important to note here that the violence that disrupts the family home not only comes from within but also has sources from outside the family home.

those that are linked with food as a source of a connection between family members, the performance of daily routines, sharing time, engaging in dinner-time conversations, producing cohesion, warmth and intimacy) merge with aspects of the diachronic family, with the actions, tastes, and smells of cooking as triggers and carriers of an embodied memory. In this regard, "the cultural significance of ethnic specific food in terms of sustaining inter-ethnic identity inter-generationally" (Reynolds 2006, 285) cannot be valued highly enough.

6.2 Home

Home is a place with an indefinite and fuzzy extension. It can be small or large, ranging from a concrete place such as a house to a village or a city; it can be an area marked out as home turf, home ground, or a homeland. In the context of the collection of family writing featured in this book, two meanings of home are particularly prominent. The first is the concept of home used as shorthand for the household, the site for family practices and the stage on which they are performed. Food and cooking are among the practices that are most closely associated with the construction of home in this sense. The second is the idea of home as having a temporal extension that designates it as a mythical place of origin and roots. Not unlike 'family', home can be described as

> a site of everyday lived experience. It is a discourse of locality, the place where feelings of rootedness ensue from the mundane and the unexpected of daily practice. [...] It signifies the social and psychic geography of space [...], a community 'imagined' in most part through daily encounter. This 'home' is a place with which we remain intimate even in moments of intense alienation from it. (Brah 2005 [1996], 4)[16]

What is true for the term 'family' is also true for the idea of 'home': both are constructed through practices. It is therefore important to "avoid assuming that the home has an essential meaning, in advance of its making" (Ahmed et al. 2003, 8). The fact that there is no fixed meaning of home entails that there is a plurality of possible meanings that can be traced in the novels. When Faith in *Fruit of the Lemon* comes back to her parents' house after she has moved out only to snatch snacks from the kitchen cupboard, home, for her, is where she

---

[16] For the meaning of home as being "fundamental to our experience of everyday life", see S. Scott (2009, 49–50), who also explores a larger range of meanings of home connected to the ways in which "social actors use the home differently to construct and perform their identities" (S. Scott 2009, 49).

knows that she will find certain food: It is a very practical and palpable place of shelter, nurture, connectivity, and care. Her newly established independence from her parents is thus counterweighted by a persisting dependence and a desire for continuity that is symbolised by the idea of home. Her shock at learning about her parents' plans of returning to Jamaica, of "going back home" (*Fruit* 44), is therefore all the more upsetting.[17] Faith's perplexity as a result of this statement also captures the ambiguity of meaning in her parents' phrase as she confuses 'home' in the sense of family household on the one hand with the idea of 'home' as a place of origin (and often imagined return), longing, and belonging on the other. Although migrant families generally share an understanding of the first idea of home, there is often an intergenerational rift that runs through their associations as regards the latter. Home, in the synchronic sense, is as essential to the structural concepts of family (that posit family as being synonymous with 'household')[18] as it is for such meaning-oriented concepts as 'doing family', since the concreteness of practices and lived interaction relies on a spatial setting constituted by the family home.[19] This 'synchronic home' is palpable and concrete, but proves to be instable to the degree to which cracks appear in the family identity across the first and second generations in the novels. Home, in the second meaning, is central to the diachronic idea of family; in this case, it is conceived of as a 'mythic' place of memory and the imagination. This second idea of home as a place and, more importantly, as a *feeling* of belonging[20] constitutes a shifting referent – or, in other words, "a simultaneously floating and rooted signifier" (Brah 2005 [1996], 3) – that might produce ambivalent or even contradictory meanings in a family and thus run counter to the idea of continuity and stability that is usually related to the notion of home.[21]

---

17 When Meena's father refers to India as home, she feels "strange that he used that word 'home' so naturally, did that mean that everything surrounding us was merely our temporary lodgings?" (*Anita* 263).
18 For a discussion of family and household see, for example, Edwards et al. (2012); Levin and Trost (1992); Crosbie-Burnett and Klein (2009).
19 It should be added, though, that family practices can also be "conducted away from the familiar sites of home and household" (Morgan 2011b, 4.8), which implies a broadened perspective of the concept in comparison to the more restrictive concepts of the family.
20 Cf. Hedetoft and Hjort's minimalist definition of home, which stresses the affective over the cognitive aspect of the concept: "home is where we *feel* we belong" (2002, vii; emphasis in the original). See also Brähler (2013, 103).
21 See also Bromley (2000, 143).

The idea of home as "a mythic place of desire in the diasporic imagination", and as "a place of no return" (Brah 2005 [1996], 188), also affects the concrete practices of 'homing'[22] among migrant communities, so that the two meanings, or places, of 'home' meet. As demonstrated in the novels, the physical homes of each of the migrant families are suffused with elements of that other home, the imaginary homeland, or the 'mythic place of desire'. In *Maps for Lost Lovers*, the first generation's "homing desire" (Brah 2005 [1996], 189) finds expression in the community's impressively comprehensive act of unofficially re-naming the streets of the new neighbourhood, linking the alien land in which they reside to the familiar places of home and thereby appropriating the strange cityscape as their home. At the family level, this sense of home is created in a similar way by painting the house in the colours of the family home that they left behind in Pakistan. In this way, a superficial layer of home is superimposed onto a place that, however, ultimately fails to provide the desired sense of safety and emotional warmth that is normally associated with home. Kaukab realises this at the end of the novel, when she reflects on how "[i]t had taken her decades to rebuild the happiness she had lost when she moved to England: she had built it around her children, and, yes, around Jugnu, but she had never realized how loosely woven a thing it was, how easily torn" (*Maps* 296). James Procter (2003, 12) highlights the inherent "tension between dwelling and diaspora", as he posits dwelling as a counter concept to "the logic of diaspora discourse, which has tended to foreground the deterritorialised, itinerant nature of migrant cultures" (Procter 2003, 12).[23] With her term 'migrant homes', Didem Kiliçkiran (2003) conjoins these two aspects, emphasising that, for migrants, "home is not only about recovering a sense of continuity and stability, and reviving their

---

[22] 'Homing' refers to the processes and practices of home-building, and emphasises the affective and meaning-related qualities of home (cf. Ahmed et al. 2003, 9). Brah (2005 [1996], 16) introduces the idea of a "homing desire, as distinct from a desire for a homeland": "The *concept* of diaspora places the discourse of 'home' and 'dispersion' in creative tension, *inscribing a homing desire while simultaneously critiquing discourses of fixed origins.*" (Brah 2005 [1996], 189; emphasis in the original)

[23] See also Procter (2003, 14): "Travelling rhetorics tend to underplay the extent to which diaspora is also an issue of settlement and a constant battle over territories: over housing and accommodation, over the right to occupy a neighbourhood, over the right to 'stay put'." Procter focuses on the experience of the first generation after their arrival in Britain in the 1950s and 60s in his analysis of the representation of housing and the 'black dwelling place', in the literary as well as non-literary discourse of the time. According to Avtar Brah (2005 [1996], 189), this tension is inherent to the concept of diaspora, which "places the discourse of 'home' and 'dispersion' in creative tension, inscribing a homing desire while simultaneously critiquing discourses of fixed origins".

'roots', but also about expressing the changes they have experienced through their displacement and resettlement" (Kiliçkiran 2003, 109).

As the children of immigrant parents grow up in this atmosphere of tension between two worlds, the cultural conflict between the different value systems and expectations is exacerbated by the intergenerational conflict between the first and second generation (cf. Korte 1999, 336). Against this background, the family house is often viewed by the second generation to be a normative place of restrictive rules that reinforce clear-cut gender role expectations. In one way or another, most of the novels analysed in this study confirm "the notion that the home site produces gendered subjects" (Mannur 2010, 19–20). In *Fruit of the Lemon* for instance, Faith's decision to move out of her parents' home is directly linked to her desire to escape the "Caribbean strictures" (*Fruit* 16) that do not apply to her brother Carl, who is also excused of all household chores because "[h]e's a man" (42). In the South Asian context of *Anita and Me* and *Maps for Lost Lovers*, gender role expectations are also very closely connected to the home site. The act of cooking here features as a crucial site for the intergenerational transmission of cultural knowledge and awareness between mother and daughter, and as an introduction to the realm of gendered and culturally prescribed life scripts.

For Kaukab, the home needs to become a fortress with strong walls that fend off the new place and time in which she has to live. She works hard to fortify the fragile togetherness of her immigrant family by constructing strong boundaries to protect the family's unity and integrity. The home that she creates through her "boundary work" (cf. Morgan 2011a, 60) inside the family house is structured by a stark contrast between inside and outside. In this way, the home becomes an important site for the production and organisation of the family's collective identity in opposition to the host society as the collective other that lies outside of this realm. In this 'us-versus-them' setting, family easily becomes over-burdened with cultural meaning as the primary (and often only) site of transmitting and putting cultural norms and values into practice. The closed spatial organisation of the family house in *Maps for Lost Lovers* symbolises a closed family system, which employs rigid boundaries that are designed to ward off outside influences and to prevent change ("deviations from a setting or a norm") and instead "reinforce stability and the maintenance of existing patterns" (Dallos and Draper 2010 [2000], 42). Kaukab's idea of family and culture is fixed and static, so that, in her eyes, even the smallest alterations in her daughter's cooking can threaten its stability and continuity. The Kumar household in *Anita and Me*, on the other hand, resembles a more open system over the course of the novel, so that the boundaries, which seemed to be very fixed at first, eventually become permeable and allow the two worlds to mingle as in the case where Meena's parents' Indian party friends spill onto the front porch (cf. *Anita* 204). This process, spurred on by Nanima's presence, is also actively shaped by Meena. The Kumar family's openness allows for the forms of productive conflict that can ultimately strengthen family ties and relationships, whereas the rigidity of Kaukab's regime leads to the disintegration of the family. This spatial production of meaning sets the first generation apart from their children, for whom the boundaries are more permeable and who are able to move more freely between the worlds of their parents and the outside world of 'white' British society. Both novels, however, emphasise the fact that the challenges and conflicts of home-building for migrants not only lie within their families but also exist in the processes of exclusion through the racism and rejection that they are met with from outside. For instance, when their village becomes the site of a racist attack against an Indian man, Meena is seen to wonder "if Tollington would ever truly be home again" (*Anita* 275; cf. *Maps* 11).[24]

The home is, of course, not only a place of belonging, it is also a location for belongings. In addition to being a site for family practices, it is also a material place and a spatial context for the significant objects that make up the interior of the house. These things, such as the "collection of appropriated materials, invested with meaning and memory, [...] are what transforms our house into our *home*" (Hecht 2001, 123; emphasis in the original; cf. also Smart 2007, 163). In Smart's view, "home and personal shared possessions within the home represent [...] forms of investment in relationships" (2007, 156).[25] Accordingly, heirlooms, keepsakes, and other nostalgic objects of memory are kept in the home in order to maintain connections across time with absent family members, whether they are living or dead, or similarly, with bygone places. Sami's study in *The Road from Damascus*, which is furnished as a shrine to his family memory, is a striking example, as are the family photo albums and the drawers of documents that lurk in the corners of each of the family houses in *Anita and Me*, *Fruit of the Lemon*, *White Teeth*, and *My Ear at His Heart*. Besides such memory objects that represent "symbolic roots into a vanished world" (Hecht 2001, 123),[26] the homes of immigrants interestingly also accommodate for the

---

24 Cf. also Brah (2005 [1996], 190).
25 Smart introduces two categories, of which the first consists of the home and the family's possessions, and food, money, and consumable goods make up the second, which "is concerned with forms of exchange within relationships" (Smart 2007, 156).
26 Since house-moving is an almost universal experience, at least in the West, this interrelation of home, objects, memory, and meaning is not specific to immigrant households; Anat

memories of uprooting. Suitcases stacked on top of cupboards are a common motif of migration literature and family writing.[27] They often serve as a memento of the event of migration, as exemplified by Kureishi's father's trunk in his memoir *My Ear at His Heart*, which, "made in India, covered in exotic labels, would dominate the little [attic] room" (*Ear* 91). The trunk is connected to the story of his father's trip to England, which, as it is often narrated, is part of the living family memory, while the trunk's role as a memorial object emphasises the importance of the event in the family narrative. On the other hand, the habit of collecting boxes, which Faith observes her parents doing but fails to fully understand, is a sign that they perceive their house to be only a transitory 'home', while they keep the idea of their homeland and the dream of return alive.[28] The boxes thus stand for the 'myth of return', which is a common denominator of the first generation's migration experience, and is in itself an expression of the 'homing desire' and of the intergenerational contestation of the idea of home.[29] In both *Maps for Lost Lovers* and *White Teeth*, the first-generation's dilemma is expressed as being connected to the attempt to found a family in the new country of residence, thereby creating ties that are indissoluble yet brittle, because of the often strained relationship with their children: "suddenly you are unsuitable to return, your children are unrecognizable, you belong nowhere" (*Teeth* 407; cf. *Maps* 146).

Suitcases and boxes are not only mementos in themselves, or metaphors for the migrant self, they also often serve as containers for other memory objects and as archives of the past, thus simultaneously symbolising the link to the past and the rupture and displacement of this link. The migrant suitcase is a powerful symbol of the economics of memory, of the question of what is a usable past that can be carried into the future, and of what amounts to being 'baggage'; it is a universal symbol that takes on a heightened meaning in the context of migration. Suitcases are 'memory boxes', characterised by mobility and strict selection due to the spatial confinement within them (cf. A. Assmann 2009 [1999],

---

Hecht's case study (2001), for example, focuses on a London resident who is born in Edinburgh.

27 Cf. Schlör (2014, 77): "This object [the suitcase], container, travel companion, and witness, plays a central role in many stories, testimonies as well as literary treatments, about migration and displacement."

28 In *White Teeth*, Irie connects her mother's boxes with a migratory mind-set rather than the actual wish to return (cf. *Teeth* 335).

29 See Brähler (2013), who offers a profound and encompassing supranational study of nostalgia and the myth of return not simply as elements of exilic literature, but as important topics of ethnic minority literature in specific (Brähler 2013, 13).

114). They serve as containers of memory objects, such as Faith's parents' trunk in *Fruit of the Lemon*, "the trunk that held the old brown photo album, a white christening shawl and several of my little ballet tutus – a waft of mothballs and memories" (*Fruit* 198). In the spatial organisation of the family house, suitcases become part of the domestic storage space, mirroring the characteristics of archives, which are, by definition, the opposites of memory boxes (cf. A. Assmann 2009 [1999], 114). According to Aleida Assmann, archives are marked by a restricted accessibility (cf. A. Assmann 2009 [1999], 344), which hints at the important dimension of generational power hierarchies within families, and corresponds with the way in which parents' memory objects become inaccessible to their children, both spatially, cognitively, and affectively. If they are no longer actively framed by stories and embodied practices, the memories invested in these objects will fade and move from the family's functional (that is, lived and shared) memory to its storage memory and thus lose their usefulness and meaning for the family identity, and, as a consequence, their reference, value, and effectiveness in the orientation of family members as they negotiate the future (cf. A. Assmann 2009 [1999], 134).

6.3 Photography

The process of intergenerational memory loss becomes tangible in *Anita and Me*, in which her parents' fragmentary transmission of stories and information from 'home' leaves Meena with a lack of cultural references, a meaningful and emotional understanding of her parents' past, and the sense that their story is also a part of her own story. Emblematic of this are her parents' photographs of their brothers and sisters who Meena learns to identify, albeit in a purely technical way. On the basis of the minimal amount of detail provided by her parents, she is unable to form an emotional attachment to the faces in these photos. In consequence, her parents' treasured mementos of their loved ones become, for Meena, merely photographs to remember names by. This scene in *Anita and Me* offers a poignant insight into the dynamics of transgenerational remembering and forgetting in families under the stress of the experience of migration: On the one hand, it shows the potential of photographs as a site of family memory for migrants, since, "in lives shaped by exile, emigration and relocation, [...] where relatives are dispersed and relationships shattered, photographs provide perhaps even more than usual some illusion of continuity over time and space" (Hirsch 2012a [1997], xi). On the other hand, the scene reveals how, if not actively transmitted from one generation to the next, these photos will lose the meaning that is originally attached to them. Photos that for one family member represent "integral pieces of a life story, full of meaning and resonance" may become "anonymous, meaningless" to another, if they are not able to identify the pictured relative (Hirsch 2012a [1997], xi). Family photos, like any other keepsake, run the risk of evolving into "depersonalized signifiers of a distant place and a bygone era" (Hirsch 2012a [1997], xi) if they are not actively incorporated into the family practices of communal storytelling and reminiscing. The disruption of what Martha Langford (2006, 225) calls the "oral-photographic framework" – the "album's roots in oral tradition" (Langford 2006, 224) and the close connection of photography with social practices of storytelling – illustrates the risk of the erosion of collective memory in (diasporic) families.[30]

Photographs play a significant role in all of the novels and memoirs analysed in this book. This is a clear indication of the seminal function that this medium holds for family life and memory preservation.[31] Photography serves as the "family's primary instrument of self-knowledge and representation – the means by which family memory would be continued and perpetuated, by which the family's story would henceforth be told" (Hirsch 2012a [1997], 6). With their symbolic expressiveness and representative potential, photographs are central to "the material culture of the family" (Gomila 2011, 63). Moreover, they play a major role in families with regard to the "performative acts at the intersections of cultural and embodied practices of production, circulation, display, viewing and reminiscing" (Arnold-de Simine and Leal 2018, 5). Over the course of the twentieth century, photography has become an increasingly accessible medium and, therefore, acts as a cornerstone for the construction, confirmation, and authentication of individual and family identity.

---

[30] Removed from its natural sphere of family reminiscing, the photographic album, according to Langford (2006, 227), becomes an "alienated object" – which resembles the way it is perceived by many second-generation characters in the novels.

[31] Given the fact that the medium of photography offers the representation of "a 'frozen' past moment" (Kuhn 2010, 304), it seems natural that most research on family photography focuses on the topic of memory (see, for example, Kuhn 2010; Kuhn 2002 [1995]; Arnold-de Simine and Leal 2018; Hirsch 2012a [1997]). See also Shevchenko (2014a; 2016) for a more general exploration of "memory and photography as mutually constitutive and interconnected" (Shevchenko 2014b, 6). By way of contrast, Rose (2010) looks at a broader range of practices that are connected with family photography, in the private/domestic sphere as well as in the public realm. Although her book's title *Doing Family Photography* may sound like a reference to the concept of 'doing family', it has more to do with Rose's interest in the activities of taking of photos, the compilation of photo albums, and the sharing of these images in and beyond the family context.

In *Anita and Me*, the "crumpled black and white photographs hoarded in a shiny suitcase" (*Anita* 35) represent a portable family memory, similar to the one that Hortense, Irie's grandmother, stores in her house in *White Teeth*. There, Irie finds pictures of her great-grandmother Ambrosia, of her great-grandfather Durham, and "photo-booth snaps of Clara in school uniform, grinning maniacally, the true horror of the teeth revealed" (*White* 399). In this assortment of photos, Clara is re-integrated into the family history, with her original teeth in place, which are a marker of family identity that Irie shares with her mother yet only gets to see now for the first time. In a metaphorical sense, the restoration of Clara's original teeth in the image re-establishes the genealogical link to the Bowden family history. Seizing on Marianne Hirsch's idea of how the photograph creates an 'illusion of continuity over space and time', we can say that, while the photos that Irie discovers create 'continuity over time', the pictures of Meena's aunts and uncles provide 'continuity through space' by including the geographically absent family members in the family home. In *Fruit of the Lemon*, Faith is surprised to find that there is a photo of her and her brother on the cupboard in her aunt Coral's front room in Jamaica – and that she already holds a presence among the family she is just getting to know. Before she flew to Jamaica, Faith, through the medium of her picture, was already part of a family transaction, as the photograph's journey preceded her own, thus demonstrating "[t]he mobility of family snaps" (Rose 2010, 4) and their significance in maintaining (transnational) family networks. The 'spatial link' that is established through family photos works both ways in connecting the transnational family. Pictures of her family even fill the first pages of her aunt's photograph album, "[p]ictures I don't remember being taken", with a bike "I never had" (*Fruit* 202). As this album illustrates, the story of the family that is told to the Jamaican part of the family is different from that which is shared within the family at home. For Faith, the album is also the beginning of her genealogical search, as her own family's pictures make way for a series of unfamiliar faces and pictures with "names and dates written on the back. Eunice, Mummy, Daddy, Auntie Matilda" (202), and so on.

Family photographs are embedded in family practices in two key ways, one having to do with the taking of the photo, and the other with the storage, viewing, and displaying of the picture.[32] As Silke Arnold-de Simine and Joanne Leal

---

[32] Cf. Gomila (2011, 63): "the meaning of family photography has to be understood in a dynamic process of family display (Finch 2007, 66) that embraces the production, the classification, the storage (albums, boxes and so on), the exhibition (in walls, in screens, in mobile phones, in handbags), the exchange and the narratives around and about them".

(2018, 5) write, "[w]e therefore need to focus on photographs not just as images (and their contents) or objects (and their material qualities) drawn together in collections (their framing and contextualization), but on the social and cultural practices in which they are embedded". When the moment of Nanima's arrival is immediately fixed in a photograph in *Anita and Me*, this is not only done in order to generate a memorable moment by creating a memento of it, it is in itself a powerful act of producing family. The act of taking a family picture here demonstrates the way "[p]hotography captures a given moment in the life of an individual, while at the same time offering a means of creating an image of our lives and selves as we would like to be seen" (Campt 2012, 5). In this photo, the reality of family life is aligned with a specific image and ideal of family that is linked with tradition, continuity, intimacy, and strong intergenerational relationships. Due to the fact that it is primarily concerned with representations (or forms of display) of family, the family photograph "blends both dimensions of the concept 'family': the *particular* and the *general*" (Gomila 2011, 64; emphasis in the original). When regarded as a "moment in the cultural construction of family" (Kuhn 2002 [1995], 20), the family photograph and the family album are intricately interconnected with cultural conventions, norms, and ideas of display, life scripts, and 'the family'.[33] In *Maps for Lost Lovers*, the photographic studio, where many immigrant families came to have their picture taken in the early years, can be read as an important part of the community's collective memory that is at risk of being lost when the studio closes down.[34] The meaning

---

[33] In this way, family photographs can be understood as a photographic genre. As an example of this, Juliane Hirsch (1981, 3) suggests that "[a] family photograph contains at least two people, though it may contain a score", with the implicit assumption that everyone represented in the photo is related. A further aspect of the genre pertains to the spectator, and concerns the specific mode of looking at family photographs in which the detection of kinship through physical likeness plays a major role (cf. J. Hirsch 1981, 3). A different understanding of the family photograph makes reference to a picture that has a specific family-related meaning for its beholder. Arnold-de Simine and Leal (2018, 3) also highlight these two aspects when they ask whether the family photograph is "defined by its modes of production, by its conventions, usually determined more by the photograph's indexical capacity than any aesthetic considerations, or by its consumption, shared among family members, confirming familial bonds, intimacy and a sense of belonging?".

[34] The novel here alludes to the Belle Vue Studio collection in the Bradford Museum photo archive, see http://photos.bradfordmuseums.org/. For the uses of family photography as a means of analysing the history of a community, in this case the African diaspora in Europe, see Tina Campt's (2012) highly interesting book *Image Matters* and her exploration of the implications held by family photographs beyond their function as historical record (cf. Campt 2012, 6–8).

of these photos here comes less from their personal significance as 'memory-texts' and more from their socio-historical relevance, in the "stereotyped and coded characteristics" (Hirsch 2012a [1997], 7) of 'family' that is displayed in them. The family photograph here falls out of the realm of the private and enters into the domain of archive storage. However, in the hands of the artist Charag, who saves the negatives from destruction, these family pictures, and the picture of his own family in particular, are imbued with the quality of hope and redemption: In these timeless stills, the families that have become separated and disjoined are again re-united. The novel thus points to the utopian aspect of family photography as a medium that may "reduce the strains of family life by sustaining an imaginary cohesion, even as it exacerbates them by creating images that real families cannot uphold" (Hirsch 2012a [1997], 7).

The recovered family picture in *Maps for Lost Lovers* is inserted into the text in the form of a schematic chart – a box in which nothing but the names of the family members convey their spatial constellation within the frame of the photograph. In reducing the particularities of the individual family, it highlights the generic qualities of the family photograph, which brings to the fore the family as a configuration: as an interlinking of relationships and inter-dependencies that are demarcated by structural constraints (cf. Morgan 2011, 41).[35] The diagrammatic illustration functions well as an effective substitute for the actual image because it can build on the fact "that family photos are often (trans)culturally recognizable and encourage identifcatory viewing" (Arnold-de Simine and Leal 2018, 5) so that mere constellation of names in the text therefore easily convey a mental image of a generic family photograph to the reader. On a formal level, the insertion of the diagram in the novel indicates a move from the thematisation of family photographs, which we find in the other novels, to an 'iconic imitation' of photographs in the text, which has the effect of a 'quasi-hybridisation' of the narrative. This categorisation by Christine Schwanecke (2012, 46–55) identifies the different forms of intermediality between narrative and photography in literature. The incorporation of photographs within texts, in the sense of a 'media combination' (Schwanecke 2012, 51), is a device that is most commonly encountered in (auto)biographical writing, and has been famously played with in Virginia Woolf's mock biography *Orlando* (1928). Within the context of relational life writing, the photographs featured in the two memoirs discussed in this book are automatically framed as family photographs, regardless of whether they qualify as such in the sense of a photographic genre.

---

[35] These are the main aspects of the definition of 'family configurations' as summarised by David Morgan in his overview of the different approaches in family studies (2011, 40ff.).

While the photos in Kay's memoir are confined to the paratextual level on the front and back cover, the images in Kureishi's book take a more prominent position, with regard to both the quantity and the quality of their incorporation into the text. Rather than being separated from the text through spatial division,[36] the pictures are embedded into the narrative in form as well as in content. The photos underline the scrapbook-like nature of the book, which can be read as a memory-text that draws attention to the processual nature, multimodality, and multimediality of family memory and the role of the material family archive (of photographs and documents) in lending substance to this memory.

6.4 The Body

The topoi of food, home and photography exemplify acts of doing family that are grounded in another medium, namely the body. As Morgan puts it, the acts are guided by the idea of a family 'we' that is performed and practiced in different configurations. "The family members who constitute the 'we' at any one point of time are embodied others who are spatially located." (Morgan 2011a, 92) He points to the way in which family relationships are embodied at a synchronic level, in the sense that they are formed through the social (and bodily) interaction of family members.[37] However, family relationships are not only performed in embodied practices in the co-presence of other family members, they are also embodied at a diachronic level, with the body acting as a link to previous generations through a shared biological heritage in terms of genetics and genealogy. As a sign of this embodied inheritance, family resemblance plays a central role. Through resemblances to other family members, "connection and recognition are constructed between relatives. It is a way of thinking about the continuity between bodies" (Marre and Bestard 2009, 77). These two general dimensions of thinking about the body in the family correspond with what Bryan Turner identifies as the two dominant sociological perspectives on the body,

---

36 The more common text-layout designates separate pages to images, while leaving the flow of the main text undisrupted, since the photographs appear to be on a distinct diegetic level. The practice of inserting images into the main text thus causes a blurring of the diegetic levels (cf. Schwanecke 2012, 136, and 175–178).
37 Issues concerning the body and embodiment feature prominently in the concept of doing family, because – with its focus on practices – it also draws attention to the physical interaction within families. David Morgan (2011a, 92) gives some examples, such as the negotiation of boundaries between the public and private sphere in families, the design of domestic space, the act of expressing emotions, corporal punishment, and care, etc.

namely "the idea of the body as representation, and embodiment as practice and experience", the first having to do with the meaning that is inscribed on the body, and the second with how the body experiences sensations or is performatively employed in practice (B. S. Turner 2008, 15).[38]

The role of the body in families, moreover, attests to the way in which these two aspects are closely interconnected, much in the same way that having a body and being a body is an indissoluble dualism of human existence (cf. Gugutzer 2015, 14–15). The three-generation photograph that Meena's father takes in *Anita and Me* illustrates this perfectly. The performative enactment of family continuity that Meena takes part in as grandmother, mother, and daughter line up elicits in her the very emotions and ideas that their pose is supposed to symbolise. The (embodied) staging of this family constellation produces an idea of the family that is invested with greater meaning in its representation as a family photograph. Through the medium's capacity of emphasising the physical likenesses between the people being photographed, it highlights their relatedness: "all of us the product of each other, linked like Russian dolls" (*Anita* 201–202). In reconstituting this link between the generations, the pose contributes to making Meena suddenly *feel* the value of family relationships and the importance of family obligation and interdependence that is a key part of her family culture. This scene brings to the fore the *performative* quality of embodiment, which can be observed here as being an essential aspect of how meaning is created in social interaction – in this case through trans-generational links in a genealogical constellation.[39]

The family photograph is a relevant case here as it provides a visual representation of the way the body serves as an index for relatedness and connectedness through the idea of family resemblances. As a medium of representation, the photograph exemplifies how family resemblances are an important form of ascribing meaning to bodies in the family context. Family photographs invite the observer to look for 'clues to kinship' (J. Hirsch 1981, 3) in the physical features of those in the picture, and to discover the "genetic traits" (J. Hirsch 1981, 81) that become visible by comparing the faces in the photograph. Likeness can be detected within the photographic text itself (intratextually), between two or

---

[38] These two dimensions may also be roughly referred to in terms of the distinction between the body as being both a product of and a producer of society, which Gugutzer (2006, 13–20) describes as the two major strands in the sociology of the body.

[39] In the context of the performative turn in social and cultural studies, there is a special focus on the way in which social reality and meaning is constructed through embodied practices (see Gugutzer 2006, 18–19).

more of the people depicted, or, from outside of the photographic text (extratextually), when, for example, someone looks for their own features in the photographs of their ancestors. Indeed, one could say that in 'reading' family photographs, "we are all photographic literates and amateur criminologists – we read the face as a history of the gene pool to which it belongs" (Langford 2008, 15). In this aspect, photography illustrates the way in which family is always the product of bodily reproduction and a key site of inheritance – the body is the carrier of relatedness and thus presents a physical link between the generations. As such, it can be endlessly invested with significance and meaning: It may be used as an important medium of *doing family* (relatedness), by serving as an indexical sign that points to a relationship that may not be established (yet) on other levels, be it with dead or living relations.[40] Yet, the body in this context is also a site of *being family* (embeddedness), in which it represents a connection that cannot be dissolved or even denied. The topic of family resemblances thus touches on this crucial issue in families, as it "raise[s] the paradoxical question of belonging to a family body and being, at the same time, an individual person" (Marre and Bestard 2009, 66).

Bodily resemblances are not only confined to specific physical features but also denote aspects of habitual behaviour and bearing, as in the case, for instance, of the laugh that Jackie Kay recognises in her half-brother, Sidney, when they meet for the first time in Nigeria. In meeting Sidney, Jackie "feel[s] a strange almost ecstatic sensation of recognition. It is nearly primitive. [...] It has completely ambushed me; I wasn't expecting it at all" (*Red* 272). Her feeling of being ambushed by this sudden and profound sense of recognition is described in terms that are suggestive of an almost visceral reaction to the meeting that emphasises the element of embodiment in their newly found relationship: in Sidney's spontaneous wholehearted embrace, in the laughter that they share, in her impression that she "could happily sniff his ears and lick his forehead", or in their walking "hand in hand, comfortable, brother and sister" (*Red* 272). The instantaneous sense of (physical and emotional) intimacy that is expressed in their body language, and which is established through their mutual "shock of recognition" (Mason 2018, 71), emphasises the fact that resemblance is a strong affective factor in family relationships, and "a force to be reckoned with" (Mason 2018, 65). The picture of Sidney that Kay will later show to her parents conveys some of these feelings, but it remains limited to capturing only the physical likeness in their features, and not the resemblance that is shared in the way that

---

40 In this context, it is significant to note that "physical resemblances are cultural perceptions of identity recognition" (Marre and Bestard 2009, 66), rather than a natural given.

their bodies move and interact.⁴¹ And yet, while the issue of family resemblances remains as an important factor throughout the memoir due to its connection with Kay's exploration of her biological relations, it is the bond of shared memory and storytelling, as the key features of her adoptive family, that are "proffered as a form of affective bonding that rivals anything to be discovered in the reassurances of biogenetic resemblance" (McLeod 2015, 218). By emphasising the way in which storytelling and reminiscing are also very much *embodied* forms of interaction in families which produce an alternative form of (physical and mental) resemblance, the memoir invites us to "speculate on resemblance beyond the consanguineous and biogenetic" (McLeod 2015, 232). In Kay's case, it even goes beyond the question of racial identity; the likeness between her and her adoptive mum is often remarked upon, to the point where she speculates that "[p]erhaps after years of unconsciously copying her physical mannerisms and gestures, I've grown to look like her" (*Red* 30).⁴²

The sensation of recognition that is experienced in meeting 'new' family members is not exclusive to the adoptive being. In *Fruit of the Lemon*, Faith instantly recognises her aunt when she picks her up from the airport in Jamaica. Again, resemblance here is embodied rather than just a question of features. It is not only due to the fact that "the way she tilted her head and folded her arms under her breasts reminded me of Mum. [... T]here were other ways in which she reminded me of Mum – ways that I could not describe or point to. She had the aura of kin." (*Fruit* 182) These examples illustrate the fact that "there is something powerful and almost magical in the sheer capacity of some resemblances [...] to *strike or hit you* as a physical and visceral sensation" (Mason 2018, 71; emphasis in the original). It is this feature of being embodied and recognised through bodily interaction that makes family resemblances so intriguing and astonishing, even to the point of being "uncanny" (Mason 2018, 71), as they often remain hard to process and grasp at a cognitive level. The texts discussed here demonstrate an acute awareness of the difference between recognising likeness in a family photograph and in an actual meeting by emphasising the

---

41 Interestingly, a similar sense of "ineffable connection" (Mason 2018, 66) is also demonstrated by the people who took part in the photo project *I'm Not a Look-Alike!* that captures resemblances between total strangers (see Mason 2018, 66; Brunelle 2004ff.). This example demonstrates that the family-related meaning we tend to ascribe to likenesses is a specific way of seeing, and that other ways of seeing and of ascribing meaning are possible.

42 In their article on family resemblances, Marre and Bestard (2009) focus specifically on the role of resemblance in adoptive families: from being an important factor in the process of child allocation in the 'matching room' right up to the ways in which it functions to create ties of relatedness in the 'kinning' process (see also Howell 2003).

peculiar quality whereby family resemblances can convey the specific effect and affect that is created by social family interaction, "with all its gestures, glances, voices, movements, sounds, textures, ways of being, demeanours, in/tangibles, auras and atmospherics" (Mason 2018, 71).[43]

While resemblances may be highly effective in the building of a relational bridge towards as yet unfamiliar family members in order to integrate them into one's network of relatedness, resemblances are also an important marker of connectedness between parents and children that can be filled with meaning in various manners and means. When Meena in *Anita and Me* traces the signs of likeness in her father's face while he is telling her the story of his experiences during the time of Partition, she endows his narrative with a specific family meaning of continuity and connectedness. Just as "that tiny teardrop shape above his lips, replicated exactly in my face" (*Anita* 71) binds the two together, his story is transferred to her and thus becomes part of her story. Her assertion that "I liked looking like him" (71) is a strong indicator of intergenerational family unity and connection. The interlinking here of this instance of an awareness of family resemblances with the practice of family storytelling is a good illustration of how such practices are "linked to the relational aspect of kinship and to a way of constructing bonds between people" rather than merely acting as a "confirmation of the biological truths of kinship" (Marre and Bestard 2009, 64).

The same novel, however, also reveals how the body can have the opposite effect when it becomes a point of contention around which dis-identification with the family is developed. As Meena becomes more fascinated with Anita Rutter, the white next-door neighbour who she wishes to emulate, her own body begins to be increasingly perceived by her to be a marker of difference and an impediment to social acceptance that shuts her off from her desires. The ensuing dis-identification with her own body implies a dis-identification with her family that can be similarly observed with regard to Irie in *White Teeth*, and Faith in *Fruit of the Lemon*. The novels examined in this study very vividly show how experiences of racism can produce racialised bodies that jar with the protagonists' self-image and therefore threaten their existing sense of self. This

---

43 See, for example, Meena's impression that she is "looking up into my mama's face" when she first meets her Nanima (200), as opposed to her rather distant relationship with the collection of family photos prior to her grandmother's arrival (*Anita* 80), or the similar "shock of sameness" that Irie experiences when she travels to her grandmother Hortense's house (*Teeth* 381). McLeod (2015, 232) also highlights the fact that family resemblances affect all aspects of the body by raising the important issue of the role of sound in this context.

threatened sense of self finds expression in a racialised perception of their own families, where the bodies of family members suddenly stand out as black (*Fruit*) or Indian (*Anita*), and thus as 'other'. In the act of 'othering' their families, Meena and Faith both align their perspective with that of their white friends in a desire to lose their own otherness (as a prerequisite to gaining a full 'social acceptance' and to participating fully in white British society). Through Irie's story line, *White Teeth* correlates the process of racialisation and the realisation of one's own difference and otherness with the larger problem of having a lack of representation in society. The novel thus emphasises the way in which bodies are socially and culturally produced and ascribed with symbolic meaning. Irie is "without reflection" in England, and consequently feels like a "stranger" (*Teeth* 266). One instance of recognition that Irie experiences in the reading of Shakespeare's Sonnet 130 is abruptly cut short by her English teacher with reference to historical probability: "There weren't any ... well, Afro-Carribee-yans in England at that time, dear." (271) In the absence of a reflection, Irie is not able to achieve an affirmative sense of self, and consequently turns towards whiteness as the standard for her self-image, a constellation that is, of course, doomed. The problem of underrepresentation is exacerbated by her mixed-race identity: "Inhabiting a body that is physiologically rooted in two places, 'belonging' to both England and Jamaica in a sense, she experiences a kind of corporeal nomadism or a not-at-homeness in her own skin" (Thompson 2005, 127).

The importance of representation and recognition in the acquisition of a healthy (bodily) self-image is also emphasised by Jackie Kay, who, in reading the works of writers such as Franz Fanon, Audre Lorde, Toni Morrison, and other important black intellectuals, manages to "change[...] the mirror that I held up to myself [..., and accordingly,] my racial awareness" (*Red* 40). As a child, she imagines her birth mother to be Shirley Bassey, and that her father was a "handsome cross between Paul Robeson and Nelson Mandela" (*Red* 67). In this way, the lack of a 'mirror image' for her own body within her family is compensated for by the introduction of father and mother figures who take on the role of a 'racial family' and thereby offer up the opportunity for a positive identification through a shared 'heritage', whether it is familial, political, or socio-cultural. In the context of a mixed-race adoptive family, the "empowering agency of this transcultural adoptive assembly of diasporic relations" (McLeod 2015, 216) cannot be regarded highly enough. By demonstrating the need for having a 'resourceful identity' in encountering a racist environment, the books discussed here stress the importance of racial socialisation, and of the role of the family in this process. While *Red Dust Road* challenges "the long-standing argument that racial matching [is] essential to adoption" (McLeod 2016, 213), Andrea Levy shows that similar issues also pertain to all-black families in *Fruit of the Lemon*. Here, Faith's racial awareness is instigated by a stranger, who, by taking the stage as a poet and thus entering the public realm, becomes a representative voice for black bodies and the black experience, an idea that she loosely connects with the notion of family and racial kinship. Her initial response to being confronted with her own racial identity is denial and rejection, in much the same way as Meena in *Anita and Me*. It is only after learning about her Jamaican ancestry that Faith finds her own position in this political coalition of racial identity, which is backed up by her newly found historical consciousness. The novels thus illustrate how, in the same way that a threatened sense of self engenders the wish to disengage from the family, a positive reevaluation of the meaning of family may help one to overcome a crisis of selfhatred.

In these books, the body is at the same time the object and the medium of identity construction. Aspects of one's "physical appearance – physique, facial expressions and gestures, clothes and movements – are used to signalise identity. These cultural signs are normatively written into bodies" (Liebsch 2017, 41, with reference to Bourdieu; my translation). How bodies are fashioned and refashioned to signify cultural, national, or religious identity is aptly illustrated in *The Road from Damascus*. Here, the body is also the primary site in which Sami's identity crisis, his downfall and the process of his 're-creation' and the complete rebuilding of his self are played out. While Sami's physical transformation is the external exhibition of his thorough internal conversion and cleansing, Irie's attempts at "fighting her genes" (*Teeth* 273) with the help of a body make-over only amounts to a superficial cover up and re-definition of the physical markers of identity.

The focus on the body has recently drawn new attention to the role of DNA, resemblance, reproduction, and physical inheritance in families due to new technical developments and a global access to digital archives. These new modalities that are deeply enmeshed with cultural and social imaginaries have opened up new processes and avenues for the act of doing family. According to this perspective, the family is the site where the past and the future of individuals are connected. The concept of family as an institution that exists not only for the transfer of genes but also of culture – of values, norms, traditions, and narratives – is particularly evident in migrant families. The first generation's fear of a 'cultural dilution' amongst the second generation is inextricably linked with the desire for the racial sameness of their children's sexual partners.[44] In the words of the narrator of *White Teeth*, "it makes an immigrant laugh to hear the fears of the nationalist, scared of infection, penetration, miscegenation, when this is small fry, *peanuts*, compared to what the immigrant fears – dissolution, *disappearance*" (*Teeth* 327; emphasis in the original).[45] This tends to put pressure on the family as it leads to the formation of anxieties of extinction, but it also nourishes the inherent conflict between the generations and their life goals and expectations. Questions of reproduction, and of choices regarding partners and family forms, are often prominent in intergenerational family narratives because they define the trans-generational life scripts that express parents' expectations of their children and their desire to control the second generation's reproductive choices. This tension between connection and emancipation lies at the heart of doing family.

*

The books analysed here offer a rich archive through which the practices, experiences, and challenges that families face due to the process of migration can be studied. In a context shaped by colonialism, globalisation, war, enforced cultural differences, and religious tensions, migration poses a huge challenge to the cohesion and continuity of family relations, involving the loss of home and carrying the wounds of displacement. The selected books highlight the fact that the family is not only the existential site where the pain and pressure of history is embodied and acted out; it is also the domain where it is processed, negotiated, and reinterpreted across generations, with the aim of transforming the historical experience and reshaping family memory in a way that opens up towards the future. These texts can thus be seen to operate in a way that Alicia Ellis (2012, 69) attributes to Andrea Levy's novel *Small Island*, namely "as an act of reconstruction, a belated intervention, which is both sequel [...] and prologue to the story of the Windrush Generation". All of the texts, to different degrees, can help us to assess the shift that John McLeod (2010) identifies in 'contemporary

---

[44] See Erll's (2014, 401) commentary on the "uneasy oscillations between nature and culture" of the discourse on first and second immigrant generations with regard to 'cultural purity' and 'mixing'.

[45] The passage continues with Alsana's recurring nightmare "visions of Millat (genetically *BB*; where *B* stands for Bengali-ness) marrying someone called Sarah (aa where 'a' stands for Aryan), resulting in a child called Michael (*Ba*), who in turn marries somebody called Lucy (aa), leaving Alsana with a legacy of unrecognizable great-grandchildren (Aaaaaaa!), their Bengali-ness thoroughly diluted, genotype hidden by phenotype" (327).

black writing in Britain'. According to McLeod, many books that have been written over the last two decades are less concerned with matters of "individuated subjectivity" (McLeod 2010, 46) and the exclusive concerns and needs of Black or Asian British identities. Rather, they introduce different ways of conceptualising the notions of belonging, home, and identity "beyond the specific parameters of Black Britishness" (McLeod 2010, 47). In bringing the realm of the migrant family to the fore, a realm which is not only inherently polyvocal but is also essentially transnational and transcultural, the texts presented here offer new modes of 'imagining the nation' as "a shared rather than subjective concern", one that shifts "attention significantly beyond the realm of subjective selfhood", and engages "with the identity of the UK conceived internationally and transculturally for the benefit of all" (McLeod 2010, 47, 48). This concern that goes beyond the individual or a specific group becomes manifest in the way in which each of these texts is "discursively pluralized" (McLeod 2015, 210) through the multiperspectivity and multidimensionality of the family. Interfusing history, memory, and the imagination, the family stories told in these texts demonstrate the need to recover and reformulate the genealogies of the post-migration nation and its communities, and the potential that practices of (af)filiation can have in redefining affinities and bonds. The texts do not present the family as a stable entity of fixed bloodlines that promotes essentialist and rooted origins; rather, they describe the family as malleable, as well as fundamentally open and inclusive, "always already inflected by broader public and generational stories, images, artefacts, and understandings that together shape identity and identification" (Hirsch and Miller 2011, 4). In the words of Marianne Hirsch and Nancy Miller (2011, 4), these texts present the family as a "multifaceted paradigm of community that acknowledges longings to belong and to return while remaining critical of a politics of identity and nation". The way in which the family is presented here as an important site of transcultural memory and as a valuable archive of shared history demonstrates that family writing has the capacity to serve as an orientation and a guide in the processes of social and political negotiations of transcultural societies and post-colonial and post-migration nations.

Works Cited

Primary Sources

Ae Fond Kiss. Dir. Ken Loach. Perf. Atta Yaqub, Eva Birthistle. 2004. DVD. Icon Home Entertainment, 2007.
Ali, Monica. *Brick Lane*. New York: Scribner, 2003.
Aslam, Nadeem. *Maps for Lost Lovers*. London: Faber and Faber, 2005 [2004].
Bend It like Beckham. Dir. Gurinder Chadha. Perf. Parminder Nagra, Keira Knightley, Jonathan Rhys Meyers, Anupam Kher. 2002. DVD. CIC Video/Paramount Home Entertainment, 2003.
Davies, Ray. "Yours Truly, Confused N10." *Thanksgiving Day*. Label: Ray Davies, 2005.
East Is East. Dir. Damien O'Donnell. Perf. Om Puri, Jimi Mistry, Linda Bassett, Jordan Routledge. 1999. DVD. Channel 4, 2007.
Evaristo, Bernardine. *Lara*. Tarset: Bloodaxe, 2009 [1997].
Grant, Linda. *The Clothes on Their Backs*. London: Virago, 2008.
Gurnah, Abdulrazak. *Dottie*. London: Bloomsbury, 2016 [1990].
Haddad, Saleem. *Guapa*. New York: Other Press, 2016.
Kay, Jackie. *Red Dust Road*. Basingstoke: Picador, 2011 [2010].
Kluger, Ruth. *Still Alive: A Holocaust Girlhood Remembered*. Foreword by Lore Segal. New York: The Feminist Press, 2001.
Kureishi, Hanif. *The Buddha of Suburbia*. London: Faber and Faber, 1990.
Kureishi, Hanif. *My Ear at His Heart: Reading My Father*. London: Faber and Faber, 2005 [2004].
Levy, Andrea. *Fruit of the Lemon*. London: Headline Review, 2004 [1999].
Mahjoub, Jamal. *Travelling with Djinns*. London: Chatto & Windus, 2003.
Mann, Thomas. *Buddenbrooks*. Berlin: S. Fischer, 1901.
Okojie, Irenosen. *Butterfly Fish*. London: Jacaranda, 2016.
Ondaatje, Michael. *Running in the Family*. London: Bloomsbury, 2010 [1982].
Phillips, Caryl. *In the Falling Snow*. London: Harvill Secker, 2009.
Pressure. Dir. Horace Ové. Perf. Herbert Norville, Oscar James, Frank Singuineau. 1976. DVD. BFI Video, 2005.
Riley, Joan. *The Unbelonging*. London: Women's Press, 1985.
Selvon, Sam. *The Lonely Londoners*. London: Penguin Books, 1965.
Seth, Vikram. *Two Lives*. Boston: Little Brown, 2005.
Shamsie, Kamila. *Kartography*. London: Bloomsbury, 2011 [2002].
Smith, Zadie. *White Teeth*. London: Penguin, 2001 [2000].
Syal, Meera. *Anita and Me*. London: Harper Perennial, 2004 [1996].
Yassin-Kassab, Robin. *The Road from Damascus*. London: Penguin, 2009 [2008].
Woolf, Virginia. *Orlando: A Biography*. London: Vintage, 2004 [1928].

Secondary Sources

Abraham, Nicolas and Maria Torok. "The Shell and the Kernel." Transl. by Nicholas Rand. *Diacritics* 9.1 (1979): 15–28.
Adams, Gerald R. and Sheila K. Marshall. "A Developmental Social Psychology of Identity: Understanding the Person-in-Context." *Journal of Adolescence* 19 (1996): 429–442.
Agazzi, Elena. "Familienromane, Familiengeschichten und Generationenkonflikte: Überlegungen zu einem eindrucksvollen Phänomen." *Gedächtnis und Identität: Die deutsche Literatur nach der Vereinigung*. Ed. Fabrizio Cambi. Würzburg: Königshausen & Neumann, 2008. 187–203.
Ahmed, Rehana. *Writing British Muslims: Religion, Class and Multiculturalism*. Manchester: Manchester University Press, 2015.
Ahmed, Sara, Claudia Castañeda, Anne-Marie Fortier, and Mimi Sheller. "Introduction: Uprootings/Regroundings: Questions of Home and Migration." *Uprootings/Regroundings: Questions of Home and Migration*. Eds. Sara Ahmed, Claudia Castañeda, Anne-Marie Fortier, and Mimi Sheller. Oxford: Berg, 2003. 1–19.
Ahmed, Sara. *The Promise of Happiness*. Durham: Duke University Press, 2010.
Al-Shawaf, Rayyan. "Reviewed: *My Ear at His Heart: Reading My Father* by Hanif Kureishi." *Washington City Paper*. 12 March 2010. http://www.washingtoncitypaper.com/arts/books/article/13038561/reviewed-my-ear-at-his-heart-reading-my-father-by-hanif-kureishi (last access 10 November 2016).
Alexander, Jeffrey C. "Toward a Theory of Cultural Trauma." *Cultural Trauma and Collective Identity*. Eds. Jeffrey C. Alexander, Ron Eyerman, Bernhard Giesen, Neil J. Smelser, and Piotr Sztompka. Berkeley, CA: University of California Press, 2004. 1–30.
Arana, Victoria and Lauri Ramey. *Black British Writing*. Basingstoke: Palgrave Macmillan, 2004.
Arnett, Jeffrey Jensen. "Broad and Narrow Socialization: The Family in the Context of a Cultural Theory." *Journal of the Marriage and the Family* 57.3 (1995): 617–628.
Arnold-de Simine, Silke and Joanne Leal. "Introduction." *Picturing the Family: Media, Narrative, Memory*. Eds. Silke Arnold-de Simine and Joanne Leal. London: Bloomsbury, 2018. 1–17.
Asendorpf, Jens B. "Genom-Umwelt-Wechselwirkungen in der Persönlichkeitsentwicklung." *Sozialisationstheorie interdisziplinär: Aktuelle Perspektiven*. Eds. Dieter Geulen and Hermann Veith. Stuttgart: Lucius & Lucius, 2004. 35–53.
Ashley, Bob, Joanne Hollows, Steve Jones, and Ben Taylor. *Food and Cultural Studies*. London: Routledge, 2005.
Assmann, Aleida. "Memory, Individual and Collective." *The Oxford Handbook of Contextual Political Analysis*. Eds. Robert E. Goodin and Charles Tilly. Oxford: Oxford University Press, 2006. 210–224.
Assmann, Aleida. *Geschichte im Gedächtnis: Von der individuellen Erfahrung zur öffentlichen Inszenierung*. München: C.H. Beck, 2007.
Assmann, Aleida. "Canon and Archive." *Cultural Memory Studies: An International and Interdisciplinary Handbook*. Eds. Astrid Erll and Ansgar Nünning, in collaboration with Sara B. Young. Berlin: de Gruyter, 2008. 97–108.
Assmann, Aleida. *Erinnerungsräume: Formen und Wandlungen des kulturellen Gedächtnisses*. Fourth, revised edition. München: C.H. Beck, 2009 [1999].
Assmann, Aleida. *Ist die Zeit aus den Fugen? Aufstieg und Fall des Zeitregimes der Moderne*. München: Carl Hanser, 2013.

Assmann, Jan. "Collective Memory and Cultural Identity." *New German Critique* 65 (1995): 125–133.

Assmann, Jan. "Communicative and Cultural Memory." *Cultural Memory Studies: An International and Interdisciplinary Handbook.* Eds. Astrid Erll and Ansgar Nünning. Berlin: de Gruyter, 2008. 109–118.

Augé, Marc. *Non-Places: Introduction to an Anthropology of Supermodernity.* Transl. John Howe. New York, NY: Verso, 1995.

Baker, Houston A., Jr., Manthia Diawara, and Ruth H. Lindeborg. "Introduction: Representing Blackness/Representing Britain: Cultural Studies and the Politics of Knowledge." *Black British Cultural Studies: A Reader.* Eds. Houston A. Baker, Jr., Manthia Diawara, and Ruth H. Lindeborg. Chicago: University of Chicago Press, 1996. 1–15.

Barfoot, Cedric C. "Blake's England and the Restoration of Jerusalem: Too Late for Green and Pleasant Idylls?" *Green and Pleasant Land: English Culture and the Romantic Countryside.* Ed. Amanda Gilroy. Leuven: Peeters, 2004. 57–71.

Barthes, Roland. "Toward a Psychosociology of Contemporary Food Consumption." *Food and Culture: A Reader.* Eds. Caroline Counihan and Penny Van Esterik. London: Routledge, 2013 [1961]. 23–30.

Bauer, Joachim. *Das Gedächtnis des Körpers: Wie Beziehungen und Lebensstile unsere Gene steuern.* Frankfurt a.M.: Eichborn, 2014 [2002].

Bauman, Zygmunt. *Liquid Modernity.* Cambridge: Polity, 2000.

Bauman, Zygmunt. *Liquid Love.* Cambridge: Polity, 2003.

Baumeister, Roy F. and Mark Muraven. "Identity as Adaptation to Social, Cultural, and Historical Context." *Journal of Adolescence* 19 (1996): 405–416.

Becher, Harriet. *Family Practices in South Asian Muslim Families: Parenting in a Multi-Faith Britain.* Basingstoke: Palgrave Macmillan, 2008.

Beck, Ulrich and Elizabeth Beck-Gernsheim. *Individualization: Institutionalized Individualism and Its Social and Political Consequences.* Transl. by Patrick Camiller. London: Sage, 2002.

Beck, Ulrich and Elizabeth Beck-Gernsheim. *The Normal Chaos of Love.* Transl. by Mark Ritter and Jane Wiebel. Cambridge: Polity, 2004 [1995].

Benjamin, Jessica. *The Bonds of Love: Psychoanalysis, Feminism, and the Problem of Domination.* New York, NY: Pantheon, 1988.

Benson, Mark J. and James E. Deal. "Bridging the Individual and the Family." *Journal of Marriage and Family* 57.3 (1995): 561–566.

Berghahn, Daniela. *Far-Flung Families in Film: The Diasporic Family in Contemporary European Cinema.* Edinburgh: Edinburgh University Press, 2013.

Beushausen, Wiebke, Anne Brüske, Ana-Sofia Commichau, Patrik Helber, and Sinah Kloß, eds. *Caribbean Food Cultures: Culinary Practices and Consumption in the Caribbean and Its Diasporas.* Bielefeld: transcript, 2014.

Bietti, Lucas M. "Sharing Memories, Family Conversation and Interaction." *Discourse & Society* 21.5 (2010): 499–523.

Birke, Dorothee. *Memory's Fragile Power: Crises of Memory, Identity and Narrative in Contemporary British Novels.* Trier: WVT, 2008.

Bohanek, Jennifer G., Kelly A. Marin, Robyn Fivush, and Marshall P. Duke. "Family Narrative Interaction and Children's Sense of Self." *Family Process* 45.1 (2006): 39–54.

Bohanek, Jennifer G., Robyn Fivush, Widaad Zaman, Caitlin E. Lepore, Shela Merchant, and Marshall P. Duke. "Narrative Interaction in Family Dinnertime Conversations." *Merrill-Palmer Quarterly* 55.4 (2009): 488–515.

Bohnenkamp, Björn, Till Manning, and Eva-Maria Silies, eds. *Generation als Erzählung: Neue Perspektiven auf ein kulturelles Deutungsmuster*. Göttingen: Wallstein, 2009.

Bookgroup Info. "Jackie Kay." May 9, 2011. *Bookgroup Info*. http://www.bookgroup.info/041205/interview.php?id=73 (accessed 24 April, 2016).

Bouquet, Mary. "Family Trees and Their Affinities: The Visual Imperative of the Genealogical Diagram." *Journal of the Royal Anthropological Institute* 2 (1996): 43–66.

Box. Sally J. "The Elucidation of a Family Myth." *Journal of Family Therapy* 1.1 (1979): 75–86.

Boyers, Robert. "The Family Novel." *Salmagundi* 26 (1974): 3–25.

Brace, Marianne. "Nadeem Aslam: A Question of Honour." *Independent*. 11 June, 2004. http://www.independent.co.uk/arts-entertainment/books/features/nadeem-aslam-a-question-of-honour-731732.html (accessed 10 January, 2014).

Bradford Museums. *Belle Vue Studio*. https://photos.bradfordmuseums.org/home (last accessed 19 July, 2017).

Brah, Avtar. *Cartographies of Diaspora: Contesting Identities*. London: Routledge, 2005 [1996].

Brähler, Susan. *Rückkehr im zeitgenössischen Migrationsroman der Karibik*. Bamberg: University of Bamberg Press, 2013.

Brinker-von der Heyde, Claudia. *Familienmuster – Musterfamilien: Zur Konstruktion von Familie in der Literatur*. Frankfurt a.M.: Lang, 2004.

Bromley, Roger. *Narratives for a New Belonging: Diasporic Cultural Fictions*. Edinburgh: Edinburgh University Press, 2000.

Bronfenbrenner, Urie. "Toward an Experimental Ecology of Human Development." *American Psychologist* (1977): 513–531.

Bronfenbrenner, Urie. "Ecological Models of Human Development." *Readings on the Development of Children*. Eds. Mary Gauvain and Michael Cole. New York, NY: Freeman, 1993. 37–43.

Brown, Mick. "Hanif Kureishi: A Life Laid Bare." *The Telegraph*. 23 February, 2008. http://www.telegraph.co.uk/culture/books/3671392/Hanif-Kureishi-A-life-laid-bare.html (last accessed 20 October, 2016).

Brunelle, François. "I'm Not a Look-Alike!" *www.francoisbrunelle.com*. 2004ff. http://www.francoisbrunelle.com/web/projet_en.html (accessed 25 June, 2018).

Bruner, Jerome and Susan Weisser. "The Invention of Self: Autobiography and Its Forms." *Literacy and Orality*. Eds. David R. Olson and Nancy Torrance. Cambridge: Cambridge University Press, 1991. 129–148.

Bruner, Jerome. "The Narrative Construction of Reality." *Critical Inquiry* 18.1 (1991a): 1–21.

Bruner, Jerome. "Self-Making and World-Making." *The Journal of Aesthetic Education* 25.1 (1991b): 67–78.

Brunow, Dagmar. *Remediating Transcultural Memory: Documentary Filmmaking as Archival Intervention*. Berlin: de Gruyter, 2015.

Buckner, Janine P. and Robyn Fivush. "Gendered Themes in Family Reminiscing." *Memory* 8.6 (2000): 401–412.

Burkitt, Ian. "The Shifting Concept of the Self." *History of the Human Sciences* 7.2 (1994): 7–28.

Burkitt, Ian. *Social Selves: Theories of Self and Society*. Second Edition. London: Sage, 2008 [1991].

Butt, Nadia. *Transcultural Memory and Globalised Modernity in Contemporary Indo-English Novels*. Berlin: de Gruyter, 2015.
Campbell-Hall, Devon. "Writing Second-Generation Migrant Identity in Meera Syal's Fiction." *Shared Waters: Soundings in Postcolonial Literatures*. Ed. Stella Borg Barthet. Amsterdam: Rodopi, 2009. 298–305.
Campt, Tina M. *Image Matters: Archive, Photography, and the African Diaspora in Europe*. Durham: Duke University Press, 2012.
Carsten, Janet. "The Substance of Kinship and the Heat of the Hearth: Feeding, Personhood, and Relatedness among Malays in Pulau Langkawi." *American Ethnologist* 22.2 (1995): 223–241.
Carsten, Janet. "Introduction: Cultures of Relatedness." *Cultures of Relatedness: New Approaches to the Study of Kinship*. Ed. Janet Carsten. Cambridge: Cambridge University Press, 2000. 1–36.
Carsten, Janet. *After Kinship*. Cambridge: Cambridge University Press, 2004.
Carsten, Janet. "Introduction: Blood Will Out." *Journal of the Royal Anthropological Institute* 19.1 (2013): 1–23.
Castañeda, Claudia. "Der Stammbaum: Zeit, Raum und Alltagestechnologie in den Vererbungswissenschaften." *Genealogie und Genetik: Schnittstellen zwischen Biologie und Kulturgeschichte*. Ed. Sigrid Weigel. Berlin: Akademie Verlag, 2002. 57–69.
Chadha, Narender K. *Integrational Relationships: An Indian Perspective*. The United Nations. http://www.un.org/esa/socdev/family/docs/egm12/CHADHA-PAPER.pdf
Chamberlain, Mary and Selma Leydesdorff. "Transnational Families: Memories and Narratives." *Global Networks* 4.3 (2004): 227–241.
Chamberlain, Mary. *Family Love in the Diaspora: Migration and the Anglo-Caribbean Experience*. New Brunswick, NJ: Transaction, 2006.
Chamberlain, Mary. "Diasporic Memories: Community, Individuality, and Creativity – A Life Stories Perspective." *The Oral History Review* 36.2 (2009): 177–187.
Chambers, Claire. *British Muslim Fictions: Interviews with Contemporary Writers*. Houndsmills, Basingstoke: Palgrave Macmillan, 2011.
Chambers, Claire. "'Sexy Identity-Assertion': Choosing between Sacred and Secular Identities in Robin Yassin-Kassab's *The Road from Damascus*." *Culture, Diaspora, and Modernity in Muslim Writing*. Eds. Rehana Ahmed, Peter Morey, and Amina Yaqin. London: Routledge, 2012. 117–131.
Chambers, Deborah. *A Sociology of Family Life: Change and Diversity in Intimate Relations*. Cambridge: Polity, 2012.
Cheal, David. *Sociology of Family Life*. New York, NY: Macmillan Education, 2002.
Chen, Serena, Helen Boucher, and Michael W. Kraus. "The Relational Self." *Handbook of Identity Theory and Research. Volume I: Structures and Processes*. Eds. Seth J. Schwartz et al. Heidelberg: Springer, 2011. 149–175.
Childs, Peter and James R. Green. *Aesthetics and Ethics in Twenty-First Century British Novels: Zadie Smith, Nadeem Aslam, Hari Kunzru and David Mitchell*. London: Bloomsbury, 2013.
Clifford, James. "Diasporas." *Further Inflections: Toward Ethnographies of the Future. Cultural Anthropology* 9.3 (1994): 302–338.
Cooper, David Graham. *The Death of the Family*. Harmondsworth: Penguin, 1976 [1971].
Côté, James E. "Sociological Perspectives on Identity Formation: The Culture-Identity Link and Identity Capital." *Journal of Adolescence* 19 (1996): 417–428.

Couser, Thomas G. "Genre Matters: Form, Force, and Filiation." *Life Writing* 2.2 (2005): 139–156.
Couser, Thomas G. *Memoir: An Introduction*. Oxford: Oxford University Press, 2012.
Couser, Thomas G. "Paper Orphans: Writers' Children Write their Lives." *Life Writing* 11.1 (2013): 21–37.
Crosbie-Burnett, Margaret and David M. Klein. "The Fascinating Story of Family Theories." *The Wiley-Blackwell Handbook of Family Psychology*. Eds. James H. Bray and Mark Stanton. Hoboken, NJ: Wiley-Blackwell. 37–52, 2009.
Csáky, Moritz. "Speisen und Essen aus Kulturwissenschaftlicher Perspektive." *Kulinarik und Kultur: Speisen als kulturelle Codes in Zentraleuropa*. Eds. Moritz Csáky and Georg Christian Lack. Wien: Böhlau, 2014. 9–36.
Dallos, Rudi and Ros Draper. *An Introduction to Family Therapy: Systemic Theory and Practice*. Fourth Edition. Maidenhead: Open University Press, 2010 [2000].
Davis, Rocío G. "Writing Fathers: Auto/biography and Unfulfilled Vocation in Sara Suleri Goodyear's *Boys Will Be Boys* and Hanif Kureishi's *My Ear at His Heart*." *Life Writing* 6.2 (2009): 229–241.
Davis, Rocío G. *Relative Histories: Mediating History in Asian American Family Memoirs*. Honolulu, HI: University of Hawai'i Press, 2010.
Douglas, Mary. *Purity and Danger: An Analysis of the Concepts of Pollution and Taboo*. London: Routledge, 2001 [1966].
Douglas, Mary. "A History of Grid and Group Cultural Theory." 2007a. Available online at http://projects.chass.utoronto.ca/semiotics/cyber/douglas1.pdf (accessed 12 August, 2012)
Douglas, Mary. "Seeing Everything in Black and White." 2007b. Available online at http://projects.chass.utoronto.ca/semotics/cyber/douglas2.pdf (accessed 12 August, 2012).
Eakin, Paul John. *How Our Lives Become Stories: Making Selves*. Ithaca, NY: Cornell University Press, 1999.
Eakin, Paul John. "Autobiography, Identity, and the Fictions of Memory." *Memory, Brain, and Belief*. Eds. Daniel L. Schacter and Elain Scarry. Cambridge, MA: Harvard University Press, 2001. 290–306.
Eakin, Paul John. *Living Autobiographically: How We Create Identity in Narrative*. Ithaca, NY: Cornell University Press, 2008.
Eckstein, Lars, Barbara Korte, Eva Ulrike Pirker, and Christoph Reinfandt. "A Divided Kingdom? Reflections on Multi-Ethnic Britain in the New Millennium." *Multi-Ethnic Britain 2000+: New Perspectives in Literature, Film and the Arts*. Eds. Lars Eckstein, Barbara Korte, Eva Ulrike Pirker, and Christoph Reinfandt. Amsterdam: Rodopi, 2008. 9–24.
Edmunds, June and Bryan S. Turner. *Generations, Culture and Society*. Maidenhead: Open University Press, 2002.
Edwards, Rosalind, Jane Ribbens McCarthy and Val Gillies. "The Politics of Concepts: Family and Its (Putative) Replacements." *The British Journal of Sociology* 63.4 (2012): 730–746.
Egan, Susanna and Gabriele Helms. "Auto/biography? Yes. But Canadian?" *Canadian Literature* 172 (2002): 5–16.
Ellis, Alicia E. "Identity as Cultural Production in Andrea Levy's *Small Island*." *EnterText* 9 (2012): 69–83.
Erll, Astrid and Ann Rigney, eds. *Mediation, Remediation, and the Dynamics of Cultural Memory*. Berlin: de Gruyter, 2009.

Erll, Astrid and Ansgar Nünning, eds. *Cultural Memory Studies: An International and Interdisciplinary Handbook*. Berlin: de Gruyter, 2008.
Erll, Astrid. "Re-Writing as Re-Visioning: Modes of Representing the 'Indian Mutiny' in British Novels, 1857 to 2000." *European Journal of English Studies* 10.2 (2006): 163–185.
Erll, Astrid."Familien- und Generationenromane: Zadie Smith." *Der zeitgenössische Roman: Genres – Entwicklungen – Modellinterpretationen*. Ed. Vera Nünning. Trier: WVT, 2007. 117–132.
Erll, Astrid. "Cultural Memory Studies: An Introduction." *Cultural Memory Studies: An International and Interdisciplinary Handbook*. Eds. Astrid Erll and Ansgar Nünning. Berlin: de Gruyter, 2008. 1–15.
Erll, Astrid. "Locating Family in Cultural Memory Studies." *Journal of Comparative Family Studies* 42.3 (2011a): 303–318.
Erll, Astrid. "Travelling Memory." *Parallax* 17.4 (2011b): 4–18.
Erll, Astrid. "Generation in Literary History: Three Constellations of Generationality, Genealogy, and Memory." *New Literary History* 45.3 (2014): 385–409.
Erll, Astrid. "Fictions of Generational Memory: Caryl Phillips's *In the Falling Snow* and Black British Writing in Times of Mnemonic Transition." *Memory Unbound: Tracing the Dynamics of Memory Studies*. Eds. Lucy Bond, Stef Craps and Pieter Vermeulen. New York: Berghahn, 2017. 109–130.
Ernst Haeckel. *Pedigree of Man*. Leipzig: Engelmann, 1874.
Esser, Hartmut, ed. *Generation und Identität: Theoretische und empirische Beiträge zur Migrationssoziologie*. Opladen: Westdeutscher Verlag, 1990.
Eyerman, Ron and Bryan S. Turner. "Outline of a Theory of Generations." *European Journal of Social Theory* 1.1 (1998): 91–106.
Eyerman, Ron. *Cultural Trauma: Slavery and the Formation of African American Identity*. Cambridge: Cambridge University Press, 2003 [2001].
Falkenhayner, Nicole. *Making the British Muslim: Representations of the Rushdie Affair and Figures of the War-On-Terror Decade*. Basingstoke: Palgrave Macmillan, 2014.
FAMILYPLATFORM. url: http://www.familyplatform.eu/ (accessed 30 April, 2014).
Fiese, Barbara H. and Marcia A. Winter. "Family Stories and Rituals." *The Wiley-Blackwell Handbook of Family Psychology*. Eds. James H. Bray and Mark Stanton. Malden, MA: Blackwell, 2009. 625–636.
Fiese, Barbara H. and Ross D. Parke. "Introduction to the Special Section on Family Routines and Rituals." *Journal of Family Psychology* 16.4 (2002): 379–380.
Fietze, Beate. *Historische Generationen: Über einen sozialen Mechanismus kulturellen Wandels und kollektiver Kreativität*. Bielefeld: transcript, 2009.
Finch, Janet. "Displaying Families." *Sociology* 41.1 (2007): 65–81.
Fink, Janet. "Private Lives and Public Issues: Moral Panics and 'the Family' in 20th Century Britain." *Journal for the Study of British Cultures* 9.2 (2002): 135–148.
Fivush, Robyn and Elaine Reese. "The Social Construction of Autobiographical Memory." *Theoretical Perspectives on Autobiographical Memory*. Eds. Martin A Conway, David C. Rubin, Hans Spinnler, and Willem A. Wagenaar. Dordrecht: Kluwer Academic, 1992. 115–134.
Fivush, Robyn and Catherine A. Haden. "Introduction: Autobiographical Memory, Narrative and Self." *Autobiographical Memory and the Construction of a Narrative Self: Developmental and Cultural Perspectives*. Eds. Robyn Fivush and Catherine A. Haden. Mahwah, NJ: Lawrence Erlbaum, 2003. vii–xiv.

Fivush, Robyn, Jennifer G. Bohanek, and Marshall Duke. "The Intergenerational Self: Subjective Perspective and Family History." *Self Continuity: Individual and Collective Perspectives.* Ed. Fabio Sani. New York, NY: Taylor & Francis, 2008. 131–143.

Fivush, Robyn, Kelly Marin, Kelly McWilliams, and Jennifer G. Bohanek. "Family Reminiscing Style: Parent Gender and Emotional Focus in Relation to Child Well-Being." *Journal of Cognition and Development* 10.3 (2009): 210–235.

Fivush, Robyn. 2008. "Remembering and Reminiscing: How Individual Lives Are Constructed in Family Narratives." *Memory Studies* 1.1 (2008): 49–58.

Fivush, Robyn. "Speaking Silence: The Social Construction of Silence in Autobiographical and Cultural Narratives." *Memory* 18.2 (2010): 88–98.

Fox, Pamela. "The 'Telling Part': Reimagining Racial Recognition in Jackie Kay's Adoptee Search Narratives." *Contemporary Women's Writing* 9.2 (2015): 277–296.

Frank, Tobias. *Identitätsbildung in ausgewählten Romanen der 'Black British Literature': Genre, Gender und Ethnizität.* Trier: WVT, 2010.

Galli, Matteo and Simone Costagli. "Chronotopoi: Vom Familienroman zum Generationenroman." *Deutsche Familienromane: Literarische Genealogien und internationaler Kontext.* Eds. Matteo Galli and Simone Costagli. München: Wilhelm Fink, 2010. 7–20.

Galvin, Kathleen M. "Diversity's Impact on Defining the Family: Discourse-Dependence and Identity." *The Family Communications Sourcebook.* Eds. Lynn H. Turner and Richard West. London: Sage, 2006. 3–20.

Gergen, Kenneth J. *Relational Being: Beyond Self and Community.* Oxford: Oxford University Press, 2009.

Geulen, Dieter. "Ungelöste Probleme im sozialisationstheoretischen Diskurs." *Sozialisationstheorie interdisziplinär: Aktuelle Perspektiven.* Eds. Dieter Geulen and Hermann Veith. Stuttgart: Lucius & Lucius, 2004. 3–20.

Giddens, Anthony. *The Transformation of Intimacy: Sexuality, Love and Eroticism in Modern Societies.* Cambridge: Polity, 1992.

Gillis, John R. *A World of Their Own Making: Myth, Ritual, and the Quest for Family Values.* New York, NY: BasicBooks, 1996.

Gillis, John R. *Our Imagined Families: The Myths and Rituals We Live By.* The Emory Center for Myth and Ritual in American Life. Working Paper No. 7, 2002. https://gdesseniorseminarfall2011.files.wordpress.com/2011/09/imagined-families.pdf (Accessed 23 April, 2014).

Gilroy, Paul. *Between Camps: Race and Culture in Postmodernity: An Inaugural Lecture.* London: Goldsmiths, 1997.

Glynn, Irial and J. Olaf Kleist. *History, Memory and Migration: Perceptions of the Past and the Politics of Incorporation.* Basingstoke: Palgrave Macmillan, 2012.

Golightly, Jennifer. *The Family, Marriage, and Radicalism in British Women's Novels of the 1790s: Public Affection and Private Affliction.* Lanham, MD: Bucknell University Press, 2012.

Gomila, Antònia. "Family Photographs: Putting Families on Display." *Families and Kinship in Contemporary Europe: Rules and Practices of Relatedness.* Eds. Riitta Jallinoja and Eric D. Widmer. Basingstoke: Palgrave Macmillan, 2011. 63–77.

Gross, Neil. "The Detraditionalization of Intimacy Reconsidered." *Sociological Theory* 23.3 (2005): 286–311.

Grossberg, Lawrence. "Identity and Cultural Studies – Is That All There Is?" *Questions of Cultural Identity.* Eds. Stuart Hall and Paul du Gay. London: Sage, 1996. 87–107.

Gugutzer, Robert. *Soziologie des Körpers*. Bielefeld: transcript, 2015.
Gunew, Sneja. "Introduction: Multicultural Translations of Food, Bodies, Language." *Journal of Intercultural Studies* 21.3 (2000): 227–237.
Gunning, Dave. *Race and Antiracism in Black British and British Asian Literature*. Liverpool: Liverpool University Press, 2010.
Gunning, Dave. "Unhappy Bildungsromane." *Andrea Levy: Contemporary Critical Perspectives*. Eds. Jeannette Baxter and David James. London: Bloomsbury, 2014. 9–22.
Halbwachs, Maurice. *On Collective Memory*. Ed. and transl. Lewis A. Coser. Chicago, IL: University of Chicago Press, 1992.
Hall, Stuart and Paul du Gay, eds. *Questions of Cultural Identity*. London: Sage, 1996.
Hall, Stuart. "Minimal Selves." *Black British Cultural Studies: A Reader*. Eds. Houston A. Baker, Jr., Manthia Diawara, and Ruth H. Lindeborg. Chicago, IL: University of Chicago Press, 1996a. 114–119.
Hall, Stuart. "New Ethnicities." *Black British Cultural Studies: A Reader*. Eds. Houston A. Baker, Jr., Manthia Diawara, and Ruth H. Lindeborg. Chicago, IL: University of Chicago Press, 1996b [1988]. 163–172.
Hanson, Clare. "Epigenetics, Plasticity and Identity in Jackie Kay's *Red Dust Road*." *Textual Practice* 29.3 (2015): 433–452.
Hansson, Leeni. "Major Trends in Family Behaviour in European Countries." *Spotlights on Contemporary Family Life: FAMILYPLATFORM – Families in Europe Vol. 2*. Eds. Linden Farrer and William Lay. Online: European Platform for Investing in Children, 2011. 21–32. http://europa.eu/epic/docs/family-platform-book-2.pdf (accessed 30 April, 2014).
Hecht, Anat. "Home Sweet Home: Tangible Memories of an Uprooted Childhood." *Home Possessions: Material Culture behind Closed Doors*. Ed. Daniel Miller. Oxford: Berg, 2001. 123–145.
Hedetoft, Ulf and Mette Hjort. "Introduction." *The Postnational Self: Belonging and Identity*. Eds. Ulf Hedetoft and Mette Hjort. Minneapolis, MN: University of Minnesota Press, 2002. vii–xxxii.
Heffl, Sissy. *Unreliable Truths: Transcultural Homeworlds in Indian Women's Fiction of the Diaspora*. Amsterdam: Rodopi, 2013.
Helfferich, Cornelia. "Agency-Analyse und Biografieforschung: Rekonstruktion von Viktimisierungsprozessen in biografischen Erzählungen." *Agency: Die Analyse von Handlungsfähigkeit und Handlungsmacht in qualifizierter Sozialforschung und Gesellschaftstheorie*. Eds. Stephanie Bettina, Cornelia Helfferich, Heiko Hoffmann, and Deborah Niermann. Weinheim/München: Juventa, 2012. 210–237.
Heneghan, Tom. "French Conservatives March Against Government 'Family-Phobia'." *Reuters*. 2 February, 2014. http://www.reuters.com/article/2014/02/02/us-france-protests-idUSBREA110AG20140202 (accessed 15 June, 2015).
Herman, David. "Introduction." *The Cambridge Companion to Narrative*. Ed. David Herman. Cambridge: Cambridge University Press, 2007. 3–21.
Highmore, Ben. "Alimentary Agents: Food, Cultural Theory and Multiculturalism." *Journal of Intercultural Studies* 29.4 (2008): 381–398.
Hill, Paul B. and Johannes Kopp. *Familiensoziologie: Grundlagen und theoretische Perspektiven*. Fifth revised edition. Wiesbaden: Springer, 2013 [1995].
Hirsch, Juliane. *Family Photographs: Content, Meaning, and Effect*. Oxford: Oxford University Press, 1981.

Hirsch, Marianne and Nancy K. Miller. "Introduction." *Rites of Return: Diaspora Poetics and the Politics of Memory*. Eds. Marianne Hirsch and Nancy K. Miller. New York, NY: Columbia University Press, 2011. 1–20.
Hirsch, Marianne. "The Novel of Formation as Genre: Between Great Expectations and Lost Illusions in Studies in the Novel." *Genre* 12.3 (1979): 293–311.
Hirsch, Marianne. "Past Lives: Postmemories in Exile." *Poetics Today* 17.4 (1996): 659–686.
Hirsch, Marianne. "The Generation of Postmemory." *Poetics Today* 29.1 (2008): 103–128.
Hirsch, Marianne. *Family Frames: Photography, Narrative, and Postmemory*. Cambridge, MA: Harvard University Press, 2012a [1997].
Hirsch, Marianne. *The Generation of Postmemory: Writing and Visual Culture after the Holocaust*. New York, NY: Columbia University Press, 2012b.
Holdenried, Michaela. "Familie, Familiennarrative und Interkulturalität: Eine Einleitung." *Die interkulturelle Familie: Literatur- und sozialwissenschaftliche Perspektiven*. Eds. Michaela Holdenried and Weertje Willms. Bielefeld: transcript, 2012. 11–23.
Howell, Signe and Diana Marre. "To Kin a Transnationally Adopted Child in Norway and Spain: The Achievement of Resemblances and Belonging." *ETHNOS* 71.3 (2006): 293–316.
Howell, Signe. "Kinning: The Creation of Life Trajectories in Transnational Adoptive Families." *Journal of the Royal Anthropological Institute* 9 (2003): 465–484. http://www.helsinki.fi/collegium/e-series/volumes/volume_1/index.htm (accessed 15 July, 2009).
Huggan, Graham. *The Post-Colonial Exotic: Marketing the Margins*. London: Routledge, 2001.
Iser, Wolfgang. *The Implied Reader: Patterns of Communication in Prose Fiction from Bunyan to Beckett*. Baltimore, MD: Johns Hopkins University Press, 1974 [1972].
Jaggi, Maya. "Beyond Belief: Review of *The Road from Damascus*." *The Guardian*. 14 June, 2008. Available at https://www.theguardian.com/books/2008/jun/14/saturdayreviewsfeatres.guardianreview9 (accessed 12 May, 2015).
Jallinoja, Riitta and Eric D. Widmer. "Introduction." *Families and Kinship in Contemporary Europe: Rules and Practices of Relatedness*. Eds. Riitta Jallinoja and Eric D. Widmer. Basingstoke: Palgrave Macmillan, 2011. 3–12.
Jamieson, Lynn. "Interpreting and Representing Families and Relationships." *Researching Families and Relationships: Reflections on Process*. Eds. Lynn Jamieson, Roona Simpson, and Ruth Lewis. Basingstoke: Palgrave Macmillan, 2011. 122–149.
Janmohamed, Abdul R. "Refiguring Values, Power, Knowledge." *Whither Marxism? Global Crises in International Perspective*. Eds. Bernd Magnus and Stephen Cullen. London: Routledge, 1995. 31–64.
Jordan, Jennifer A. "Investigating the Edible: Points of Inquiry in the Study of Food, Culture, and Identity." *Kulinarik und Kultur: Speisen als kulturelle Codes in Zentraleuropa*. Eds. Moritz Csáky and Georg Christian Lack. Wien: Böhlau, 2014. 37–50.
Jorgenson, Jane and Arthur P. Bochner. "Imagining Families through Stories and Rituals." *Handbook of Family Communication*. Ed. Anita L. Vangelisti. Mahwah, NJ: Lawrence Erlbaum, 2003. 513–538.
Jureit, Ulrike and Michael Wildt. *Generationen: Zur Relevanz eines wissenschaftlichen Grundbegriffs*. Hamburg: Hamburger Edition, HIS-Verlag, 2005.
Kansteiner, Wulf. "Moral Pitfalls of Memory Studies: The Concept of Political Generations." *Memory Studies* 5.2 (2012): 111–113.

Kashima, Yoshihisa and Margaret Foddy. "Time and Self: The Historical Construction of the Self". *Self and Identity: Personal, Social, and Symbolic*. Eds. Yoshihisa Kashima, Margaret Foddy, and Michael Platow. Mahwah, NJ: Lawrence Erlbaum, 2002. 181–206.

Kashima, Yoshihisa, Emiko Kashima, and Anna Clark. "Interpersonal Dynamics of the Self: The Doubly Distributed Approach." *The Social Self: Cognitive, Interpersonal, and Intergroup Perspectives*. Eds. Joseph P. Forgas and Kipling D. Williams. New York, NY: Psychology Press, 2002. 233–254.

Kershen, Anne J., ed. *Food in the Migrant Experience*. Aldershot: Ashgate, 2002.

Kershen, Anne J. "Introduction: Food in the Migrant Experience." *Food in the Migrant Experience*. Ed. Anne J. Kershen. Aldershot: Ashgate, 2002. 1–13.

Keupp, Heiner et al. *Identitätskonstruktionen: Das Patchwork der Identitäten in der Spätmoderne*. Reinbek bei Hamburg: Rowohlt, 2008.

Kiliçkiran, Didem. "Migrant Homes: Ethnicity, Identity and Domestic Space Culture." *Constructing Place: Mind and Matter*. Ed. Sarah Menin. London: Routledge, 2003. 99–110.

Kilroy, James F. *The Nineteenth-Century English Novel: Family Ideology and Narrative Form*. Basingstoke: Palgrave Macmillan, 2007.

Kimmich, Dorothee and Schamma Schahadat. "Vorwort: Essen." *Essen*. Eds. Dorothee Kimmich and Schamma Schahadat. Bielefeld: transcript, 2012. 7–18.

King, Bruce. "*My Ear at His Heart*: Review." *World Literature Today* 79.2 (2005): 89.

King, Russel, Anastasia Christou, and Peggy Levitt, eds. *Links to the Diasporic Homeland: Second Generation and Ancestral 'Return' Mobilities*. Abingdon: Routledge, 2014.

Koenig Kellas, Jody and April R. Trees. "Family Stories and Storytelling: Windows into the Family Soul." *The Routledge Handbook of Family Communication*. Second Edition. Ed. Anita L. Vangelisti. New York, NY: Routledge, 2013. 391–406.

Korte, Barbara and Klaus Peter Müller, eds. *Unity in Diversity Revisited? British Literature and Culture in the 1990s*. Tübingen: Gunter Narr, 1998.

Korte, Barbara. "Generationsbewußtsein als Element 'schwarzer' britischer Identitätsfiktion." *Literaturwissenschaftliches Jahrbuch* 40 (1999): 331–350.

Korte, Barbara and Eva Ulrike Pirker. *Black History – White History: Britain's Historical Programme between Windrush and Wilberforce*. Bielefeld: transcript, 2011.

Kraft, Andreas and Mark Weißhaupt. *Generationen: Erfahrung – Erzählung – Identität*. Konstanz: UVK Verlagsgesellschaft, 2009.

Kramer, Anne-Marie. "Kinship, Affinity and Connectedness: Exploring the Role of Genealogy in Personal Lives." *Sociology* 45.3 (2011): 379–395.

Kramer, Anne-Marie. "The Genomic Imaginary: Genealogical Heritage and the Shaping of Bioconvergent Identities." *Media Tropes* 1 (2015): 80–104. http://www.mediatropes.com/index.php/Mediatropes/article/view/22137 (accessed 12, April 2017).

Küey, Levent. "Trauma and Migration: The Role of Stigma." *Trauma and Migration: Cultural Factors in the Diagnosis and Treatment of Traumatised Immigrants*. Ed. Meryam Schouler-Ocak. London: Springer, 2015. 57–68.

Kuhn, Annette. *Family Secrets: Acts of Memory and Imagination*. London: Verso, 2002 [1995].

Kuhn, Annette. "Memory Texts and Memory Work: Performances of Memory in and with Visual Media." *Memory Studies* 3.4 (2010): 298–313.

Künemund, Harald and Marc Szydlik. "Generationen aus Sicht der Soziologie." *Generationen: Multidisziplinäre Perspektiven*. Eds. Harald Künemund and Marc Szydlik Wiesbaden: VS Verlag für Sozialwissenschaften, 2009. 7–22.

Kureishi, Hanif. 2004. "Things I Never Knew About My Father." *The Guardian*. 21 August, 2004. https://www.theguardian.com/books/2004/aug/21/biography.features (accessed 20 October, 2016).

Kureishi, Yasmin. "'Keep Me Out of Your Novels': Hanif Kureishi's Sister Has Had Enough." *Independent*. 4 March, 2008. http://www.independent.co.uk/arts-entertainment/books/features/keep-me-out-of-your-novels-hanif-kureishis-sister-has-had-enough-790839.html (accessed 20 October, 2016).

Kwak, Kyunghwa. "Adolescents and Their Parents: A Review of Intergenerational Family Relations for Immigrant and Non-Immigrant Families." *Human Development* 46 (2003): 115–136.

Laing, Ronald D. "The Family and the 'Family'." *The Politics of the Family, and other Essays*. London: Routledge, 1971 [1969]. 3–20.

Landsberg, Alison. *Prosthetic Memory: The Transformation of American Remembrance in the Age of Mass Culture*. New York, NY: Columbia University Press, 2004.

Langellier, Kristin M. and Eric E. Peterson. *Storytelling in Daily Life: Performing Narrative*. Philadelphia, PA: Temple University Press, 2004.

Langellier, Kristin M. and Eric E. Peterson. "Family Storytelling as Communication Practice." *The Family Communications Sourcebook*. Eds. Lynn H. Turner and Richard West. London: Sage, 2006. 109–128.

Langford, Martha. "Speaking the Album: An Application of the Oral-Photographic Framework." *Locating Memory: Photographic Acts*. Eds. Annette Kuhn and Kirsten Emiko McAllister. New York, NY: Berghahn, 2006. 223–246.

Langford, Martha. "Imagined Memories." *I Am My Family: Photographic Memories and Fictions*. Ed. Rafael Goldchain. New York, NY: Princeton Architectural Press, 2008. 10–15.

Lauer, Gerhard. "Einführung." *Literaturwissenschaftliche Beiträge zur Generationsforschung*. Ed. Gerhard Lauer. Göttingen: Wallstein, 2010. 7–21.

Lawler, Steph. *Identity: Sociological Perspectives*. Second Edition. Cambridge: Polity, 2014 [2008].

Lee-Von, Kim. "Scenes of Af/filiation: Family Photographs in Postcolonial Life Writing." *Life Writing* 12.4 (2015): 401–415.

Lemke, Cordula. "Racism in the Diaspora: Nadeem Aslam's *Maps for Lost Lovers* (2004)." *Multi-Ethnic Britain 2000+: New Perspectives in Literature, Film and the Arts*. Eds. Lars Eckstein et al. Amsterdam: Rodopi, 2008. 171–183.

Lenz, Claudia. "Genealogy and Archaeology: Analyzing Generational Positioning in Historical Narratives." *Journal of Comparative Family Studies* 42.3 (2011): 319–327.

LetsOpenOurWorld. "momondo – The DNA Journey." *YouTube*, 1 June, 2016. https://www.youtube.com/watch?v=tyaEQEmt5ls (accessed 24 April, 2017).

Levin, Irene and Jan Trost. "Understanding the Concept of Family." *Family Relations* 41.3 (1992): 348–351.

Lévi-Strauss, Claude. "Kleine Abhandlung in kulinarischer Ethnologie." *Theorien des Essens*. Eds. Kikuko Kashiwagi-Wetzel and Anne-Rose Meyer. Berlin: Suhrkamp Taschenbuch Wissenschaft, 2017 [1968]. 334–354.

Lévi-Strauss, Claude. "The Culinary Triangle." *Food and Culture: A Reader*. Eds. Caroline Counihan and Penny Van Esterik. London: Routledge, 2013 [1966]. 40–47.

Levy, Andrea. "This Is My England." *The Guardian*. 19 February, 2000. https://www.theguardian.com/books/2000/feb/19/society1 (accessed 23 May, 2014).

Liebsch, Katharina. "Identität." *Handbuch Körpersoziologie. Band 1: Grundbegriffe und theoretische Perspektiven*. Eds. Robert Gugutzer, Gabriele Klein, and Michael Meuser. Heidelberg: Springer, 2017. 39–43.
Lillge, Claudia and Anne-Rose Meyer. "Interkulturelle Dimensionen von Mahlzeiten." *Interkulturelle Mahlzeiten: Kulinarische Begegnungen und Kommunikation in der Literatur*. Eds. Claudia Lillge and Anne-Rose Meyer. Bielefeld: transcript, 2008. 11–22.
Lumsden, Allison. "Jackie Kay's Poetry and Prose: Constructing Identity." *Contemporary Scottish Women Writers*. Eds. Aileen Christianson and Allison Lumsden. Edinburgh: Edinburgh University Press, 2000. 79–94.
Lusin, Caroline. "Curry, Tins and Grotesque Bodies: Food, Cultural Boundaries and Identity in Anglo-Indian Life-Writing." *English Studies* 94.4 (2013): 468–488.
Lutosch, Heide. *Ende der Familie – Ende der Geschichte: Zum Familienroman bei Thomas Mann, Gabriel García Márquez und Michel Houellebecq*. Bielefeld: Aisthesis, 2007.
Macho, Thomas. "Stammbäume, Freiheitsbäume und Genlereligion: Anmerkungen zur Geschichte genealogischer Systeme." *Genealogie und Genetik: Schnittstellen zwischen Biologie und Kulturgeschichte*. Ed. Sigrid Weigel. Berlin: Akademie Verlag, 2002. 15–43.
Mannheim, Karl. "The Sociological Problem of Generations." *Younger than Jesus: The Generation Book*. Eds. Lauren Cornell, Massimiliano Gioni, Laura Hoptman, and Brian Sholis. Göttingen: Steidl, 2009 [1928; 1952]. 163–195.
Mannur, Anita. *Culinary Fictions: Food in South Asian Diasporic Culture*. Philadelphia, PA: Temple University Press, 2010.
Marre, Diana and Joan Bestard. "The Family Body: Persons, Bodies and Resemblance." *European Kinship in the Age of Biotechnology*. Eds. Jeanette Edwards and Carles Salazar. New York, NY: Berghahn, 2009. 64–78.
Mason, Jennifer. *Affinities: Potent Connections in Personal Life*. Cambridge: Polity, 2018.
Maza, Sara. "Only Connect: Family Values in the Age of Sentiment: Introduction." *Eighteenth-Century Studies* 30.3 (1997): 207–212. http://muse.jhu.edu/journals/eighteenth-century_studies/v030/30.3maza.html (accessed 24 April, 2014).
McAdams, Dan P. "Identity and the Life Story." *Autobiographical Memory and the Construction of a Narrative Self: Developmental and Cultural Perspectives*. Eds. Robyn Fivush and Catherine A. Haden. Mahwah, NJ: Lawrence Erlbaum, 2003. 187–207.
McAdams, Dan P. "The Problem of Narrative Coherence." *Journal of Constructivist Psychology* 19 (2006): 109–125.
McCrum, Robert. "Hanif Kureishi Interview: 'Every 10 Years You Become Someone Else'." *The Observer*. 19 January, 2014. https://www.theguardian.com/books/2014/jan/19/hanif-kureishi-interview-last-word (last accessed 22 June, 2016).
McCulloch, Fiona. *Cosmopolitanism in Contemporary British Fiction: Imagined Identities*. Houndsmills, Basingstoke: Palgrave Macmillan, 2012.
McLeod, John. "Extra Dimensions, New Routines: Contemporary Black Writing of Britain." *Wasafiri* 25.4 (2010): 45–52.
McLeod, John. *Life Lines: Writing Transcultural Adoption*. London: Bloomsbury, 2015.
McLeod, John. "Adoption Aesthetics." *The Cambridge Companion to British Black and Asian Literature (1945-2010)*. Ed. Deirdre Osborne. Cambridge: Cambridge University Press, 2016. 211–224.
Mennell, Stephen. *All Manners of Food: Eating and Taste in England and France from the Middle Ages to the Present*. Basingstoke: Blackwell, 1985.

Mergenthal, Silvia. "Acculturation and Family Structure: Mo's *Sour Sweet*, Kureishi's *The Buddha of Suburbia*, Ishiguro's *A Pale View of Hills*." *Defining New Idioms and Alternative Forms of Expression*. Ed. Eckhard Breitinger. Amsterdam: Rodopi, 1996. 119–127.

Meyer, Anne-Rose. "Einführung: Essen und Theorien des Essens. Interdisziplinäre Perspektiven." *Theorien des Essens*. Eds. Kikuko Kashiwagi-Wetzel and Anne-Rose Meyer. Berlin: Suhrkamp Taschenbuch Wissenschaft, 2017. 15–66.

Meyer, Scarlett. "Ritual and Narrative in the Intercultural British Novel at the Turn of the 21st Century." *Ritual and Narrative: Theoretical Explorations and Historical Case Studies*. Eds. Vera Nünning, Jan Rupp, and Gregor Ahn. Bielefeld: transcript, 2013. 217–236.

Minkmar, Nils. "Habt keine Angst!" *Frankfurter Allgemeine Sonntagszeitung* 30 March, 2014. 37.

Mirza, Heidi Safia. *Black British Feminism: A Reader*. London: Routledge, 1997.

Misztal, Barbara A. *Theories of Social Remembering*. London: Open University Press, 2003.

Mitchell, Marilyn. "Fitting Issues: The Visual Representation of Time in Family Tree Diagrams." *Sign Systems Studies* 42.2–3 (2014): 241–280.

Mitchell, W.J.T., ed. *On Narrative*. Chicago, IL: University of Chicago Press, 1981.

Montanari, Massimo. *Food Is Culture*. New York, NY: Columbia University Press, 2006. Online Edition: Ebrary. https://ebookcentral.proquest.com/lib/ub-heidelberg/detail.action?docID=908243 (last accessed 12 March, 2017).

Moore, Lindsey. "British Muslim Identities and Spectres of Terror in Nadeem Aslam's *Maps for Lost Lovers*." *Postcolonial Text* 5.2 (2008): 1-19.

Morgan, David H. J. *Family Connections: An Introduction to Family Studies*. Cambridge: Polity, 1996.

Morgan, David H. J. *Rethinking Family Practices*. Basingstoke: Palgrave Macmillan, 2011a.

Morgan, David H. J. "Locating 'Family Practices'." *Sociological Research Online* 16.4.14 (2011b): n.p. http://www.socresonline.org.uk/16/4/14.html (accessed 3 May, 2014).

Murdock, Peter. *Social Structure*. New York, NY: Free Press, 1949.

MyHeritage. https://www.myheritage.com (accessed 24 April, 2017).

Narayan, Uma. "Eating Cultures: Incorporation, Identity and Indian Food." *Social Identities: Journal for the Study of Race, Nation and Culture* 1.1 (1996): 63–86.

Nave-Herz, Rosemarie, ed. *Kontinuität und Wandel der Familie in Deutschland: Eine zeitgeschichtliche Analyse*. Stuttgart: Lucius & Lucius, 2007.

Nave-Herz, Rosemarie, ed. *Familiensoziologie: Ein Lehr- und Studienbuch*. München: de Gruyter, 2014.

Nave-Herz, Rosemarie. *Ehe- und Familiensoziologie: Eine Einführung in Geschichte, theoretische Ansätze und empirische Befunde*. Basel: Beltz, 2013.

Neisser, Ulric. "Five Kinds of Self-Knowledge." *Philosophical Psychology* 1.1 (1988): 35–59.

Nelson, Katherine and Robyn Fivush. "The Emergence of Autobiographical Memory: A Social Cultural Development Theory." *Psychological Review* 111.2 (2004): 486–511.

Nelson, Katherine. "Narrative and the Emergence of a Consciousness of Self." *Narrative and Consciousness: Literature, Psychology, and the Brain*. Eds. Gary D. Fireman, Ted E. McVay Jr., and Owen J. Flanagan. Oxford: Oxford University Press, 2003. 17–36.

Neti, Leila. "Siting Speech: The Politics of Imagining the Other in Meera Syal's *Anita and Me*." *British Asian Fiction: Framing the Contemporary*. Eds. Neil Murphy and Wai-chew Sim. Amherst, NY: Cambria Press, 2008. 97–118.

Neumann, Birgit and Ansgar Nünning. *An Introduction to the Study of Narrative Fiction*. Stuttgart: Klett, 2008.

Neumann, Birgit. "Literatur, Erinnerung, Identität." *Gedächtniskonzepte der Literaturwissenschaft: Theoretische Grundlegung und Anwendungsperspektiven*. Eds. Astrid Erll and Ansgar Nünning. Berlin: de Gruyter, 2005. 149–178.

Nünning, Ansgar and Kai Marcel Sicks, eds. *Turning Points: Concepts and Narratives of Change in Literature and Other Media*. Berlin: de Gruyter, 2012.

Nünning, Ansgar, Marion Gymnich, and Roy Sommer, eds. *Literature and Memory: Theoretical Paradigms, Genres, Functions*. Tübingen: Francke, 2006.

Nünning, Ansgar. "'With the Benefit of Hindsight': Features and Functions of Turning Points as a Narratological Concept and as a Way of Self-Making." *Turning Points: Concepts and Narratives of Change in Literature and Other Media*. Eds. Ansgar Nünning and Kai Marcel Sicks. Berlin: de Gruyter, 2012. 31–58.

Nünning, Vera and Ansgar Nünning. "Von 'der' Erzählperspektive zur Perspektivenstruktur narrative Texte: Überlegungen zur Definition, Konzeptualisierung und Untersuchbarkeit von Multiperspektivität." *Multiperspektivisches Erzählen: Zur Theorie und Geschichte der Perspektivenstruktur im englischen Roman des 18. bis 20. Jahrhunderts*. Eds. Vera Nünning and Ansgar Nünning. Trier: WVT, 2010. 3–38.

Nünning, Vera and Jan Rupp. "Ritual and Narrative: An Introduction." *Ritual and Narrative: Theoretical Explorations and Historical Case Studies*. Eds. Vera Nünning, Jan Rupp, and Gregor Ahn. Bielefeld: transcript, 2013. 1–24.

Nünning, Vera. "From Theory to Practice: New Approaches to Narrative." *New Approaches to Narrative: Cognition – Culture – History*. Ed. Vera Nünning. Trier: WVT, 2013. 1–20.

O'Reilly Herrera, Andrea, Elizabeth Mahn Nollen, and Sheila Reitzel Foor, eds. *Family Matters in the British and American Novel*. Bowling Green, OH: Bowling Green State University Popular Press, 1997.

O'Riley, Michael F. "Postcolonial Haunting: Anxiety, Affect, and the Situated Encounter." *Postcolonial Text* 3.4 (2007): 1–15.

Osborne, Deirdre, ed. *The Cambridge Companion to British Black and Asian Literature (1945-2010)*. Cambridge: Cambridge University Press, 2016.

Ott, Christine. *Identität geht durch den Magen: Mythen der Esskultur*. Frankfurt a.M.: S. Fischer, 2017.

Parasecoli, Fabio. "Savoring Semiotics: Food in Intercultural Communication." *Social Semiotics* 21.5 (2011): 645–663.

Parnes, Ohad, Ulrike Vedder, and Stefan Willer. *Das Konzept der Generation: Eine Wissenschafts- und Kulturgeschichte*. Frankfurt a.M.: Suhrkamp, 2008.

Parry, Benita. "Problems in Current Theories of Colonial Discourse." *The Post-Colonial Studies Reader*. Eds. Bill Ashcroft, Gareth Griffiths, and Helen Tiffin. London: Routledge, 1995. 36–44.

Parsons, Talcott. "The American Family: Its Relations to Personality and to the Social Structure." *Family, Socialization and Interaction Process*. Eds. Talcott Parsons and Robert F. Bale. Glencoe, IL: The Free Press, 1955. 3–33.

Pérez Fernández, Irene. "Exploring Hybridity and Multiculturalism: Intra and Inter Family Relations in Zadie Smith's *White Teeth*." *Odisea* 10 (2009): 143–154.

Petronio, Sandra. *Boundaries of Privacy: Dialectics of Disclosure*. Albany, NY: State University of New York Press, 2002.

Plahl, Silvia. "Familienbande: Die Rolle der Vorfahren in der Psychotherapie." *SWR 2 Wissen*. 25 May, 2016. http://www.swr.de/swr2/programm/sendungen/wissen/familienbande-

vorfahren-in-der-psychotherapie/-/id=660374/did=17258252/nid=660374/8a2rnc/index.html (accessed 3 Dec, 2016).
Prillinger, Horst. *Family and the Scottish Working-Class Novel 1984–1994: A Study of Novels by Janice Galloway et al.* Frankfurt a.M.: Peter Lang, 2000.
Procter, James. *Dwelling Places: Postwar Black British Writing.* Manchester: Manchester University Press, 2003.
Procter, James. "New Ethnicities, the Novel, and the Burdens of Representation." *A Concise Companion to Contemporary British Fiction.* Ed. James F. English. Malden, MA: Blackwell, 2006. 101–120.
Rashid, C.E. "British Islam and the Novel of Transformation: Robin Yassin-Kassab's *The Road from Damascus.*" *Journal of Postcolonial Writing* 48.1 (2014): 92–103.
Reichl, Susanne. *Cultures in the Contact Zone: Ethnic Semiosis in Black British Literature.* Trier: WVT, 2002.
Reynolds, Tracey. "Family and Community Networks in the (Re)Making of Ethnic Identity of Caribbean Young People in Britain." *Community, Work and Family* 9.3 (2006): 273–290.
Rimmon-Kenan, Shlomith. "Concepts of Narrative." *The Travelling Concept of Narrative.* Eds. Matti Hyvärinen, Anu Korhonen, and Juri Mykkänen. Helsinki: Helsinki Collegium for Advanced Studies, 2006. 10–19.
Rogers, Edna L. "Introduction: A Reflective View on the Development of Family Communication." *The Family Communications Sourcebook.* Eds. Lynn H. Turner and Richard West. London: Sage, 2006. xv–xx.
Rose, Gillian. *Doing Family Photography: The Domestic, the Public and the Politics of Sentiment.* Surrey: Ashgate, 2010.
Roseman, Mark. "Generationen als 'Imagined Communities': Mythen, generationelle Identitäten und Generationenkonflikte in Deutschland vom 18. bis zum 20. Jahrhundert." *Generationen: Zur Relevanz eines wissenschaftlichen Grundbegriffs.* Eds. Ulrike Jureit and Michael Wildt. Hamburg: Hamburger Edition, 2005. 180–199.
Rothberg, Michael. "Remembering Back: Cultural Memory, Colonial Legacies, and Postcolonial Studies." *The Oxford Handbook of Postcolonial Studies.* Ed. Graham Huggan. Oxford: Oxford Handbooks Online, 2013. doi: 10.1093/oxfordhb/9780199588251.013.0027.
Ru, Yi-ling. *The Family Novel: Toward a Generic Definition.* Frankfurt a.M.: Lang, 1992.
Rüggemeier, Anne. *Die relationale Autobiographie: Ein Beitrag zur Theorie, Poetik und Gattungsgeschichte eines neuen Genres in der englischsprachigen Erzählliteratur.* Trier: WVT, 2014.
Rupp, Jan. *Genre and Cultural Memory in Black British Literature.* Trier: WVT, 2010.
Rupp, Jan. "Fictions of Cultural Memory and Generations: Challenging Englishness in Zadie Smith's *White Teeth* (2000) and Nadeem Aslaam's *Maps for Lost Lovers* (2004)." *The English Novel in the 21st Century: Cultural Concerns – Literary Developments – Model Interpretations.* Eds. Vera Nünning and Ansgar Nünning. Trier: WVT, 2017.
Rutherford, Jennifer. *Zombies.* London: Routledge, 2013.
Sabourin, Teresa C. "Theories and Metatheories to Explain Family Communication." *The Family Communications Sourcebook.* Eds. Lynn H. Turner and Richard West. London: Sage, 2006. 43–59.
Sáez, Elena Machado. "Bittersweet (Be)Longing: Filling the Void of History in Andrea Levy's *Fruit of the Lemon.*" *Anthurium: A Caribbean Studies Journal* 4.1 (2006): Article 5.
Schachter, Elli P. "Context and Identity Formation: A Theoretical Analysis and a Case Study." *Journal of Adolescent Research* 20.3 (2005): 375–395.

Schacter, Daniel L. and Endel Tulving. "Memory, Amnesia, and the Episodic/Semantic Distinction." *The Expression of Knowledge: Neurobehavioral Transformations of Information into Action*. Eds. Robert L. Isaacson and Norman E. Spear. New York, NY: Plenum Press, 1982. 33–65.
Schäfer, Stefanie. "'Looking Back, You Do Not Find What You Left Behind': Postcolonial Subjectivity and the Role of Memory in *White Teeth* and *The Inheritance of Loss*." *'Hello, I say, It's Me': Contemporary Reconstructions of Self and Subjectivity*. Eds. Jan D. Kucharzewski, Stefanie Schäfer and Lutz Schowalter. Trier: WVT, 2009. 107–127.
Schier, Michaela and Karin Jurczyk. "'Familie als Herstellungsleistung' in Zeiten der Entgrenzung." *Sozialwissenschaftlicher Fachinformationsdienst soFid* 1 (2008): 9–18.
Schier, Michaela. "Räumliche Entgrenzung von Arbeit und Familie: Die Herstellung von Familie unter Bedingungen von Multilokalität." *Informationen zur Raumentwicklung* 1.2 (2009): 55–66.
Schlör, Joachim. "Means of Transport and Storage: Suitcases and other Containers for the Memory of Migration and Displacement." *Jewish Culture and History* 15.1–2 (2014): 76–92.
Schneider, David. *American Kinship: A Cultural Account*. Chicago, IL: University of Chicago Press, 1968.
Schneider, David. *A Critique of the Study of Kinship*. Ann Arbor, MI: University of Michigan Press, 1984.
Schneider, Norbert. "Familie in Westeuropa." *Handbuch Familiensoziologie*. Eds. Paul Bernhard Hill and Johannes Kopp. Wiesbaden: Springer, 2015. 21–53.
Scholliers, Peter, ed. *Food, Drink and Identity: Cooking, Eating and Drinking in Europe since the Middle Ages*. Oxford: Berg, 2001.
Schouler-Ocak, Meryam, ed. *Trauma and Migration: Cultural Factors in the Diagnosis and Treatment of Traumatised Immigrants*. London: Springer, 2015.
Schwanecke, Christine. *Intermedial Storytelling: Thematisation, Imitation and Incorporation of Photography in English and American Fiction at the Turn of the 21st Century*. Trier: WVT, 2012.
Scott, Jaqueline, Judith Treas, and Martin Richards. "Preface." *The Blackwell Companion to the Sociology of Families*. Eds. Jaqueline Scott, Judith Treas, and Martin Richards. Malden, MA: Blackwell, 2003. xv–xxv.
Scott, Susie. *Making Sense of Everyday Life*. Cambridge: Polity, 2009.
Seemann, Daphne. "The Re-Construction and Deconstruction of a Family Narrative: Eva Menasse's *Vienna*." *Transitions: Emerging Women Writers in German-Language Literature*. Eds. Valerie Heffernan and Gillian Pye. Amsterdam: Rodopi 2013. 35–51.
Segrin, Chris and Jeanne Flora. *Family Communication*. Second Edition. London: Routledge, 2011.
Sesay, Kadija, ed. *Write Black, Write British: From Post-Colonial to Black British Literature*. Hertford: Hansib,2005.
Sesay, Kadija. "Transformations within the Black British Novel." *Black British Writing*. Eds. R. Victoria Arana and Lauri Ramey. New York: Palgrave Macmillan, 2004. 99–108.
Shaw, Alison. *Kinship and Continuity: Pakistani Families in Britain*. London: Routledge, 2000.
Shevchenko, Olga, ed. *Double Exposure: Memory & Photography*. New York: Transaction, 2014a.
Shevchenko, Olga. "Memory and Photography: An Introduction." *Double Exposure: Memory & Photography*. Ed. Olga Shevchenko. New York, NY: Transaction, 2014b. 1–18.

Shevchenko, Olga. "'The Mirror with a Memory': Placing Photography in Memory Studies." *Routledge International Handbook of Memory Studies*. Eds. Anna Lisa Tota and Trever Hagen. London: Routledge, 2016. 272–287.

Shore, Bradd. "Family Time: Studying Myth and Ritual in Working Families." *The Emory Center for Myth and Ritual in American Life*. Working Paper No. 27, 2003. http://citeseerx.ist.psu.edu/viewdoc/summary?doi=10.1.1.194.3370 (accessed April 14, 2014).

Sinha, Cynthia B. "Dynamic Parenting: Ethnic Identity Construction in the Second-Generation Indian American Family." *Sociology Dissertations*, 2010. Paper 59.

Smart, Carol. *Personal Life: New Directions in Sociological Thinking*. Cambridge: Polity, 2007.

Smart, Carol. "Families, Secrets and Memories." *Sociology* 45.4 (2011a): 539–553.

Smart, Carol. "Relationality and Socio-Cultural Theories of Family Life." *Families and Kingship in Contemporary Europe*. Eds. Riitta Jallinoja and Eric D. Widmer. Basingstoke: Palgrave Macmillan, 2011b. 13–28.

Snoek, Jan A. M. "Defining 'Rituals'." *Theorizing Rituals, Vol.1: Issues, Topics, Approaches, Concepts*. Eds. Jens Kreinath, Jan Snoek, and Michael Strausberg. Leiden: Brill, 2006. 3–14.

Sobral, Ana. *Opting Out: Deviance and Generational Identities in American Post-War Cult Fiction*. Amsterdam: Rodopi, 2012.

Sollors, Werner. "First Generation, Second Generation, Third Generation …: The Cultural Construction of Descent." *Beyond Ethnicity: Consent and Descent in American Culture*. Ed. Werner Sollors. Oxford: Oxford University Press, 1986. 208–236.

Sommer, Roy. *Fictions of Migration: Ein Beitrag zur Theorie und Gattungstypologie des zeitgenössischen interkulturellen Romans in Großbritannien*. Trier: WVT, 2001.

Sontag, Susan. *On Photography*. Harmondsworth: Penguin, 1977.

Spivak, Gayatri Chakravorty. "Imperialism and Sexual Difference." *Oxford Literary Review* 8.1 (1986): 225–244.

Stano, Simona. "Introduction: Semiotics of Food." *Semiotica* 211 (2016): 19–26.

Stein, Mark. "The Black British *Bildungsroman* and the Transformation of Britain: Connectedness across Difference." *Unity in Diversity Revisited? British Literature and Culture in the 1990s*. Eds. Barbara Korte and Klaus Peter Müller. Tübingen: Gunter Narr, 1998. 89–105.

Stein, Mark. "Bildungsroman." *Companion to Contemporary Black British Culture*. Ed. Alison Donnell. London: Routledge, 2002. 34–35.

Stein, Mark. *Black British Literature: Novels of Transformation*. Columbus, OH: The Ohio State University Press, 2004.

Strathern, Marilyn. *After Nature: English Kinship in the Late Twentieth Century*. Cambridge: Cambridge University Press, 1992.

Sundholm, John. "The Cultural Trauma Process, or the Ethics and Mobility of Memory." *Memory and Migration: Multidisciplinary Approaches to Memory Studies*. Eds. Julia Creet and Andreas Kitzmann. Toronto: University of Toronto Press, 2011. 120–134.

Sürig, Inken and Maren Wilmes. *The Integration of the Second Generation in Germany: Results of the TIES Survey on the Descendants of Turkish and Yugloslavian Migrants*. Amsterdam: Amsterdam University Press, 2015.

Thomas, Susie. "Hanif Kureishi's *My Ear at His Heart*: 'When a Writer Is Born a Family Dies'." *Changing English: Studies in Culture and Education* 13.2 (2006): 185–196.

Thompson, Blair, Jody Koenig Kellas, Jordan Soliz, Amber Epp, Jason Thompson, and Paul Schrodt. "Family Legacies: Constructing Individual and Family Identity through Intergenerational Storytelling." *Narrative Inquiry* 19.1 (2009): 106–134.
Thompson, Molly. "'Happy Multicultural Land'? The Implications of an 'Excess of Belonging' in Zadie Smith's *White Teeth*." *Write Black, Write British: From Post Colonial to Black British Literature*. Ed. Kadija Sesay. Hertford: Hansib, 2005. 122–140.
Toates, Frederick. "The Embodied Self: A Biological Perspective." *Understanding the Self*. Ed. Richard Stevens. London: Sage, 1996. 35–88.
Toplu, Şebnem. "Home(land) or 'Motherland': Transnational Identities in Andrea Levy's *Fruit of the Lemon*." *Anthurium: A Caribbean Studies Journal* 3.1 (2005): Article 6.
Tournay-Theodotou, Petra. "Some Connection with the Place: Jackie Kay's *Red Dust Road*." *Wasafiri* 29.1 (2014): 15–20.
Turner, Bryan S. *The Body & Society: Explorations in Social Theory*. Third Edition. London: Sage 2008.
Turner, Jonathan. *Contemporary Sociological Theory*. London: Sage, 2013.
Turner, Lynn H. and Richard West. "Preface." *The Family Communications Sourcebook*. Eds. Lynn H. Turner and Richard West. London: Sage, 2006. ix–xiv.
Upstone, Sara. *British Asian Fiction: Twenty-First-Century Voices*. Manchester: Manchester University Press, 2010.
van den Berghe, Pierre L. "Ethnic Cuisine: Culture in Nature." *Ethnic and Racial Studies* 7.3 (1984): 387–397.
Vangelisti, Anita L. "Preface." *Handbook of Family Communication*. Ed. Anita L. Vangelisti. Mahwah, NJ: Lawrence Erlbaum, 2003. ix–xii.
Veracini, Lorenzo. "Historylessness: Australia as a Settler Colonial Collective." *Postcolonial Studies* 10.3 (2007): 271–285.
Visser, Irene. "Introduction." *Family Fictions: The Family in Contemporary Postcolonial Literatures in English*. Eds. Irene Visser and Heidi van den Heuvel-Disler. Groningen: Centre for Development Studies, 2005. 5–13. https://www.rug.nl/research/globalisation-studies-groningen/cds/publications/familyfictions.pdf (last accessed 1 May, 2017)
Walters, Tracey L. "'We're All English Now Mate Like It or Lump It': The Black/Britishness of Zadie Smith's *White Teeth*." *Write Black, Write British: From Post Colonial to Black British Literature*. Ed. Kadija Sesay. Hertford: Hansib, 2015. 314–322.
Waterman, David. "Memory and Cultural Identity: Negotiating Modernity in Nadeem Aslam's *Maps for Lost Lovers*." *Pakistaniaat: A Journal of Pakistan Studies* 2.2 (2010): 18–35.
Weedon, Chris. *Identity & Culture: Narratives of Difference & Belonging*. Maidenhead: Open University Press, 2004a.
Weedon, Chris. "Identity and Belonging in Contemporary Black British Writing." *Black British Writing*. Eds. R. Victoria Arana and Lauri Ramey. Basingstoke: Palgrave Macmillan, 2004b. 73–97.
Weedon, Chris. "Tropes of Diasporic Life in the Work of Nadeem Aslam." *Metaphor and Diaspora in Contemporary Writing*. Ed. Jonathan P. A. Sell. Basingstoke: Palgrave Macmillan, 2012. 20–38.
Weedon, Chris. "British Black and Asian Writing since 1980." *The Cambridge Companion to British Black and Asian Literature (1945–2010)*. Ed. Deirdre Osborne. Cambridge: Cambridge University Press, 2016. 40–56.
Weigel, Sigrid. "Generation, Genealogie, Geschlecht: Zur Geschichte des Generationenkonzepts und seiner wissenschaftlichen Konzeptualisierung seit dem Ende des 18. Jahrhun-

derts." *Kulturwissenschaften: Forschung – Praxis – Positionen*. Eds. Lutz Musner and Gotthard Wunberg. Wien: WUV, 2002. 161–190.

Weigel, Sigrid. "Familienbande, Phantome und die Vergangenheitspolitik des Generationsdiskurses: Abwehr von und Sehnsucht nach Herkunft" *Generationen: Zur Relevanz eines wissenschaftlichen Grundbegriffs*. Eds. Ulrike Jureit and Michael Wildt. Hamburg: Hamburger Edition, 2005. 108–126.

Weigel, Sigrid. *Genea-Logik: Generation, Tradition und Evolution zwischen Kultur- und Naturwissenschaften*. München: Wilhelm Fink, 2006.

Weingarten, Jutta. "Die Emanzipation der Subalternen: Monica Alis interkultureller Familienroman *Brick Lane*." *Die interkulturelle Familie: Literatur- und sozialwissenschaftliche Perspektiven*. Eds. Michaela Holdenried and Weertje Willms. Bielefeld: transcript, 2012. 177–193.

Weingarten, Jutta. *Narrating Generations: Representations of Generationality and Genealogy in Contemporary British Asian Narratives*. Giessen: GEB – Giessener Elektronische Bibliothek, 2014. Available at: http://geb.uni-giessen.de/geb/volltexte/2014/11017/ (accessed 3 November, 2015).

Welzer, Harald. "Schön unscharf: Über die Konjunktur der Familien- und Generationenromane." *Literatur: Beilage zum Mittelweg* 36.1 (2004): 53–64.

Wessendorf, Susanne. *Second-Generation Transnationalism and Roots Migration: Cross-Border Lives*. London: Routledge, 2013.

Widmer, Eric D. *Family Configurations: A Structural Approach to Family Diversity*. London: Ashgate, 2010.

Willer, Stefan, Sigrid Weigel, and Bernhard Jussen. "Erbe, Erbschaft, Vererbung: Eine aktuelle Problemlage und ihr historischer Kontext." *Erbe: Übertragungskonzepte zwischen Natur und Kultur*. Eds. Stefan Willer, Sigrid Weigel, and Bernhard Jussen. Berlin: Suhrkamp, 2013. 7–36.

Wilson, Janet. "The Family and Change: Contemporary Second-Generation British-Asian Fiction." *Family Fictions: The Family in Contemporary Postcolonial Literatures in English*. Eds. Irene Visser and Heidi van den Heuvel-Disler. Groningen: Centre for Development Studies, 2005. 109–120. https://www.rug.nl/research/globalisation-studies-groningen/cds/publications/familyfictions.pdf (last accessed 1 May, 2017)

Winter, Jay. *Remembering War: The Great War Between Memory and History in the Twentieth Century*. New Haven, CT: Yale University Press, 2006.

Winter, Jay. "Thinking about Silence." *Shadows of War: A Social History of Silence in the Twentieth Century*. Eds. Efrat Ben-Ze'ev, Ruth Ginio, and Jay Winter. Cambridge: Cambridge University Press, 2010. 3–31.

Winter, Jay. "Foreword." *History, Memory and Migration: Perceptions of the Past and the Politics of Incorporation*. Eds. Irial Glynn and J. Olaf Kleist. Basingstoke: Palgrave Macmillan, 2012. viii–xi.

Winter, Jay. "From Silent Film to Filmic Silence: Thinking about Silence in Film." *Schweigen*. Eds. Aleida Assmann and Jan Assmann. München: Wilhelm Fink. 245–271.

Wolin, Steven J. and Linda A. Bennett. "Family Rituals." *Family Process* 23.3 (1984): 401–420. doi: 10.1111/j.1545-5300.1984.00401.x (accessed May 29, 2014)

Yaqin, Amina. "Muslims as Multicultural Misfits in Nadeem Aslam's *Maps for Lost Lovers*." *Culture, Diaspora, and Modernity in Muslim Writing*. Eds. Rehana Ahmed, Peter Morey and Amina Yaqin. London: Routledge, 2012. 101–116.

Yassin-Kassab, Robin. "*Maps for Lost Lovers* and Writerly Responsibility." *qunfuz* 06 February, 2008. Available at http://qunfuz.blogspot.de/ 2008/02/maps-for-lost-lovers-and-writerly.html (accessed 12 May, 2015).

Zerubavel, Eviatar. *Time Maps: Collective Memory and the Social Shape of the Past*. Chicago, IL: University of Chicago Press, 2003.

Zerubavel, Eviatar. *Ancestors & Relatives: Genealogy, Identity, & Community*. Oxford: Oxford University Press, 2012.

Zielke, Barbara and Jürgen Straub. "Culture, Psychotherapy, and the Diasporic Self as Transitoric Identity: A Reply to Social Constructionist and Postmodern Concepts of Narrative Psychotherapy." *Meaning in Action: Constructions, Narratives, and Representations*. Eds. Toshio Sugiman, Kenneth J. Gergen, Wolfgang Wagner and Yoko Yamada. Tokyo: Springer, 2008. 49–72.

Index

Abraham, Nicolas 65
Adams, Gerard 37, 39f.
Adichie, Chimamanda Ngozi 215
adoption narrative 213, 218ff., 223
Ae Fond Kiss 6
African American Lives, TV series 71
Ahmed, Rehana 141, 143, 168
Ahmed, Sara 92, 94, 240, 242, 244
Alexander, Jeffrey C. 149
Ali, Monica
– *Brick Lane* 14f.
ancestry 22, 48, 71f., 74, 76, 110, 120, 128
Anderson, Benedict 31
anthropology 20f., 23, 43, 46
Arana, Victoria 13, 74
archive 55, 120, 201f., 209, 233, 247f., 251ff., 259f.
Arnett, Jeffrey 41
Arnold-de Simine, Silke 249ff.
Asendorpf, Jens B. 45
Aslam, Nadeem 166
– *Maps for Lost Lovers* 18, 60, 62f., 78, 143, 145, 149f., 159, 166, 185ff., 238, 241, 244ff., 251f.
Assmann, Aleida 9, 51, 55, 57, 60f., 70, 73, 75, 88, 105, 213, 230, 247f.
Assmann, Jan 57, 61
Augé, Marc 227
auto/biography 10, 188

Barthes, Roland 236f.
Bauer, Joachim 65, 75
Bauman, Zygmunt 25
Baumeister, Roy F. 45
Beck, Ulrich 24ff.
Beck-Gernsheim, Elizabeth 24ff.
Belle Vue Studio photo archive 251
Bend It like Beckham 6, 41, 87
Benjamin, Jessica 38
Bennett, Linda A. 34
Benson, Mark J. 37, 39
Berghahn, Daniela 4, 8, 13, 25, 27, 238
Bestard, Joan 253, 255ff.

bildungsroman 6f., 17f., 81, 101ff., 122, 139, 167, 180
– Black British *bildungsroman* 4, 81, 102, 122, 140
Black and Asian British writing 6, 13, 18f., 70, 74, 81, 87, 122, 141
– generations of Black and Asian British writing 3ff., 16
Black British 2ff., 142, 261
Black-ish, TV series 20
Blake, William
– *Jerusalem* 112, 128
blood relation 45, 84, 211f., 232
Bochner, Arthur 11, 30ff., 60, 213
body 5ff., 44f., 64, 93f., 96, 114, 126, 137, 159f., 162, 164, 171, 182, 219, 235f., 238, 240, 253ff., 257ff.
Bohanek, Jennifer 49, 54, 59
boundaries 35, 66, 143, 146, 150f., 154, 179, 186, 245, 253
Bouquet, Mary 129f.
Bourdieu, Pierre 44
Box, Sally J. 32f.
Boyers, Robert 17
Brah, Avtar 242ff., 246
Brähler, Susanne 117, 243, 247
Brien, Lee 237
Brinker-von der Heyde, Claudia 2, 11
British Empire 18, 62, 67, 123, 150, 193
British Islam 141f., 172
British Muslim writing 18, 141f.
British Muslims 2, 141f., 145, 166, 172
Bromley, Roger 13, 95, 97, 102, 114, 119f., 129, 139f., 243
Bronfenbrenner, Urie 40, 45
Bruner, Jerome 10, 50f., 78f.
Brunow, Dagmar 15f.
Burkitt, Ian 38, 42, 44f.
Butt, Nadia 3, 15, 69

Campt, Tina 251
Carsten, Janet 11, 20, 46f., 62, 202, 240
Castañeda, Claudia 71, 76, 130

Index

Chamberlain, Mary 49, 53, 70, 109, 117ff., 130
Chambers, Claire 141f., 144f., 167, 173
Chambers, Deborah 11, 22, 24ff., 36, 39, 47
Chen, Serena 38
Childs, Peter 142f., 148
Clifford, James 148
collectivism and individualism 25, 46, 72, 84f.
colonialism 62, 67, 98, 111, 127, 136, 150, 260
communication studies 30, 34, 49, 58
Cooper, David Graham 20
Costagli, Simone 17
Côté, James 41
Couser, Thomas G. 188ff., 192, 202, 209, 233f.
Csáky, Moritz 237, 239

Davies, Ray
– "Yours Truly, Confused N10" 112
Davis, Rocío G. 147f.
Deal, James E. 37, 39
Derrida, Jacques 44, 147
detraditionalisation 22, 25, 27
diaspora 15, 69, 86f., 103, 121, 148, 150, 244, 251
diasporic self 224
DNA 46, 48, 70f., 211, 220, 239, 259
Douglas, Mary 150f., 239

Eakin, John Paul 5, 8, 10, 22, 38, 40, 42, 45, 48f., 51, 53, 88, 188f., 208
East Is East 6, 41
Eckstein, Lars 13
Edwards, Rosalind 11, 20, 27f., 243
Elias, Norbert 44
Ellis, Alicia E. 106, 124, 260
embeddedness 22, 37, 42f., 49, 52, 72, 165, 188, 190, 195, 231, 255
Emory Center for Myth and Ritual in American Life 32
Empire Windrush 74, 105
Englishness 4, 82f., 93, 106f., 110, 112ff., 117, 120f., 125f., 128, 135
epigenetics 45, 65, 75, 220

Erll, Astrid 10, 12, 15ff., 19, 28, 51ff., 57, 61ff., 68f., 72, 74f., 122ff., 131, 136f., 140, 260
Evaristo, Bernardine
– *Lara* 6, 18
Eyerman, Ron 9, 117, 149

family
– concept of family 8, 11, 22, 27, 29, 36, 77, 235, 251
– death of the family 20, 27
– decline of the family 22, 25, 27, 29, 31, 36
– diachronic family 13f., 21f., 28, 34, 47, 56, 70, 78, 112, 159, 190, 242f.
– displaying family 11, 28, 35f., 239f., 250f.
– doing family 11, 29, 32, 35, 42, 44, 75, 77ff., 189, 199, 203, 213, 235f., 239, 241, 243, 249, 253, 255, 259f.
– families we live by 31, 35, 157, 213
– family as imagined community 31
– family configurations 11, 14, 28
– family history 4ff., 18, 21, 48f., 52, 64, 72f., 78, 88, 90, 98, 103, 105, 109ff., 113ff., 118ff., 123ff., 127, 129ff., 135f., 138f., 160, 164, 177ff., 185, 190, 201ff., 206, 213ff., 229ff., 233
– family imaginary 31ff., 35, 42, 60, 157, 236
– family interaction 30, 33, 59, 61
– family legacy 32, 49, 51, 55f., 64, 75, 85, 98, 136, 161, 164, 168, 173ff., 177, 184, 186, 192ff., 200f.
– family myth 14, 31ff., 36, 48, 55, 60, 79, 106, 124, 136, 139, 185, 205, 207ff., 221, 232ff., 238
– family of choice 21, 127
– family of origin 21, 43, 127, 155, 159
– family of procreation 155, 159, 218
– family photo album 108, 110, 246, 248, 250
– family photographs 31f., 57, 87, 90, 96, 128, 133ff., 177f., 185, 197, 201ff., 206f., 228, 231, 233, 236, 248ff.
– family practices 22, 28ff., 33, 35ff., 41f., 49, 60, 83, 86f., 159, 193, 199, 211, 236, 239f., 242f., 246, 249f.
– family resemblances 6, 45, 253ff., 259
– family rituals 31ff., 35f., 48, 60, 85f., 213, 217, 233
– family routines 33, 60, 213

- family sociology 22f., 26, 28f., 42
- family stories 30, 32, 35f., 48, 51, 55ff., 67, 78, 98, 102, 118, 121, 132, 213ff., 217ff.
- family storytelling 30f., 33f., 49, 58ff., 64, 78, 88, 118, 131, 213, 215ff., 221, 223, 233, 249, 256f.
- family studies 20, 32, 34, 37, 41, 46
- family tree 71, 75f., 103, 105, 111, 113, 118ff., 128ff., 139
- nuclear family 7, 11, 24, 27f., 49, 73, 81, 111
- synchronic family 13f., 21f., 34, 47, 49, 56, 70, 112, 159, 190, 241, 253
family memoir 19, 189f., 209, 232f.
family novel 7, 15ff., 63, 82, 122, 139
family writing 17f., 242, 247, 261
Farnell, Piatti 237
fictions of migration 3, 81
Fiese, Barbara 33f., 36f., 58f., 216f., 220
filiation 72, 189f., 204, 234
- narratives of filiation 189f., 234
Finch, Janet 11, 29, 35, 43, 240, 250
Fink, Janet 22
Fivush, Robyn 49, 51, 53f., 56ff., 65f., 85, 138, 213, 217f.
Flora, Jeanne 54, 178, 235
food 29, 47, 83, 86f., 110, 161, 182, 236ff., 243, 246, 253
Foucault, Michel 44
Frank, Tobias 13, 81ff., 90, 96f., 100, 102, 104, 106, 112, 114, 116, 119

Galli, Matteo 17
Galvin, Kathleen M. 11, 32f., 35
Gates, Henry Louis 71
gender 12, 27, 38, 47, 54, 160, 238f., 245
genealogy 4, 9, 16, 21, 43, 48f., 52, 70ff., 74, 76, 105, 113, 123, 126, 130, 140, 142, 163, 210f.
- genealogical imagination 49, 72, 76
- genealogical research 48, 71, 120
generation
- family generations 9, 17, 25, 73, 144
- generational memory 55
- generational places 230, 234
- generational relations 73
- generationality 16f., 123, 158

- intergenerational conflict 6, 12f., 17, 41, 81, 87, 92, 123, 158, 200, 240, 245
- intergenerational dynamics 73
- social generations 9, 73, 144
- the concept of generation 7f., 73
genetic inheritance 5, 45f., 48, 218, 253
Gergen, Kenneth J. 38
Geulen, Dieter 39
Giddens, Anthony 24, 26
Gillis, John 31f., 60, 213
Gilroy, Paul 86
Glynn, Irial 70, 111
Gomila, Antònia 249ff.
Grant, Linda
- *The Clothes on Their Backs* 19
green and pleasant land 112, 125
Green, James R. 148
Gross, Neil 24, 26f., 36
Gugutzer, Robert 254
Gunew, Sneja 238
Gunning, Dave 13, 81, 102
Gurnah, Abdulrazak
- *Dottie* 6
Gymnich, Marion 10

Haddad, Saleem
- *Guapa* 157
Haden, Catherine A. 51, 53
Haeckel, Ernst
- *Pedigree of Man* 129
- *Tree of Life* 76
Halbwachs, Maurice 51ff., 68
Hall, Stuart 1, 142
Hanson, Clare 219ff.
haunting 1, 43, 156, 164, 179, 181, 186f., 204
hauntology 147
Hecht, Anat 246f.
heirlooms 113, 178, 246
Helfferich, Cornelia 12
heredity 2, 65, 130
heritability 45
heritage 2, 106, 109f., 123, 126, 128, 137, 141, 169, 225f., 231, 258
- family heritage 110, 172, 174, 204
- family heritage industry 48, 76
Herman, David 50
Hill, Paul B. 28, 39

Hirsch, Juliane 251, 254
Hirsch, Marianne 32, 64f., 74, 108, 122, 140, 167, 248ff., 252, 261
history
- entangled history 15, 63, 120ff., 136, 170, 187
- global history 68
- history and family memory 15, 19, 61, 63, 138, 163f., 168, 170, 175, 187, 214, 230, 260f.
- oral history 120, 129, 139
historylessness 111, 124f.
Holdenried, Michaela 12f., 16
home 47, 236, 240ff., 250, 253, 260
- dwelling 244
- family home 152ff., 157, 241, 243ff., 248
- migrant homes 244
homing desire 244, 247
Howell, Signe 220
Huggan, Graham 13

identity
- intersection of individual and collective identities 8, 21, 36, 61, 79
- narrative identity 9f., 38, 50
- performative identity 6, 93, 139, 240
- relational identity 8, 22f., 37f., 41
imagined communities 9, 74
individualisation 22, 24
individualisation thesis 23f., 26, 29, 37, 42
inheritance 65, 73, 75, 130, 186, 200, 211, 218, 234, 253, 255, 259
intermediality 252
intimacy 11, 23f., 27f., 66, 77, 154, 159, 206, 212, 242, 251, 255
Iser, Wolfgang 221
Islamophobia 142, 172

Jallinoja, Riitta 11, 37
James, William 37
Jorgenson, Jane 11, 30ff., 60, 213
Jurczyk, Karin 77
Jureit, Ulrike 9

Kay, Jackie
- *Red Dust Road* 18, 59, 190f., 210, 212, 215, 218, 233, 239, 255f., 258

- *The Adoption Papers* 5, 210
Kershen, Anne J. 237ff.
Keupp, Heiner 44
Kiliçkiran, Didem 245
Kimmich, Dorothee 237f.
kinship 8, 24, 41, 43, 46f., 70ff., 76, 108, 110, 119, 121, 131, 138, 155, 160ff., 212, 257, 259
- milk kinship 47
kinship studies 42f., 46, 239
Kleist, J. Olaf 70, 111
Klüger, Ruth
- *Still Alive* 89
Koenig Kellas, Jody 30, 32f., 49, 54, 56, 59f., 213, 215, 217f.
Kopp, Johannes 28, 39
Korte, Barbara 3, 15f., 110, 245
Kramer, Anne-Marie 48, 72, 75
Küey, Levent 155
Kuhn, Annette 67, 202, 251
Kureishi, Hanif
- *My Beautiful Laundrette* 197f.
- *My Ear at His Heart. Reading My Father* 18, 62, 190ff., 204, 208, 246f.
- *The Buddha of Suburbia* 4, 14, 106, 191, 198
Kureishi, Yasmin 194

Laing, Ronald D. 31
Landsberg, Alison 56, 67
Langellier, Kristin M. 30, 48f., 60
Langford, Martha 249, 255
Lauer, Gerhard 9
Lawler, Steph 37, 44ff., 48, 50, 72, 138
Leal, Joanne 249ff.
Lenz, Claudia 73f.
Lévi-Strauss, Claude 237
Levy, Andrea
- *Fruit of the Lemon* 4, 6, 18, 62f., 81, 102, 104, 106, 108, 117, 119f., 125, 132, 134f., 138ff., 242f., 245f., 248, 250, 256ff.
- *Small Island* 260
- *The Long Song* 110
Leydesdorff, Selma 49, 53
life scripts 51, 54f., 85, 173ff., 177, 245, 251, 260
life writing 188, 210

Lillge, Claudia 237f.
Lusin, Caroline 237, 240

Macho, Thomas 129
Mahjuob, Jamal
– *Travelling with Djinns* 18
Mann, Thomas
– *Buddenbrooks* 17
Mannheim, Karl 9
Mannur, Anita 240, 245
Marre, Diana 220, 253, 255ff.
Marshall, Sheila 37, 39f.
Mason, Jennifer 43, 255ff.
Maza, Sara 21
McAdams, Dan P. 10, 42, 50f.
McLeod, John 2, 4f., 7, 19, 210ff., 214f., 219, 222f., 232, 256ff.
Mead, George Herbert 37f.
Mead, Margaret 41
meaning-making 22f., 26, 33, 36, 42, 45, 47, 72, 75, 79, 150, 185, 201, 236
memory
– autobiographical memory 10, 53, 58, 88
– collective memory 10, 15, 51f., 55ff., 60f., 63, 65, 68ff., 149, 213, 249, 251
– communicative memory 17, 57, 61, 120, 217
– corporeal/body memory 64, 156, 160, 162
– cultural memory 10, 15f., 57, 61, 67, 174, 238f.
– family memory 5, 10, 12, 15f., 22, 33, 49, 51f., 55ff., 60ff., 67, 69f., 78, 88, 113, 126, 177, 209, 212f., 246ff., 253, 260
– family reminiscing 52, 54, 56ff., 60, 212ff., 216f., 249, 256
– memory and narrative 8ff., 49f., 53
– memory boxes 247f.
– memory studies 9, 12, 43, 52, 63, 68, 235
– memory work 201ff., 208
– memory-text 252f.
– national memory 15, 61ff., 67f.
– objects of memory 113, 121, 133, 177f., 180, 246ff.
– prosthetic memory 56
– social frameworks of memory 52ff., 57, 68
– transcultural memory 3, 15, 19, 68f., 261
Mergenthal, Silvia 14
Meyer, Anne-Rose 237f.

migration
– family and migration 2, 12f., 18, 25, 36, 41, 49, 63, 67, 69f., 78, 236, 243ff., 259ff.
migration literature 2f., 5f., 12f., 15f., 19, 41, 62, 74, 247
Miller, Nancy K. 261
Mirza, Heidi 107f.
Misztal, Barbara 43, 51, 53, 55ff., 64f., 68
Mitchell, Marilyn 130
Mitchell, W. J. T. 50
Modern Family, TV series 20
Montanari, Massimo 236
Moore, Lindsey 147f., 150
Morgan, David H. J. 11, 23, 28f., 31, 33, 35, 41, 66, 79, 236, 239f., 243, 245, 252f.
multi-/generational novel 15ff., 63, 82, 140
multiculturalism 3, 63, 70, 74, 124, 136, 138, 142, 144, 167, 169, 237f.
Muraven, Mark 45
Murdock, Peter 27
myth of return 117, 243, 247

Naipaul, V. S. 3
narrative 50, 88, 121, 131, 185
– counter-narrative 62, 136, 139, 176
– family narrative 17, 30, 50f., 54, 59, 61, 65, 67, 70, 78, 86, 89f., 98, 101, 103ff., 111, 115, 118ff., 131, 133, 138, 141, 143, 164, 177f., 180, 185ff., 193, 196, 204, 210, 214, 247, 260
– narrative of origin 33, 74, 159, 175, 185, 213, 220, 223
– self-narrative 65, 109, 115, 157, 168, 174, 187, 218
– self-narratives 51
nature versus nurture 2, 45, 123, 210, 218, 220
nature/culture divide 46f., 236f.
Nave-Herz, Rosemarie 28
Neisser, Ulric 45
Nelson, Katherine 10, 53f., 88
Neti, Leila 93f., 100
Neumann, Birgit 50
non lieux 227
non-places 227, 229
novel of transformation 6, 81, 122
Nünning, Ansgar 10, 50, 59, 78

Nünning, Vera 33, 50, 59, 78, 185
nurture 159, 161, 220, 239, 243

O'Riley, Michael F. 147f.
Okojie, Irenosen
– *Butterfly Fish* 19
Ondaatje, Michael
– *Running in the Family* 19
Osborne, Deirdre 13
Ott, Christine 238f.

Parasecoli, Fabio 237
Parke, Ross D. 33f., 36f.
Parsons, Talcott 27, 39
Partition 88f., 149f., 163, 187
pedigree 71, 75, 120, 128, 130f.
Pérez Fernández, Irene 121, 126f.
personal life 11, 28, 36, 38, 41f., 47, 49
perspective structure 59, 145, 158
Peterson, Eric E. 30, 48f., 60
Petronio, Sandra 66
phantom 65
Phillips, Caryl
– *In the Falling Snow* 19
photography 32
Pirker, Ulrike 15f., 110
Plahl, Silvia 75
postcolonial studies 3, 7, 13, 15, 81, 98
postmemory 32, 64f., 74
Pressure 87, 107
Procter, James 3, 13, 142, 244
psychology 21, 23, 34, 36ff., 42f., 50, 53

racialisation 6, 108, 119, 257
Ramey, Lauri 13, 74
Rashid, C. E. 166f., 172, 181
Rashkin, Esther 65
Reichl, Susanne 13, 83, 94, 98f., 110
relatedness 22f., 35, 37, 43, 46f., 71, 76, 151, 159f., 185, 190, 202, 210, 212, 220, 231, 234, 254, 256f.
relational autobiography 18, 188f.
relational being 38
relational self 7ff., 23, 38, 40, 42, 44, 48, 53, 188f., 192, 205f., 212, 232
relationality 22, 37f., 42f., 52, 97, 139, 190, 212

Reynolds, Tracey 242
Ricoeur, Paul 50
Rigney, Ann 10
Riley, Joan
– *The Unbelonging* 3
Rimmon-Kenan, Shlomith 50
Rogers, Edna L. 30
Rothberg, Michael 15
Ru, Yi-ling 17
Rüggemeier, Anne 188f., 193, 196, 203, 206, 208
Rupp, Jan 9, 13, 15, 33, 74, 105
Rushdie Affair 142f., 166, 169
Rushdie, Salman 3, 142, 166

Sabourin, Teresa C. 33
Sáez, Elena Machado 106, 109f., 115f., 118f.
Schachter, Elli P. 37
Schacter, Daniel L. 88
Schahadat, Schamma 237f.
Schier, Michaela 77
Schlör, Joachim 247
Schneider, David 45, 47
Schouler-Ocak, Meryam 155
Schwanecke, Christine 252f.
Scott, Jacqueline 12, 20f., 23
Scott, Susie 236, 239, 242
secrets 47f., 64ff., 89ff., 93, 132ff., 137, 141, 143, 153, 157, 163ff., 177ff., 181, 183, 186f., 228, 230
Seemann, Daphne 65, 99
Segrin, Chris 54, 178, 235
self-narrative 55
Selvon, Sam
– *The Lonely Londoners* 3
September 11 attacks 142f., 172, 183
Sesay, Kadija 3f.
Seth, Vikram
– *Two Lives* 19
sexuality 24, 91, 196, 198f., 205, 207, 226, 260
Shamsie, Kamila
– *Kartography* 19
Shaw, Alison 161
Shevchenko, Olga 249
Shore, Bradd 32ff.
Shotter, John 38

silence 64ff., 99, 111, 114, 140f., 143, 153, 157, 164f., 180, 183, 186f., 196, 198
Smart, Carol 11, 20, 24, 26, 29ff., 37f., 41ff., 47, 51, 65, 67, 78, 115, 132, 157, 178, 189, 212, 241, 246
Smith, Zadie 28
– *White Teeth* 4ff., 15, 17f., 63, 82, 121ff., 125, 127, 132, 135, 137, 140f., 235, 246f., 250, 257ff.
Snoek, Jan A. M. 33f.
Sobral, Ana 9
social individuality 38
socialisation 13, 23, 37, 39, 41, 54
– narrative socialisation 54
– racial socialisation 258
Sollors, Werner 9
Sommer, Roy 3, 81
Sontag, Susan 31f.
spectrality 223
Spivak, Gayatri Chakravorty 136
Stano, Simona 237
Stein, Mark 2, 4, 6, 13, 16, 81, 100ff., 122
Strathern, Marilyn 47, 72
Straub, Jürgen 224
Stryker, Sheldon 50
substance 47, 70, 239f.
Sundholm, John 149
Surkamp, Carola 59
Syal, Meera
– *Anita and Me* 14, 18, 62f., 81ff., 86, 90, 92ff., 101, 103f., 107, 132, 138ff., 238, 240f., 243, 245f., 248, 250f., 254, 257ff.
symbolic interactionism 30, 37, 50

Thompson, Blair 49
Thompson, Molly 122
Toplu, Şebnem 104
Torok, Maria 65
Tournay-Theodotou, Petra 215, 217, 224, 226f.
transcultural studies 68
transculturality 21, 68, 238
Transparent, TV series 20

trauma 32, 64, 73ff., 88, 117, 149, 155, 158, 164f., 171, 186f.
– cultural trauma 149f., 155
Trees, April R. 30, 33, 49, 54, 56, 59f., 215, 217f.
Tulving, Endel 88
Turner, Bryan S. 9, 253f.
Turner, Jonathan 50
Turner, Lynn H. 30

Upstone, Sara 13, 81

van den Berghe, Pierre L. 236f., 239
Vangelisti, Anita L. 5, 30, 65ff.
Veracini, Lorenzo 111
Visser, Irene 8, 14f.

Warburg, Aby 69
Waterman, David 149f.
Weedon, Chris 2ff., 6, 13, 146
Weigel, Sigrid 9, 61, 73, 75f., 130
Weingarten, Jutta 15, 144f., 149f., 158
Welzer, Harald 62f.
West, Richard 30
White, Hayden 50
Who Do You Think You Are?, TV series 48, 71
Widmer, Eric D. 11, 27, 37
Wildt, Michael 9
Willer, Stefan 75
Wilson, Janet 14
Windrush Generation 74, 105, 260
Winter, Jay 61f., 65, 69
Winter, Marcia A. 58f., 216f., 220
Wolin, Steven J. 34

Yaqin, Amina 143, 147
Yassin-Kassab, Robin 166
– *The Road from Damascus* 18, 143, 166, 185ff., 246, 259

Zerubavel, Eviatar 49f., 53, 70ff., 74, 76, 119, 128ff., 132, 234
Zielke, Barbara 224

www.ingramcontent.com/pod-product-compliance
Lightning Source LLC
Chambersburg PA
CBHW031759220426
43662CB00007B/468